"'Small plates, big hearts' could easily be an alternate title for this ebullient, gorgeous, and delicious book. Ben and Zikki's food radiates love, generosity, and good taste, infused with the unique fusion of cultures that makes them and their cooking so special."
—**Adeena Sussman,** *New York Times* **bestselling author of** *Shabbat*

"If you want to master the art of hosting; make everyone feel welcome at your table; and impress your guests with homemade dips, breads, salads, desserts, and beyond, Ben and Zikki created the perfect cheat sheet for us. *Eat Small Plates* is here to shape the way we host and dine with a collection of incredibly fresh and vibrant dishes."
—**Carolina Gelen,** *New York Times* **bestselling author of** *Pass the Plate*

"These two! Incredible people and cooks by themselves but absolutely deadly as a team . . . so stoked to cook from this one."
—**Brad Leone,** *New York Times* **bestselling author of** *Field Notes for Food Adventure*

"Hosting a dinner party can be overwhelming, even for an experienced chef. This is the kind of food you want at your next gathering—fun, interesting, and all conversation starters. You can't help but smile after picking up and flipping through this book."
—**Joe Sasto, chef and Food Network star**

"I so admire Ben's expert but loving approach to food. His and Zikki's first cookbook is a love letter to joyful Israeli cooking everywhere, with beautiful recipes for the whole family."
—**Michael Solomonov, James Beard–award winning chef and author of** *Zahav*

EAT
small
plates

EAT small plates

vibrant, shareable dishes for daily joy

ben & zikki siman-tov
@bengingi and @chefzikki

AVERY · AN IMPRINT OF PENGUIN RANDOM HOUSE · NEW YORK

AVERY

an imprint of Penguin Random House LLC
1745 Broadway, New York, NY 10019
penguinrandomhouse.com

Copyright © 2025 by Ben Siman-Tov

Photographs on pages 5, 6 (top left), 10, 12, 15 (top left, bottom left, bottom right), and 16 by Omer Kaplan. All other photographs by Dan Perez.

Penguin Random House values and supports copyright. Copyright fuels creativity, encourages diverse voices, promotes free speech, and creates a vibrant culture. Thank you for buying an authorized edition of this book and for complying with copyright laws by not reproducing, scanning, or distributing any part of it in any form without permission. You are supporting writers and allowing Penguin Random House to continue to publish books for every reader. Please note that no part of this book may be used or reproduced in any manner for the purpose of training artificial intelligence technologies or systems.

Avery with colophon is a trademark of Penguin Random House LLC

Book design by Ashley Tucker

Library of Congress Cataloging-in-Publication Data
Names: Siman-Tov, Ben, author. | Siman-Tov, Zikki, author.
Title: Eat small plates / Ben Siman-Tov and Zikki Siman-Tov.
Description: New York : Avery, an imprint of Penguin Random House, [2025] | Includes index.
Identifiers: LCCN 2024044605 (print) | LCCN 2024044606 (ebook) | ISBN 9780593716793 (hardcover) | ISBN 9780593716809 (epub)
Subjects: LCSH: Cooking, Middle Eastern. | Cooking, Mediterranean. | Appetizers. | LCGFT: Cookbooks.
Classification: LCC TX725.M628 S56 2025 (print) | LCC TX725.M628 (ebook) | DDC 641.59/1822—dc23/eng/20241029
LC record available at https://lccn.loc.gov/2024044605
LC ebook record available at https://lccn.loc.gov/2024044606

Printed in China
10 9 8 7 6 5 4 3 2 1

The authorized representative in the EU for product safety and compliance is Penguin Random House Ireland, Morrison Chambers, 32 Nassau Street, Dublin D02 YH68, Ireland, https://eu-contact.penguin.ie.

To our tiny T, our little superhuman who made us a family—the ultimate team. You are the engine that keeps us moving every day.

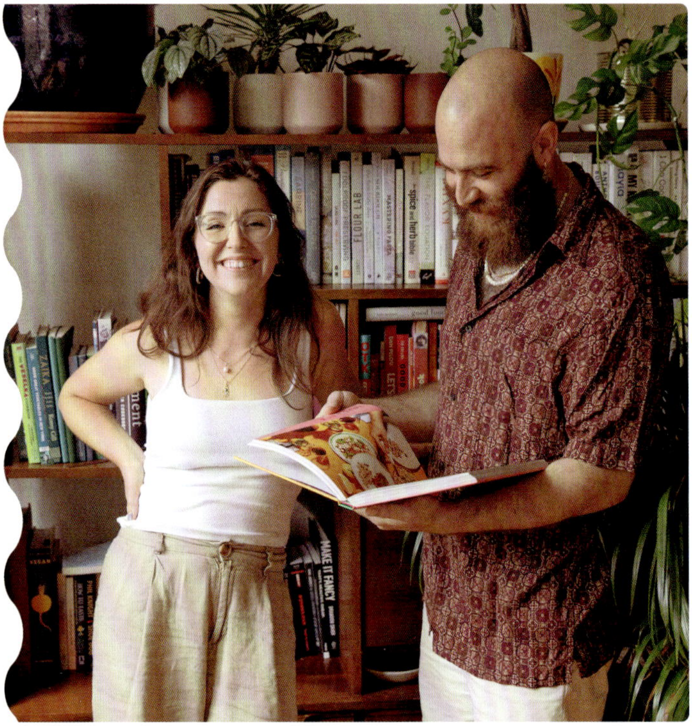
FLOUR LAB
MAKE IT FANCY

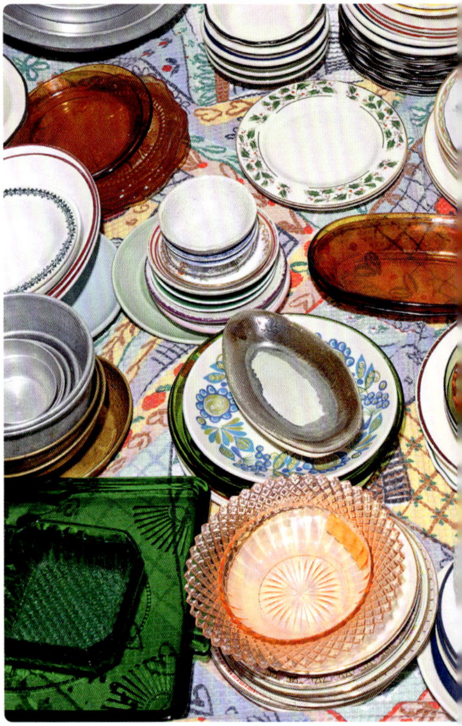

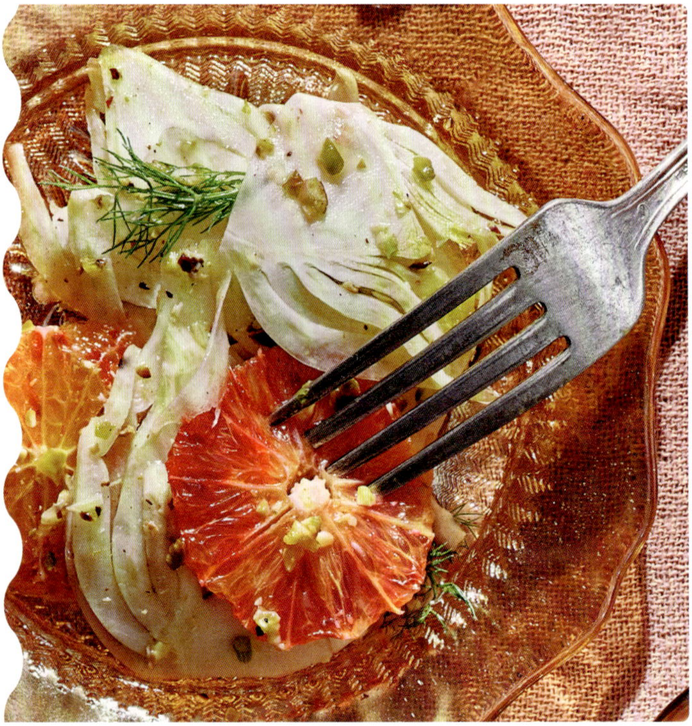

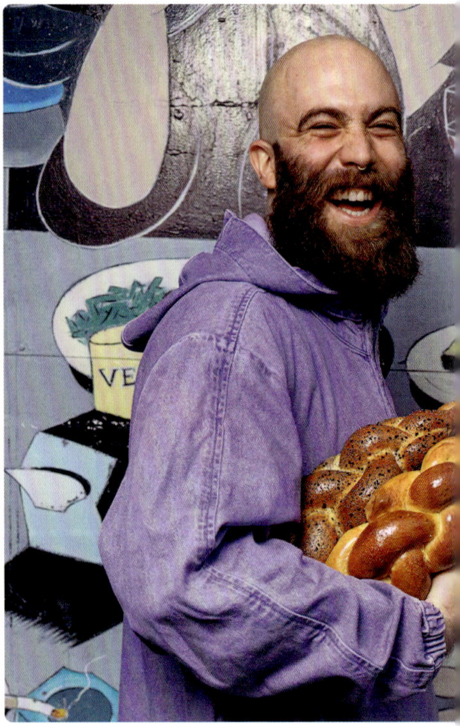

contents

9   introduction
19 the small plates pantry & essentials
27 hosting 101

44 **dips & spreads**
104 **breads**
132 **salads**
194 **veggie bites**
240 **animal bites**
278 **something sweet**

304 tips, tricks & sample menus
308 acknowledgments
312 index

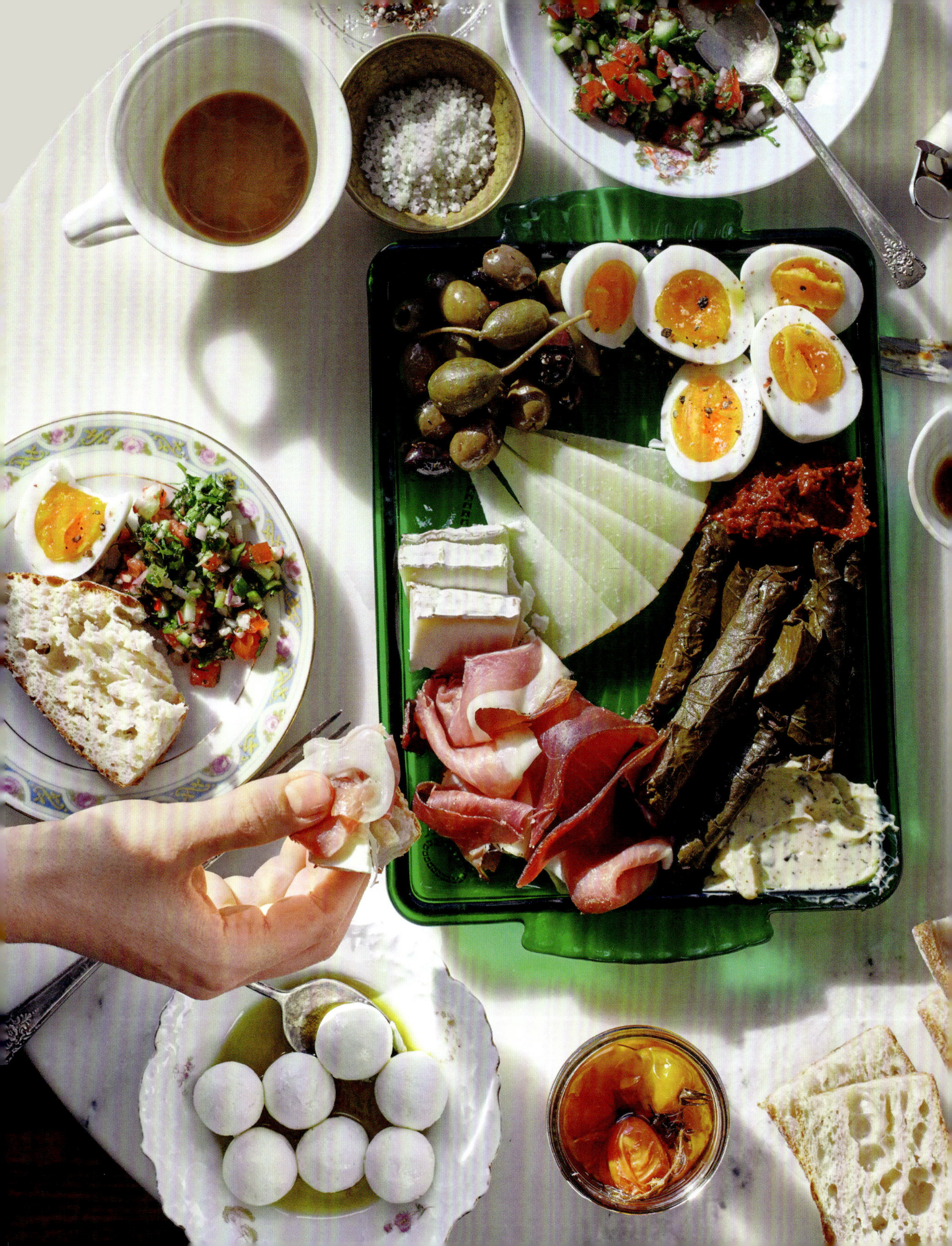

INTRODUCTION

You may know me as BenGingi, the vivacious baker shouting "YASSS" at the end of my Instagram tutorials, which take complex baking techniques and simplify them for home bakers. But my journey with food didn't start at home and in front of the camera. This adventure began many years ago, during my gap year trip around the world before my anticipated studies for a degree in engineering in Israel.

My first stop on that trip was New York City, where my uncle and lifelong mentor Tal took me on the best culinary tour maybe EVER. At that point in my life, to say I was a picky eater was an understatement. My wife and culinary partner, Zikki, still jokes that she really considered not marrying me because I didn't eat fruit when we first met. So, my uncle took this picky-eating boy and threw him into the depths of the culinary world, taking me to all of New York's gastronomic wonders—Union Square Greenmarket, Il Buco Alimentari, Katz's Deli, and Prince Street Pizza, just to name a few. To say the least, I fell in love with everything New York had to offer!

During that time in the US, I spent three months in upstate New York working on a idyllic dairy farm. Upon

so why bengingi?

In Hebrew, *gingi* means "redhead." But for me, redhead is more of a personality than a hair color. The people I've met with red hair are outgoing, adventurous, creative, and passionate, and they have a fiery temperament—all the things I have aspired to be. When I opened my first Instagram account, right before moving to Italy, I called myself BenGingi. I thought to myself, "Now everyone I'll meet in Italy will know me as the Gingi." When I became bald and was left only with my red beard, it was official; I literally grew into the name. And I love it.

my return to New York City, before heading out on the next leg of my journey to Vietnam, Thailand, and India, my uncle sat me down and encouraged me to continue my travels, but through the lens of food. He urged me to try foods I had never experienced before, to engulf my senses in the gastronomic unknown. But most important, my uncle Tal encouraged me to work in a kitchen after my trip—just for the hell of it. Maybe I'd learn a thing or two.

After leaving New York for Asia, I went on to eat the most aromatic and truly nurturing pho of my life in Hanoi. I would spend my nights in the live markets in Bangkok jumping from one street food vendor to another, searching for the best khao soi. In India, I found myself eating fresh dosa daily, dipping this fermented savory "crepe" made from ground white gram and rice in a variety of local chutneys. Unknowingly, I was already infatuated with doughs and batters. Go figure.

Upon my return to Israel, I took my uncle Tal's advice and I began working at North Abraxas in Tel Aviv under Eyal Shani, one of the revolutionary founders of Israeli cuisine, known for his wild food philosophy and sensational hospitality. He places a strong emphasis on the dining experience, having an open kitchen at the heart of the restaurant so that the customers can see where and how their food is prepared. People feast on vegetable-forward dishes characterized by low ingredient count, fresh market produce, and the occasional riddance of cutlery. The environment within any of his establishments is heavily focused on the most intuitive transformation of a vegetable into its peak moment.

What started as a one-off opportunity quickly evolved into one of the biggest turning points in my life. When I began, I barely knew how to hold a knife, and within a couple of weeks, I had been warmly initiated into the kitchen family.

Soon after, I started at HaSalon, Eyal's high-end restaurant in Tel Aviv. On my first day, I came to work alongside the legends; I prepped all day, and when service began—to my disbelief—the chef asked me to sit down at the bar and just "enjoy the service." You can imagine my shock.

That evening, they served me the whole menu paired with their exceptional, everflowing wine, so I could better understand their unique approach to food and hospitality. Classical music played in the background, and I watched as a divine synergy bubbled among the cooks, waiters, and diners. *That* was the moment I understood I wanted to be around food for the rest of my life.

That night on my way back home, I realized I was over the moon in love and impulsively canceled my enrollment to the engineering school at Tel Aviv University. Although that was a crazy moment in my life, I knew intuitively it would lead me to the next chapter. My father bid me farewell, saying, "Whatever you choose to do in life, just be the best in it."

I took those words to heart and did exactly that. I enrolled in the undergraduate program at the Slow Food University of Gastronomic Sciences in Pollenzo, and soon I was off to Italy to live in the Alps. Little did I know what life had in store for me.

During the second year of my undergraduate program, I found myself in a dark moment in my life, unsure of my next move and missing home. It was around the same time that my father called me and encouraged me to bake some bread, as he had just taken a class and found it deeply therapeutic. It was at that moment, after baking

BRA, ITALY • 2019

my first loaf, that I found my curiosity and sense of purpose strangely charged. It was also around that same time, too, that I met my (now) wife and business partner, Zikki, by chance on a street in our tiny town. She had traveled from the US to study in Italy, and she was also deeply infatuated with the world of food.

Soon Zikki and I became lovebirds, sipping life like wine, while surrounded by delicious food and the romance of the Italian Alps. From the very beginning, Zikki and I shared the same passions—we loved cooking and hosting friends and family at any opportunity. Even though we were from different backgrounds, countries, and languages, we somehow never ran out of things to talk about.

When it comes to food, I am always inspired by the way Zikki understands flavors. The core difference between us is that as a picky eater, I explored my palate later in life and made new discoveries. Zikki, on the other hand, is a naturally gifted food lover and cook.

Having grown up on the Lower East Side of Manhattan in the Ukrainian Village, Zikki was exposed to NYC's wild restaurant and bodega scene from the earliest days of her childhood, snacking on wasabi peas as a five-year-old and eating dinners out with her parents weekly. Simultaneously, as a resident of the Ukrainian Village and member of the diaspora, Zikki was always surrounded by an abundance

meet zikki

For as long as I can remember, my life has been about food, flavor, and the community surrounding it. To understand my approach to food and hosting is to understand who came before me: my beloved mother, Marta Kostyk. An artist, community organizer, and the woman to whom I've dedicated my entire life's work. My eternal source of light, clarity, and passion.

But truthfully, her magic was in the way she hosted, a gene passed down to all of us "Kostyk girls" from my grandmother Baba Lu. My mother was the most generous woman, maybe ever. My earliest memories are flooded with her eternal kindness and inclusion, specifically around the table. Whether she was inviting all of the kids from the neighborhood upstate for lunch during the summer or serving us ice water in wineglasses to make us feel special, she always showed love through food, and from her, I learned everything.

—zikki

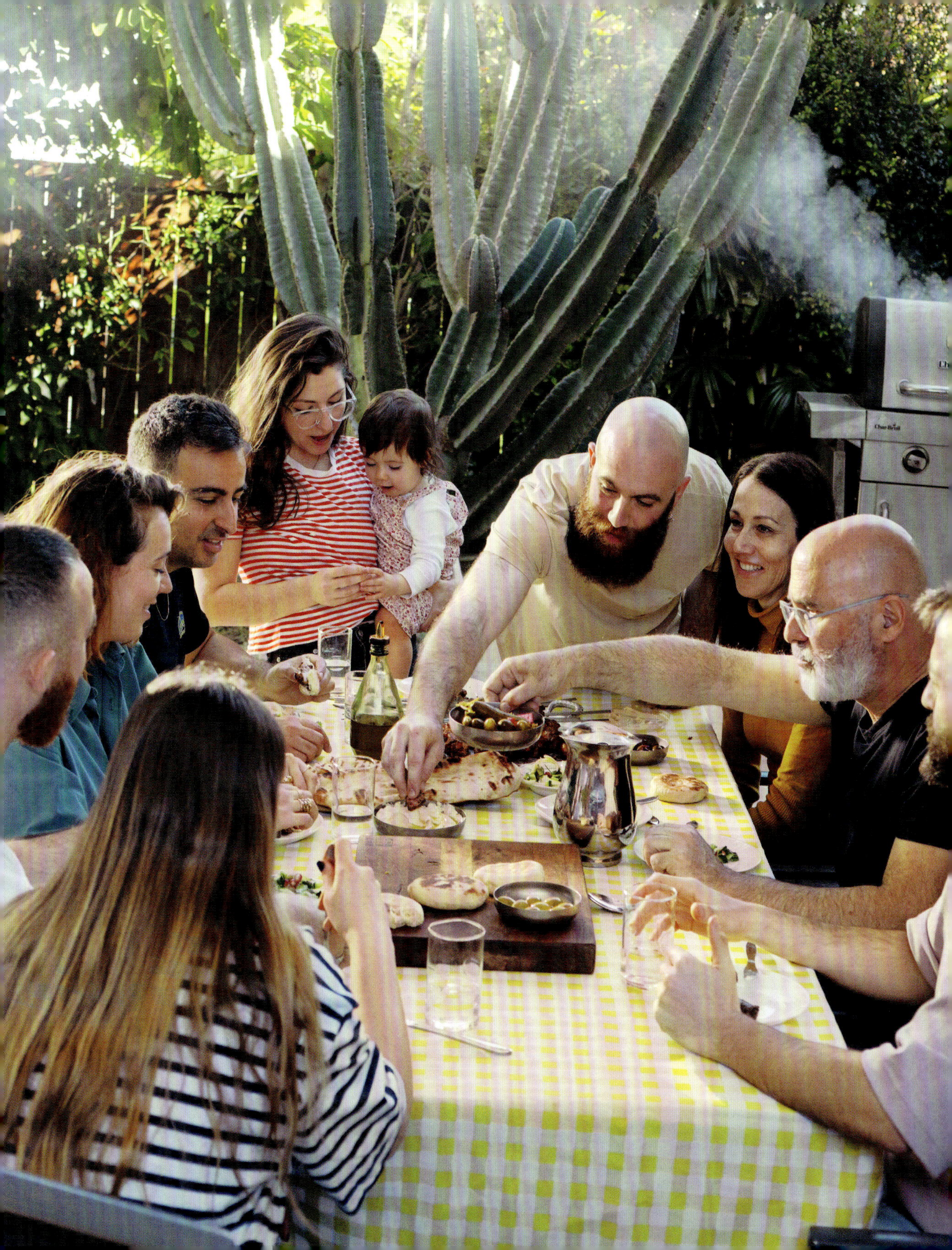

of community. Zikki grew up alongside her grandmother Baba Lu, who served as the lead caterer in their community. Baba Lu's kitchen was right next door to her parents' office, so Zikki spent endless hours with her grandmother, watching as she prepared for events, making hundreds of varenyky and holubtsi for festivals and weddings.

Later on in life, Zikki headed west to San Diego for her college years, where she learned all about seasonality and agriculture. Her exposure to so many different culinary cultures in New York combined with her love of the coastal California kitchen set her on a path to study and live through and for food.

Soon after Zikki and I met, life took yet another turn, and the world experienced the COVID pandemic. We decided to move together to New York and get married.

As I was waiting for my green card to be approved, I couldn't work legally. So I found myself baking all day, recording and documenting my journey. Every day, I would make a new baked good from around the world and would try to simplify the process and make it accessible to the home baker. Almost overnight, I found myself with an exponentially exploding online community looking to learn and engage.

As this online community grew, so did our new life in New York. We found ourselves hosting friends, family, strangers, followers, clients, and simply people we love—always over a good meal. The shelves of our refrigerator often held a container of freshly simmered matbucha and a jar of garlic confit I'd make to go along with the bread I baked. Zikki would come back from the market with seasonal veggies impeccably chosen to curate the perfect salad, fish to cure, and beans for soaking overnight. She'd prepare the creamiest hummus for lunch the following day and ferment krauts, roots, and lemons. A yogurt and salt mixture always hung in a cloth from a hook in our kitchen, in our pursuit of the tangiest labneh. You get the gist. We created a food kingdom in NYC, and we were inspired to share it with others. For us, food and community are a way of life.

Israeli cuisine has exciting influences from all over the world, and it is blessed with Arabic hospitality and magic. When I was growing up, we would host guests by "opening the table"—we'd put out an abundance of tantalizing small plates and serve them with bread like pita, laffa, challah, or Tel Avivian focaccia. It has always been my favorite way to eat. To this moment, it is the way Zikki and I eat daily and the way we like to cook for our loved ones when we gather.

We hope this book will inspire you to

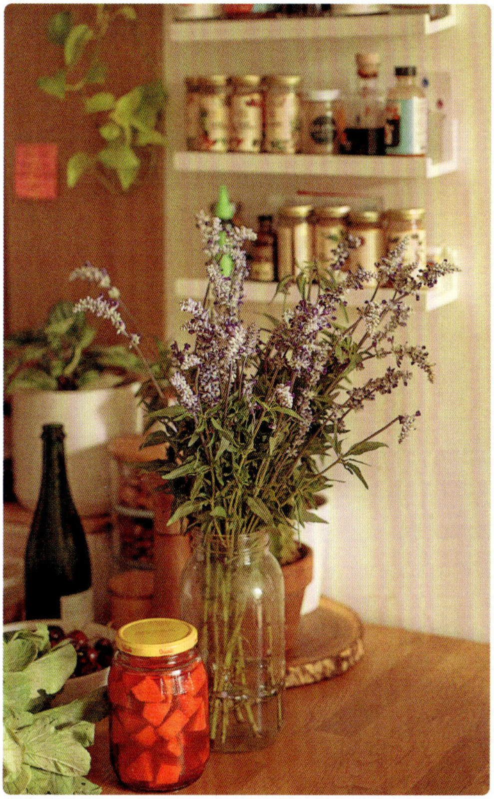
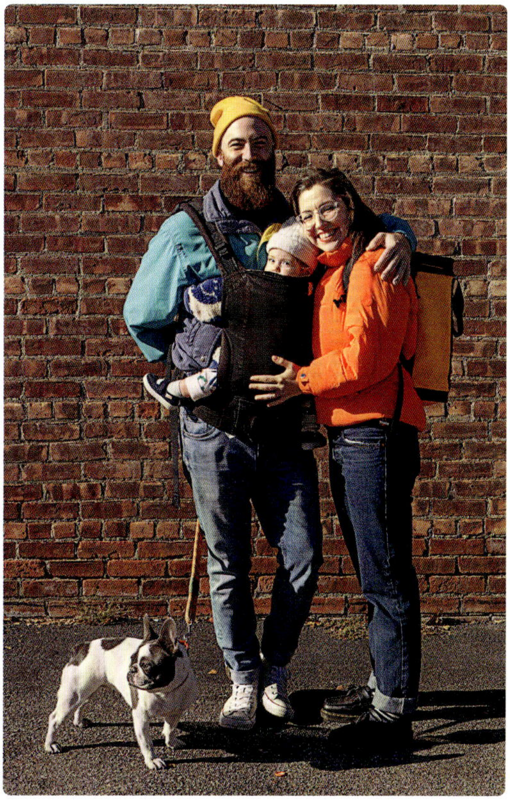
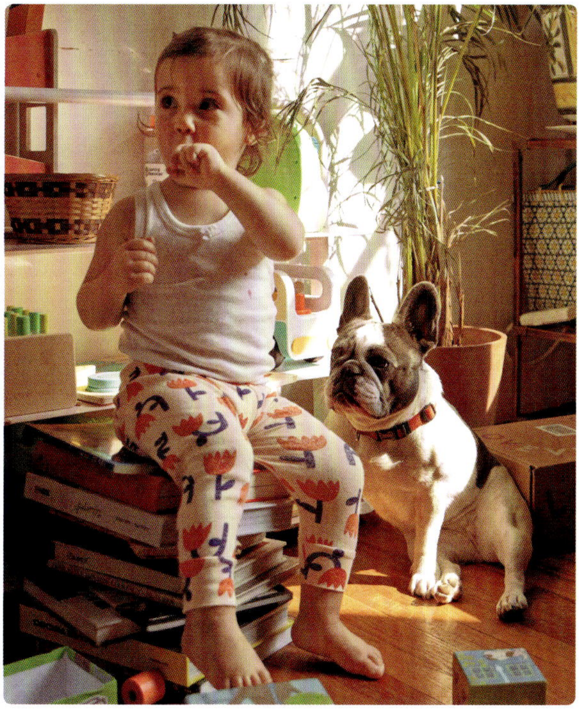
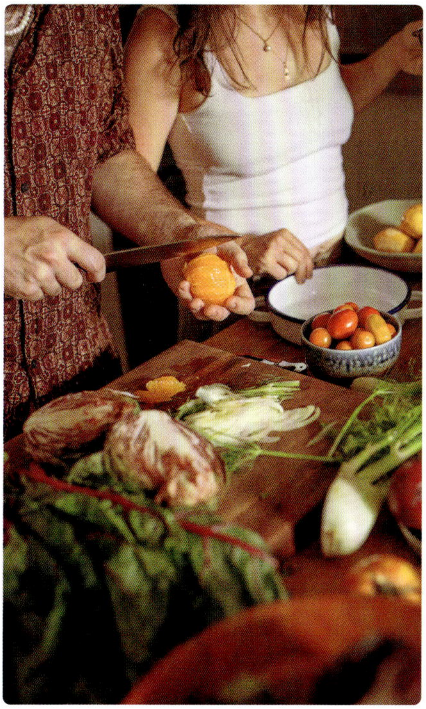

"open your table" too. It contains more than one hundred of our favorite small plates, some of which are classic Middle Eastern and Mediterranean-inspired dishes and others that are unique to our own culinary journey, as partners and as individual culinary creators. Most of these recipes can be made ahead of time and served within minutes so that you, too, can join in the eating and hosting easily—anytime. Our recipes are a simple and delicious solution to feeding two people—or one hundred!

"everyday cooking"

Since the day Ben and I met, we've been looking for a way to bring our strongest culinary capabilities together, to unite into some grand force. Ben has always been precise and wildly committed to perfection—characteristics that define an extraordinary baker. I, on the other hand, leaned into my mother's creativity and magic building, developing dishes spontaneously and focusing only on flavor and the feeling the food gave the eaters. As we grew into our life, family, and business together, our strengths naturally complemented one another, and we both evolved into better versions of ourselves in the kitchen and beyond.

The recipes in this book are for things that we've eaten together daily a million times, prepped weekly, and served to both our neighbors for Shabbat dinner and to our clients for big events. Whether we are making a quick Breakfast Salad for our family, loaded with fresh cucumbers, tomatoes, and eggs, or simply boiling gorgeous queen artichokes in salty water for Double-Dip Artichokes, our recipes have ultimately been designed to be eaten every day. They are healthy, easy to make, family friendly, and just so happen to be totally, irresistibly shareable. Through this book, you will learn techniques for cooking that you can use constantly to improve your general comfort and excitement in the kitchen. The recipes are simple enough to make on a weeknight for one, yet still so decadent and delicious that they are sure to impress all your friends and family for any occasion.

—zikki

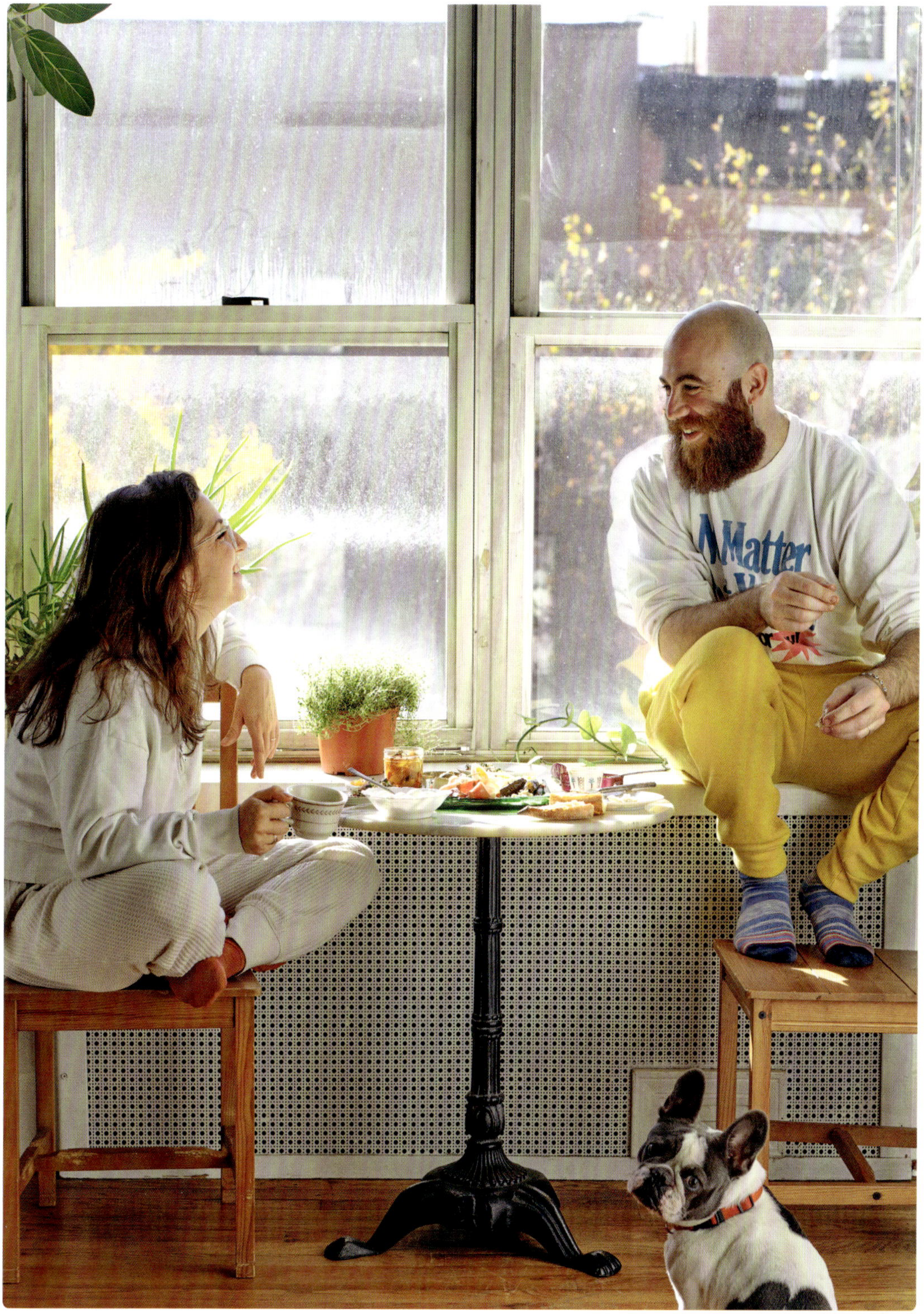
Matter

BEIRUT
KESHK
Milk Powder, Salt, Ground Wheat
Lightly SMOKED
SARDINES
IN OLIVE OIL
PRODUCT OF MOROCCO
Ingredients:
Lightly-smoked sardines,
vegetable oil, salt.
HAWAYEJ
Dehydrated Sourdough
BAHARAT
Allspice, cinnamon, and clove blend for chicken liver and vegetables.
Cloves
Clover Trèfle
250g
Miód + cytryny
275 g
w cukrze
MARMA

THE SMALL PLATES PANTRY & ESSENTIALS

Look into someone's pantry and you will learn a world about them. Zikki and I love to collect foods from everywhere we travel. Whether it's an ingredient from a local shop in the East Village or the rolling hills of the Western Galilee, our pantry is stocked with our favorites. We always bring home spices and olive oil from Israel and honey, teas, and sunflower products from Ukraine. And often friends and family will gift us their favorite spice or jam from whatever place they've traveled to. Our pantry is a snapshot of the flavors that color our life: canned fish, olives, nuts, spices, jams, syrups, oils, and of course, tahini.

In addition to telling a story, a stocked pantry will ensure you never go hungry or get bored in the kitchen. But we want to preface this section by letting you know that all you **REALLY** need to cook this book or to be a terrific host is salt, lemon, and an excellent extra virgin olive oil. Everything else is a super-sexy added bonus.

the essentials

extra virgin olive oil

When it comes to extra virgin olive oil, there are no compromises. For us, extra virgin olive oil is as important as a spice or other flavor enhancer: It's not just a fat. It is our seasoning oil, our finisher. We always have at least five different types of extra virgin olive oil at home, sourced from various countries and olive varieties. When buying your seasoning olive oil, always make sure to choose a single-origin extra virgin olive oil (not a blend) and ensure that it hasn't been bottled for more than a year. After a year, the oil tends to go rancid and lose its flavor and aroma. The biggest risks to extra virgin olive oil quality are temperature and direct light, so it is best to store it in a cool, dark space.

other oils

We almost exclusively use extra virgin olive oil at our house, but when we are feeling particularly wild, we pull out Zikki's favorite pantry item in the world: toasted sunflower oil. Zikki discovered it when she was in Ukraine writing her graduate thesis in 2019, and I must admit, it is a salad game changer. This oil is made with the precision and attention given to olive oil and adds a decadence and unexpected earthy twist to any dish! How do you know you've stumbled upon the real stuff? The aroma is absolutely intoxicating. It is hard to find, but most eastern European supermarkets carry it. It is worth the chase.

When frying, we use organic canola oil. It is the best for frying in our opinion, as it has a high smoke point and totally neutral flavor.

Our seasoning olive oil is different from the olive oil we use to cook. For example, to pan-sear lamb kebabs, we use a regular olive oil. It is far less aromatic and less expensive but still much healthier and tastier than cooking with neutral oils like canola.

gray atlantic sea salt

If you thought we were particular about our olive oil, we are even more choosy when it comes to salt. We have two main types of salt at home: fine sea salt for salting water for artichokes or pasta, and coarse Atlantic gray sea salt for seasoning. It's important to stick with one type of seasoning salt because different salts tend to have varying levels of saltiness; it is much easier to season precisely and not overwhelm the dish if you understand the proper salt levels. We love Atlantic gray salt because it is unprocessed and still retains important minerals such as magnesium, iron, calcium, potassium, manganese, and zinc. If you find something that really works, stick with it!

freshly cracked black pepper

Freshly cracked. That's the only way we use black pepper. We buy whole black peppercorns, load them into our pepper grinder, and freshly crack it for every meal. Cracking it on the spot keeps the fruity-spicy notes of the black pepper present. Our recommendation? Never get preground black pepper. It has lost all its magic and will absolutely make you sneeze.

other really fun pantry items

tahini

Tahini is raw sesame paste. It is like the cooler, more sophisticated older brother of peanut butter. We always have a jar at home, and we use it for everything. When combined with water, it opens up and is the most luxurious and creamy condiment, ever. And it is vegan.

acid

One of the most important fundamentals of food seasoning is acid. We like to pay special attention to this. For most of our salads, we usually use a freshly squeezed lemon, which immediately adds a brightness to every dish. In the past couple of years, we discovered vinegars are also an amazing way to diversify our acid game, adding totally new dimensions to our food. Sherry, apple cider, champagne, and sometimes tomato vinegar are main characters in the story of our salads. Yes, they all taste totally different, yet they add magnitudes of complexity to the dish.

When buying vinegar, make sure that the ingredient list includes only the vinegar. No sugar. No preservatives. No additives. Why, you may ask? Vinegar is naturally self-preserving—which is why vinegar is used to preserve other foods. The really good stuff will have only the fundamental ingredients.

irish butter

Number one, it's just downright delicious. Number two, it's genuinely made with the best interests of both the cows and the consumer in mind. Irish butter comes from grass-fed cows that graze on lush pastures, leading to higher-quality milk and a more flavorful butter. The cows are often treated more humanely, benefiting from a natural, pasture-based diet. The result is a product with a richer, creamier taste, higher butterfat content, and fewer additives, making it both indulgent and wholesome.

nuts

It's nuts how much we love nuts. I know this joke is not funny, but I had to drop it somewhere. When buying nuts, we always prefer to go with organic raw nuts so that we can salt and toast them to our own liking. You might be surprised, but we've discovered that the best way to roast nuts is actually in the microwave. They will look the same but will be toasted to perfection inside! We love all nuts, but our favorites are pistachios, hazelnuts, and almonds.

how to toast nuts

When toasting nuts you have two options: the oven or the microwave. The oven provides a very well-rounded, classic toasted nutty flavor and texture. The microwave is the faster, less fussy option.

1. To toast in the oven: Preheat the oven to 425°F (220°C). Spread the nuts evenly on a parchment paper–lined baking sheet and bake for 10 minutes, or until golden brown. Remove from the oven and cool.

2. To toast in the microwave: Spread the nuts in one layer on a microwave-safe plate and heat for 2 minutes 30 seconds. Remove from the microwave and toss. Microwave for another 1 minute

30 seconds. Remove and cool (if the nuts do not look/smell finished, repeat this process in 1-minute intervals until you've achieved the desired result). You will be able to tell that they are finished as the warm aroma of the toasted nuts will overcome your senses with glee!

spices

Zikki and I love to cook with spices. We learned how to incorporate them into our dishes in a delicate way so that they add a lot of flavor but not so much that it overwhelms whoever is not into spiced food (my mom). Here are the ones we use the most in our kitchen (and in this book):

sumac

This is hands down my absolute favorite spice in the entire world. Sumac (from the Arabic *summaq*, which means "dark red") is a berry, which is then dried and ground into a fine powder. It has fruity, acidic notes, and we use it any time we want to add an acidic touch to our dishes without adding more liquid (lemon or vinegar). It works exceptionally well in salads or sprinkled on dips and raw fish dishes!

za'atar

When you don't know what to add to a dish to make it special, sprinkle it with za'atar. This incredible blend of thyme, sesame seeds, sumac, and salt is made differently depending on the family, region, and tradition. No matter the origin, it adds a bright, herby pop to any dip, spread, or bread.

baharat

Baharat, which translates to "spices" in Arabic, is a direct reflection of how versatile and unique this blend can be based on the region of its origin. However, every "baharat" has one thing in common: it undeniably gives the feeling of warmth. Whenever we want to add warmth to a dish, primarily a cooked meat or stuffed vegetable, we add baharat. It is a blend of cinnamon, cardamom, black pepper, cumin, nutmeg, cloves, and coriander.

hawaij

Hawaij is the spice that adds (yellow) color to our life, quite literally. With turmeric as one of the main ingredients, this classic Yemeni spice blend adds a bright yellow color to everything it touches. There are many variations of hawaij (including one that is made specifically for coffee), but the one we use the most is a blend made for savory treats that includes turmeric, fenugreek, cumin, chili, coriander, mustard seed, cinnamon, and nutmeg.

cumin

Cumin is a staple in Israeli kitchens and is most notably used to give hummus its signature flavor. The powdered stuff at the store is not a good representation of this fantastic earthy spice, so we use raw cumin seeds instead, toast them in a pan, and crush them in a mortar with a pestle.

dukkah

Dukkah is a traditional Egyptian spice blend or condiment. It is a mix of nuts, seeds, and spices toasted and crushed individually in varying sizes and mixed together to create an excellent topper for any dip, spread, or salad. Our dukkah includes pistachios, sesame seeds, cumin seeds, coriander seeds, and gray salt. Recipes for dukkah vary by region.

hot stuff

When I first moved to the US, I could not understand the obsession Americans have with hot sauce, but as time passed and I integrated into society, I became a convert. The truth is, everything is more fun with a little heat. In our home and in our kitchen, we use zhug and harissa to add heat. Additionally, when we need to add a fresher kick of heat to a dish, we always use the long green hot chili (also known as the Anaheim chili). It is spicy yet very balanced, and an excellent addition to any dish where you're looking for a pop of color and spice.

sweet stuff

You will rarely find us reaching for white sugar in order to make something sweet. In our pantry, we have an abundance of honeys, jams, syrups, waters, and halva (but of course). You will also find silan (date honey), acacia raw honey, rose water and orange blossom water, grape and pomegranate syrups, and fig and apricot jams.

tinned fish and canned things

Nothing like cracking open a can of something truly decadent, meal boosting, and classically shelf stable. Smoked trout, sardines, tuna in olive oil, preserved anchovies, and marinated artichokes, to name a few. We often collect specialty canned foods from wherever we travel since they are always vastly diverse and a great conversation starter with whomever you are hosting!

THE SMALL PLATES PANTRY & ESSENTIALS

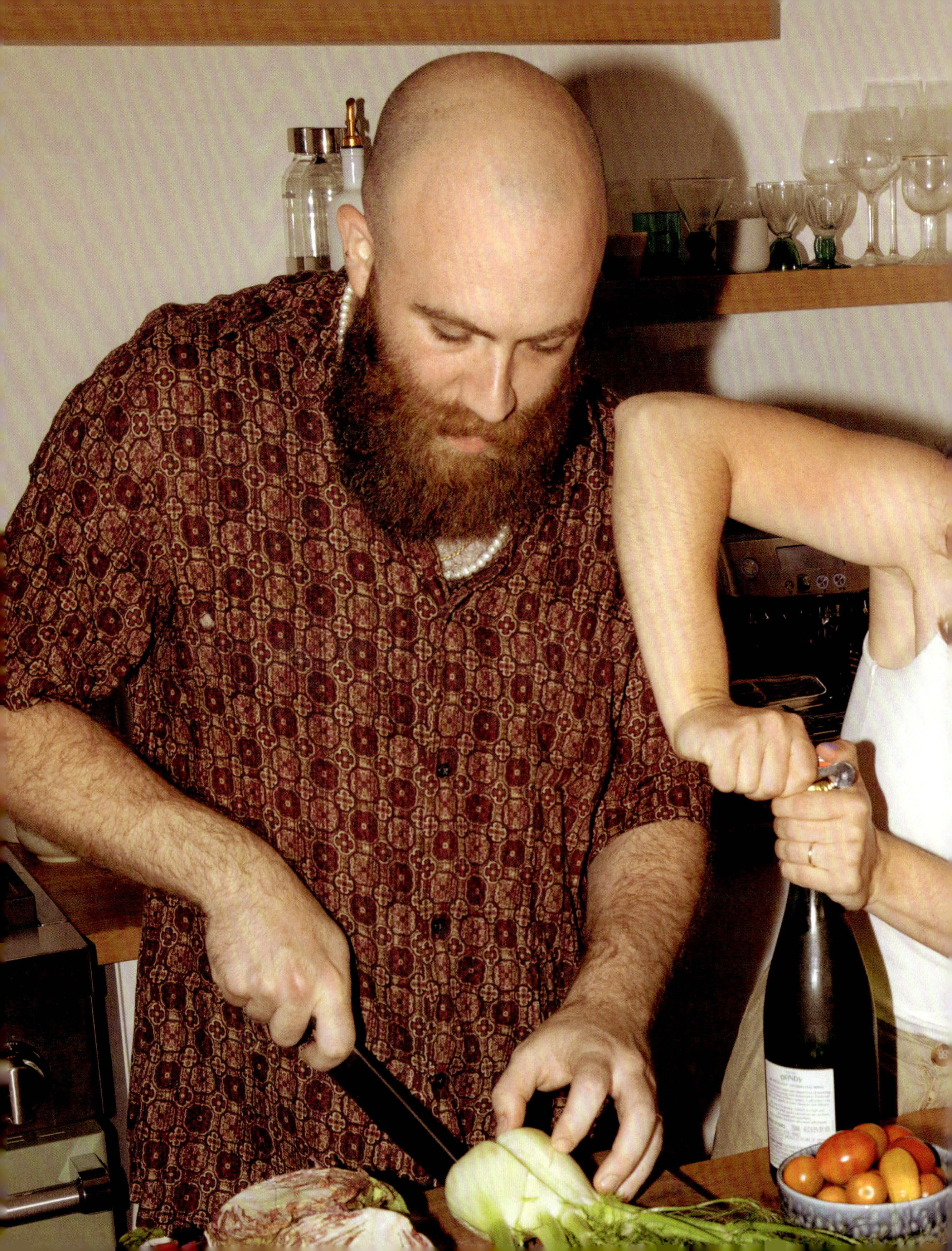

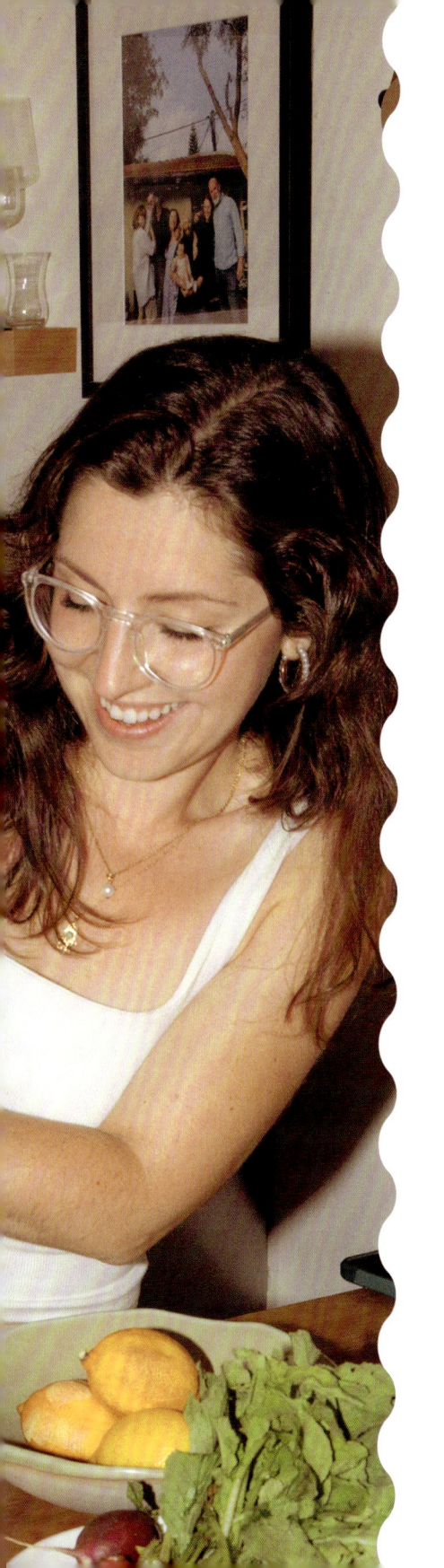

HOSTING 101

Hosting is something that has come naturally to us as a pair since the day we met. When we were living in Bra, Italy (where we were crazy enough to move in together only a few months after we met!), we cooked for Shabbat dinners, Saturday brunch, late-night Eurovision watch parties, yoga classes and wellness lunches, video shoots, and twelve-hour marathon study parties for finals.

Now that we are in NYC, hosting still brings us to our happiest place. Welcoming people into our home gives us joy, builds community, and offers us a daily opportunity to share our life's work. Our kitchen is the heart of our home—when we moved into our apartment in the East Village, we tore down a wall (quite literally) to create an open kitchen, and we chose every detail carefully, from the tile, drawers, shelves, and appliances to the huge kitchen island that Zikki hauled all the way from Pittsburgh on the roof of our car! We wanted it to feel warm and welcoming.

Whether it's a five-minute quick hello bite or a three-hour meal to savor, our goal is to make people feel loved and appreciated through food. We hope that with this book we will inspire you to have friends over and share a moment over culinary glories, big and small.

Cooking and sharing food with others does not need to be daunting! Here are some tricks we've learned along the way that have made everything much easier. We call them the Hosting Fundamentals.

hosting fundamentals

1 Always have sparkling water on hand. Sparkling water is AMAZING because it can make someone feel like they are having a special experience for no other reason than that they are drinking something cold with bubbles in it. Not to mention that sparkling water is a great foundation to build mocktails and cocktails.

2 Keep your refrigerator and pantry stocked with simple, snackable treats. Sometimes you are at the store and you wonder, "Why would I buy this beautiful and random container of tinned fish?" Here's how we see it: if you buy something with the intention of sharing it with the ones you love, there is no greater joy. Cheese, crackers, nuts, olives, and a yummy jam. That's it. Everything else is just a bonus.

3 Never skip the bookends. More on this below, but in short: Never skip the Welcome Olives or dessert. Unknowingly and especially over time, people remember the opening and closing of an experience more than anything. They remember most how they feel upon arriving at your home and how they feel when the evening is over. Our goal as good hosts is to make sure they always feel welcome.

4 If you have the right tools, you don't need much. Our friend Charlie told us this years ago in reference to buying a good vacuum cleaner, and it has stuck with me since that day. And it very much applies to hosting. EVERYTHING will be much easier if you have the right tools, starting with the right plates and glassware. It seems silly, but this makes an enormous difference in the way people experience your food and hospitality. It does not need to be fancy, but it MUST be intentional, coming into your home with a purpose.

hosting today? let's go through the day together.

Early in the day:

1 Ensure the wine and sparkling water are chilled, and stock up on plenty of ice.

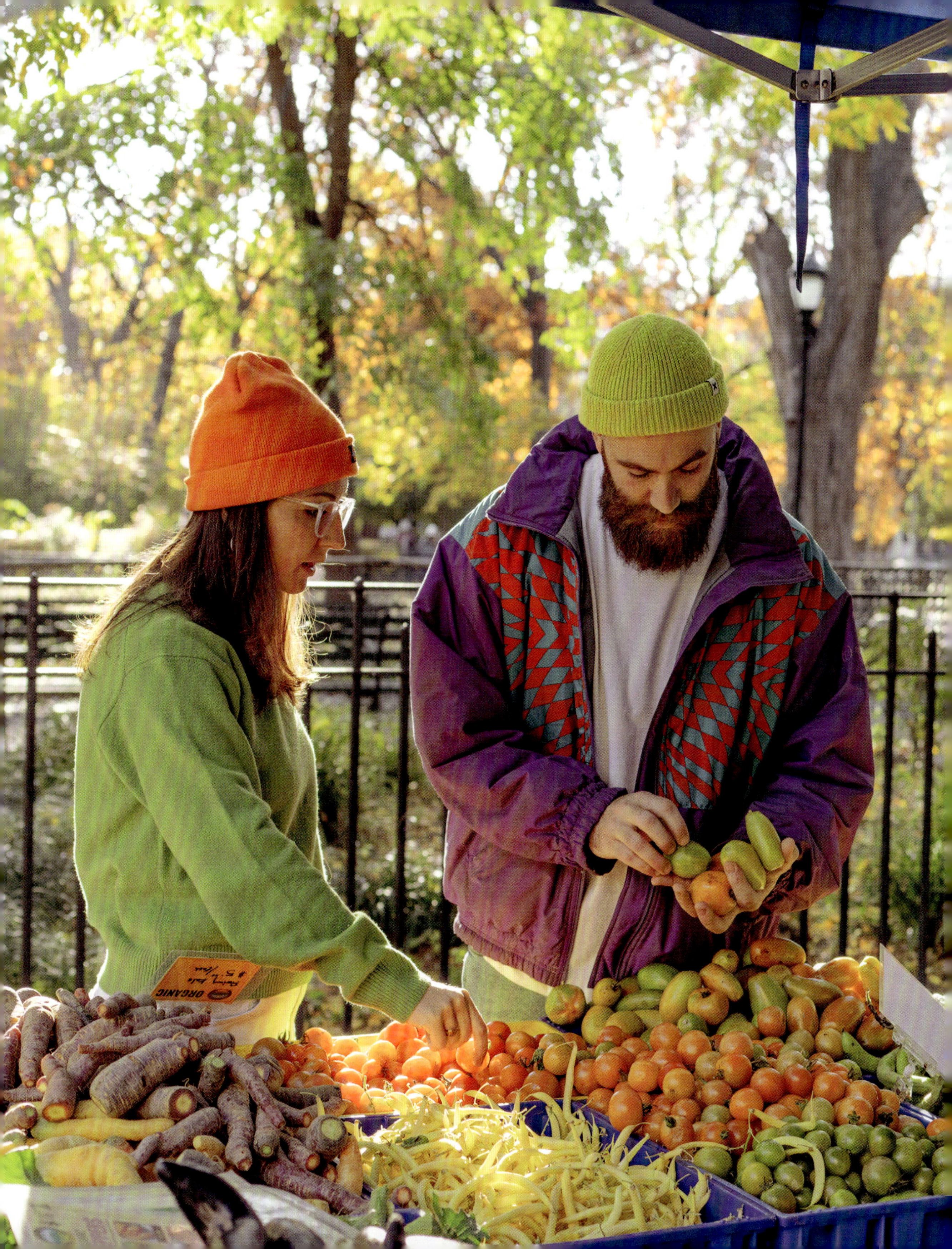
ORGANIC

2 This is the time to prep your dips, spreads, and dressings if you are serving any.

Before they arrive: Set out the Welcome Olives (page 39).

Guests need something to nosh on right away. We call this essential snack Welcome Olives, and it can be as simple as putting out a bowl of olives, a sliced block of really good cheese, some nuts toasted in the microwave, and some yummy crackers. Or you can get creative with some meats, tinned fish, or one of our simpler small plates (see page 39). This does not need to be an over-the-top production. On the contrary, it's just to get things going. A small bite to "calm down," as we say. You would be shocked how far some olives and nuts go when people come in ravenous. And you immediately look like a generous and gracious host.

When they arrive: Keep. It. Simple.

1 Offer something to drink. Make sure it is cold or hot but absolutely not room temperature (unless it's a glass of red wine). Have an alcoholic and nonalcoholic option.

2 Offer them THE snack, the Welcome Olives.

3 Now, this is IMPORTANT. Once they are snacking, walk them through the experience they are about to have. Tell them about the menu and the process you used to make the dishes. People LOVE to know the plan—it makes them feel in control and creates a sense of anticipation. Between us, there is nothing worse than arriving for a meal and not knowing what you'll be offered. And if the plan changes, talk them through it!

4 Be ready with the first "dish" within fifteen minutes of arrival. This can be just a dip or something simple you prepared earlier that day. But that first bite will help you gauge how hungry your guests are and will set the speed for the evening.

As they eat and the evening winds down: Never. Skip. Dessert.

1 You may not get through all the dishes you planned, but that is okay. People may find that they are full and ready for another glass of wine or a walk around the block. What matters is that they are satisfied.

2 But still: Never. Skip. Dessert. Dessert is as integral to the hosting experience as the Welcome Olives. These are the bookends of the meal and likely the most remembered moments of the experience. Even if someone is running out the door, make sure they have something sweet in hand. Dessert does not have to be a grand display. It is that final sweet bite of the meal that closes the evening. It could be a pint of ice cream, fruit, or our crazy-delicious Ma'amoul cookies (page 288).

how to prevent hosting burnout (why does no one talk about this?)

Between the two of us, we have hosted many gatherings in our lives. And there is truly nothing less fun than being left with having to manage or close the party all on your own. Over the years, we've come up with a couple of strategies that have really taken the pressure off hosting. Because yes, hosting burnout is a THING. These little tips may seem obvious in retrospect, when you are standing in your living room wearing yellow rubber gloves and holding a garbage bag. However, if you happen to be a person who likes to plan ahead, these are nonnegotiable things that will absolutely change the game.

1 Make sure your dishwasher is empty when your guests arrive. Easy cleanup is absolutely essential when hosting. In general, have a cleanup plan in place for the end of the party. This can range from asking a friend to help clean up to hiring someone to wash dishes!

2 Ask friends to bring things, but make them intentional. It can be salad ingredients, a bottle of wine, or a dessert from the local bakery, but make sure whatever you ask guests to bring fits with the meal you envision. Not only is this great because it takes things off your shoulders, it also helps the person coming over feel relaxed and included in the process—making the whole experience way more fun and holistic.

3 Let the food lead you . . . Hosting doesn't always have to be a huge production. Often you invite people first, and then plan the menu. But the food can also lead the way, and that's what often drives our gatherings. For example, on shooting days we have ample amounts of treats left over from the day's work, so we casually invite our neighbors over for a freshly baked snack and coffee. Hosting needs to be a joy. When it stops being a joy, it is time to reassess.

4 Invite a social butterfly. Hosting is about the food, but it is also about the people. When you are inviting people over, make sure you have a "middle." This is someone who typically sits at the middle of the table and has the magical ability to play well with anyone, keeping the conversation flowing all night long! Maybe it's your best friend who knows how to spark a conversation with any guest, or a charming neighbor who has a way with words. This person will take the pressure off YOU because they handle the social aspect of the meal, while you focus on the culinary journey.

how do i scale up? meet . . . the feast table

So far, we've touched on all the basics of how to host your loved ones in a small group gathering, including the best snacks to welcome them with and how to begin and end every gathering situation so you look like the best host in town.

Now we want to take all these tips and step it up a notch. Let's talk about how to host a big group of people. How big, you ask? Throw out a number, we can cover it. It doesn't mean you won't need help here, in prep or shopping. It just means you will learn how to scale food for a small gathering into a feast that can feed as many people as you like. Hence the genesis of the name . . . feast table.

Feast tables are a way of hosting. Think small plates with colorful foods, in different textures and looks, covering the entire table, tied together with a variety of breads, flowers, and fruits, setting the vibe of abundance, generosity, and fun. Not only does it give your guests a chance to pick and pair flavors to their liking, it is also a joy for the eyes.

Let's just jump in and walk through the fundamentals of setting up a feast table:

1 Choose a table that fits the size of your party. Depending on the number of people you are hosting, choose an appropriately sized table, which will allow your guests to freely roam around. It will also ensure that you avoid waste because a properly sized spread will quickly be devoured!

2 Prep enough food for the feast. Prep is important, and we want to make sure you get it right. The recipes in this book (especially the dips and spreads) typically yield three small plates, individually plated and garnished, which is perfect for serving two plates and having one extra for refill. Based on how many people you plan to host, this is how many dishes, breads, and small plates we recommend. For a party of 6–8—we recommend making 2–3 recipes + a bread. A sample menu might include Pita, Fattoush Salad, Hummus, and Lamb Kebab OR Tel Avivan Foccacia, Tuna & Grapes, Labneh, and the Best Salad of Your Life drizzled with our delectable Tarragon Silk. Then these recipes can be divided up amongst small plates so everyone has a chance to taste them!

6–8 people	25-person cocktail party
1 loaf of bread	3 or 4 loaves of bread
2 to 3 recipes	10 to 12 recipes
6 to 9 small plates	30 to 36 small plates

3 Cover the table with a tablecloth or, even better, brown paper. When covering your table with small plates or treats that are placed directly on the table, you will want to make sure that it does not get too messy. We love using brown kraft paper as it makes for easy cleanup. Simply remove all the plates from the table at the end of the meal and toss the kraft paper directly into the trash. Clean and efficient.

4 First, flowers. Besides the fact that flowers make us truly happy, they are crucial to creating a beautiful experience for your feast table and make for an excellent centerpiece. You can choose any flowers that speak to you—we encourage working with seasonal local flowers. For example, during the fall, we love to decorate our table with Brussels sprout branches, cabbage flowers, and artichokes!

5 Be strategic with the cutlery and serving plates. In order to avoid a huge line of people waiting to dive into the table, place the cutlery and serving plates in two locations on the table. This will create glorious organic flow around the table.

6 Group and serve with consideration. Make sure that the food you place on the table can last (and not get soggy) until people come in and start to eat. There is absolutely no need to dress and plate the table more than 30 to 60 minutes before the event begins. Keep in mind certain foods can sit out longer than others. For example, when building your feast table, bread can be placed on the table early on, while leafy salads should be dressed, plated, and brought to the table as close as possible to your guests' arrival.

We like to divide our menu into groups and place them on the table in this order:

* Spreads, dips, and butters
* Charcuterie and veggie bites
* Fruits and nuts
* Breads and crackers
* Salads and animal bites (especially if needed to be served hot or cold)

7 Let's cover the table! As mentioned for the cutlery and serving plates, make

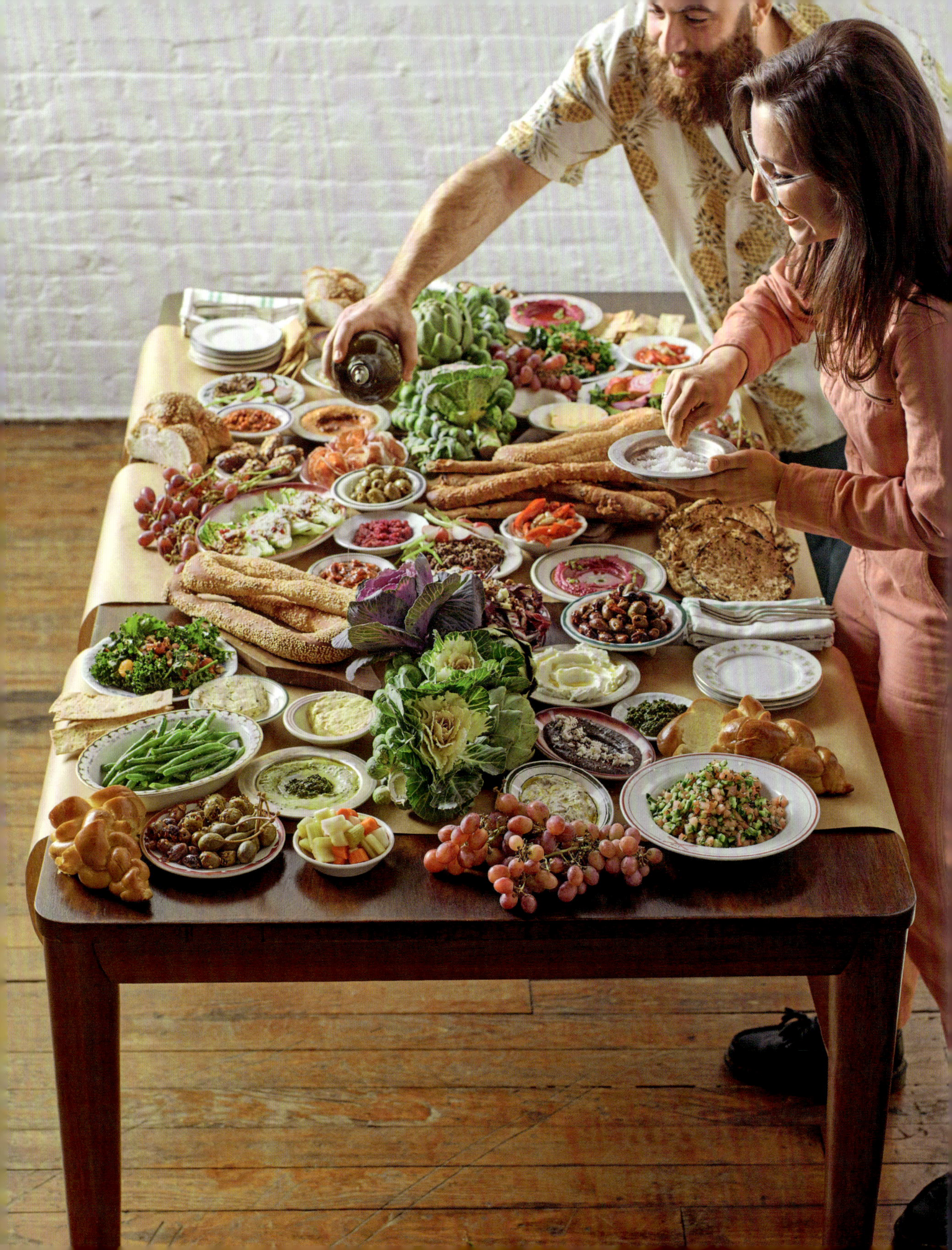

sure you spread out your food in a few locations on the table. That means that every salad, dip, spread, pickle, or any other food you serve should be plated on two or more plates and placed in different areas on the table for easy access. Give attention to the color of your food and try to take it into consideration when giving it space on the table. Remember—the eyes always eat first. You want the food to attract the guests to the table, and color is a great way to do this.

8 Fill in the gaps and cracks. Once you've plated the entire table, you want to fill in all the empty gaps so that you can barely see down to the table (#abundance). Use big voluptuous grapes, strawberries, oranges with their leaves still attached, nuts in their shells, additional crackers, and anything else that is craveable AND clean.

9 Welcome the guests and maintain the feast. Once your guests arrive, welcome them to the table and explain what you served so the whole experience is more approachable. As needed, remove empty plates from the table, refill them, and place them back into their spot.

THE FEAST TABLE

choose your table

lay your

now for the dips & spreads . . .

veggie bites, animal bites & salads

finish with

paper

lay centerpiece & flatware

lay your bread & butter

salt & olive oil

invite your friends to devour

invite your friends to clean ;)

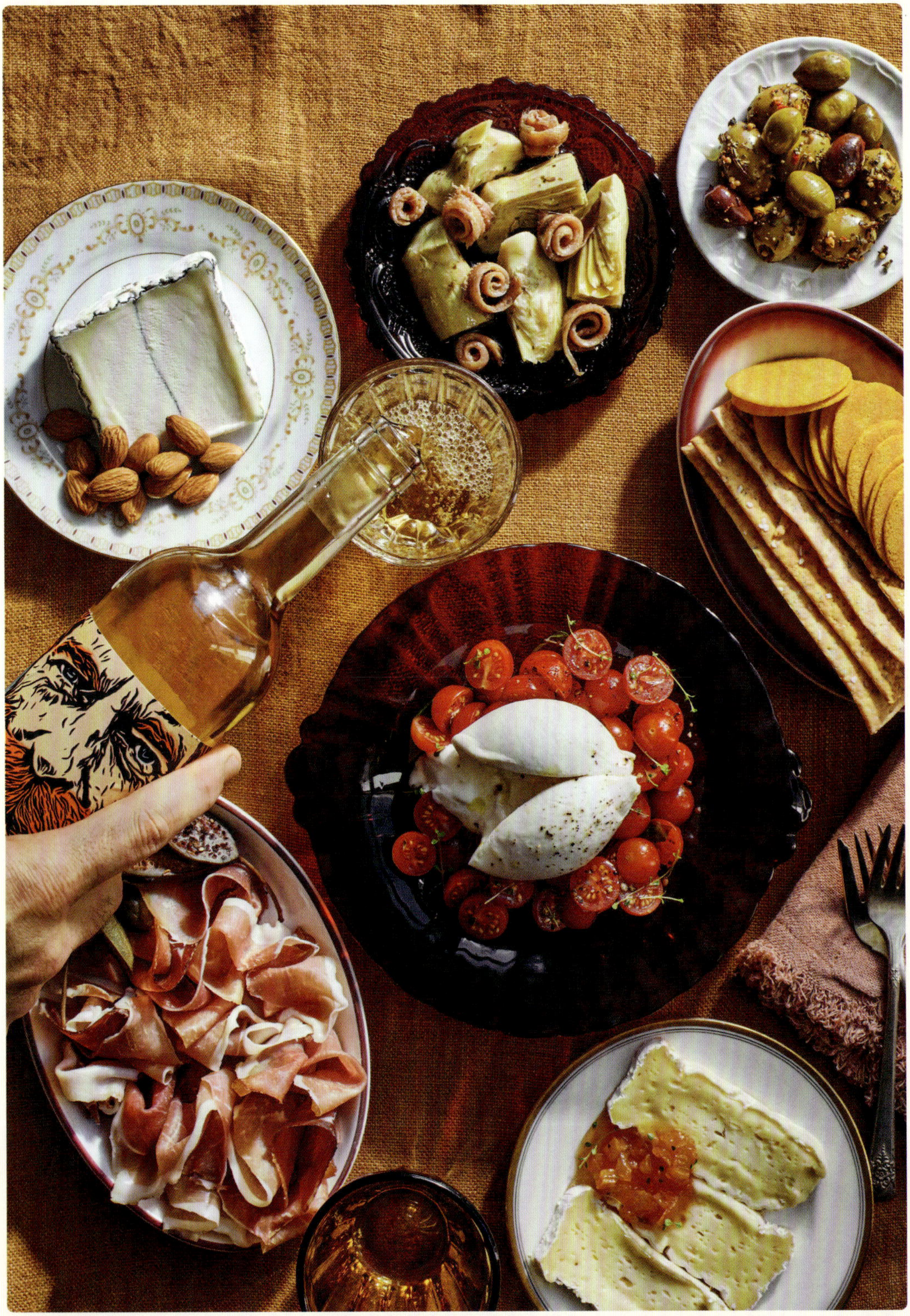

welcome olives

The Welcome Olives can truly be any treat to welcome your guests. The good news for you is that this entire book is dedicated to small plates, all of which fit into this category of "Welcome Olives," but in case that feels overwhelming and you'd prefer to buy everything, we also have you covered.

I don't want to cook, but I can buy.

Yes, you can! My mom (who does not cook) always says, "It is not how you cook, but rather how you buy." I agree, but let's take it one step further: it is really about how you plate. Buy and arrange the following ingredients and you'll have the perfect "welcome" setup!

1. **nuts.** Always buy raw nuts and give them a roast right before serving. The heat and aroma from the nuts will activate many senses and will set the mood for the house like freshly baked cookies. Follow our directions for microwaving nuts (page 22). Serve once cooled and pair alongside your favorite sharp cheese.

2. **charcuterie.** Take a piece of any salumi, loosely fold it into a wave, and place it onto a plate. Repeat until the plate is totally full and drool-worthy. (Prosciutto plates are our favorite.)

3. **creamy cheese.** Burrata is great for crowds and always feels royal. Cut some baby tomatoes in half and distribute them evenly on a beautiful plate. Place a burrata on top and slice into the center to reveal the creamy surprise inside. Finish with extra virgin olive oil, freshly cracked black pepper, and gray salt.

4. **tinned fish.** Anchovies are such a joy and best served taken out of the jar, rolled up into little rounds, and served alongside something tangy and pickled, like quartered artichokes or capers.

5. **funky cheese.** Don't plate the whole cheese. Evenly divide it into thick slices and serve alongside your favorite jam. Not only will it require less and go much further, it will also feel like a dish at a restaurant.

continues

6. something sweet to balance. I would argue that fig or apricot jam can fix all problems. It is important that you balance all the saltiness in your Welcome Olives with something sweet. This can be a jam, any type of dried fruit, or a vine of seedless sweet green grapes.

7. crackers. The secret here is to choose high-quality crackers in a mixed variety. We recommend low-ingredient-count crackers (yes, worth the $9): seeded, herb-based, sourdough-based, and corn crackers are among our favorites.

8. olives. Anything salty and sour on a small plate goes a long way to satisfy your guests. We have at least three different varieties of olives or pickled goodies available at our home for immediate hosting at any point.

---

mix & match

Choose one from each section for your very own Welcome Olives board!

something salty and tangy	charcuterie	cheese	something tinned	crunchy	sweet
olives	prosciutto	burrata	anchovies	crackers	jam
pickles/fermented treats	smoked salmon	labneh	smoked trout	almonds or hazelnuts	dried dates or other dried fruit
canned artichokes	log of salami	humboldt fog	sardines	toasted bread	seedless green grapes

Finish the whole board with a drizzle of extra virgin olive oil and gray salt!

continues

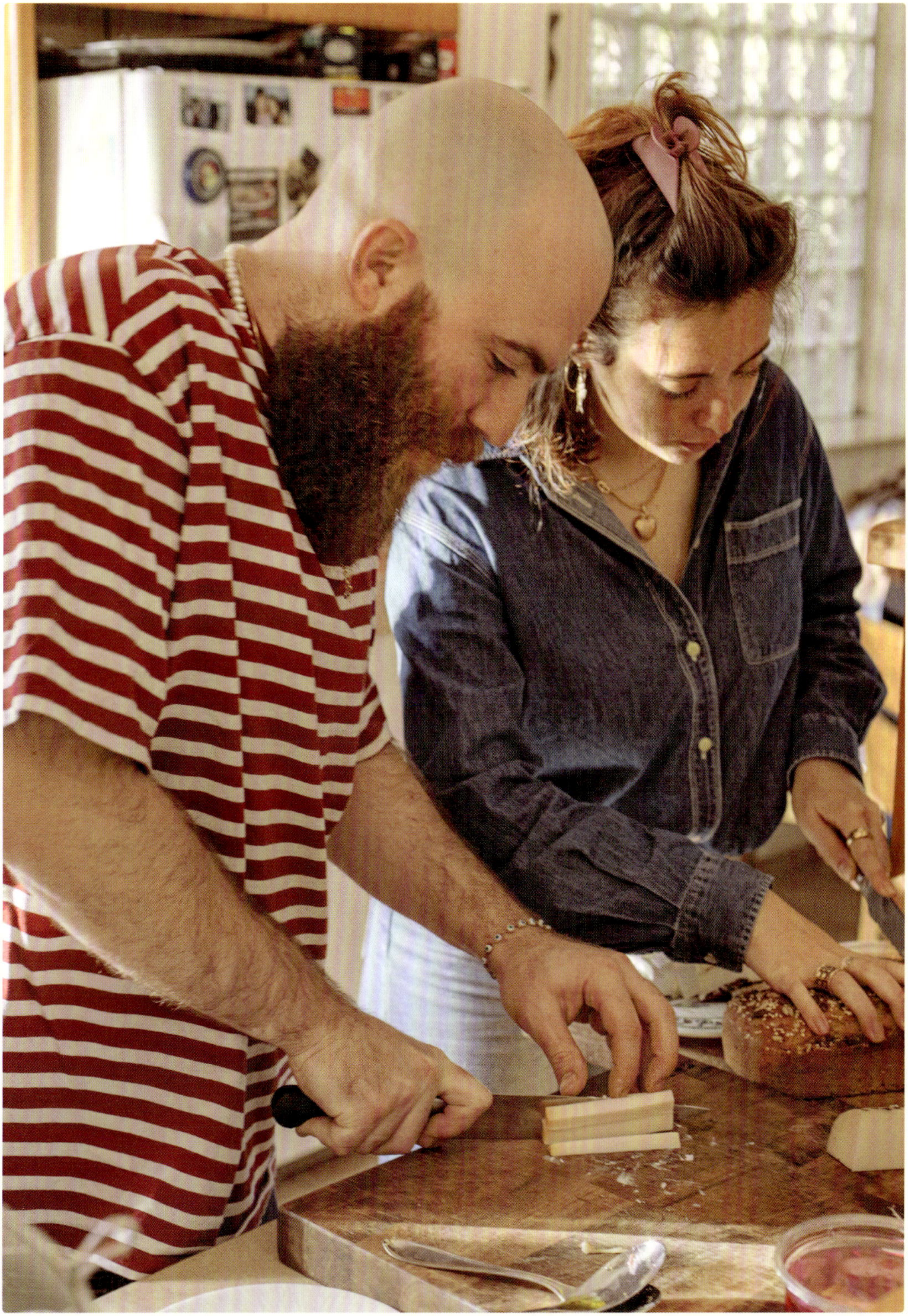

5-minute goat cheese stuffed dates

I don't want to cook, but I am down to combine some ingredients to make something super sexy, quick, and delicious.

Serve fresh bread and a small bowl of . . .

1. **za'atar olive oil:** Combine 1 tablespoon za'atar, 2 tablespoons extra virgin olive oil, and a sprinkle of gray salt.

2. **that tomato sauce:** Combine 3 grated Campari tomatoes, 2 tablespoons extra virgin olive oil, 1 teaspoon vinegar (apple cider or tomato), a sprinkle of gray salt, and a few cracks of black pepper.

And/or serve a few:

1. **5-minute goat cheese stuffed dates:** Pit a container of dates and stuff them with 1 tablespoon of goat cheese. Close them into a sandwich and roll the exposed goat cheese into toasted and crushed pistachios.

2. **sumac cucumber spears:** In a medium bowl, combine 5 speared Persian cucumbers, 1 teaspoon sumac, 1 teaspoon gray salt, and 1 tablespoon extra virgin olive oil. Toss and serve.

3. **spiced jammy eggs:** Place 3 large eggs into boiling water and cook for 7 minutes. Remove and run under cold water. Peel underwater and cut in half. Season with a sprinkle of hawaij, dukkah, harissa powder, or za'atar. Finish with extra virgin olive oil and gray salt.

dips & spreads

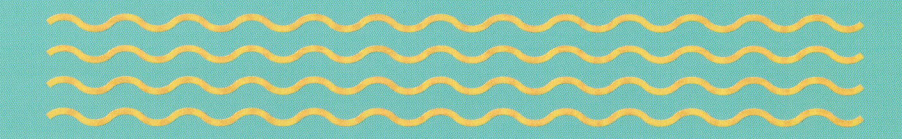

Ben and I have at least two dips or spreads in the refrigerator at all times. To tell you the truth, this is the ultimate hosting hack.

Imagine you get a last-minute call from a friend who just so happens to be in the neighborhood and wants to come over to say hello. No sweat off your back. All you have to do is spoon the dips and spreads you had prepped in advance onto a sexy small plate and drizzle them with some olive oil and sprinkle with gray salt. Add a ladle of olives from your massive bucket of olives (because of course you have one) and slice up a fresh loaf. And that's it, you are ready to go.

These dips, spreads, and gorgeous pantry staples are our absolute go-tos and have been eaten in copious amounts by all the people we love. Not to mention . . . these recipes are easy to make and last a while!

Whether you are serving our ten-minute Tza-Zikki (page 87) or building a Spicy Plate (page 51) to elevate your meal, these recipes will quickly imprint on your culinary cortex.—*zikki*

RECIPES

my grandfather's zhug

harissa

our hassle-free matbucha

the smoothest tahini dip

preserved lemon

zikki's quick amba

garlic lovers ONLY toum

three confits
garlic confit • tomato confit • leek & sage confit

compound butters
sumac, lemon & oregano butter • preserved lemon butter • sage & leek butter

jams
cranberry & sumac jam • silan & onion jam • persimmon & thyme jam

chopped liver, better than your grandma's

classic hummus

my uncle tal's lentil masabacha

labneh 3 ways

tza-zikki

beet & goat cheese dip

let's burn a veggie and make a spread
white baba • black baba • zaalouk • mashwiya

a cashew basil dip everyone will talk about

cilantro pistachio artichoke dip

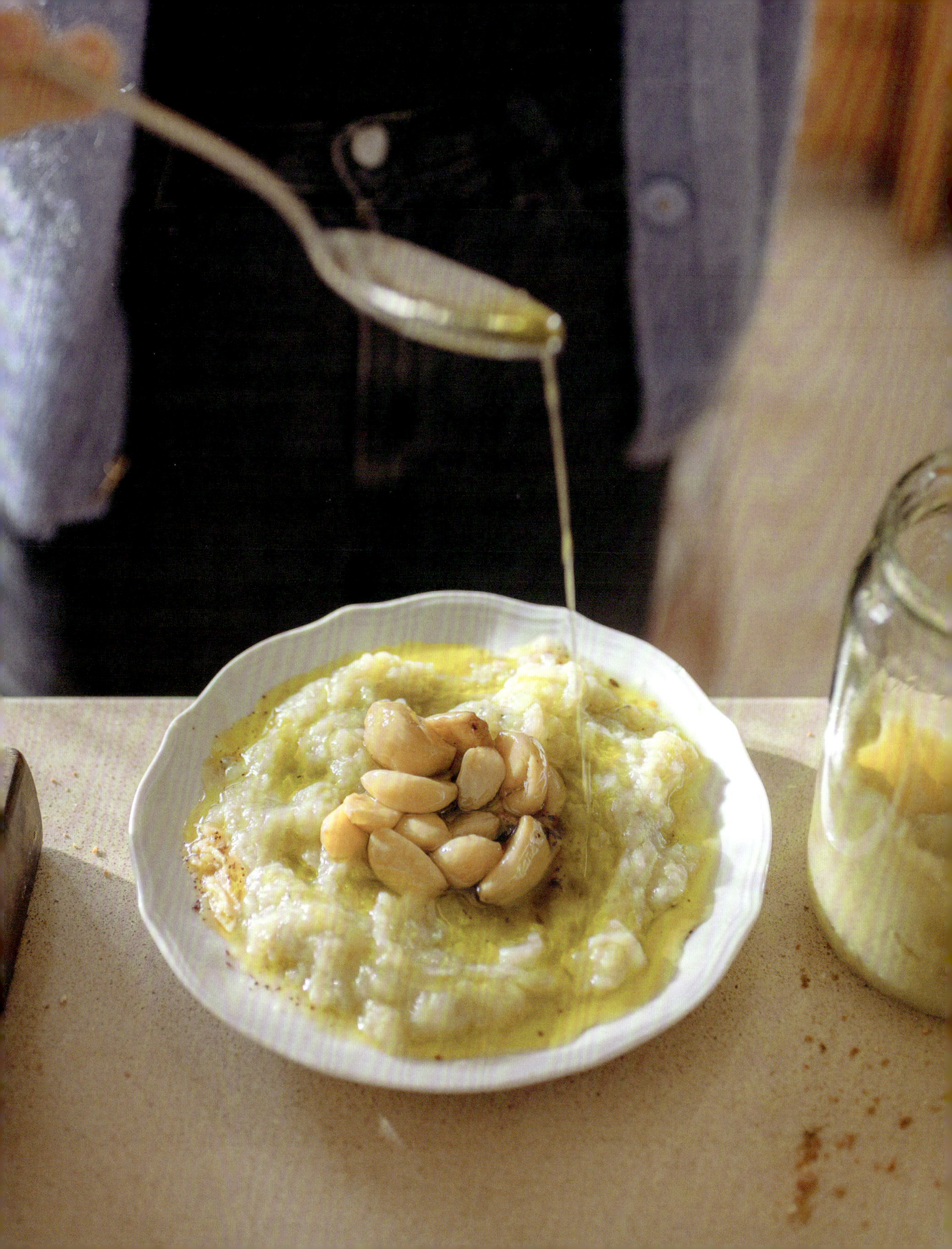

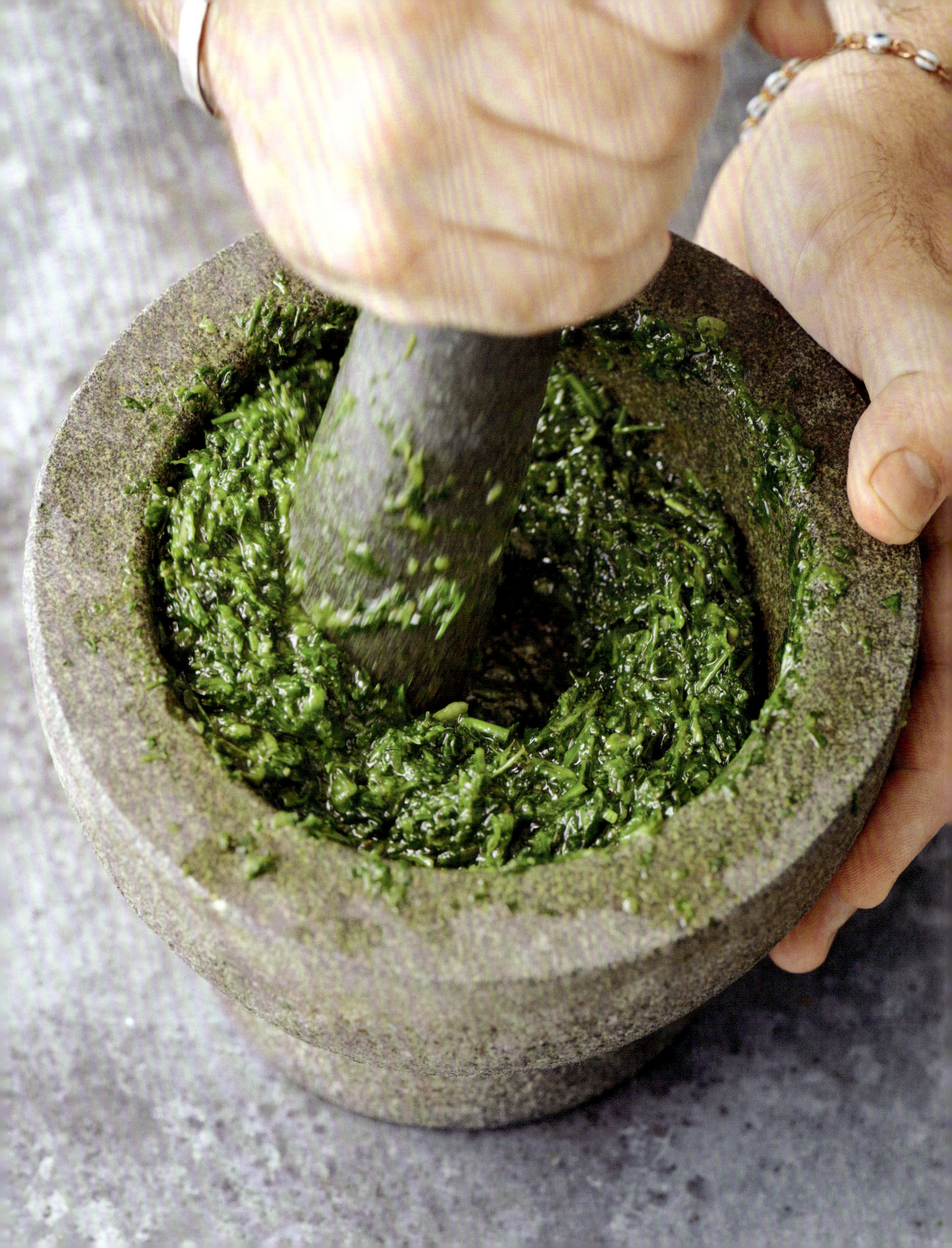

My Grandfather's Zhug
Yemenite Spicy Cilantro Chutney

One of the core memories from my childhood is brunching on Saturdays at my grandparents' house. Safta and Saba (my grandmother and grandfather) were and still are notorious for planning a glorious feast that feeds our entire family. My Saba is quite the cook, and in his kitchen you'll find a huge array of jars scattered everywhere that hold his pickled treasures. Saba always "opens" the table with olives, pickles, tahini, bread, and of course, zhug. Some people make it spicy, but he does not. He balances the bright flavors of the garlic, cilantro, chili, and cumin perfectly to make the zhug bold and delicious. This Yemenite condiment is the perfect addition to any dip, spread, grilled veggie, meat, or fish! —Ben

Serve it with: Zhug & Zucchini (page 211), Charred Eggplant with Labneh, Zhug & Dukkah (page 233), My Uncle Tal's Lentil Masabacha (page 79)

Yield: One 16-ounce jar or two 8-ounce jars

Total time: 10 minutes

Special tools: food processor

8 garlic cloves, peeled

1 teaspoon ground cumin

5 long green hot chilies, halved and seeded

2 bunches of cilantro

1 bunch of mint, stemmed

1 teaspoon gray salt

½ cup extra virgin olive oil

1. In a food processor, add the garlic, cumin, and chilies. Process until the mixture is evenly combined. Add the cilantro, mint, and salt and blend until the leaves have broken down and are incorporated into the chili paste.

2. With the food processor running on low, slowly pour in the olive oil. Process the mixture for 1 minute, or until combined into a smooth spread.

3. Transfer to a jar with a tight-fitting lid and store in the refrigerator for up to 1 month.

HARISSA
smoky hot pepper paste

Harissa is one of the most underrated spreads in your pantry. It's also very hard to find a good-quality harissa in the store. But luckily, for the enormous amount of flavor it adds to a dish, it requires very little effort to make from scratch. Just don't forget to wear a pair of gloves when removing the seeds from the dried chilies. —ben & zikki

Serve it with: Deconstructed Sabich (page 143), The Smoothest Tahini Dip (page 55), Pita (page 109), Falafel (page 215), Vetrena Fries (page 227)

Yield: One 8-ounce jar

Total time: 45 minutes

Special tools: kitchen gloves, food processor

1.7 ounces dried hot chilies

3.5 ounces dried sweet red peppers

4¼ cups boiling water

3 garlic cloves, peeled

1 teaspoon gray salt

2 teaspoons ground cumin

¼ cup extra virgin olive oil

---

1. Wearing kitchen gloves, slice the hot and sweet peppers in half and remove all the seeds and stems.

2. Place the peppers in a large heatproof bowl and rehydrate them by pouring the boiling water into the bowl, ensuring they are fully submerged. Let sit to rehydrate for 30 minutes, stirring every few minutes to make sure that they are plumping evenly.

3. After 30 minutes, remove the peppers from the water and pat them dry using a towel. Place the peppers into your food processor along with the garlic, salt, and cumin. Pulse and slowly add the olive oil while pulsing until the mixture becomes smooth.

4. Transfer to a jar with a tight-fitting lid and store in the refrigerator for up to 6 months.

our hassle-free matbucha

harissa

my grandfather's zhug

spicy plate

In Israel, we like to serve a "spicy plate" alongside a meal. It is a plate or platter made up of different spicy things—all varying in texture, flavor, and heat level. Learning to use a spicy plate will elevate your table and can provide a different perspective to any dish!

OUR HASSLE-FREE MATBUCHA
spicy tomato spread

Our hassle-free matbucha (see photo, page 51) is the kind of condiment that needs to be the highlight of everything. It is a hot tomato sauce that cooks slowly throughout the day into a candied hot tomato paste. We use it in our house very frequently and our guests love it. Matbucha is traditionally made with old tomatoes, but in this recipe, we are using whole canned tomatoes. We discovered that when cooked down, they provide the best texture for matbucha, saving you hours of labor-intensive tomato scoring, flash cooking, and peeling. Simply use the canned tomatoes and focus your energy on perfectly browning your flavor boosters: the garlic and chili.—ben & zikki

Serve it with: The Smoothest Tahini Dip (page 55), Black or White Baba (pages 92 and 94), Pita (page 109), My Grandfather's Zhug (page 49)

Yield: Serves 6 to 8, makes 1 quart

Total time: At least 1 hour

¼ cup extra virgin olive oil

20 large garlic cloves, peeled

2 long green hot chilies, sliced into ¼-inch rounds

1 teaspoon ground cumin

2 (28-ounce) cans whole tomatoes

1 heaping teaspoon gray salt

---

1. In a medium saucepan over medium heat, add the olive oil and garlic and bring to a simmer. Simmer without stirring for 2 minutes, or until fragrant. Add the chilies and stir to combine. Continue to cook for 1 minute, or until the chilies begin to change color and before the garlic turns brown. Add the cumin and stir.

2. Keeping the heat on medium, add the canned tomatoes to the mixture and stir. Add the salt and stir to combine again.

3. Bring the tomato mixture to a boil over high heat and cook, stirring continuously, for 5 minutes, then reduce the heat to medium and simmer for at least 1 hour, stirring occasionally, until the water from the tomatoes has evaporated and they have reduced to a thick paste.

4. After 1 hour, increase the heat to high and cook the matbucha for 5 more minutes, stirring constantly (it is okay if it sticks to the bottom slightly).

5. Remove from the heat and cool to room temperature. Serve or transfer to an airtight container and store in the refrigerator for up to 1 week.

Essential Tips:

Don't skip the high-heat step. It will add a sexy, charred smoky flavor to the matbucha, saving you hours of slow cooking. But if you happen to have more time, you can continue cooking the matbucha on low heat for up to 3 hours. It will deepen the flavor.

This should be the first thing you put on to cook when you are preparing a feast. It is simple to prep and just needs a quick stir every 15 minutes to ensure it is not burning on the bottom of the pot. It's a great dish to cook in the background while you work on other things in the kitchen.

the smoothest
tahini dip

+ harissa

+ my grandfather's
zhug

THE SMOOTHEST TAHINI dip

To us, tahini is a way of life. It is one of the lightest yet most satisfying spreads ever. The base of this tahini dip is just two ingredients: water and raw tahini. Many people "open" raw tahini by adding water to the paste to transform it into a dip (Israelis use the term "open" to describe this transformation). But in our method, we add the raw tahini to water and whisk until we have reached the consistency we are looking for. This way you skip the weird clumpy phase when the water is fully absorbed into the raw tahini and looks like you've done something wrong. This method takes you straight to a smooth dip.

    We love to season our tahini dip using only lemon juice and salt, but we also have two variations we like to make, using one of two additional condiments to make an extra-dreamy spread. Once you know how to open the tahini from raw to sauce, watch as it transforms the way you eat! —bEN & zikki

Serve it with: Our Hassle-Free Matbucha (page 52), Black or White Baba (pages 92 and 94), Zaalouk (page 95), Kebab (page 266)

Yield: Serves 6 to 12, makes 1 cup or 4 small bowls

Total time: 5 minutes

½ cup (4.5 ounces) cold water

Juice of ¼ lemon

½ teaspoon gray salt, plus more to taste

8 ounces raw tahini

1. In a small bowl, whisk together the water, lemon juice, and salt.

2. Continue whisking as you slowly add the raw tahini, until the mixture reaches a smooth, sauce-like consistency.

3. Serve immediately or transfer to an airtight container and store in the refrigerator for up to 2 days.

ESSENTiAL Tips:

How to adjust the consistency: The consistency of your tahini dip will define its use. If you want to use it in a pita, then it should be a relatively thin sauce. If you want to use it as a spread, then add more raw tahini to thicken it up. Add either raw tahini or water 1 teaspoon at a time to adjust the consistency.

How to get the most out of your raw tahini: If you have reached the bottom of a raw tahini jar and want to make use of those last bits, simply add around 3 tablespoons of water and shake the jar instead of trying to loosen it with a kitchen tool!

recipe continues

ZHUG/HARISSA/ANY-DIP-YOU-LIKE TAHINI

Yield: 1 small plate

Zhug and harissa are our favorite condiments to mix with tahini, but feel free to use your favorite sauces or dips instead. Tahini is a great vehicle for all good flavors.

½ cup The Smoothest Tahini Dip (page 55)
1 tablespoon My Grandfather's Zhug (page 49) or Harissa (page 50)

Add your tahini dip to a bowl and mix in the zhug or harissa until combined. Serve immediately.

preserved lemon

In Israel, preserved lemon is as much of a staple in someone's home as a jar of peanut butter is in a New York pantry. It wasn't until I moved abroad that I realized that in order to enjoy this flavor at home, I actually had to make the preserved lemon myself. The shelf-stable preserved lemon available in the grocery store tends to have a very soapy aftertaste and overwhelms whatever dish it is served with. When you make your own, the result is a bright, tangy, and salty condiment that adds a citrusy freshness to any dish. The truth is, it takes a few minutes to prep and lasts forever. All you need is salt, lemons, and a jar. Let's ride. —ben

Serve it with: Preserved Lemon Butter (page 69), Akko Crudo (page 247), Middle Eastern Caesar (page 187), Double-Dip Artichoke (page 198)

Yield: Four 8-ounce jars or one 24-ounce jar

Total time: 15 minutes, plus 1 week for preservation

Special tools: One 24-ounce sterilized wide-mouth mason jar or four 8-ounce sterilized wide-mouth mason jars (see page 72)

7 organic lemons, scrubbed

Gray salt (about 1 cup)

1. Slice the lemons into ¼-inch rounds, remove the seeds, and lightly coat each slice with salt on both sides. Shake off the excess salt.

2. Layer and distribute the lemon slices tightly and evenly into the sterilized jar(s), pressing down each layer with your hands so that the slices release some of their juices. It is important that the juice reaches the top of the jar so that it covers the entirety of the packed lemons. If it does not, add more lemon juice as needed and seal the container. Let the jar rest at room temperature and out of the sunlight for 2 days.

recipe continues

dips & spreads

3. After 2 days, flip the jar upside down and place it on a sturdy plate to catch any spillage. Leave the jar upside down for an additional 5 days.

4. After the jar rests for a total of 7 days, flip the jar upright. Place the jar in the refrigerator as is or blend into a paste using a food processor and then refrigerate for up to 6 months.

Essential Tips:

Use quality lemons: When preparing pickled lemons, it is imperative that the lemons be organic and from the cleanest source possible, as we want to preserve their most authentic citrus essence. If you buy lemons from the supermarket, make sure to scrub them with soap and water to remove the supermarket wax and glaze.

Using as a preserved lemon paste: As a blended paste, the preserved lemon can be the base of any sauce, added to a vinaigrette or stew, or served as a basic spread on your sandwich. We add it to yogurt whenever we are looking for a quick dip for veggies or bread!

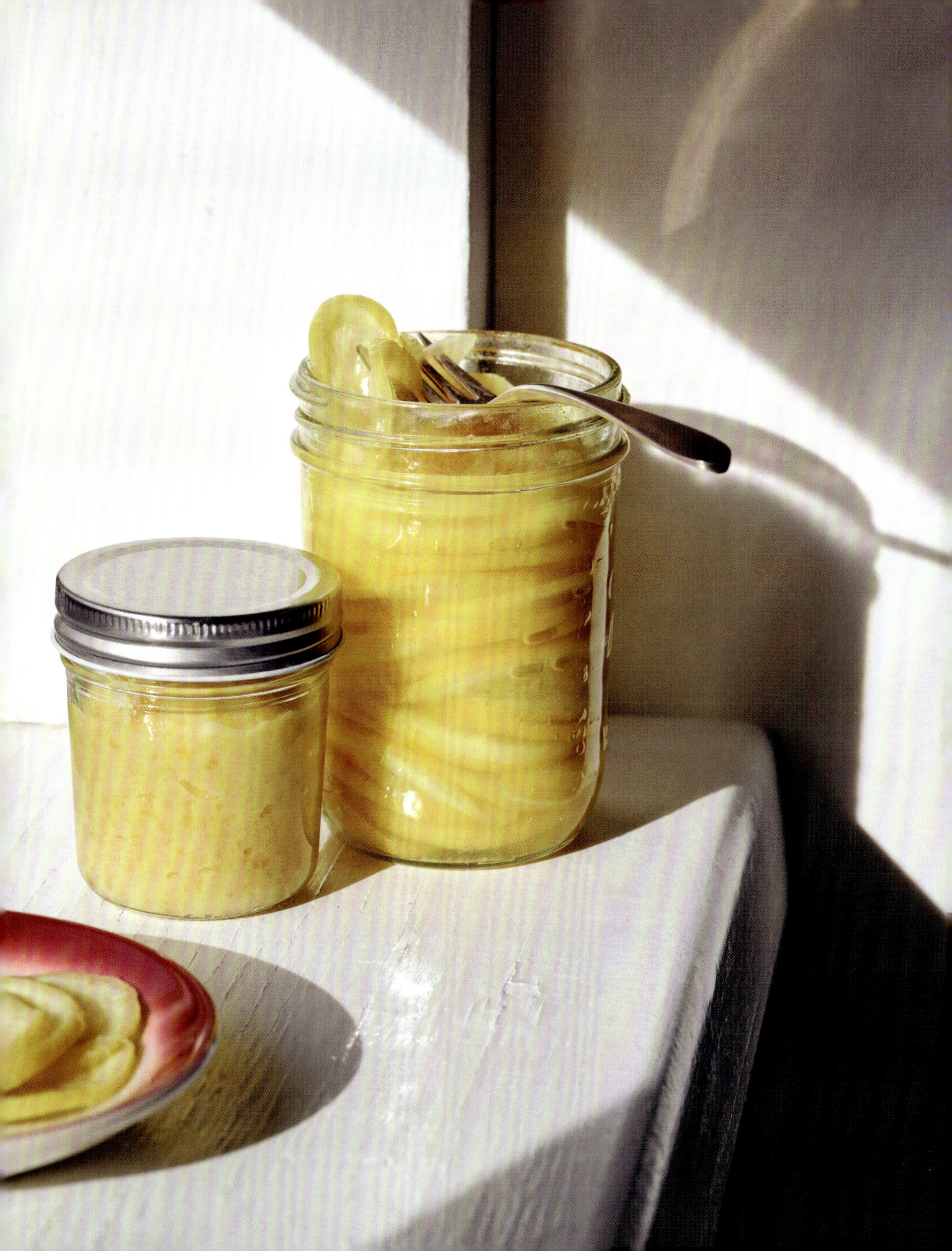

zikki's quick amba
middle eastern spiced pickled mango sauce

I remember when Zikki tasted amba sauce on her very first sabich pita at Hakosem (The Magician) in Tel Aviv. Her mind was blown. Arguably, amba is the signature taste of the sabich pita—it infuses the dish with its most notable flavors and textures.

When we returned to New York, amba was nowhere to be found, but Zikki remembered the sensation and flavor profile well, almost as if she had a photographic memory. Using ingredients available at our local spice store, she was able to recreate amba at home. Though amba is traditionally fermented for weeks, Zikki's version can be executed in a matter of minutes without compromising the unique flavors. This tangy and bright condiment is perfect on any pita sandwich or grilled meat, and especially delicious on anything fried. I would argue Zikki's is almost better than the ones we've had in Israel. —ben

Serve it with: Deconstructed Sabich (page 143), Kebab (page 266), Chicken Shawarma Salad (page 153)

Yield: One 8-ounce jar

Total time: 10 minutes

Special tools: food processor

---

2 very ripe mangoes, peeled and pitted

2 tablespoons tirshi powder (see note)

½ teaspoon ground fenugreek

½ teaspoon citric acid (see note)

1 teaspoon honey

1 teaspoon gray salt

1. In a food processor, add the mangoes, tirshi powder, fenugreek, citric acid, honey, and salt. Process until smooth.

2. Transfer to a jar with a tight-fitting lid and store in the refrigerator for up to 1 month.

essential tips:

Tirshi powder is a Middle Eastern spice mix that is equal parts ground cumin, turmeric, cayenne, fenugreek, and salt. If you can't find it in the store, it is easy to make at home.

Citric acid plays a key role in the quick-curing process of the "quick amba," giving the ripe mangoes the tang typically achieved by curing green mango with salt over a longer period of time. As a result, the citric acid cannot be substituted.

Garlic Lovers Only Toum

Garlic toum is made from only four ingredients: garlic, salt, lemon, and olive oil. This means that it is imperative to use the best ingredients available: fresh garlic, extra virgin olive oil (see page 20), gray salt, and freshly squeezed organic lemon juice.

Magic happens when these ingredients are blended together in a specific order with a strong attention to detail, especially when it comes to the texture. If done correctly, you will create a light and fluffy whipped garlic spread that is perfectly balanced in flavor.
—ben & zikki

Serve it with: Kebab (page 266), Black Baba (page 94)
Yield: One 8-ounce jar
Total time: 15 minutes
Special tools: food processor

1 cup whole garlic cloves, peeled

2 teaspoons gray salt

3 cups extra virgin olive oil

Juice of 4 organic lemons

1. In a food processor, add the garlic and salt. Blend, scraping down the sides with a spatula as needed to incorporate any unblended pieces of garlic.

2. With the food processor running, slowly pour in the olive oil, 1 tablespoon at a time, then turn off the food processor and scrape down the sides. Repeat this process until the garlic mixture becomes creamy.

3. Once the mixture is creamy and with the food processor still running, pour in 1 tablespoon of lemon juice, followed by 1 tablespoon of the remaining olive oil. Continue alternating the ingredients until both ingredients are fully used. Blend for 5 minutes, until the mixture is fully homogeneous and fluffy in texture.

4. Serve alongside some toasted bread and olives or transfer to an airtight container and store in the refrigerator for up to 3 months.

Essential Tip:

Follow the blending process: It is really important that you alternate between the olive oil and the lemon juice as soon as the garlic and olive oil have emulsified to achieve the airy and fluffy consistency of toum.

tomato confit

garlic confit

leek & sage confit

THREE CONFITS

There is always at least one type of confit in our refrigerator. It is incredibly easy to prep and absolutely the most impressive thing to whip out for some impromptu hosting.

When making a confit, it is important to remember that you are not frying the ingredients in the oil; you are slow cooking them so that the hot oil gently permeates the raw layers and transforms the base vegetable into a decadent, perfectly balanced, and spreadable condiment. Pair with fresh bread and flaky sea salt, or use as a hummus topper with sumac and za'atar. The best part? It preserves itself and doubles as a flavorful oil!—*zikki*

GARLIC CONFIT

Serve it with: Sourdough bread, Classic Hummus (page 77)
Yield: One 16-ounce jar or two 8-ounce jars
Total time: 45 minutes

1½ cups whole garlic cloves
1½ cups extra virgin olive oil

1. In a small saucepan over medium heat, heat the garlic and olive oil. Once the garlic and oil are hot but not boiling, reduce the heat to low.

2. Continue cooking heat for 30 to 45 minutes, until the cloves are soft and tender. Be careful to not let the garlic brown as it can become bitter.

3. Once the garlic is softened, remove from the heat and allow the confit to cool to room temperature before transferring it to a jar with a tight-fitting lid.

4. Transfer the garlic confit to a jar, fully submerging it in oil to prevent spoilage. Refrigerate for up to 2 weeks (see note, page 65).

recipe continues

TOMATO CONFIT

Serve it with: Labneh Spread (page 84), Pita (page 109)
Yield: One 16-ounce jar or two 8-ounce jars
Total time: 45 minutes

1 (10-ounce) container cherry tomatoes
3 sprigs of thyme
1½ cups extra virgin olive oil

1. Using a sharp chef's knife, make a small slit in the side of each tomato so that they don't burst as they cook.

2. In a small saucepan over medium heat, heat the tomatoes, thyme, and olive oil. Once the oil is hot but not boiling, reduce the heat to low.

3. Continue cooking over low heat for 30 to 45 minutes, until the tomatoes are soft and tender.

4. Once the tomato skin has crinkled and the tomatoes have softened, remove from the heat and allow the confit to cool to room temperature before transferring to a jar with a tight-fitting lid.

5. When transferring the tomato confit to the jar, make sure that the tomatoes are fully submerged in the oil to prevent early spoilage. Store in the refrigerator for up to 2 weeks (see note, opposite).

LEEK & SAGE CONFIT

Serve it with: Ricotta, Labneh Spread (page 84)
Yield: One 16-ounce jar or two 8-ounce jars
Total time: 1 hour

2 leeks
10 sage leaves
1 long green hot chili, sliced into ½-inch rounds
1½ teaspoons gray salt
1½ cups extra virgin olive oil

1. To remove the sediment from the leeks, peel back the outer leaves and fully submerge the leeks in a large bowl filled with water for 10 minutes, then drain.

2. Using a chef's knife, cut off the top 2 inches of the leek and the root. Then slice the leeks into ½-inch rounds.

3. In a medium saucepan over medium heat, combine the leeks, sage, chili, salt, and ¼ cup of the olive oil. Cook for 2 minutes, until all the salt is dissolved. Add the remaining 1¼ cups olive oil and increase the heat to medium-high. Once the oil is hot but not boiling, reduce the heat to low.

4. Continue cooking over low heat for 45 minutes, or until the leeks are soft and tender.

5. Once the leeks are completely limp and softened, remove from the heat and allow the confit to cool to room temperature before transferring to a jar with a tight-fitting lid.

6. When transferring the leek confit to the jar, ensure that the solids are fully submerged in the oil to prevent early spoilage. Store in the refrigerator for up to 2 weeks (see note).

essential tips (for all confits):

How to eat: You can choose to keep these confits in a jar to be eaten as they are on a sexy piece of toast topped with ricotta, or feel free to blend them into a gorgeous paste that can then be used as a spread or a base to start a stew or pasta! You can also reuse the preserving oil to cook or season with, or you can simply discard it.

Storing the confit: If you want to make this confit last more than a few days, sterilize your jars before adding the confit and then seal them in a simple water bath. To sterilize, wash the jars and lids in hot, soapy water; rinse well. Fill them up to the brim with boiling water and then pour out the water (see page 72).

Preparing in bulk: Confit is an excellent condiment to make in bulk during peak tomato, garlic, and leek season. Make it in the summer, then seal it in sterilized jars (using a water bath) to use in the fall and winter.

silan & onion jam

sage & leek butter

cranberry & sumac jam

persimmon & thyme jam

sumac, lemon & oregano butter

preserved lemon butter

this is our bread & butter— & jam

This part of the book was given its wildly original title as it is literally the bread and butter of our life. And jam. To build up a bread, butter, and jam board, all you need to do is pull the butters and jams from the refrigerator 1 hour before your guests arrive, allowing them to come to room temperature and, hence, becoming perfectly spreadable. Our jams change seasonally depending on what is abundant and available. Arrange your butters and your jams in small little bowls and top with flaky sea salt. Serve alongside a freshly baked loaf.

—ben & zikki

compound butters

Compound butter is another term for "super-fancy butter" or "butter mixed with random spices and ingredients from your refrigerator." As a baker, I really lean into making compound butters not only because it is really fun but because it provides a bright condiment for a plain loaf of bread. Additionally, butter is an incredible vehicle for any overwhelming flavor that may need to be gently toned down or given a big crank up! —ben

Serve it with: Challah (page 117), Absolutely Love a Breakfast Spread (page 304), sourdough bread

sumac, lemon & oregano butter

Yield: One 8-ounce jar
Total time: 10 minutes

8 ounces salted Irish butter, softened to room temperature

½ teaspoon sumac

½ organic lemon, seeded and finely chopped

10 sprigs of oregano, stemmed

½ teaspoon gray salt

1. In a small bowl, add the softened butter, sumac, lemon, oregano, and salt. Using a spatula, fold until evenly combined.

2. Transfer the butter to a jar with a tight-fitting lid and refrigerate overnight or for up to 2 months (see note, opposite). One hour before serving, remove the butter from the refrigerator to soften and come to room temperature.

ESSENTIAL TIP (FOR ALL BUTTERS):

Storing the butter:
If you want to make this butter last longer, sterilize your jar before adding the butter and then seal it in a simple water bath. To sterilize, wash the jar and lid in hot, soapy water; rinse well. Fill it up to the brim with boiling water and then pour out the water (page 72).

PRESERVED LEMON BUTTER

Yield: One 8-ounce jar
Total time: 10 minutes

8 ounces salted Irish butter, softened to room temperature
1 heaping tablespoon Preserved Lemon paste (page 57)

1. In a small bowl, add the softened butter and preserved lemon paste. Using a spatula, fold until evenly combined.

2. Transfer the butter to a jar with a tight-fitting lid and refrigerate overnight or for up to 2 months (see note). One hour before serving, remove the butter from the refrigerator to soften and come to room temperature.

SAGE & LEEK BUTTER

Yield: One 8-ounce jar
Total time: 10 minutes

8 ounces salted Irish butter, softened to room temperature
½ cup Leek & Sage Confit (page 64), drained

1. In a small bowl, add the softened butter and leek and sage confit. Using a spatula, fold until evenly combined.

2. Transfer the butter to a jar with a tight-fitting lid and refrigerate overnight or for up to 2 months (see note). One hour before serving, remove the butter from the refrigerator to soften and come to room temperature.

JAMS

Jams are my jam. But seriously. They are perfect to spread on toast, whisk into dressings, or to serve alongside something decadent because they up the richness perfectly! A little secret? Don't overcook the jam. Once you see the twinkle of carmelized sugar coating, you are finished! —*zikki*

CRANBERRY & SUMAC JAM

Serve it with: Absolutely Love a Breakfast Spread (page 304), Welcome Olives (page 309), sourdough bread

Yield: One 8-ounce jar

Total time: 40 minutes

1 pound fresh cranberries

1 cup sugar

1 tablespoon sumac

1 teaspoon lemon juice

1. In a small saucepan over medium-low heat, combine the cranberries, sugar, sumac, and lemon juice. Cook uncovered for 40 minutes, stirring every few minutes to break up the cranberries and keep the mixture from burning on the bottom.

2. The jam will be finished when the liquid has thickened to a molasses-like consistency. When this happens, remove the pan from the heat. Let the jam cool to room temperature before transferring it to a jar with a tight-fitting lid.

3. Store the jam in the refrigerator until you are ready to enjoy, up to 1 month (see note, page 72).

ESSENTIAL TIP:

How to buy silan:
Searching for silan may sound intimidating, but it is actually widely available at most supermarkets. If you cannot find it in the baking or sugar section, you may find it in the "global foods" aisle. It also goes by the name date honey. If you cannot find silan, you can substitute it here with 2 tablespoons of regular honey plus a teaspoon of balsamic vinegar.

SILAN & ONION JAM

Serve it with: Absolutely Love a Breakfast Spread (page 304), Welcome Olives (page 309), sourdough bread

Yield: One 8-ounce jar

Total time: 40 minutes

4 white onions, sliced

1½ cups sugar

2 teaspoons gray salt

2 tablespoons silan (date honey)

1. In a medium saucepan over medium-low heat, combine the onions, sugar, and salt. Cook uncovered for 40 minutes, stirring often to prevent sticking.

2. The jam will be finished when the liquid has thickened to a molasses-like consistency. When this happens, remove the pan from the heat and stir in the silan. Let the jam cool to room temperature before transferring it to a jar with a tight-fitting lid.

3. Store the jam in the refrigerator until you are ready to enjoy, up to 1 month (see note, page 72).

PERSIMMON & THYME JAM

Serve it with: Absolutely Love a Breakfast Spread (page 304), Welcome Olives (page 309), sourdough bread

Yield: One 8-ounce jar

Total time: 40 minutes

4 persimmons, peeled and finely diced

1 cup sugar

3 sprigs of thyme, stemmed

recipe continues

ESSENTIAL TIP (FOR ALL JAMS):

Storing the jam: If you want to make this jam last longer, sterilize your jar before adding the jam and then seal it in a simple water bath. To sterilize, wash the jar and lid in hot, soapy water; rinse well. Fill up to the brim with boiling water and then pour out the water (see below).

1. In a small saucepan over medium-low heat, combine the persimmons, sugar, and thyme. Cook uncovered for 40 minutes, stirring often to break up the persimmons and keep the mixture from burning on the bottom.

2. The jam will be finished when the liquid has thickened to a molasses-like consistency. When this happens, remove the saucepan from the heat. Let the jam cool to room temperature before transferring it to a jar with a tight-fitting lid.

3. Store the jam in the refrigerator until you are ready to enjoy, up to 1 month (see note).

---

storing your goods for a long time

to sterilize

1. Wash the jar and lid in hot, soapy water.
2. Rinse well to remove all soap residue.
3. Fill the jar up to the brim with boiling water.
4. Pour out the boiling water after a few moments to complete the sterilization.
5. Now your jar is sterilized and ready for use!

to seal and store

1. Fill the jar with confit, butter, or jam.
2. Remove air bubbles by gently tapping the jar with a utensil.
3. Clean the edges of the jar to remove any residue.
4. Seal the jar by putting on the lid tightly.
5. Boil water in a large pot.
6. Place the jars into the boiling water using rubber-edged tongs.
7. Boil the jars for 10 minutes.
8. Turn off the heat and let the water cool down.
9. Leave the jars in the pot for about 1 hour, until they are completely cooled.
10. Remove the jars and place them on a towel to rest for 24 hours.
11. Store the jars in a cool, dry place.

chopped liver, better than your grandma's

We're talking OLD-SCHOOL comfort food.

I have to be honest with you here: I discovered chopped liver later on in life. I did not grow up eating it with my grandparents during the holidays. Also, like many people, I thought chopped liver requires a lot of time and is very difficult to make. But I've since learned that this isn't the case. Using only a few simple ingredients, this recipe creates a quick and wildly enticing spread that is hard to resist. It can make anyone into a chopped liver convert. Every time I prepare this chopped liver, I always make a little extra because I can't stop eating it. And somehow, Zikki's dad always knows when it's being made, so I prepare a bit more for him, too—it's his favorite. —ben

Serve it with: Challah (page 117), Chrain (page 204), hard-boiled eggs, Silan & Onion Jam (page 71), My Dad's Fermented Cucumbers (page 233)

Yield: Serves 6 to 8, makes 4 small plates

Total time: 1 hour

For the Chopped Liver:

3 leeks

1 (18-ounce) container chicken livers, cleaned, with tendons removed, and patted dry

2 teaspoons gray salt

1½ teaspoons freshly cracked black pepper

6 tablespoons extra virgin olive oil, plus more as needed

1 tablespoon beef fat (optional)

1 tablespoon hot honey

1. Prep the leeks: Soak the leeks in water for at least 30 minutes to loosen any sediment at the root or in the outer leaves. After soaking, rinse thoroughly and remove the first three layers. Cut off the roots and the top fibrous section (about 4 inches from the top). Then thinly slice and set aside.

2. Prep the livers: In a medium bowl, combine the cleaned chicken livers with 1 teaspoon of the salt and 1 teaspoon of the pepper. Allow the livers to come to room temperature (see note).

3. In a large skillet over medium heat, heat 3 tablespoons of the olive oil and the beef fat (if desired). Add the leeks and cook for about 1 hour (stirring occasionally, until they melt, lose their volume, and caramelize). Set aside.

4. While the leeks are frying, in a medium skillet, heat the remaining 3 tablespoons olive oil. Line a plate with paper towels. When the oil is hot enough (about 1 minute), sear the livers in small batches, making sure there is only one layer of livers in the pan and that they are not

recipe and ingredients continue

dips & spreads

For Serving:

4 hard-boiled eggs

4 cucumbers from My Dad's Fermented Cucumbers (page 233)

4 tablespoons Chrain (page 204)

1 loaf Challah (page 117), sliced and toasted

stacked on top of one another. This ensures that they get the proper color and crust! Fry for 3 to 5 minutes, or until they are seared on one side, then flip and fry the other side for an additional 3 to 5 minutes. Transfer the seared livers to the paper towel–lined plate. Add an additional tablespoon of olive oil to the skillet if necessary and repeat until you have seared all the livers.

5. Once you are finished cooking, transfer the livers to a cutting board and roughly chop them.

6. Assemble the chopped liver: In a medium bowl, combine the chopped liver, caramelized leeks, remaining 1 teaspoon salt, remaining ½ teaspoon pepper, and hot honey and mix until combined.

7. Serve immediately in a small bowl alongside the hard-boiled eggs, fermented cucumbers, chrain, and challah or store in an airtight container in the refrigerator for up to 3 days.

Essential Tips:

Cook the chicken livers at room temperature: Bring the chicken livers to room temperature before cooking as they might explode if seared right out of the refrigerator.

How to incorporate the eggs: Do you chop your liver with or without the eggs? This is a personal preference. Truthfully, it's absolutely delicious either way. Just keep in mind that if you mix your hard-boiled eggs into the mixture, it will not last as long in the refrigerator.

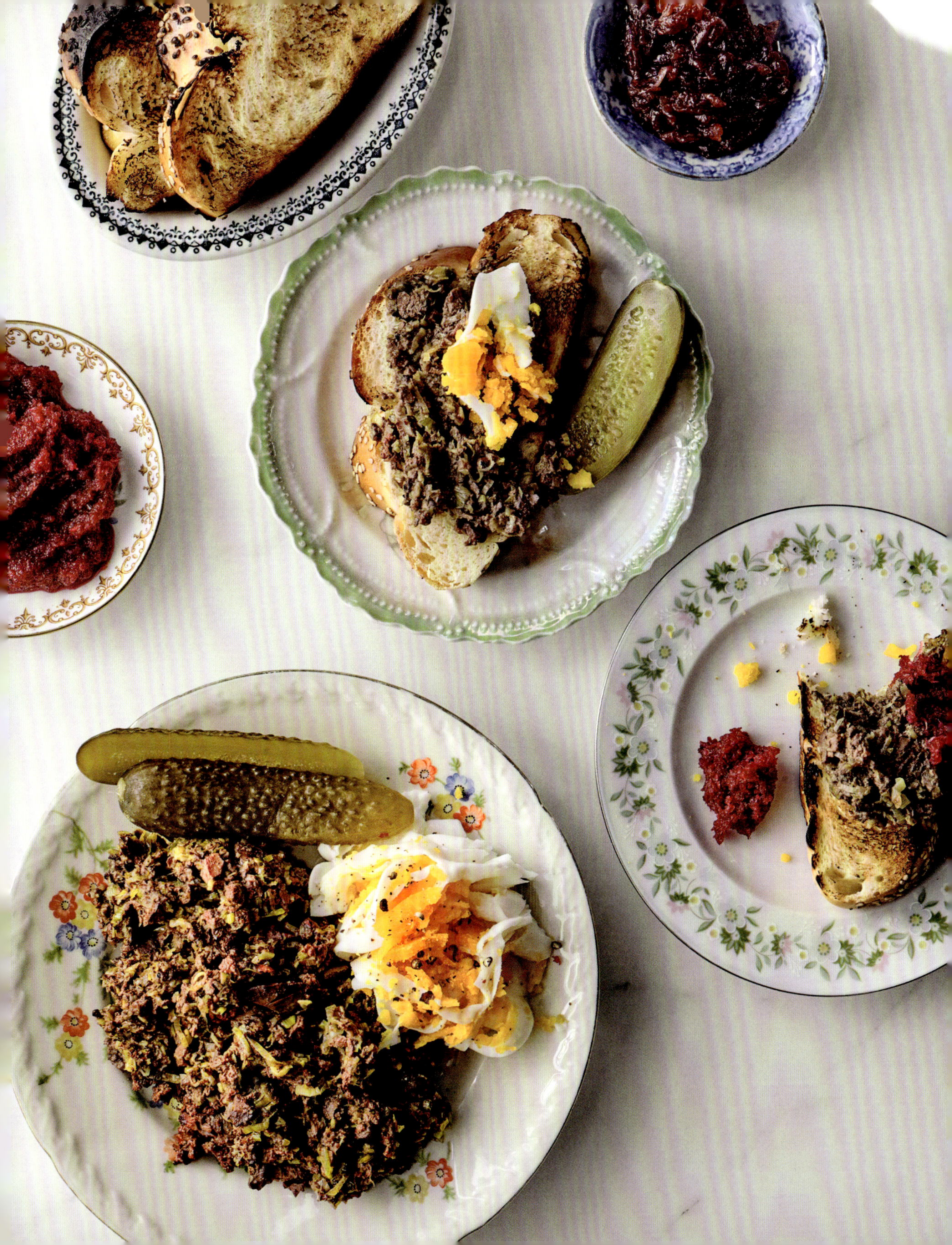

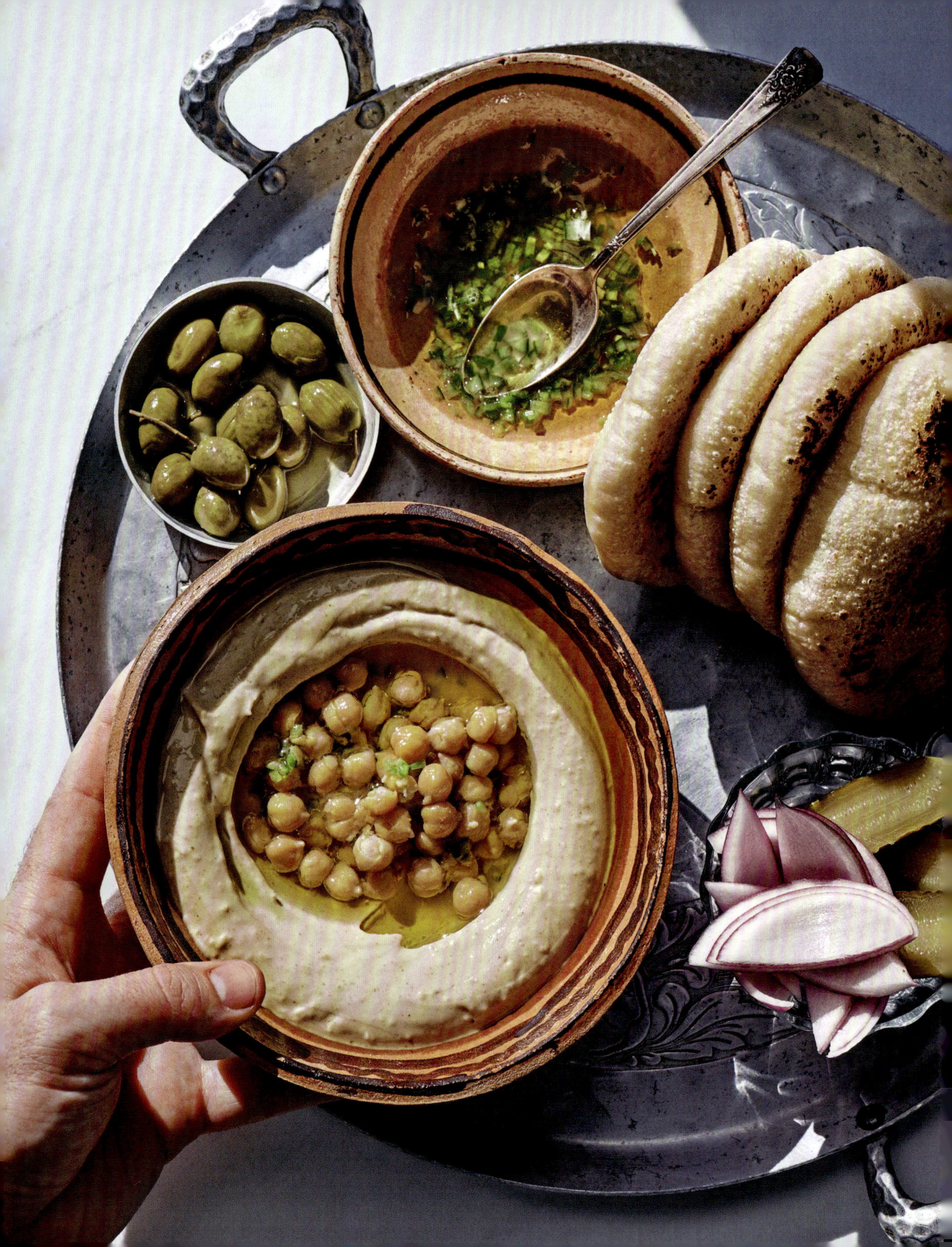

Classic Hummus

In Israel, everyone claims they make the best hummus. While methods vary, one thing is certain: once you've had homemade hummus, supermarket brands can't compare. Freshly made hummus is preservative-free, smooth, and warm—really, one of the best dips you can ever have. We like to top ours with extra chickpeas, a serving method called hummus gargirim. You can top the hummus as you like, but the most common versions in Israel are the following:

Hummus pitriot: hummus served with either sautéed onions or mushrooms

Hummus tehina: hummus topped with tahini

Hummus basar: hummus topped with a quick beef stew—BEN

Serve it with: Pita (page 109), olives, quartered red onion, pickles

Yield: Serves 3 to 5, makes 1 quart

Total time: 4 hours, plus at least 12 hours soaking

Special tools: food processor

For the Hummus:

- 2 cups dried chickpeas
- 1 onion, halved with skin on
- 5 garlic cloves, peeled
- 1 small carrot, peeled
- 1 teaspoon baking soda
- Juice of 1 lemon
- ½ teaspoon ground cumin
- Gray salt
- 1½ cups raw tahini

1. In a large bowl, add the chickpeas and cover with cold water at least twice their volume. Let soak overnight, or at least 12 hours.

2. Prep the chickpeas: Drain the chickpeas and pour them into a large pot. Add the onion, garlic, and carrot. Cover with water at least twice their volume.

3. Bring the water to a boil, then lower the heat to medium and cook for about 1 hour, skimming off any foam that floats to the surface with a shallow, wide spoon. After 1 hour, the chickpeas will be halfway cooked.

4. Drain the chickpeas, reserving the cooking water. Discard the onion, carrot, and garlic. Run the chickpeas under cold water for 1 minute and massage them with your fingers to remove or loosen as many of the skins as possible (see note).

5. Place the peeled chickpeas and cooking water back into the same pot over medium-high heat. Bring to a simmer and add the baking soda. Continue to cook the chickpeas, stirring occasionally and skimming the top for floating chickpea skins every few minutes, for about 1 hour, or until they are completely softened.

recipe and ingredients continue

dips & spreads

Tiny Tangy Chili Oil (Makes One 8-Ounce Jar):

2 long green hot chilies, diced super tiny

Juice of 1 lemon

1 teaspoon gray salt

½ cup extra virgin olive oil

For Serving:

½ cup cooked chickpeas (enough for 4 small plates or bowls)

¼ cup Tiny Tangy Chili Oil

6. Turn off the heat and allow the chickpeas to cool in the water, then drain, once again reserving the cooking water. Set aside ½ cup of the cooked chickpeas for plating.

7. In a food processor, add the remaining chickpeas and ¼ cup of the cooking water. Blend until the mixture is smooth, then add the lemon juice, cumin, and salt to taste. Blend on low, slowly pouring in the raw tahini until you reach the desired smooth and creamy consistency. Set aside while you prepare the chili oil.

8. Make the chili oil: Combine the chilies, lemon juice, and salt in an 8-ounce jar, shake to mix, and marinate for 10 minutes. Add olive oil, stir, and use immediately or refrigerate for up to 1 week.

9. Assemble the hummus: Plate the hummus in a shallow, wide bowl or plate using the rounded side of a wide spoon to spread it evenly, leaving a slight hollow in the center. Rotate the bowl as you drag the spoon for a clean, even finish. Spoon the leftover cooked chickpeas on top and finish with the chili oil.

Essential Tips:

Soaking the chickpeas: To soak chickpeas, cover them with cold water, at least twice their volume, and leave them in the refrigerator overnight.

Removing the chickpea skins: This step requires patience. Some skins will come off in the first wash under the cold water, but it mostly just loosens them. The skins fully come off and will float to the surface when you boil the chickpeas with baking soda. Skim the mixture periodically throughout the boiling process, removing the floating skins and stirring to loosen any remaining skins.

Storing the hummus: Fresh hummus should be eaten within 24 hours. For longer storage, stop at step 5, refrigerate the cooked chickpeas, and complete the recipe when ready to serve.

My Uncle Tal's Lentil Masabacha

Tal, my uncle, has influenced me very much throughout my life. One of the things that I admire most about him is his extraordinary ability to cook. He has such a deep understanding of food and has surprised me many times in my life with flavors that seem almost impossible to replicate. One of the best-known things about Tal is that he makes a dish only once. He will make this one dish, talk about it, reflect on it, and take feedback, but it is likely that he will never make it again. I would argue that this is magic.

One weekend morning, we were visiting Tal in New Jersey and he made us a lentil masabacha. Masabacha, or "swimming chickpeas," is a dish similar to hummus but made with mashed rather than fully blended chickpeas. This method creates a more rustic texture while maintaining the creamy richness of traditional hummus. Tal took the same idea but swapped the chickpeas for dark black lentils, giving the hummus a deep, sexy, and intriguing charcoal color. This recipe takes only 35 minutes from start to finish—unlike traditional masabacha, you don't need to soak chickpeas overnight. Zikki and I both remember vividly the day Tal made this dish. True to form, he never made it again, sealing its magical legacy. —Ben

Serve it with: Jeweled Celery Salad (page 136), A Cashew Basil Dip Everyone Will Talk About (page 99), Tel Avivian Focaccia (page 113)

Yield: Serves 4 to 8, makes 1 quart

Total time: 45 minutes

Special tools: mortar and pestle or immersion blender

---

1 cup dried black lentils

1 heaping teaspoon gray salt

1 garlic clove, grated

½ cup raw tahini

For Serving:

Tiny Tangy Chili Oil (page 78)

---

1. Pour the lentils into a medium pot and cover with 3 cups of water. Add the salt. Bring to a boil, then lower the heat and simmer for 40 minutes, or until the water has been fully absorbed and the lentils are soft and tender.

2. Add an additional ½ cup of water to the lentils and let them simmer for 5 more minutes, stirring as the water evaporates. Turn up the heat and add an additional ½ cup water to the pot, stirring constantly.

3. Add the garlic and slowly pour in the raw tahini as you continue mixing for another minute. Watch as it thickens and the raw tahini

recipe continues

turns dark gray, as the lentils break down and fully integrate with the raw tahini. If you find that your lentils aren't breaking down in the pot, add 1 cup of the lentils and tahini mixture to a mortar and grind with a pestle until simultaneously coarse and homogenous.

4. Plate the masabacha and finish with a spoonful of tiny tangy chili oil. Serve immediately.

ESSENTIAL TIPS:

Serving and storing: This dish is best if served immediately, but if you choose to store it in the refrigerator, plan to serve it later. Twenty minutes before serving, heat it in a saucepan with an additional cup of water, stirring constantly until you've reached the desired thickness.

Try it with an egg: This masabacha is wonderful when served with a grated hard-boiled egg on top.

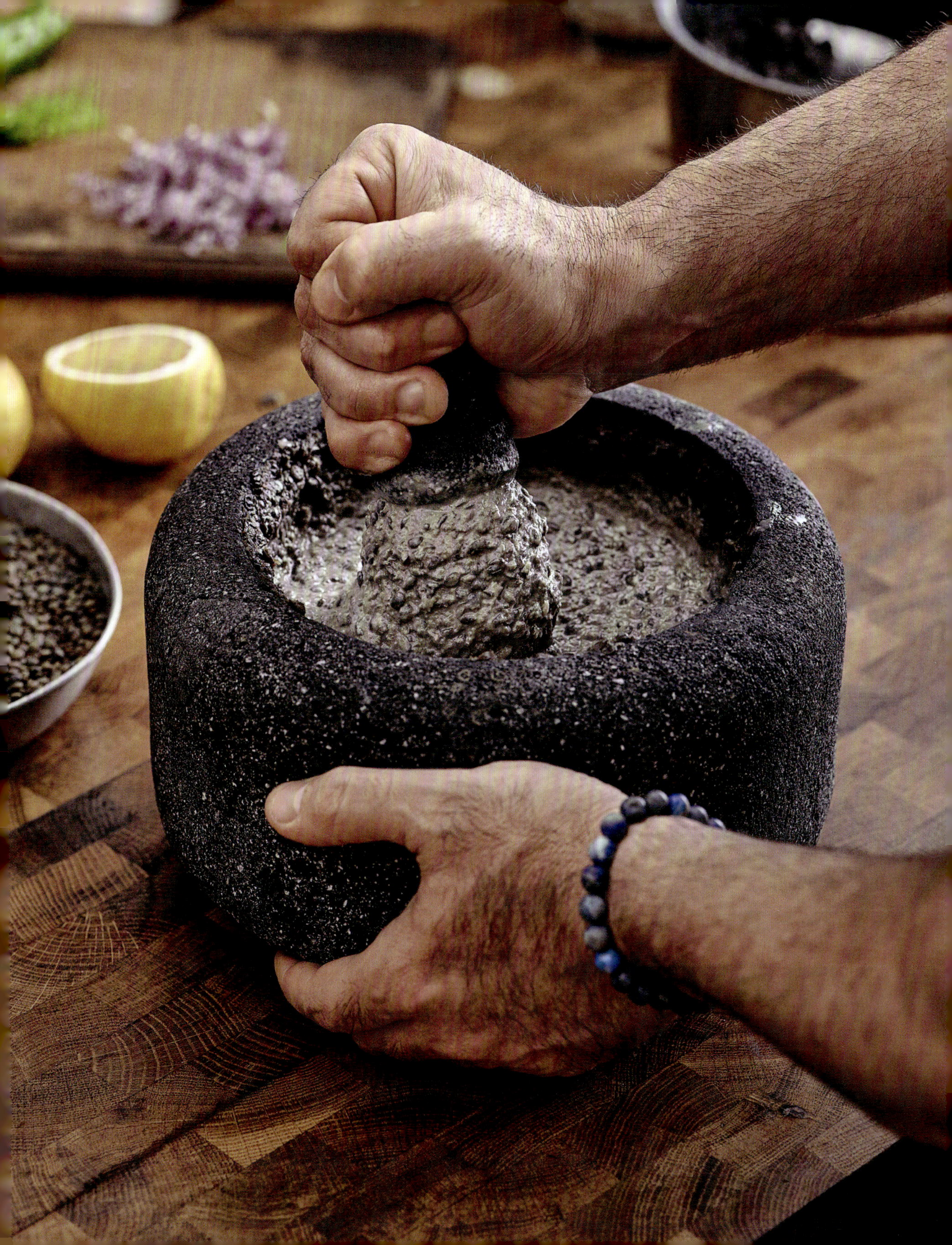

labneh 3 ways

salty tangy yogurt cheese

Where do we even start? We have been making labneh since the early days of our life together. We found strange places to hang this sack of salty yogurt goodness in our homes when we lived in Italy and Israel, and we did the same in our little studio apartment in New York (we sometimes even used our shower!). It just recently occurred to me that it's just as easy to hang labneh from a wooden spoon in a narrow mixing bowl. More practical, but maybe less fun?

But wait, Ben and Zikki. What is labneh? Right. Let's rewind. Labneh is a yogurt-based cheese, originally made from sheep's or goat's milk. It has just two ingredients: yogurt and salt.

You can customize the texture of labneh based on your preference or how you plan to use it in a recipe—creamy labneh is perfect to spread on bread, and harder labneh balls are great to add to salads (#IsraeliCaprese). The texture you are looking for will determine how long you hang the labneh. On the following pages, we've outlined a three-part recipe on how to make labneh into three different products: a spread, a cheese ball submerged in oil, and a hard cheese, or yogurt stone. The hard cheese is a perfect replacement for Parmigiano Reggiano or Pecorino Romano. It has more tang and adds a gorgeous freshness to almost every dish.—ben & zikki

Special tools: **cheesecloth or a thin kitchen towel, long wooden spoon**

continues

ESSENTIAL TIPS:

Why whole-fat yogurt is best: Make sure that you use a yogurt with a high fat content; otherwise most of the weight will drain out in the process.

How to adjust the salt: We love our labneh salty and usually aim for an amount of salt that's about 3 percent of the weight of yogurt. We suggest that you try the labneh this way first. If it is too salty for you, decrease the salinity next time by reducing the quantity of salt to 2 percent.

labneh spread

Serve it with: Absolutely Love a Breakfast Spread (page 304), Charred Eggplant with Labneh, Zhug & Dukkah (page 223)
Yield: Serves 6 to 8, makes 1 quart or 4 small plates
Total time: 15 minutes, plus 12 hours draining

32 ounces (900 grams) whole-fat Greek yogurt
1 ounce (27 grams) gray salt
Sumac, for garnish
Za'atar, for garnish
Extra virgin olive oil, for garnish

1. In a medium bowl, whisk together the yogurt and salt until completely combined. Set aside.

2. Spread your cheesecloth or thin towel over the edges of a medium bowl (you are going to use the bowl to help you center the yogurt in the middle of the towel). Pour the yogurt into the center of the towel and then place a long wooden spoon across the bowl. Quickly tie each edge of the towel around the length of the wooden spoon to create a hanging sack of yogurt.

3. Let the salted yogurt drain for at least 12 hours.

4. Once it has drained, untie the cheesecloth or towel and scrape the yogurt into a bowl for serving.

5. To serve: You can spread the labneh onto a plate and top with sumac, za'atar, and extra virgin olive oil. Or you can substitute the yogurt for labneh in both the Tza-Zikki (page 87) and the Beet & Cherry Salad (page 149).

6. To store: Pack the labneh into an airtight container and store in the refrigerator for up to 2 weeks.

labneh balls

Serve it with: Israeli Caprese (page 179), Welcome Olives (page 39)
Yield: Makes 2 quarts of rolled balls in olive oil or 40 balls of labneh
Total time: 15 minutes, plus 24 hours draining

32 ounces (900 grams) whole-fat Greek yogurt
1 ounce (27 grams) gray salt
Sumac, for garnish (optional)
Za'atar, for garnish (optional)
Extra virgin olive oil

1. Follow steps 1 through 2 for the Labneh Spread. Allow the hanging sack of salted yogurt to drain for at least 24 hours.

2. After the yogurt hangs, untie the cheesecloth or towel and scrape the yogurt into a bowl.

3. Wet your hands and scoop a tablespoon of labneh into your hands. Roll into a ball and set aside. Repeat until you roll all the labneh.

4. Roll the balls in either sumac or za'atar, if desired, and serve immediately or place them gently into an airtight container and fill to the top with olive oil so that all the balls are submerged.

5. Serve with Israeli Caprese or alongside your Welcome Olives!

yogurt stone

Serve it with: Fig Carpaccio (page 169)
Yield: Makes 40 small balls of yogurt stone
Total time: 30 minutes, plus 5 days refrigeration

1 recipe Labneh Balls (recipe precedes)
Sumac, for garnish (optional)
Za'atar, for garnish (optional)

1. Roll your labneh balls in sumac or za'atar, if desired, or leave them plain.

2. Instead of submerging them in oil, place the balls on a paper towel–lined plate in the refrigerator and let sit uncovered for 5 days, or until hard like a stone.

3. To serve: Using a Microplane, grate this yogurt stone over a fresh salad or a carpaccio or use as garnish for any dip!

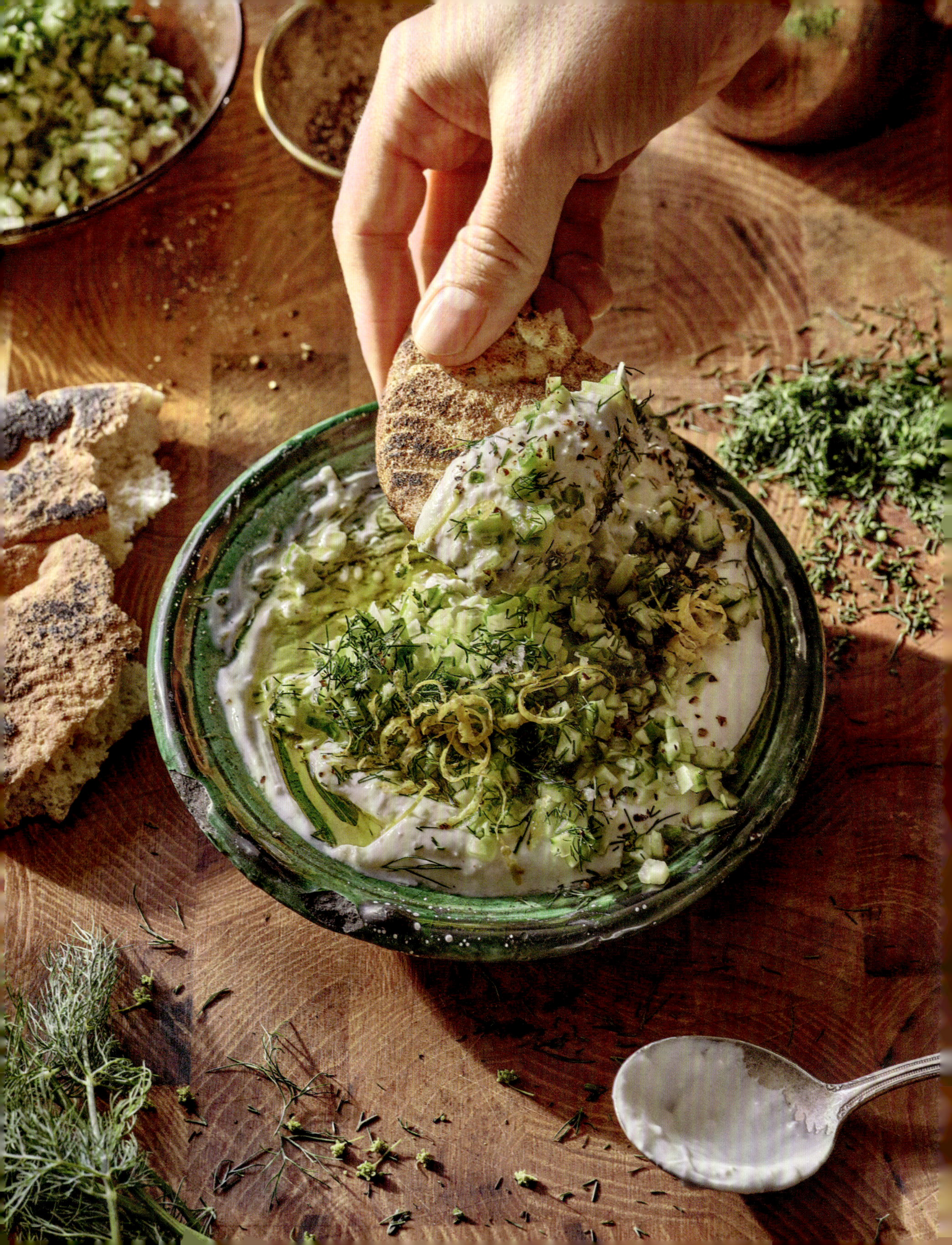

TZA-zikki
deconstructed cucumber & yogurt dip

This is my go-to for a quick small plate if I've got friends coming over on short notice. Small effort for big claps. This dish originated during that funny limbo time in my life when I was living in California for a hot minute between jobs during the peak of COVID. My friends in San Diego were hosting me for a month and my vow was to feed them and do it REALLY well. When I first made this dish, my intention was to toss it all together into a dip, but I found that I was able to better preserve the integrity of all the ingredients by simply stacking them. Not to mention that it was far more beautiful. —*zikki*

Serve it with: Beet & Goat Cheese Dip (page 88), A Cashew Basil Dip Everyone Will Talk About (page 99), Pita (page 109)

Yield: Serves 4 to 6, makes 2 small plates

Total time: 10 minutes

Special tools: Microplane

½ cup Labneh Spread (page 84) or whole-fat Greek yogurt (see note)

3 Persian cucumbers, finely diced

2 tablespoons chopped dill

1 lemon

½ teaspoon gray salt

Freshly cracked black pepper

4 tablespoons extra virgin olive oil

---

1. Evenly divide the labneh between two small plates, spreading it across the plates by using the rounded side of a wide spoon. Top each plate generously and evenly with the cucumbers. Garnish each plate with 1 tablespoon of the dill. Using a Microplane, zest the lemon over each plate and season with ¼ teaspoon salt per plate and pepper to taste.

2. If serving right away, juice half of the lemon and drizzle 2 tablespoons of your best olive oil over each plate. If you will be enjoying later, store in an airtight container in the refrigerator and, before serving, finish with the lemon juice and olive oil.

ESSENTIAL TIPS:

Using yogurt vs. labneh: If you choose to use whole-fat Greek yogurt and not labneh, we recommend seasoning with an additional pinch of salt and mixing before spreading it on the plate.

How to zest a lemon: When zesting a lemon, hold the lemon steady in your hand and move the Microplane from one axis to the other. This will ensure that you zest the entire lemon evenly.

dips & spreads

beet & goat cheese dip

Without a doubt, this dip will be a showstopper at your next gathering. From the intriguing hot-pink color to the smooth and silky texture, beets and goat cheese are a match made in heaven. This crowd-pleaser is sweet and charred from the beets, bright and tangy from the goat cheese, and strangely reminiscent of the early 2000s hit salad: beet and goat cheese spinach salad. But that might just be me . . . Regardless, it is absolutely glorious, and with a little spoonful of the Tiny Tangy Chili Oil, you are set. —*zikki*

Serve it with: Tza-Zikki (page 87), Pita (page 109), A Cashew Basil Dip Everyone Will Talk About (page 99), Akko Crudo (page 247)

Yield: Serves 6 to 8, makes 1 quart or 4 small plates

Total time: 2 hours

Special tools: parchment paper, food processor, kitchen gloves

---

3 large beets

¼ cup extra virgin olive oil, plus more for drizzling

1 (10.5-ounce) log goat cheese

1 tablespoon hot honey

1 teaspoon gray salt

Juice of ¼ lemon

Tiny Tangy Chili Oil (page 78), for garnish

---

1. Preheat the oven to 500°F (260°C). Line a baking sheet with parchment paper.

2. Place the unpeeled beets on the prepared baking sheet and roast for about 1 hour 30 minutes, or until the skin cracks upon touch. Remove the beets from the oven and let them cool for 10 minutes.

3. Wearing kitchen gloves, peel the beets.

4. In a food processor, add the beets and olive oil and blend until coarse. Add the goat cheese, hot honey, salt, and lemon juice and continue blending for about 5 minutes, or until silky and smooth.

5. Spread the dip evenly onto four small plates using the rounded side of a wide spoon. Serve immediately topped with a spoonful of tiny tangy chili oil, or store in an airtight container in the refrigerator for up to 3 days.

tiny tangy chili oil

beet & goat cheese dip

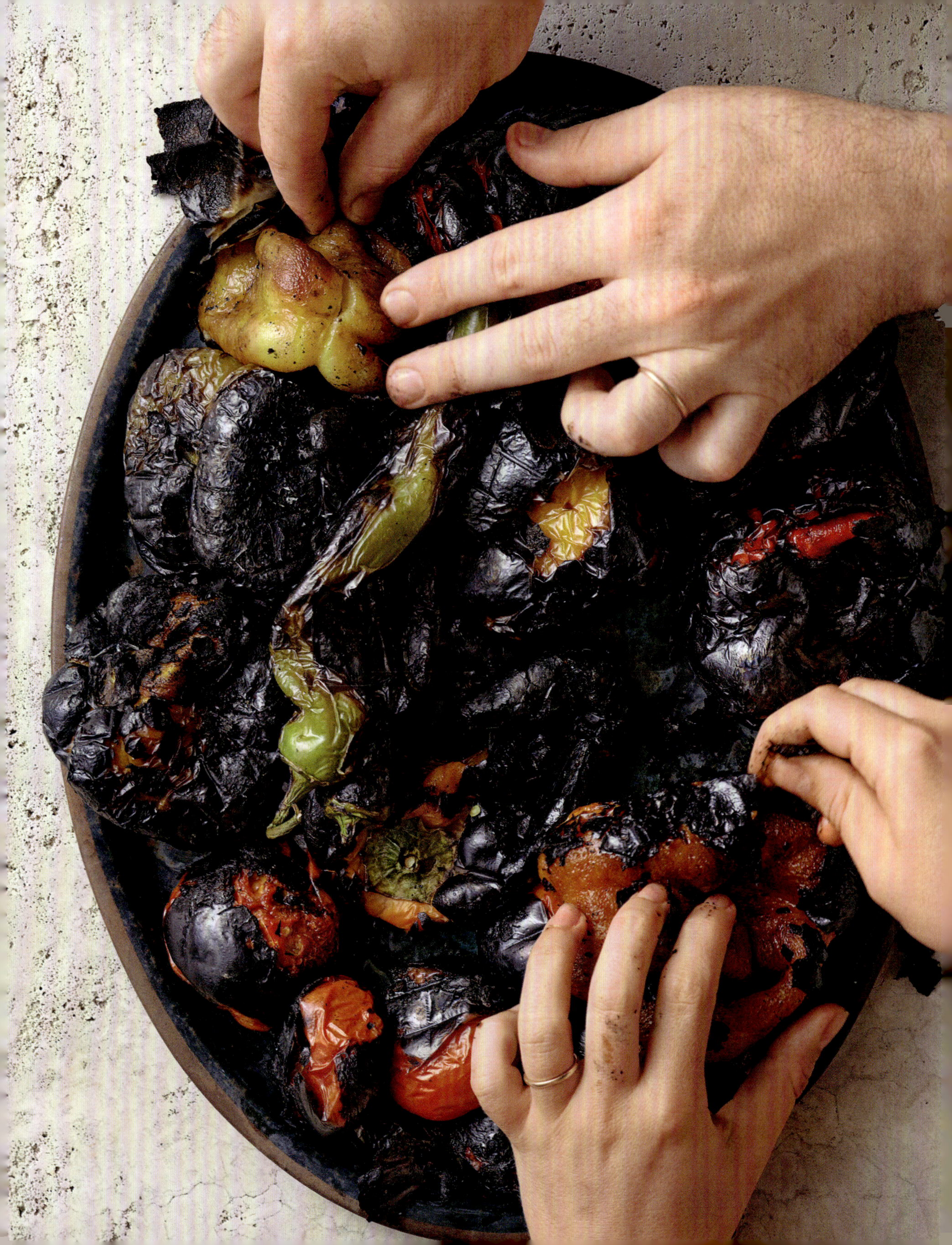

let's burn a veggie and make a spread

When I see an open fire, I just *have* to burn vegetables. It is deep in my blood. When the flame hits the raw skin of vegetable, the transformation begins. The vegetable takes on a completely different persona, turning from crisp, fresh, and juicy to sweet, smoky, and absorbant, serving as a wonderful foundation for a dip or spread. Cooking vegetables directly on top of your gas range or grill until they are charred and collapsed yields the silky, fire-kissed result that a broiler simply can't achieve, and is a defining element among our favorite recipes such as the Baba(s), Mashwiya, and Zaalouk.

how to char a veggie

1. **Prepare the vegetable:** Wash it and dry thoroughly.

2. **Heat the grill or gas stovetop:** Preheat a grill or turn the gas on to high heat.

3. **Char the vegetable:** Place the vegetable directly on the grill or flame. Let the skin blacken and blister. Using rubber tongs, turn occasionally to expose a new side to the flame and char all sides evenly.

4. **Cool and peel:** Once fully charred and blackened, place the vegetable into an airtight container or a bowl covered with plastic wrap or lid. Let it steam for at least 20 minutes, or up to 24 hours in the refrigerator. This helps loosen the skin.

5. **Remove the skin:** Once cool enough to handle, peel off the charred skin using your hands.

6. **Use in your dip:** Chop or mash the vegetable and mix it into your dip for a smoky flavor.

WHITE BABA

Our version of the classic. Burnt eggplant deserve a standing ovation. The unique texture and flavor profile of eggplant pairs unimaginably well with smoke. The most famous dish using burnt eggplants is baba ganoush. Baba ganoush is a Levantine appetizer (of Lebanese origin) popular all over the Middle East consisting of eggplant, olive oil, lemon juice, various seasonings, and sometimes tahini.

Zikki and I love a simple baba seasoned with lemon, olive oil, salt, and tahini. If we are feeling extra frisky, we will go the extra mile and make our Black Baba, which uses the charred skin of the eggplant for a deeper smoky element and yogurt or labneh to brighten it up!—BEN

Serve it with: Pita (page 109), Tza-Zikki (page 87), Our Hassle-Free Matbucha (page 52), Moroccan Carrots (page 201), My Grandfather's Zhug (page 49)

Yield: Serves 6 to 8, makes 1 quart or 4 small plates

Total time: 15 minutes

---

4 large Charred Eggplants (page 218)

½ cup raw tahini

Juice of ¼ lemon

½ teaspoon gray salt

½ teaspoon sumac, for garnish

Extra virgin olive oil, for finishing

---

1. Place the cooled, charred eggplants on a cutting board so that they are lying flat. For each eggplant, place your nondominant hand on the far side and, using a sharp chef's knife with your dominant hand, gently run the knife directly under the skin on the opposite end to remove the burnt outer layer of skin from the cooked eggplant flesh.

2. Using a spoon, gently scoop the eggplant flesh to detach it from the burnt skin on the bottom, but leave the remaining skin of the eggplant intact as a sort of bowl to contain the flesh.

3. Place only the eggplant flesh into a medium bowl and, using a fork, mash it into a paste. If the eggplant is fully cooked, breaking it apart with a fork will be very easy.

4. Slowly drizzle in the raw tahini as you continue whisking the eggplant mixture with the same fork. Once the mixture is homogeneous, squeeze in the lemon juice and add the salt. Whisk again until combined and taste. Adjust the flavors to your liking.

5. Plate the baba and garnish with the sumac and a drizzle of olive oil. Serve immediately or store in an airtight container in the refrigerator for up to 3 days.

black baba

white baba

black baba

A little smokier, a little darker, and just a pinch brighter.—ben & zikki

Yield: Serves 6 to 8, makes 1 quart or 4 small plates

Total time: 30 minutes

Special tools: food processor, Microplane

4 large Charred Eggplants (page 218)

¼ cup raw tahini

½ teaspoon gray salt

¼ cup whole-fat Greek yogurt or Labneh Spread (page 84)

Yogurt Stone (page 85), for garnish

Sumac, for garnish

1. Place two of the cooled, charred eggplants on a cutting board so that they are lying flat. For each eggplant, place your nondominant hand on the far side and, using a sharp chef's knife with your dominant hand, gently run the knife directly under the skin on the opposite end to remove the burnt outer layer of skin from the cooked eggplant flesh.

2. Using a spoon, gently scoop the eggplant flesh to detach it from the burnt skin and place only the flesh into the food processor. Set aside.

3. Place the remaining two charred eggplants on a cutting board and, using a sharp knife, remove just the stems, keeping the skin intact.

4. Place the unpeeled eggplants into the food processor along with the peeled eggplants. Blend until smooth.

5. As the processor continues to run, slowly pour in the raw tahini and add the salt. Once the mixture is homogeneous, add the yogurt and pulse just until it is combined.

6. Spread the baba evenly on four small plates. Using a Microplane, garnish with the yogurt stone and sprinkle sumac over the plates to finish. Serve immediately or store in an airtight container in the refrigerator for up to 3 days.

I will start by saying this—the magic of the vegetables in these two spreadable salads is that there are only two steps: burn and chop. The texture is really up to you, but no matter how coarse or fine the Zaalouk or Mashwiya is, you and your guests will find yourself transported to the Middle East. These flavors are timeless.

To balance the smoky acidity of the Zaalouk and Mashwiya, we recommend serving them along with something decadent and creamy, such as a bowl of The Smoothest Tahini Dip (page 55) and a plate of crispy, crunchy, and fresh Persian cucumbers cut into spears and tossed with sumac, gray salt, and extra virgin olive oil. —zikki

zaalouk

Zaalouk (see photo, page 96) is a traditional Moroccan spreadable "salad," or what we call a dip in the States. Traditionally, you would prepare zaalouk by cooking down the eggplant with tomatoes, garlic, cumin, and cilantro. Ours is a little different. We burn all our vegetables to bring a big, bold, smoky element. Additionally, we don't slow cook the vegetables in oil; instead, we marinate them in hot oil, which makes this spread much lighter and more delicate.
—ben & zikki

Serve it with: The Smoothest Tahini Dip (page 55), Tel Avivian Focaccia (page 113), Sumac Cucumber Spears (page 43), Kebab (page 266)

Yield: Serves 4 to 6, makes 1 pint or 2 small plates

Total time: 25 minutes

Special tools: gas range

---

1 eggplant

3 plum tomatoes

1 teaspoon ground cumin

1 teaspoon hot paprika

¼ cup extra virgin olive oil

1. Prep the veggies: Place a small oven rack over your gas range. Place the eggplant on top of the rack and follow the instructions for Charred Eggplant 101 (page 218). Once you've removed the finished eggplant, place the tomatoes on the rack with the stems down first. Keep a close eye on the tomatoes and, using a pair of tongs, gently move them to ensure that their entire surface area receives a kiss from the open fire. Once blackened, remove from the heat and let cool.

recipe and ingredients continue

mashwiya

zaalouk

sumac
cucumber
spears

2 garlic cloves, minced

2 tablespoons minced cilantro

Juice of ¼ lemon

1 teaspoon gray salt

2. When the eggplant and tomatoes have cooled enough to touch, peel and discard their skins. Place the eggplant and tomatoes on a cutting board and, using a chef's knife, finely chop the veggies and place them into a medium bowl. Set aside.

3. Make a quick-spiced oil: In a small nonstick skillet, add the cumin and paprika. Heat the pan over medium heat for about 1 minute, or until it is hot. As the pan heats, stir the spices often until they become fragrant. Add the olive oil and garlic. Turn the heat down to low and cook for 2 minutes, or until fragrant. Remove from the heat.

4. Assemble the zaalouk: Add the spiced-oil mixture to the bowl with the eggplant and tomatoes and stir to combine. Stir in the cilantro, lemon juice, and salt.

5. Spread the zaalouk evenly onto two small plates using the rounded side of a wide spoon. Serve immediately or store in an airtight container in the refrigerator for up to 1 week.

MASHWiYA

Salat mashwiya is a staple in Tunisian homes. In Arabic it translates to "grilled salad." This salsa-like spread features burnt peppers, onions, and tomatoes that are finely chopped and tossed with copious amounts of extra virgin olive oil. In Israel, this spread is part of the all-star lineup for classic "salatim" served at the beginning of an extravagant meat-heavy meal because it breaks up the fat perfectly. In our recipe, we omit the tomato in order to really focus on the peppers!—ben & zikki

Serve it with: The Smoothest Tahini Dip (page 55), Tel Avivian Focaccia (page 113), Sumac Cucumber Spears (page 43), Kebab (page 266)

Yield: Serves 4 to 6, makes 1 pint or 2 small plates

Total time: 25 minutes

Special tools: gas range

---

1 green bell pepper, charred, peeled, and diced (see page 91)

1 yellow bell pepper, charred, peeled, and diced (see page 91)

1 red bell pepper, charred, peeled, and diced (see page 91)

1 long green hot chili, charred, peeled, and minced (see page 91)

½ medium red onion, charred, peeled, and finely diced (see page 91)

1 teaspoon gray salt

1½ teaspoons freshly cracked black pepper

3 tablespoons extra virgin olive oil

---

1. In a small bowl, combine the bell peppers, green chili, and onion. Add the salt, pepper, and olive oil. Mix to combine.

2. Spread the mashwiya evenly onto two small plates using the rounded side of a wide spoon. Serve immediately or store in an airtight container in the refrigerator for up to 1 week.

A cashew basil dip everyone will talk about

I will admit that when Zikki first told me about this dip, I was skeptical. The idea of using soaked cashews sort of confused me. However, when soaked cashews are blended with loads of gorgeous fresh basil, garlic, lemon, and extra virgin olive oil, they take on a new flavor and texture. This recipe is outrageously delicious and perfect for anyone who is vegan or may have a sensitivity to dairy but is craving something super creamy! Use basil that is in season for an incredible color. —ben

Serve it with: Beet & Goat Cheese Dip (page 88), Zikki's Eggplant (page 224), Double-Dip Artichoke (page 198)

Yield: Serves 6 to 8, makes 1 quart or 4 small plates

Total time: 40 minutes

Special tools: immersion blender

---

10 ounces raw cashews

2 teaspoons gray salt

1 garlic clove (optional)

¼ cup extra virgin olive oil

80 basil leaves (or 1 large bunch, stemmed)

3 or 4 ice cubes

---

1. Place the cashews into a small saucepan. Fill the pot with enough water so that the cashews are fully submerged by 1 inch. Bring to a boil.

2. Boil the cashews for 2 minutes and then lower the heat and simmer for 15 minutes. Remove from the heat and allow the cashews to cool completely in the water.

3. Drain the cashews, reserving ½ cup of the cooking water.

4. Place the cooled cashews, reserved cooking water, ½ cup of cold water, the salt, and garlic (if using), into a tall plastic quart container and blend until coarse using the immersion blender. Add the olive oil and continue blending until smooth.

5. Once the mixture is homogeneous in texture, add a handful of basil leaves and 1 small ice cube at a time to the mixture as you continue to blend. Repeat this step, adding the basil leaves in batches, then blend the mixture on the highest speed for 5 minutes, until the basil is fully incorporated and there is no sign of the actual leaves.

recipe continues

6. Evenly spread the dip onto four small plates using the rounded side of a wide spoon. Serve immediately or store in an airtight container in the refrigerator for up to 3 days.

ESSENTIAL TIPS:

Using a food processor vs. an immersion blender: I know you might be tempted to use a food processor instead of an immersion blender. But an immersion blender is best here because the blade of a food processor might overheat and cause the basil leaves to "burn," turning the paste to a dull, dark gray color. Adding the basil in small increments using a lower-heat blender (immersion) will help create a bright, light green color. Make sure to take breaks during the blending process if you feel the mixture is overheating.

Creating the right texture: The strength of your immersion blender and sharpness of your blade will change the texture. We recommend an estimated 80 basil leaves in the ingredient list; however, you can continue to add more until you reach the desired consistency.

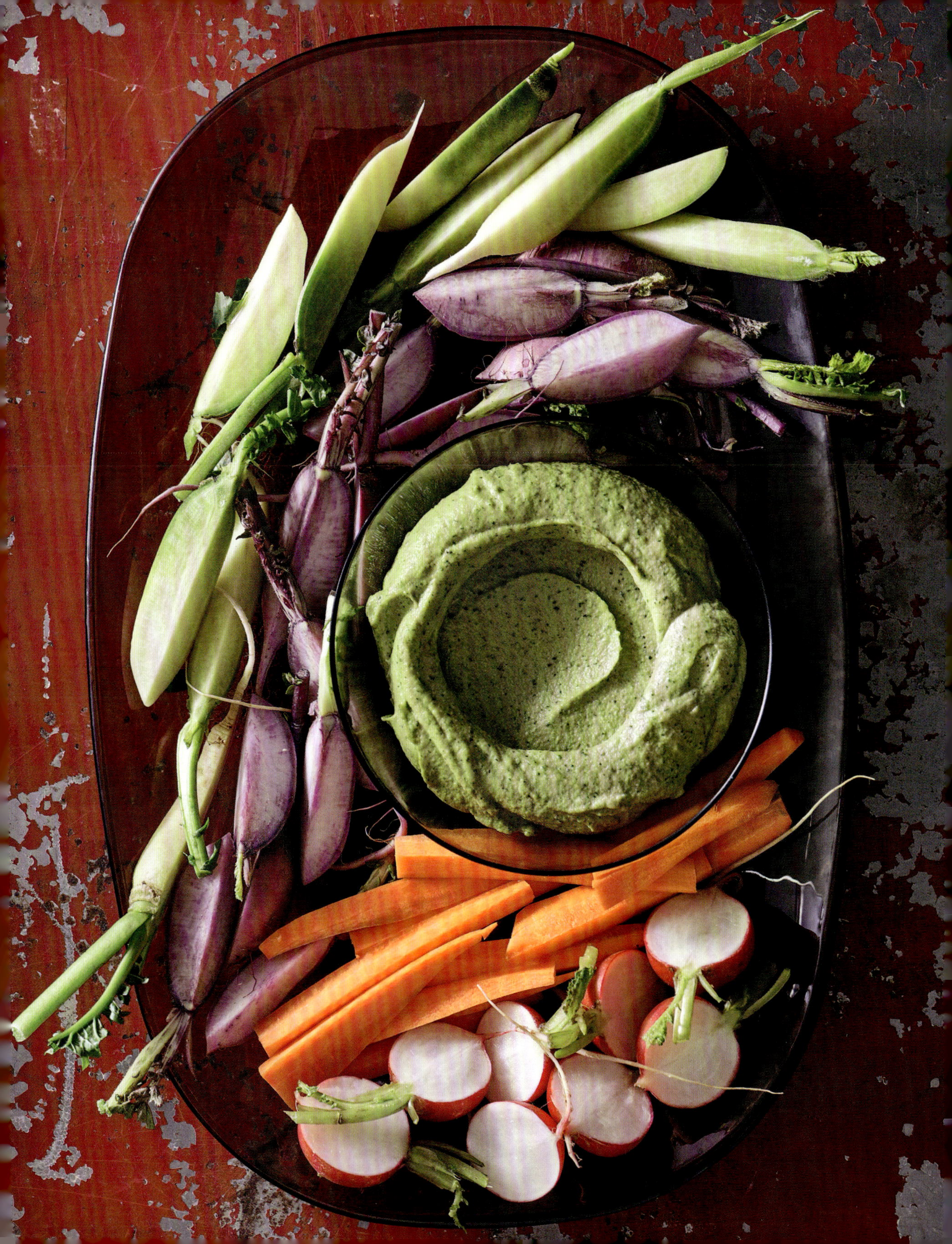

fennel, citrus & pistachio salad

cilantro pistachio artichoke dip

cilantro pistachio artichoke dip

You know when you make something by accident and it turns out to be the best thing you've ever tasted? Yep. Well, this spread was born exactly that way. I had just given birth and Ben was home with our little one while I went to host a gorgeous fortieth birthday party for one of our clients. What started out as a kind-of-improvised-Middle-Eastern-pesto dip turned out to be a HUGE crowd-pleaser among our clients and our team. It's decadent and fatty from the nuts and olive oil, bright and fresh from the cilantro and lemon, and wonderfully spicy from the classic long green hot chili. Not only does this dish deserve a seat at your table, it deserves exclusive rights to be a permanent member of your refrigerator pantry!—*zikki*

Serve it with: Jerusalem Bagel (page 120), Mackerel, Cucumber & Arugula Crudo (page 255), Labneh Spread (page 84)

Yield: Serves 6 to 8, makes 1 quart or 4 small plates

Total time: 30 minutes

Special tools: parchment paper, food processor or blender

---

1 cup raw shelled pistachios

2 garlic cloves

2 long green hot chilies, sliced into 1-inch rounds (with seeds)

½ cup extra virgin olive oil

1 teaspoon gray salt

Juice of ¼ lemon

1 (14-ounce) jar marinated artichoke hearts, drained

1 bunch of cilantro, chopped

---

1. Preheat the oven to 425°F (220°C). Line a baking sheet with parchment paper.

2. Spread the pistachios evenly on the prepared baking sheet and bake for 10 minutes, or until golden brown. Remove from the oven, cool, and coarsely crush with a knife.

2. In a food processor or blender, add the pistachios, garlic, chilies, ¼ cup of the olive oil, and the salt. Process until smooth. With the food processor running, slowly pour in the remaining ¼ cup olive oil and the lemon juice. Add ½ cup of water and the marinated artichoke hearts. Blend until fully homogeneous. Add the cilantro and blend until smooth.

3. Evenly spread the dip onto four small plates using the rounded side of a wide spoon. Serve immediately or store in an airtight container in the refrigerator for up to 3 days.

ESSENTIAL TIP:

Blending troubleshooting: If you are using a blender and it's stalling, make sure to remove the lid and scrape down the excess ingredients on the sides with a spatula.

breads

I can easily argue that almost everything in my life as an adult has happened because I chose to become a baker. Life is just better with bread. Bread is the missing piece of every culinary puzzle. It is there for you to dip in any creamy spread, to soak up the last of a crazy-delicious sauce, or simply to satiate hunger at any point in the meal.

I chose seven of my favorite breads for this chapter. Each one is perfect for any occasion yet still unique in flavor and texture. My intention was to give you a diverse array of techniques, taking you out of your comfort zone as a host and into the "learning new skills" zone. Bread is more than just flour and water. It is patience, precision, and most of all, a perfect practice.

We encourage you all to lean in and get your hands dirty because, let's be honest, there is absolutely nothing better than serving fresh bread to your guests.—BEN

RECIPES

pita

tel avivian focaccia

challah

jerusalem bagel

breadsticks

murtabak

lahuh

my baking commandments

1. When the dough gets sticky, don't rush to add flour. Instead, wet your hands with water or oil and see the magic—the dough won't stick to your hands. Keep wetting your hands as needed.

2. The dough wants to be kneaded quickly and confidently. If you work on the dough slowly, it will likely stick to your hands. Speeding up the kneading process (when done by hand) will help prevent the dough from sticking.

3. If you knead the dough by hand and the recipe calls for 10 to 12 minutes of kneading, but you get tired before finishing, don't worry! Cover the dough with plastic wrap and let it rest for 5 minutes. This rest allows the dough to relax and become smoother without further kneading. This is exactly the rationale behind no-knead bread.

4. The way I determine if the dough has finished kneading, regardless of the kneading time, is by taking the dough and rounding it into a tight ball. If the surface of the ball is smooth and shiny (referred to in recipes as kneading "until smooth and elastic") and doesn't tear apart, you can stop kneading. If it still tears a bit, knead for an additional minute and check again.

5. I highly recommend getting a kitchen scale. Honestly, I don't even think I need to convince you; it's one of the most useful tools in the kitchen and is very affordable. It will elevate all your baking to a whole new level. The baking recipes in this book call for weight, not volume. When you measure flour with a cup, it can vary in density (sometimes packed, sometimes loose). When you measure flour on a scale, the weight will always be accurate.

6. When following baking recipes, use your common sense to adjust them. Each oven behaves differently, affecting baking temperature and duration. My challah might be ready in 25 minutes, while yours might be done in 22 or even 30 minutes. Getting to know your oven takes a couple of trials, but once you understand it, you can adjust accordingly.

7. When proofing the dough, I always recommend using a bowl that is twice the size of the dough before proofing. This makes it easy to see when the dough has doubled in size. If the bowl is smaller, you might be tempted to use the dough before it finishes proofing; if larger, it might overproof.

8. While using a towel is a common method, it can allow some of the dough's moisture to evaporate, potentially drying out the surface. Better options include a lidded box (twice the size of the pre-proofed dough) or plastic wrap. Whichever method you choose, I recommend adding a few drops of olive oil on top of the dough before proofing to prevent it from drying out and sticking to the plastic wrap or box lid.

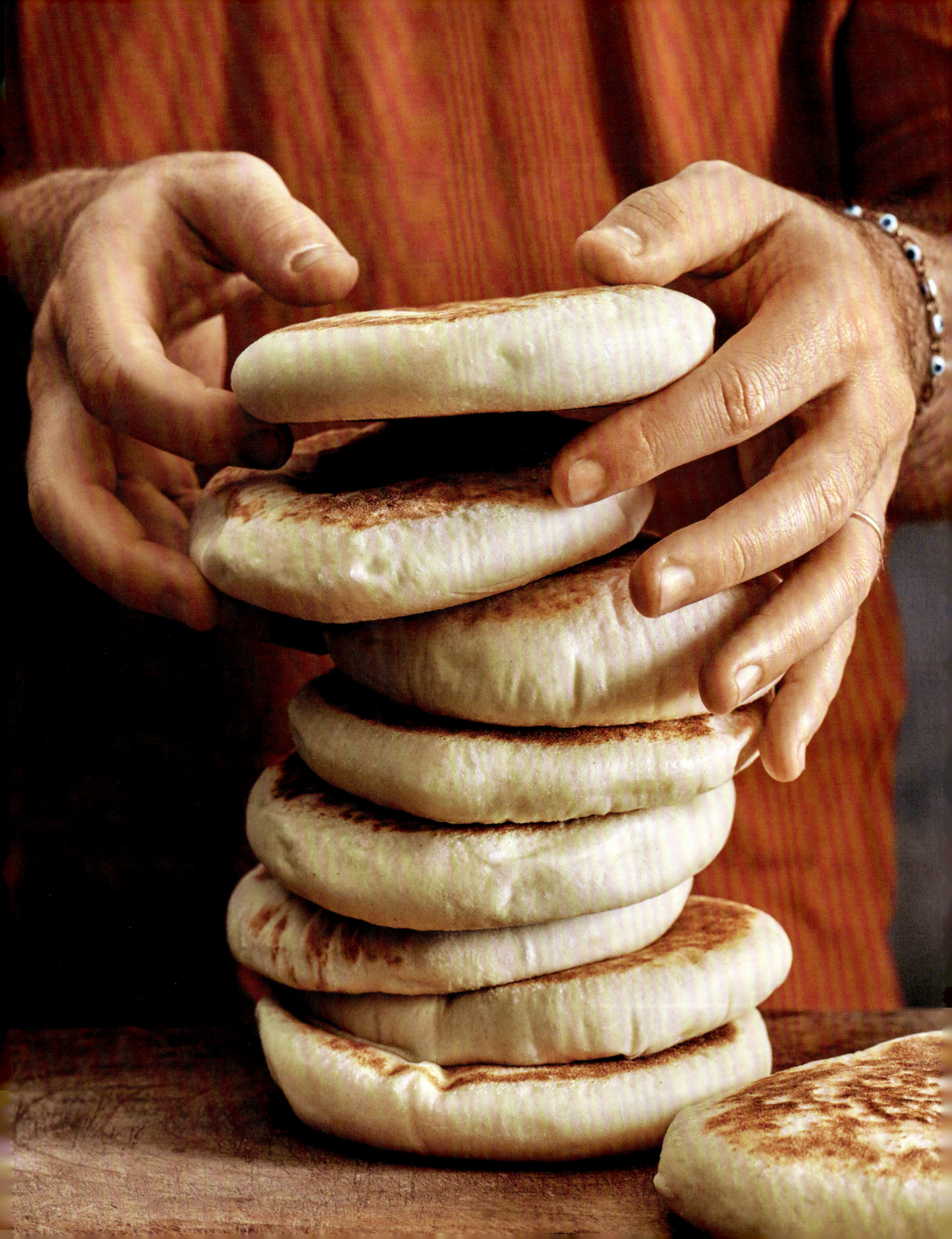

PITA

If I had to choose one type of bread I could survive on for the remainder of my life, it would unquestionably be pita. Whether you know it or not, pita is one of the oldest types of breads in the world. One of the reasons for this, and what endows it with such significance is that it doesn't really require specialized tools for preparation. The dough is forgiving and remarkably easy to work with just your hands. (Ironically, I use a mixer in this recipe for efficiency, but you can absolutely do it by hand!)

In America, the majority of pitas I encounter are thin and designed more for dipping than serving as sandwich bread. The Israeli version of pita, however, is thicker and heartier and can accommodate an array of add-ins, which creates a flawless sandwich. Don't get me wrong; this pita serves its dipping purpose admirably as well. It is remarkably versatile and suits any occasion. Without a doubt, it is my absolute favorite bread, and soon it shall be yours as well. —BEN

Serve it with: Classic Hummus (page 77), Tza-Zikki (page 87), Zaalouk (page 95), Black or White Baba (pages 92 or 94)

Yield: Serves 8 to 10, makes 8 pitas

Total time: 2 hours 30 minutes

Special tools: stand mixer, rolling pin

---

500 grams bread flour

300 grams lukewarm water [between 105°F (40°C) and 115°F (46°C)]

25 grams sugar

10 grams active dry yeast

10 grams fine sea salt

Olive oil, for coating the bowl

---

1. Make the dough: In the bowl of a stand mixer fitted with the dough hook, add the flour, water, sugar, yeast, and salt. Knead on the lowest speed for 12 minutes.

2. Remove the dough from the bowl and round it into a tight ball. Using a paper towel, lightly oil a large bowl. Place the dough in the bowl and cover with plastic wrap. Let the dough rest until it has doubled in size, at least 1 hour 30 minutes.

3. After the dough has doubled in size, remove it from the bowl, deflate it, and divide it into 8 equal portions. You can achieve even portions by using a kitchen scale. Each portion should weigh roughly 100 grams. Round each piece of dough into a tight ball and set aside, covered with a kitchen towel, for 15 minutes.

4. Using a rolling pin, roll out each ball into a ⅓-inch-thick disk.

recipe continues

1

2

3

4

5

6

7

8

9

10

11

12

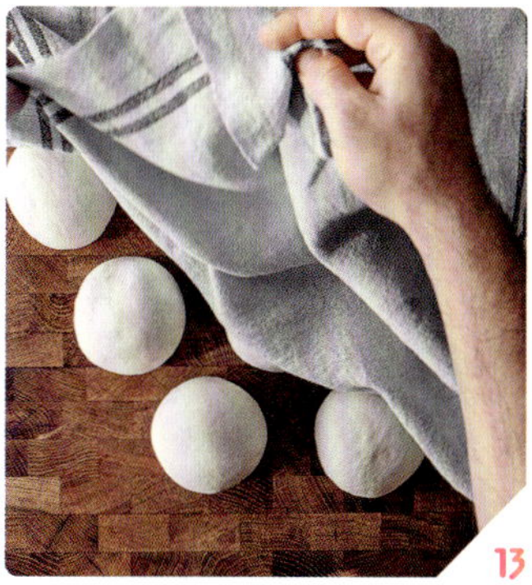
13

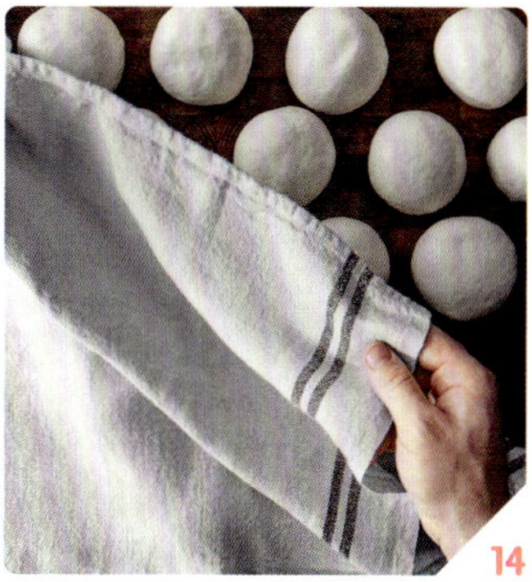
14

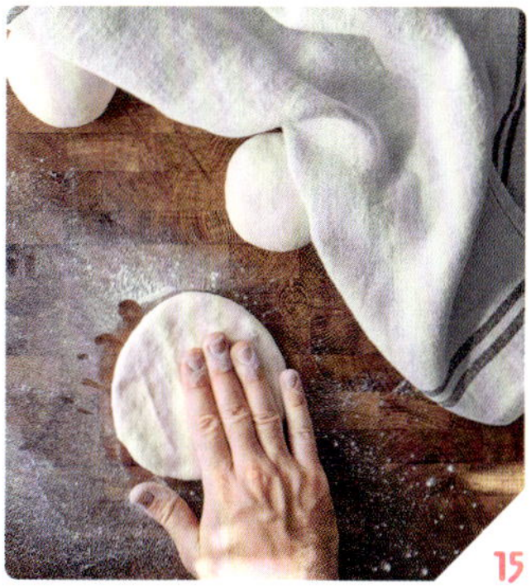
15

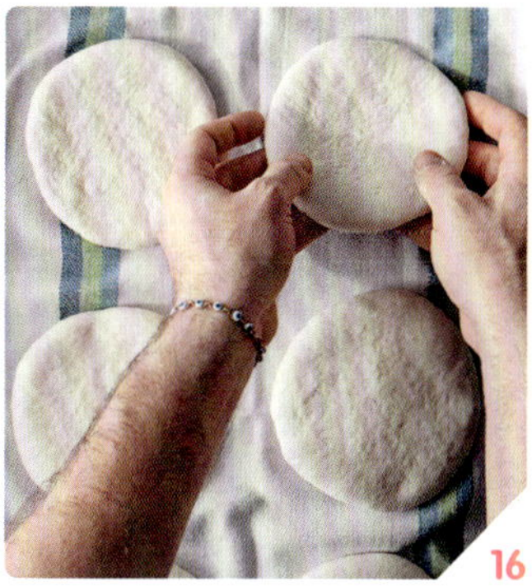
16

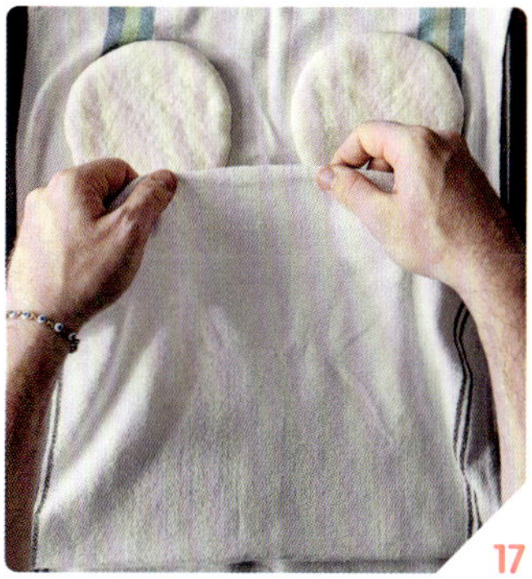
17

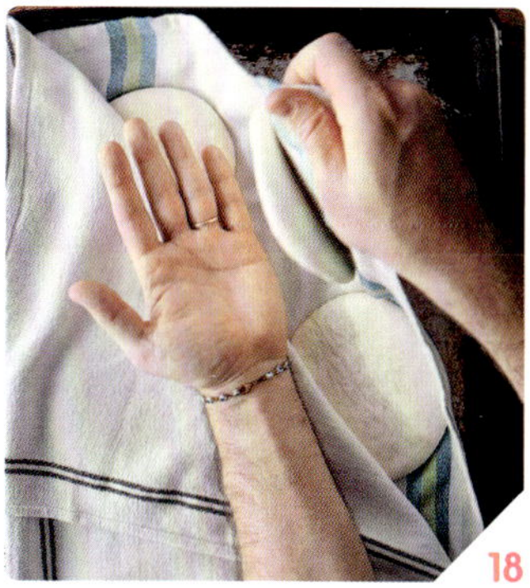
18

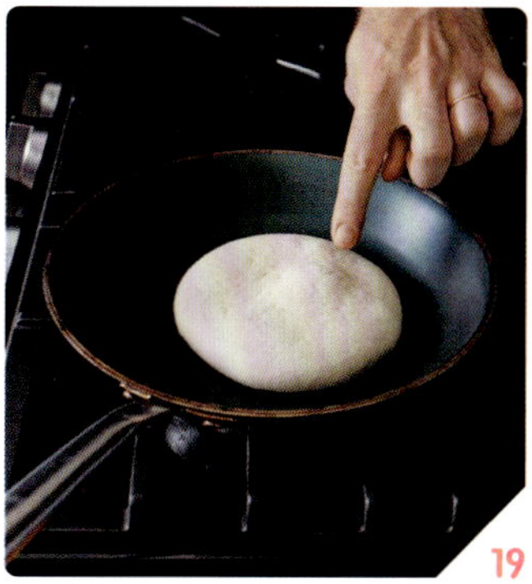
19

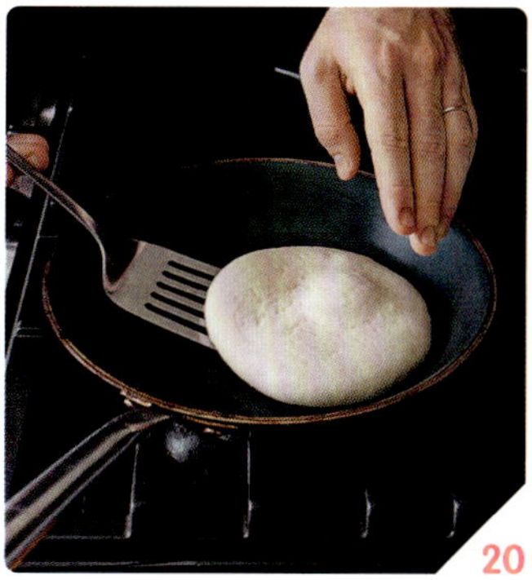
20

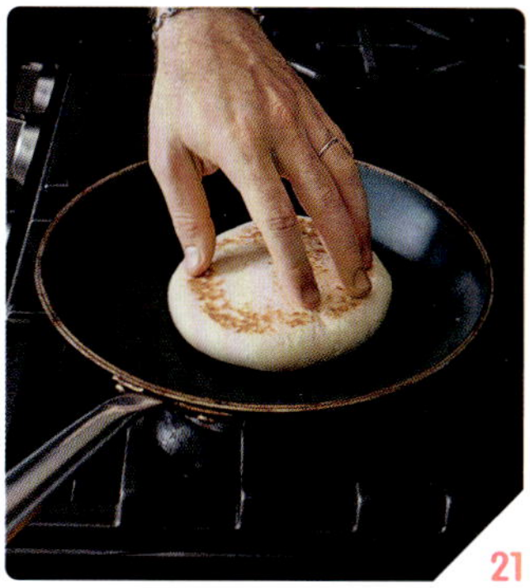
21

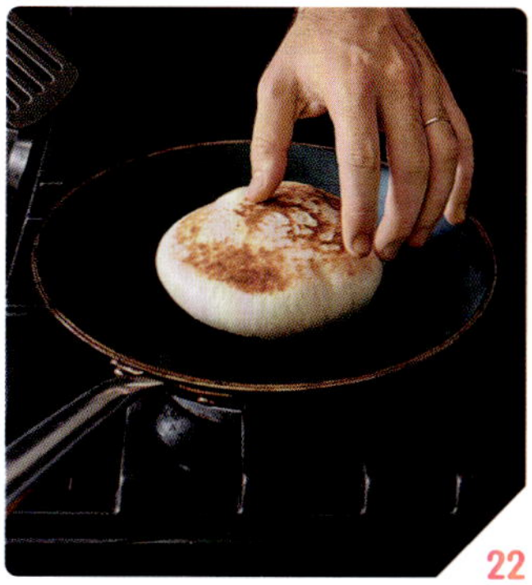
22

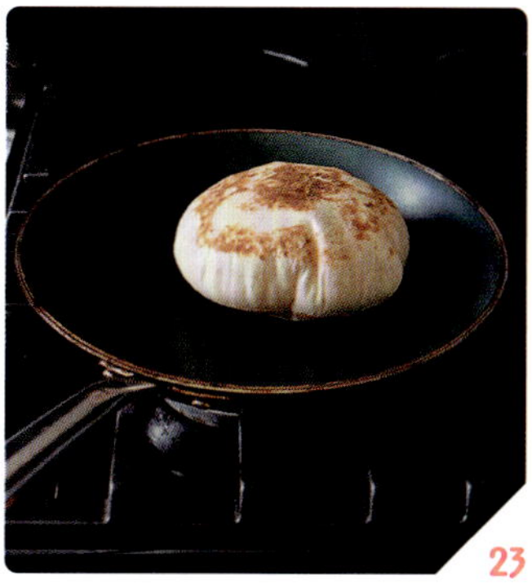
23

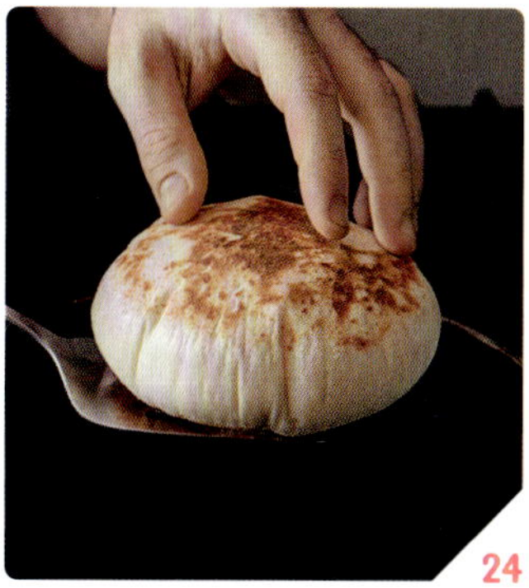
24

Place each of the rolled-out dough disks 2 inches apart on a kitchen towel and cover with another kitchen towel to proof for 20 minutes (use as many kitchen towels as necessary to space the pita properly; it shouldn't take more than two for the bottoms and two for covering). Ensure that the dough is resting close to your stove, making it easier to transfer the dough disks to the pan for cooking.

5. Heat a medium pan over medium-low heat for 1 minute. Working one at a time, gently transfer a dough disk to the pan. The easiest way to transfer the pita dough from the towel to the pan without deflating it is to remove the top towel, hold the edge of the bottom towel, and flip the pita onto your hand. Cook until the first bubble starts to form in the bread, then gently flip it using tongs with smooth edges. Continue flipping the dough every 30 seconds until the pita puffs up. Each pita should take 2 to 3 minutes. Ensure that you adjust the heat accordingly. For example, lower the heat if the pita colors too quickly or raise the heat if the process is taking more than 3 minutes.

6. Transfer the pita to a basket or a bowl covered with a kitchen towel until you're ready to serve. This will prevent the pita from drying out and hardening. If saving leftovers, store the pita in a tightly sealed plastic bag at room temperature for up to 2 days or in the freezer for up to 2 months. To thaw, wrap in a paper towel and place in a sealed container in the refrigerator overnight or place directly into a toaster for 3 minutes.

Tel Avivian Focaccia

Focaccia is undoubtedly one of the best-known and most-loved breads. What's remarkable about it is the possibilities it offers for savory or sweet toppings. Some sweet options include grapes, honey, or a sprinkle of sugar. For a savory twist, try toppings like olives, rosemary, cherry tomatoes, or onions. Or you can just keep it simple with extra virgin olive oil and sea salt. What I also appreciate about focaccia is how easy it is to prepare, making it so well suited for beginner bakers. The mixing is the hardest part! Unlike most focaccias that are baked in trays, you freely shape Israeli focaccia as you stretch the dough. Each loaf has its own unique form, so you can't make a mistake! The result is a distinctive, amazing vessel for all the goodness that a small plates meal has to offer. —Ben

Serve it with: That Tomato Sauce (page 43), Tza-Zikki (page 87), Akko Crudo (page 247)

Yield: Serves 4 to 6, makes 6 focaccias

Total time: 2 hours 30 minutes (plus a 24-hour rest)

Special tools: stand mixer, pastry brush

---

370 grams lukewarm water [between 105°F (40°C) and 115°F (46°C)]

12 grams active dry yeast

500 grams 00 pizza flour

15 grams extra virgin olive oil

12 grams fine sea salt

Olive oil, for brushing and oiling

---

1. In the bowl of a stand mixer fitted with the dough hook, add the water, yeast, and flour. Knead on the lowest speed for 8 minutes.

2. Slowly add the olive oil a little at a time as the stand mixer continues to run, allowing the oil to be fully incorporated into the dough. If the oil is not incorporating fully, turn the stand mixer off and knead the dough by hand in the bowl. Once the oil has been incorporated, add the salt. Continue kneading on low speed for an additional 4 minutes, until it becomes elastic and smooth.

3. Remove the dough from the bowl and round it into a tight ball. Using a paper towel, lightly oil a large bowl. Place the dough in the bowl and cover with plastic wrap. Let the dough rest in the refrigerator overnight, or up to 24 hours.

4. Two hours before you wish to bake the focaccia, remove the bowl from the refrigerator and let it rest for about 1 hour, or until the dough has come to room temperature.

5. Divide the dough into six equal portions. To ensure even portions, use a digital kitchen scale. First, weigh the entire dough to determine

recipe continues

its total weight. Then, divide that number by 6 to calculate the approximate weight for each portion. Pinch off pieces of dough, place them on the scale, and adjust until each portion roughly matches the target weight. Once you have evenly sized portions, round each piece of dough into a tight ball, brush with olive oil using a pastry brush, and set aside, covered with a kitchen towel, for 30 to 40 minutes.

6. While the dough is resting, place a large baking pan in the oven and preheat the oven to 500°F (260°C) or its maximum temperature.

7. On a lightly oiled surface, pinch the sides of each dough ball with your thumbs and gently tap as you stretch the dough on the work surface into a long, oval shape, about 12 inches long and ½ inch thick.

8. Carefully remove the hot pan from the oven and gently transfer each stretched dough to the hot baking pan in batches (there is no need to grease the pan). Bake for 6 to 8 minutes, until the focaccia is light in color and the bread remains soft and springy. Repeat with the remaining dough.

9. Store the focaccia whole in a tightly sealed plastic bag at room temperature for up to 2 days or in the freezer for up to 2 months.

Essential Tips:

For a darker focaccia: This focaccia should be baked only until it is light in color; otherwise it will become overbaked and hard. To add a bit more color while not compromising on the softness, broil for less than a minute before removing from the oven.

Resting in the refrigerator is best: Letting the dough rest overnight in the refrigerator will result in a richer flavor and better texture of the final bread. You can let the dough double in size at room temperature instead, but the flavor and texture will be different.

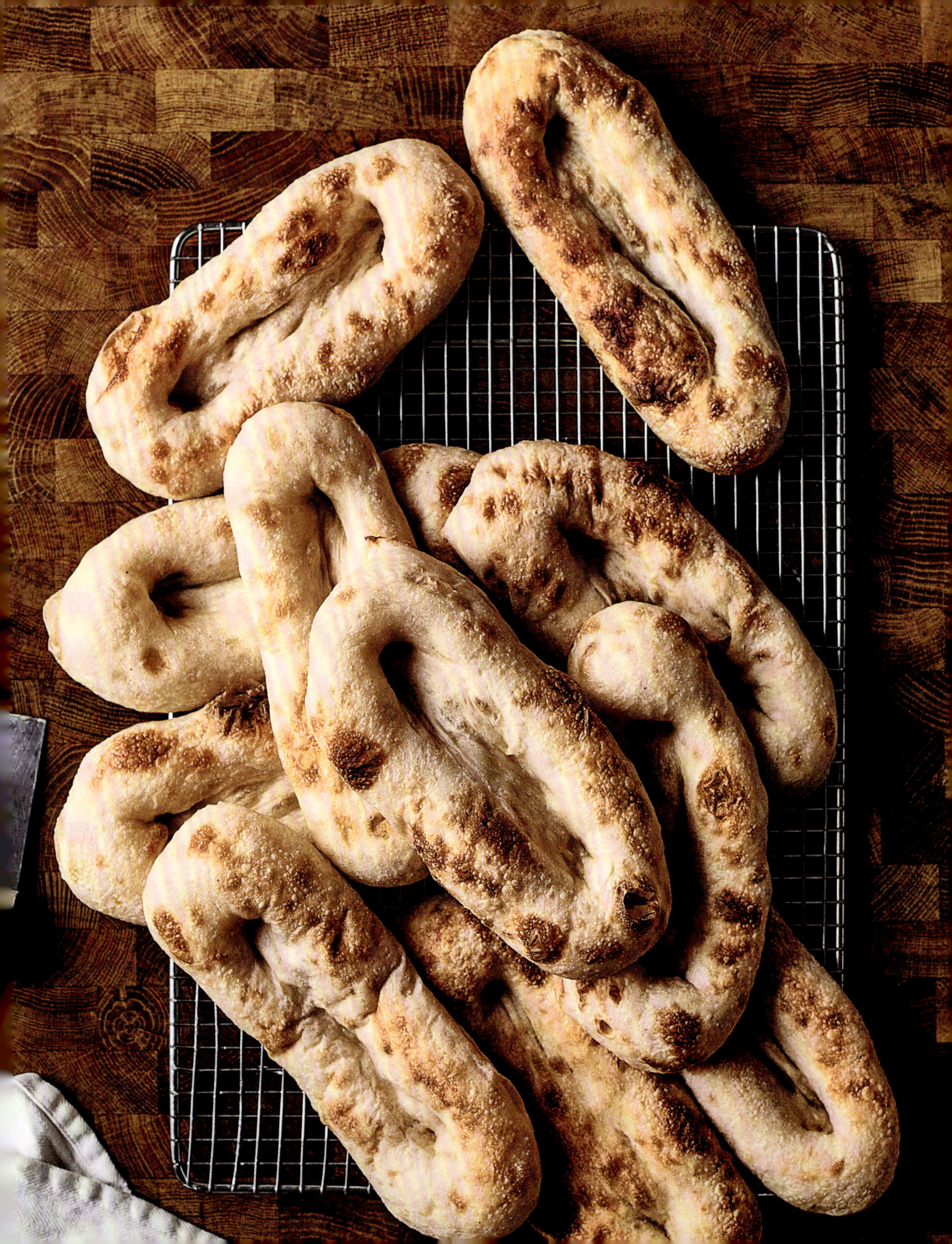

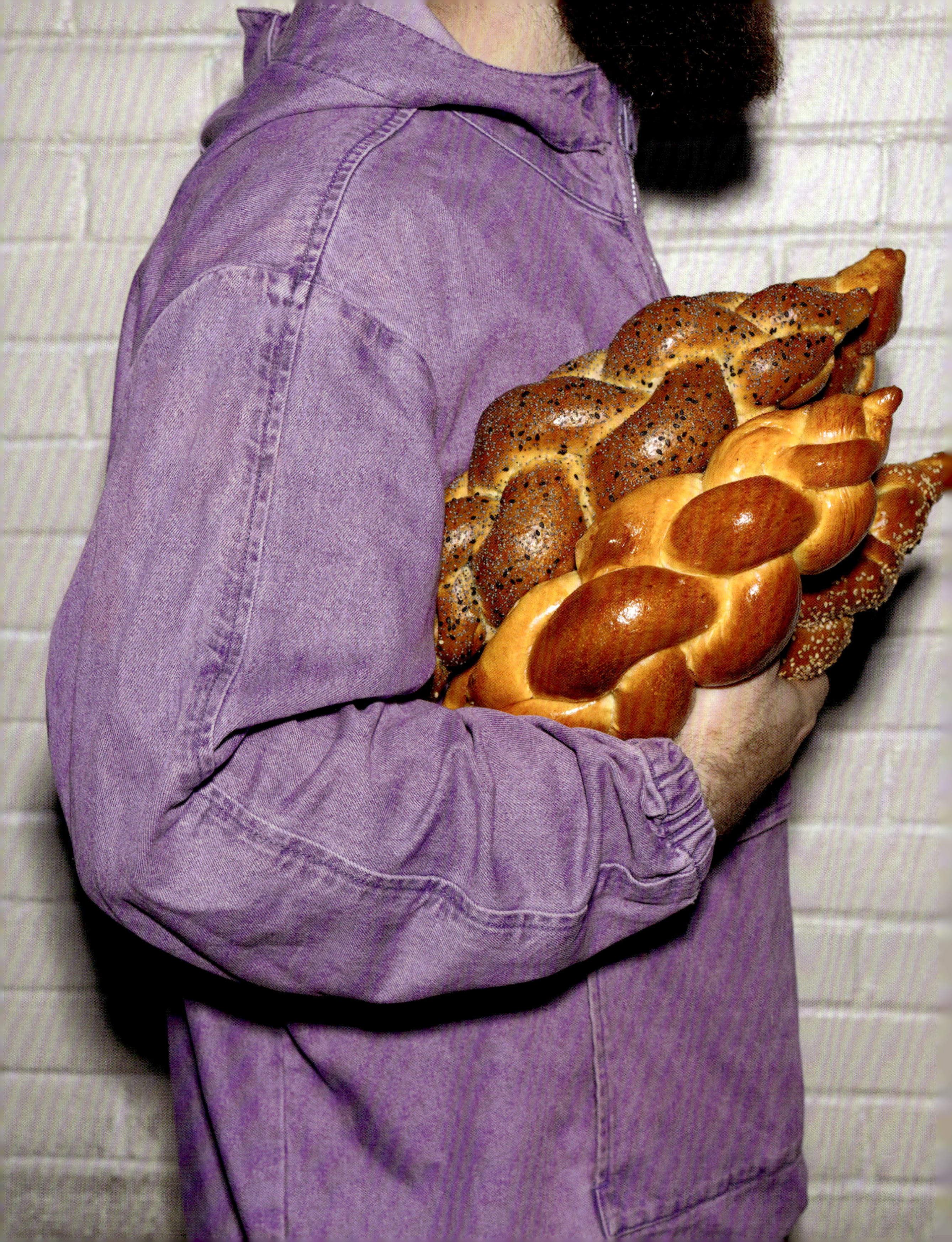

CHALLAH

As an Israeli, I can't think of another bread that reminds me more of my childhood than challah. Every Friday in kindergarten, my friends and I would braid a challah for Shabbat and bring it home to our parents that evening. Shabbat is our day of rest in Israel, and there is nothing more symbolic than baking a loaf of challah to begin the sabbath on Friday evening. Challah is a bread that smells like family—like togetherness and freedom. It always carries a sense of celebration. And for good reason, as historically it is a rich bread enriched with extra virgin olive oil and eggs—considered a luxury at the time of its creation. It was meant to be enjoyed for weekend celebrations.

There are endless ways to braid the challah and to decorate it. My favorite is a four-braid challah adorned with golden sesame seeds, but you can also incorporate poppy seeds. It is the ultimate bread for sopping up sauces at the end of a stew, making a sandwich, or indulging in French toast on a Saturday morning. —BEN

Serve it with: The Smoothest Tahini Dip (page 55), Black or White Baba (pages 92 and 94), Our Hassle-Free Matbucha (page 52), Chopped Liver, Better Than Your Grandma's (page 73), Cucumber, Dill, Labneh & Onion Salad (page 165)

Yield: Serves 10 to 14, makes 2 medium challahs

Total time: 3 hours

Tools: stand mixer, parchment paper, pastry brush, spray bottle, digital kitchen thermometer

FOR THE CHALLAH:

225 grams lukewarm water [between 105°F (40°C) and 115°F (46°C)]

50 grams sugar

10 grams active dry yeast

1 large egg

500 grams bread flour

50 grams extra virgin olive oil

15 grams fine sea salt

1. Make the dough: In the bowl of a stand mixer fitted with the dough hook, add the water, sugar, yeast, egg, flour, and olive oil (in this order). Knead on the lowest speed for 10 minutes. Add the salt and continue to knead for an additional 2 minutes. The dough should be smooth and elastic.

2. Remove the dough from the bowl and round it into a tight ball. Using a paper towel, lightly oil a large bowl. Place the dough in the bowl and cover with plastic wrap. Let the dough rest until it has doubled in size, 1 hour to 1 hour 30 minutes.

3. After the dough has doubled in size, remove it from the bowl and divide it into 8 equal portions. To ensure even portions, use a digital kitchen scale. First, weigh the entire dough to determine its total weight. Then, divide that number by 8 to calculate the approximate weight for each portion. Pinch off pieces of dough, place them on

recipe and ingredients continue

Olive oil, for coating the bowl

For Coating:

1 large egg yolk

1 tablespoon sesame seeds

1 tablespoon poppy seeds

2 tablespoons everything bagel seasoning

the scale, and adjust until each portion roughly matches the target weight. Once you have evenly sized portions, round each piece of dough into a tight ball and set aside, covered with plastic wrap, for 15 minutes.

4. Flip the dough balls upside down. Press each ball into a flat disk shape. Then, roll the dough into itself to form a tight cylinder. Cover the cylinders with a towel and set these dough cylinders aside for 10 minutes.

5. Using your hands, roll each of your dough pieces into a 15-inch-long strand, dusting the strands with flour so that they will stay separate from each other when baked. Place the first four strands parallel to one another and pinch the tops of the strands together so that they are connected and form one end. Repeat for the second four strands.

6. Working with one set of four dough strands, take the strand that is farthest to the right and braid it over the other three strands so it is on the opposite side from where it started. Then, take the second from the left strand and place it on the opposite side, all the way to the right. Take the farthest left strand and place it between the two middle strands. This is the first step of the repeating pattern. Take the second strand on the right and place it on the opposite left side. Repeat the steps until all the dough is braided.

7. Line a large baking sheet with parchment paper and place the two braided challahs on the baking sheet. Cover with a kitchen towel and set aside for about 30 minutes, or until the braided dough has doubled in size. In the meantime, preheat the oven to 375°F (190°C).

8. Make the egg wash: In a small bowl, whisk together the egg yolk and 1 tablespoon of water. Once the challahs have doubled in size, use a pastry brush to lightly and evenly brush the tops and sides of the loaves with the egg wash. Avoid adding an excess of egg wash.

9. Decorate the challahs: In another small bowl, combine the sesame seeds, poppy seeds, and everything bagel seasoning. Sprinkle evenly over the challahs.

10. Lightly spray the dough with water using a spray bottle and bake for 20 to 25 minutes, until golden brown. The internal temperature of the challah should reach 195°F (90°C) on a digital kitchen thermometer. When the proper temperature is reached, remove the loaves from the oven and cover each challah with one or two towels until they cool to room temperature.

11. Store the challahs whole in a tightly sealed plastic bag at room temperature for up to 2 days or sliced in the freezer for up to 2 months.

Essential Tips:

Shaping the strands: When shaping the dough cylinders into strands, I like to form the ends of the strands to be thinner than the center. This will give more volume to the center of the challah and crispier edges once baked.

Don't skip spraying the challah with water before baking: This helps the dough stay elastic and expand properly in the oven, preventing the strands from tearing apart and ensuring a beautifully shaped challah when it's done baking.

Covering the challah: Covering the challah with a towel right after baking traps the steam from the hot loaves, preventing it from escaping and helping to create a soft, tender crust—just the way a perfect challah should be.

Jerusalem Bagel

This bagel brings back so many memories from my childhood. On the sidewalks of Jerusalem, there are bagel carts with huge piles of oval-shaped, sesame-coated bagels wrapped in that day's newspaper with a little bag of za'atar. Unlike New York bagels, Jerusalem bagels are not boiled, but rather dipped in a sweet syrup before they are coated with sesame seeds and then baked. They have a beautiful mix of sweet and savory notes in every bite. Enjoy these with a bit of olive oil and za'atar and you will be transported directly to the old city of Jerusalem. —Ben

Serve it with: A Cashew Basil Dip Everyone Will Talk About (page 99), Beet & Goat Cheese Dip (page 88), Black Baba (page 94)

Yield: Serves 6 to 12, makes 6 Jerusalem bagels

Total time: 3 hours 30 minutes

Special tools: kitchen scale

For the Dough:

285 grams lukewarm water [between 105°F (40°C) and 115°F (46°C)]

30 grams sugar

10 grams active dry yeast

400 grams bread flour

100 grams whole wheat flour

40 grams extra virgin olive oil

10 grams fine sea salt

Olive oil, for coating the bowl

1. Make the dough: In a medium bowl, add the water, sugar, yeast, bread flour, and whole wheat flour. Pour the olive oil on top and mix well until all the ingredients are incorporated. Add the salt and continue to knead the dough using your hands for 8 to 10 minutes, until it is elastic and smooth.

2. Round the dough into a tight ball. Using a paper towel, lightly oil a large bowl. Place the dough in the bowl and cover with plastic wrap. Let the dough rest until it has doubled in size, 1 hour to 1 hour 30 minutes.

3. Make the simple syrup for the topping: While the dough is rising, in a small saucepan over medium heat, add the water and the sugar. Stir until the sugar is dissolved. Set aside to cool.

4. After the dough has doubled in size, remove it from the bowl and divide it into six 150-gram pieces using a kitchen scale. Round each piece into a tight ball and set aside, covered with a kitchen towel, for 10 to 15 minutes.

5. Roll each ball into a thin, long strand. Connect the top and bottom of the strand together and roll the ends together to seal it into a long oval bagel shape.

recipe and ingredients continue

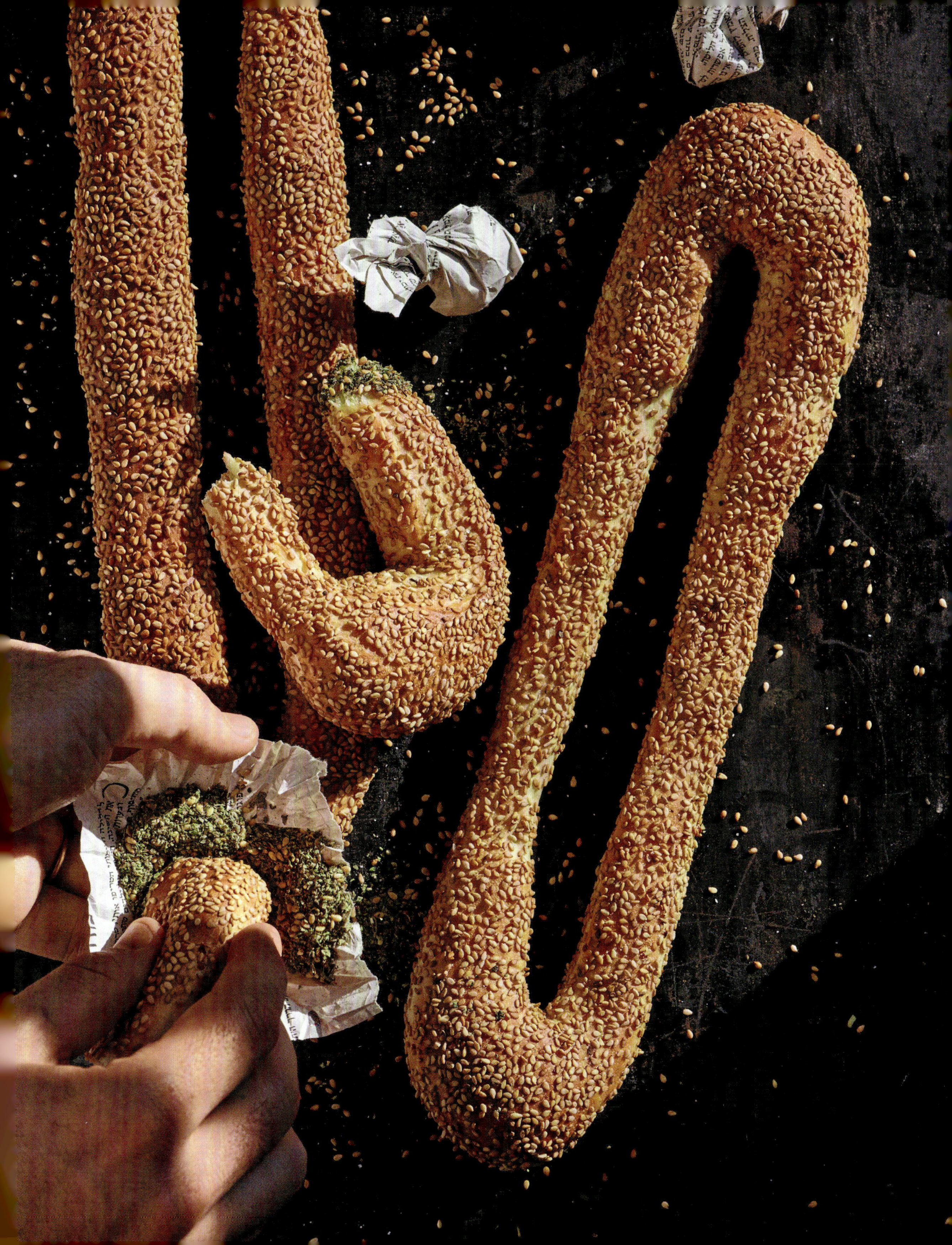

For the Topping:

400 grams water

200 grams sugar

1 cup sesame seeds

For Dipping:

2 tablespoons za'atar

Extra virgin olive oil

6. Coat the bagels: Pour the simple syrup and sesame seeds into two separate baking trays. First, dip the bagel into the syrup, ensuring that all sides are coated with an even layer of syrup. Then, coat the entire bagel evenly with sesame seeds, flipping once (you may have leftover seeds). Repeat until all the bagels are coated.

7. Place the bagels about 2 inches apart on a large baking sheet. Cover with a kitchen towel and set aside for 30 minutes, or until the bagels have doubled in size. In the meantime, preheat the oven to 400°F (200°C).

8. Once your bagels have doubled in size, bake them for 18 to 20 minutes, until golden brown. Remove the bagels from the oven and let cool on a rack.

9. Serve the bagels fresh with a small dipping bowl filled with the za'atar and a small dipping bowl of your favorite olive oil.

breadsticks

This bread is really close to our hearts. Breadsticks, also known as grissini, originated in Piemonte, the region in northwestern Italy where Zikki and I met. Wherever you go in Piemonte, you will find these golden, crispy breadsticks coated with a rustic layer of semolina welcoming you to any meal. Breadsticks are common in bakeries in Israel, too, but they are on the softer side and made for dipping into spreads. We love incorporating olives and cheese into our breadsticks and enjoying them as a flavorful, standalone snack. —BEN

Serve it with: Beef Tartare (page 259), Preserved Lemon Butter (page 69), Garlic Confit (page 63), Shrimp in Grated Tomato Butter (page 276)

Yield: Serves 7 to 9, makes 14 to 18 breadsticks

Total time: 3 hours 30 minutes

Special tools: rolling pin, pastry brush, pizza wheel

---

270 grams lukewarm water [between 105°F (40°C) and 115°F (46°C)]

15 grams honey

10 grams active dry yeast

400 grams all-purpose flour

100 grams whole wheat flour

50 grams extra virgin olive oil

15 grams fine sea salt

100 grams olives, chopped

1. In a large bowl, add the water, honey, yeast, all-purpose flour, whole wheat flour, olive oil, and salt. Mix well until all the ingredients are incorporated. Continue to knead the dough for 10 minutes, or until it is elastic and smooth. Add the olives, cheddar, and rosemary and knead for an additional 2 minutes.

2. Round the dough into a tight ball. Using a paper towel, lightly oil a large bowl. Place the dough in the bowl and cover with plastic wrap. Let the dough rest until it has doubled in size, 1 hour to 1 hour 30 minutes.

3. Preheat the oven to 500°F (220°C).

4. After the dough has doubled in size, remove it from the bowl. Sprinkle semolina flour on the work surface and, using a rolling pin, roll out the dough into a long rectangular shape. The final shape should be about the size of a half-sheet pan (13 × 18 inches) with a ⅓-inch thickness.

recipe and ingredients continue

50 grams cheddar, grated

7 grams dried rosemary

Olive oil, for brushing and coating the bowl

Semolina flour, for dusting

Gray salt, for topping (optional)

5. Using a pastry brush, evenly brush the top of the dough with olive oil. Using a pizza wheel and cutting perpendicular to the long edge of the dough, cut the dough evenly into ½-inch-thick strips. This should give you 14 to 18 breadsticks. Then twist each strip with your hands by rolling each end in the opposite direction.

6. Place the breadsticks about 1 inch apart on a large baking sheet. If desired, brush each stick with a light coat of olive oil and sprinkle gray salt on top. Put the breadsticks directly into the oven and bake for 10 minutes, or until golden brown.

7. Remove the breadsticks from the oven and brush with another light layer of olive oil. Allow to cool to room temperature and serve standing up in a vase or tall jar.

ESSENTIAL TIP:

Texture of the breadsticks: After the breadsticks cool to room temperature, they might lose their stiff persona and soften. If you let them sit at room temperature for a day, they will dry out and the texture will be more like grissini. Both are delicious, depending on your preference!

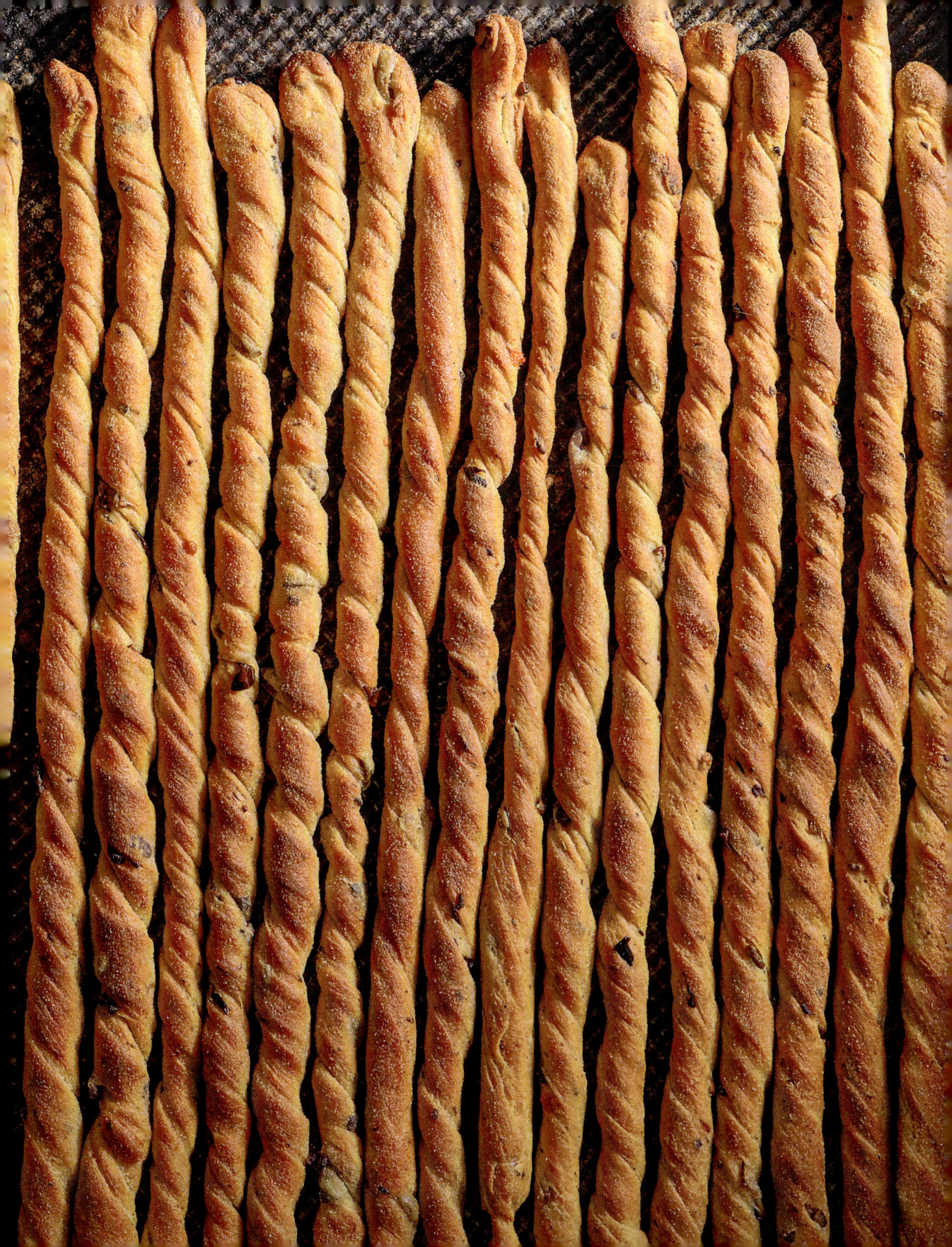

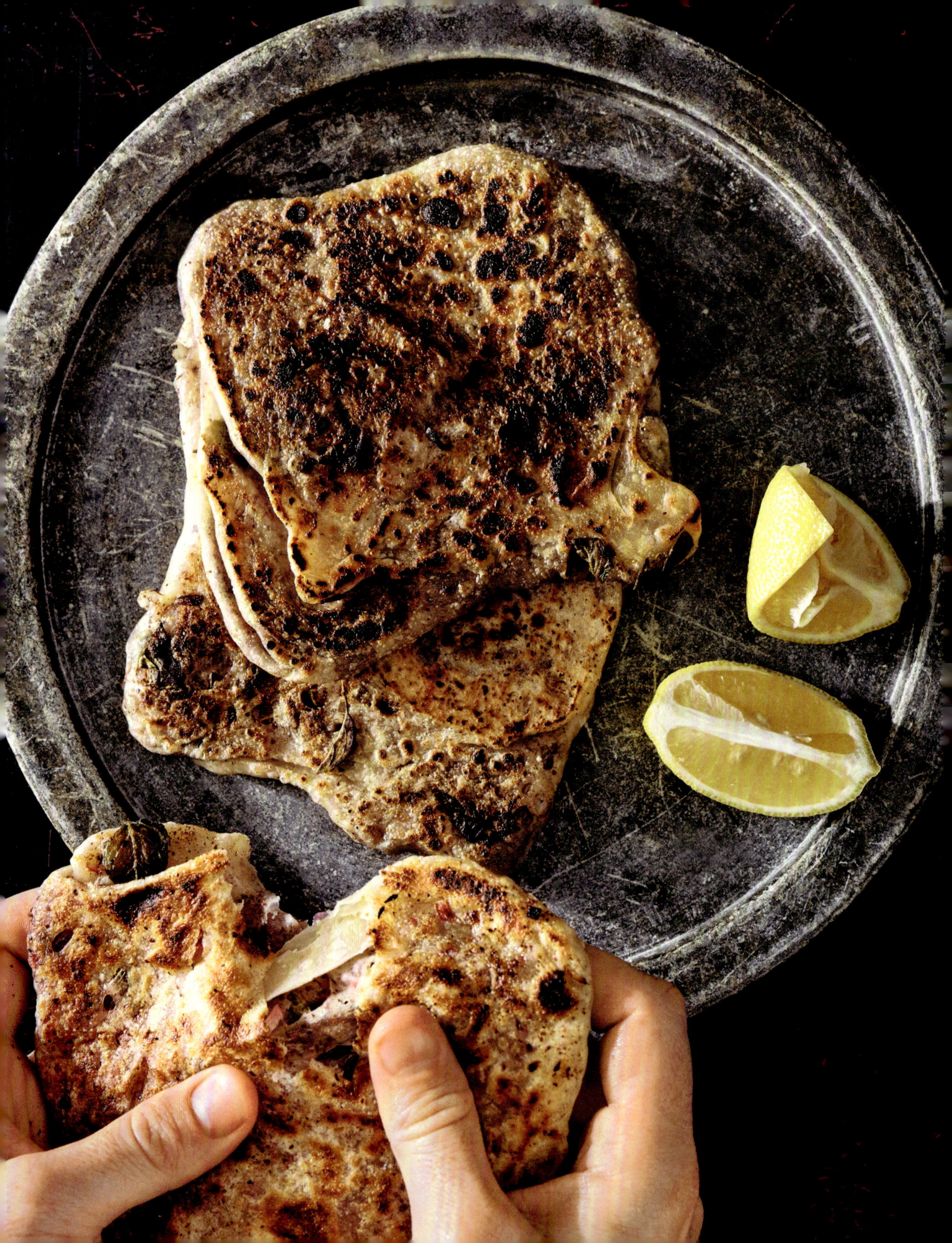

MURTABAK

On a trip to Israel as a family, we traveled to Akko, one of the oldest port cities in the world. Akko is known for its mixed Arab and Jewish population, and thus it has an outstanding food scene. It is filled with colorful markets full of smells and spices, authentic hummus shops, and rich fish stands offering a wonderful variety of treasures from the sea. Not far from the market, an Arabic woman named Fatima runs baking workshops. We visited her class, and she taught us how to make an easy and versatile flatbread called murtabak, which means "folded" in Arabic. As the name implies, this is a simple dough that is stuffed with either a savory or sweet filling and then folded onto itself. Fatima's version was baked, but I found it much easier to cook it directly in a pan on the stove. This murtabak recipe uses our favorite filling from that workshop: onion, sumac, and fresh oregano leaves. —BEN

Serve it with: The Smoothest Tahini Dip (page 55), Tza-Zikki (page 87), Labneh Spread (page 84)

Yield: Serves 6 to 8, makes 4 murtabaks

Total time: 2 hours 30 minutes

Special tools: rolling pin

FOR THE DOUGH:

500 grams all-purpose flour

350 grams water

10 grams fine sea salt

4 tablespoons olive oil, plus more for coating the bowl

FOR THE FILLING:

2 red onions, thinly sliced

1 bunch of oregano, stemmed

1 tablespoon sumac

1. Make the dough: In a medium bowl, add the flour, water, and salt. Knead the dough for 12 minutes, or until it is elastic and smooth.

2. Round the dough into a tight ball. Using a paper towel, lightly oil a large bowl. Place the dough in the bowl and cover with plastic wrap. Let the dough rest for 1 hour.

3. Make the filling: In a separate small bowl, combine the onions, oregano, sumac, lemon juice, and salt and set aside.

4. After the dough has rested, remove it from the bowl and divide it into 4 equal pieces. To ensure even portions, use a digital kitchen scale. First, weigh the entire dough to determine its total weight. Then, divide that number by 4 to calculate the approximate weight for each portion. Pinch off pieces of dough, place them on the scale, and adjust until each portion roughly matches the target weight. Once you have evenly sized portions, round each piece into a tight ball and set aside, covered with a kitchen towel, for 20 minutes.

recipe and ingredients continue

Juice of 1 lemon

1 teaspoon fine sea salt

For Serving:

1 lemon, cut into quarters

5. Work on each piece of dough separately. Using a rolling pin, roll the dough ball out as thin as possible. Once you are not able to get the dough any thinner with the rolling pin, continue to spread the dough by using the tips of your fingers, palm side up, to lightly lift the edges of the dough and stretch it. Ensure that your hands are flat so you don't poke a hole in the dough.

6. Assemble the murtabak: Once the dough is rolled as thin as possible, spread 2 to 3 tablespoons of the filling evenly onto the dough. Fold the top third of the dough to the center. Add 1 tablespoon of filling on this piece of dough and fold the bottom third on top of it. Fill and fold the sides the same way. The dough should end up folded into a square. Repeat with the remaining pieces of dough.

7. When you are ready to cook the murtabak, set a medium pan over medium-low heat. Flatten each folded dough to the size of the pan using your hands. Add 1 tablespoon of olive oil to the skillet and transfer one folded dough onto the skillet. Cook for 4 to 5 minutes, flipping it every 30 seconds. If the color of the dough darkens too quickly, lower the heat. Once the dough is golden brown, remove it from the skillet and repeat with the remaining dough and oil.

8. Serve the murtabak hot, either whole or cut into quarters, with a slice of lemon.

Essential Tip:

For a sweet variation: Fill the murtabak with equal parts brown sugar and crushed hazelnuts, and season with cinnamon to taste. For 1 cup of brown sugar and 1 cup of crushed hazelnuts, we recommend adding ½ teaspoon of cinnamon.

Lahuh

I'm so happy to introduce you to one of the coolest flatbreads in the world: lahuh. My hometown, Rehovot, is known for its Yemenite population, which has a major influence on the local cuisine. And so although I'm not Yemenite, I'm very familiar with their food. Lahuh is one of the staple breads of the Yemenite diet. It is similar to a crumpet, a small griddle bread made from a batter of water or milk, flour, and yeast. However, lahuh is much thinner and served mostly with savory dishes. What I find unique about this bread is that in between each batch, you must rinse the pan under cold water to cool it down because lahuh must be cooked on a cold nonstick skillet to keep its light color and delicate, fluffy texture. Our favorite way to serve lahuh is with freshly grated tomatoes, zhug, and hard-boiled eggs. —BEN

Serve it with: Freshly grated tomatoes, My Grandfather's Zhug (page 49), hard-boiled eggs

Yield: Serves 10 to 12, makes 10 to 12 mini lahuh

Total time: 3 hours

---

850 grams lukewarm water [between 105°F (40°C) and 115°F (46°C)]

500 grams all-purpose flour

100 grams semolina flour

10 grams active dry yeast

30 grams sugar

15 grams fine sea salt

Olive oil, for coating the pan

---

1. In a medium bowl, combine the water, all-purpose flour, semolina flour, yeast, sugar, and salt. Whisk for 5 minutes, or until the mixture reaches the consistency of pancake batter. Cover with plastic wrap and set aside until the batter has doubled in size, 1 hour to 1 hour 30 minutes.

2. After the batter has doubled in size, whisk again for another 2 to 3 minutes. Set aside and cover with plastic wrap for an additional 30 minutes.

3. Whisk one more time for 2 to 3 minutes (so you are whisking three times total) and set aside the covered batter for 30 more minutes.

4. Using a paper towel, lightly oil a cold nonstick small skillet. Fill a ladle halfway with the batter and pour it into the pan. Turn the temperature to high and cook the lahuh for 1 to 2 minutes, until bubbles form on top and it has almost completely dried. Transfer the cooked lahuh to a kitchen towel and cover with another towel to keep it soft and moist.

recipe continues

5. Rinse the bottom of the pan under cold water until the pan is completely cooled. Repeat step 4 until all of the lahuh have been cooked. After every couple of rounds of cooking the lahuh, recoat the pan with the oiled paper towel.

6. Serve fresh off the pan or soon after alongside some grated tomatoes, zhug, and hard-boiled eggs.

Essential Tip:

Whisking multiple times when making lahuh ensures air is incorporated, fermentation is even, lumps are prevented, and the yeast is reactivated for a light, spongy texture.

that tomato sauce

zhug

salads

If you are anything like us, you love a salad at any point of the day. Whether you're whipping up a quick-fix Jeweled Celery Salad (page 136) for a quaint dinner with your girlfriends or looking to make something simple yet grand, like the Best Green Salad of Your Life (page 184), this chapter has a recipe for every occasion and mood.

This chapter is—neurotically—broken down by concept and texture so that you never feel like you are just crunching away at a pile of leaves. You will always be biting into something unexpected, refreshing, and wildly satisfying.—*zikki*

RECIPES

chopped
jeweled celery salad
when in doubt chopped salad
tabbouleh (2 ways)

semicooked
deconstructed sabich
marinated peppers
beet & cherry salad
herby marinated eggplants
chicken shawarma salad
breakfast salad

crispy, crunchy, or crushed
fennel, citrus & pistachio salad
not your typical "crisp veg"
cucumber, dill, labneh & onion salad
pear, mustard green, mint & challah crouton salad
fig carpaccio
not your grandma's fruit salad

tomato based
fattoush salad
peach & tomato salad with mozzarella & basil
israeli caprese
zikki's peeled tomato salad
salat dudu

leafy
the best green salad of your life
middle eastern caesar
radicchio, blue cheese & hazelnut salad
kale salad with roasted tomatoes & almonds

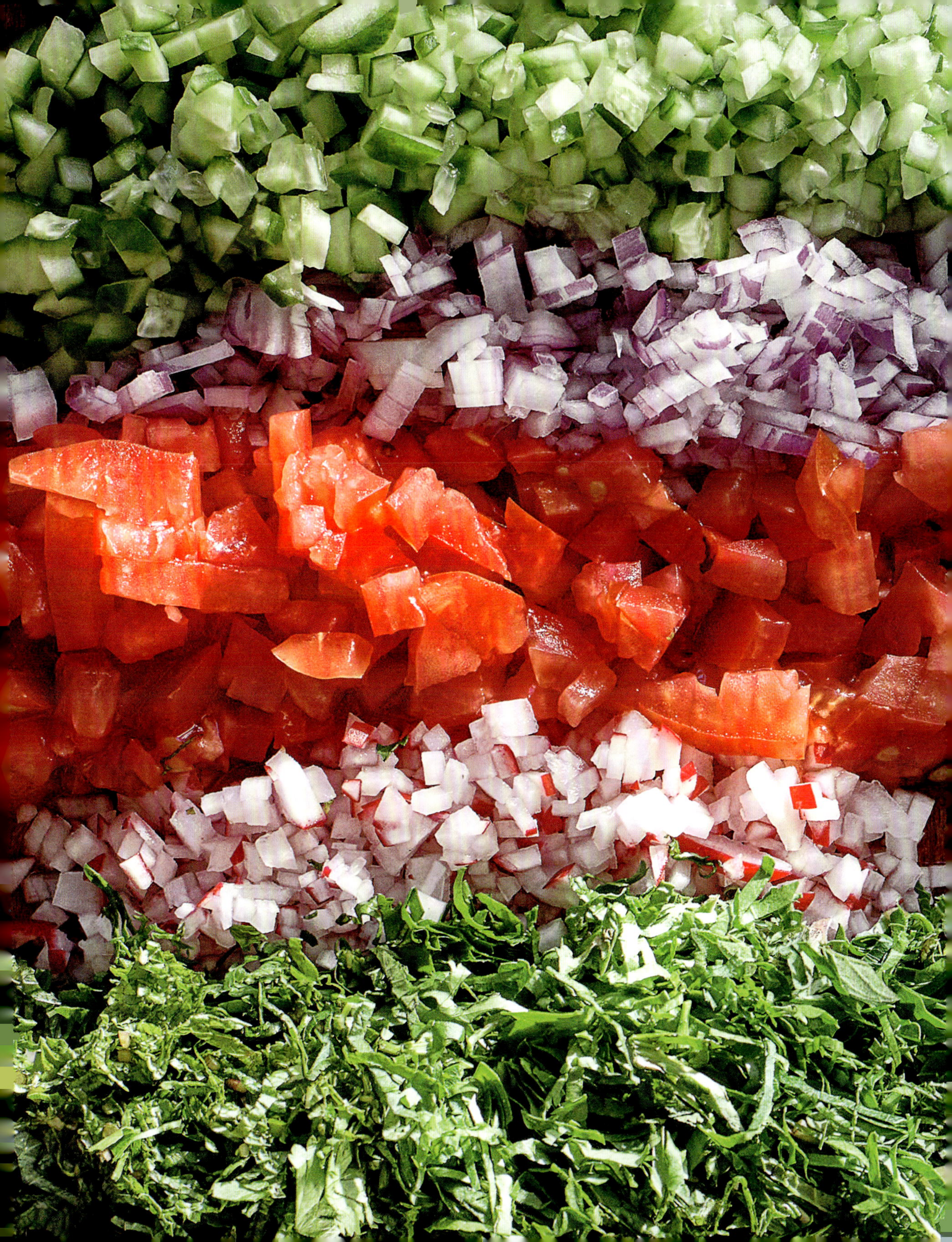

jeweled celery salad

chopped

You didn't realize you needed this salad until now. We used to call this the leftover salad because it was born out of all our leftovers from a big night of cooking: herbs, nuts, dried fruit, and celery (because who doesn't have leftover celery?). But the more we made this salad, the more it became a menu staple. And then it became the most important salad we ever served. This salad is fresh and bountiful from the abundance of herbs, satisfying and decadent from the freshly toasted almonds, tart and sweet from the dried fruit, and pulled together using the celery, which is the ultimate vehicle for crunch. To add even more color, toss in an additional cup of pomegranate seeds. —*zikki*

Serve it with: My Uncle Tal's Lentil Masabacha (page 79), Zikki's Eggplant (page 224), Jerusalem Bagel (page 120)

Yield: Serves 3 to 6, makes 3 heaping small plates

Total time: 15 minutes

- 1 cup raw almonds, toasted and roughly chopped (see page 22)
- 2 cups raw celery, sliced into small ¼-inch pieces
- 1 cup dried cranberries, roughly chopped
- ½ bunch of flat-leaf parsley, roughly chopped
- ½ bunch of cilantro, roughly chopped
- 1 bunch of mint, chopped
- 1 cup pomegranate seeds (optional, highly recommended)
- Juice of 1 lemon
- 2 tablespoons extra virgin olive oil
- 1 tablespoon honey
- 1 teaspoon gray salt, plus more to taste

In a medium bowl, add the almonds, celery, cranberries, parsley, cilantro, mint, pomegranate seeds (if desired, but highly recommended), lemon juice, olive oil, honey, and salt. Toss until combined, adjust the salt as needed, and serve immediately.

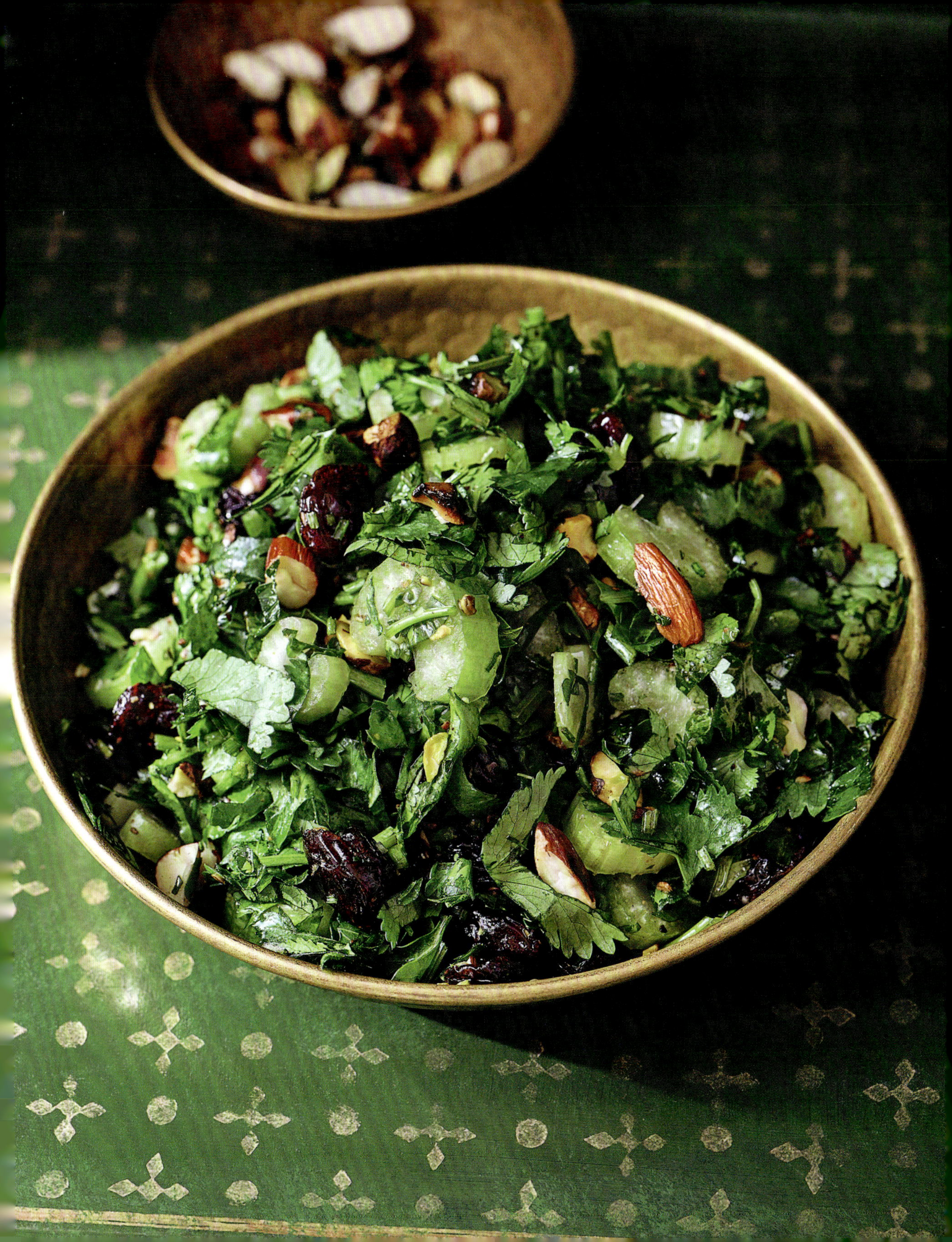

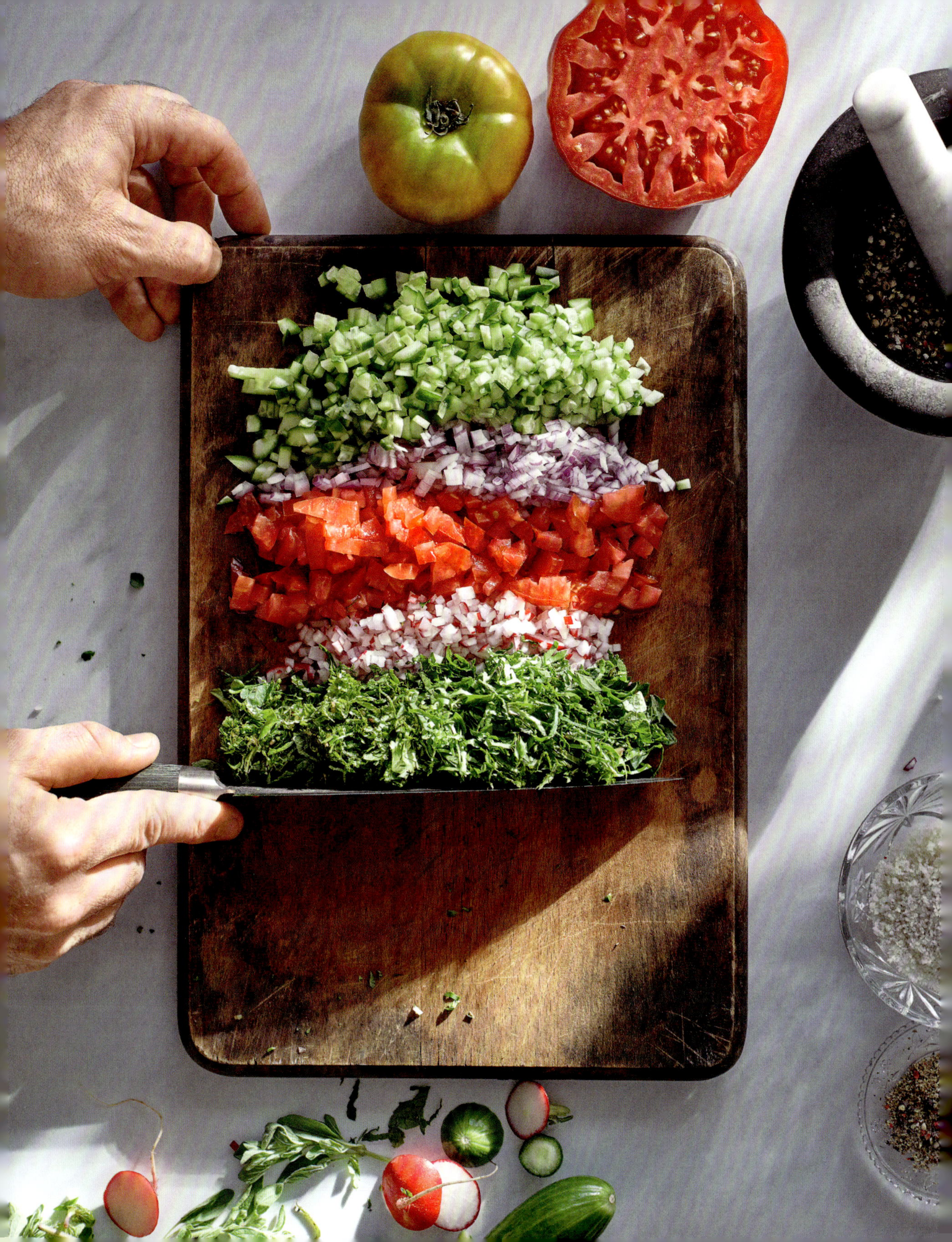

when in doubt chopped salad

The first word that comes to mind when I think of Israeli salad is FRESH. Saturdays during my childhood were spent at my Saba Judah's house, where we always enjoyed a large lunch as a family. Something I remember profoundly is my Saba's chopped salad, which was chock-full of fresh veggies meticulously cut to perfection. Being who I am, I deeply respected and enjoyed the time and effort he put into making this salad for all the grandkids. It was not easy work!

As an adult, I crave this salad Every. Single. Day. When you are in doubt about what to serve, this is always a crowd-pleaser! It is an extraordinarily fun salad to make, too, as you get to practice your knife skills. Zikki and I frequently compete to see who can chop the ingredients the fastest and most precise. It is colorful, fresh, lemony, and goes with literally everything. —Ben

Serve it with: Ben's Schnitzel Fingers (page 265), Vetrena Fries (page 227), Arabic Ceviche (page 256), Stuffed Onions (page 270), The Smoothest Tahini Dip (page 55)

Yield: Serves 3 to 5, makes 3 small plates

Total time: 15 minutes

chopped

- 4 Persian cucumbers, finely diced
- 1 large red heirloom tomato, finely diced and drained
- ¼ small red onion, finely diced
- 3 red radishes, finely diced
- ¼ bunch of flat-leaf parsley, stemmed and finely chopped
- 20 mint leaves, finely chopped
- ¼ bunch of cilantro, stemmed and finely chopped
- 2 tablespoons extra virgin olive oil
- Juice of ½ lemon
- 1 teaspoon sumac
- Gray salt

In a medium bowl, add the cucumbers, tomato, onion, radishes, parsley, mint, cilantro, olive oil, lemon juice, sumac, and salt to taste. Toss and serve immediately.

essential tip:

Drain the salad: When making this recipe for a large group or ahead of time, drain your tomatoes after you dice them, and before you add them to the whole mix. This will ensure that your salad stays fresh and light, without accumulating too much juice at the bottom.

Tabbouleh (2 ways)

chopped

Tabbouleh is one of those salads that you forget how much you love until you taste it again, especially when it's made to perfection. It may look simple, but it is a salad that elicits pure satisfaction. What I love about our take on this classic is the addition of mint (mint is not a traditional ingredient because if it's not fresh, it can blacken the salad). It elevates the herb mixture tremendously. The second recipe is for anyone looking for a lighter, gluten-free version of this salad—it switches out bulgur for cauliflower rice and pomegranate. The addition of the pomegranate seeds feels simply royal, and each bite bursts with tangy sweetness. —BEN

Serve it with: The Smoothest Tahini Dip (page 55), Kebab (page 266), Burnt Beets & Feta (page 207)

Yield: Serves 2 to 4, makes 2 small plates

Total time: 15 minutes

Using Bulgur

1 small heirloom tomato, finely diced

3 Persian cucumbers, finely diced

1 bunch of mint, stemmed and finely chopped

1 bunch of flat-leaf parsley, finely chopped

1 bunch of cilantro, finely chopped

1 cup bulgur, cooked and drained according to package instructions

Juice of ½ lemon

2 tablespoons extra virgin olive oil

1 teaspoon gray salt

¼ teaspoon cumin seeds, toasted and crushed

In a medium bowl, add the tomato, cucumber, mint, parsley, cilantro, bulgur, lemon juice, olive oil, salt, and crushed cumin seeds. Toss until combined and serve immediately.

recipe continues

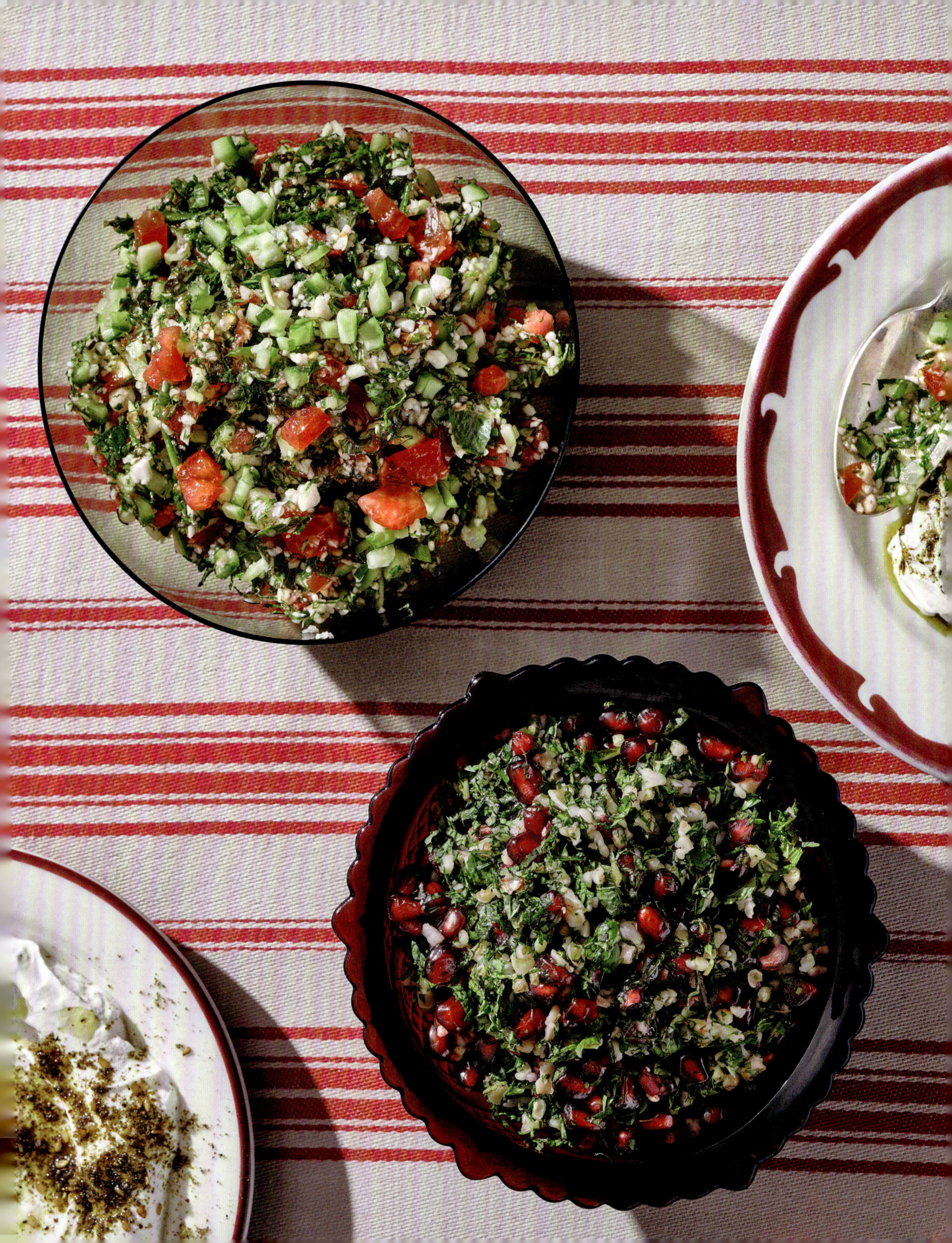

USING CAULIFLOWER RICE

2 Persian cucumbers, finely diced

½ cup pomegranate seeds

1 bunch of mint, stemmed and finely chopped

1 bunch of flat-leaf parsley, finely chopped

1 bunch of cilantro, finely chopped

1 cup raw cauliflower rice

Juice of ½ lemon

1 teaspoon honey

2 tablespoons extra virgin olive oil

1 teaspoon gray salt

In a medium bowl, add the cucumbers, pomegranate seeds, mint, parsley, cilantro, cauliflower rice, lemon juice, honey, olive oil, and salt. Toss until combined and serve immediately.

deconstructed sabich

semi-cooked

There are many legends about the genesis of the famous sabich pita sandwich. The true story is that sabich came from Iraq and landed in Israel through the migration of Jewish Iraqis. In modern times, people say the word *sabich* in Hebrew is an acronym for "salat, baytsa, v hatsil," which translates to "salad, eggs, and eggplant." It sounds simple, but when these ingredients are strategically prepared and smothered in tahini and amba, they are the heartbeat of lunchtime in Israel. Sabich is a great vegetarian alternative to falafel, typically served in pita, but Zikki and I love to serve it deconstructed along with freshly baked pita.

This dish does require some heavy lifting on the front end, but if you prep most of the ingredients in advance, then all you have left to do is fry the eggplant and toss the salad once your guests arrive! Trust me, if you haven't experienced fried eggplant, it is a game changer. —ben

Serve it with: Pita (page 109), Harissa (page 50)

Yield: Makes 4 pitas

Total time: 1 hour 30 minutes

Special tools: digital kitchen thermometer

FOR THE EGGPLANT:

2 large eggplants, cut into 1-inch cubes

2 tablespoons kosher salt

Canola oil, for frying (about 2 cups)

FOR THE SALAD:

15 cherry tomatoes, halved

4 Persian cucumbers, finely diced

¼ small red onion, thinly sliced

1. Prep the eggplant: In a medium bowl, toss the eggplant cubes with the kosher salt. Place the eggplant cubes in a colander and allow them to sit for 30 minutes in order to release water. Then run the cubes under cold water to wash off the excess salt. Place the rinsed eggplant onto a dry kitchen towel and pat dry, pressing out all the moisture. Set aside until you are ready to fry.

2. In a large skillet, heat about 2 inches of canola oil over medium-high heat until it reaches 350° to 375°F (175° to 190°C) on a digital kitchen thermometer. Check the temperature periodically. Line a baking sheet with paper towels.

3. Once the oil is ready, add one layer of eggplant into the skillet. Fry for 3 minutes on one side and then, using a slotted spoon, flip the eggplant cubes. Fry on that side for an additional 3 minutes, or until fully golden brown.

recipe and ingredients continue

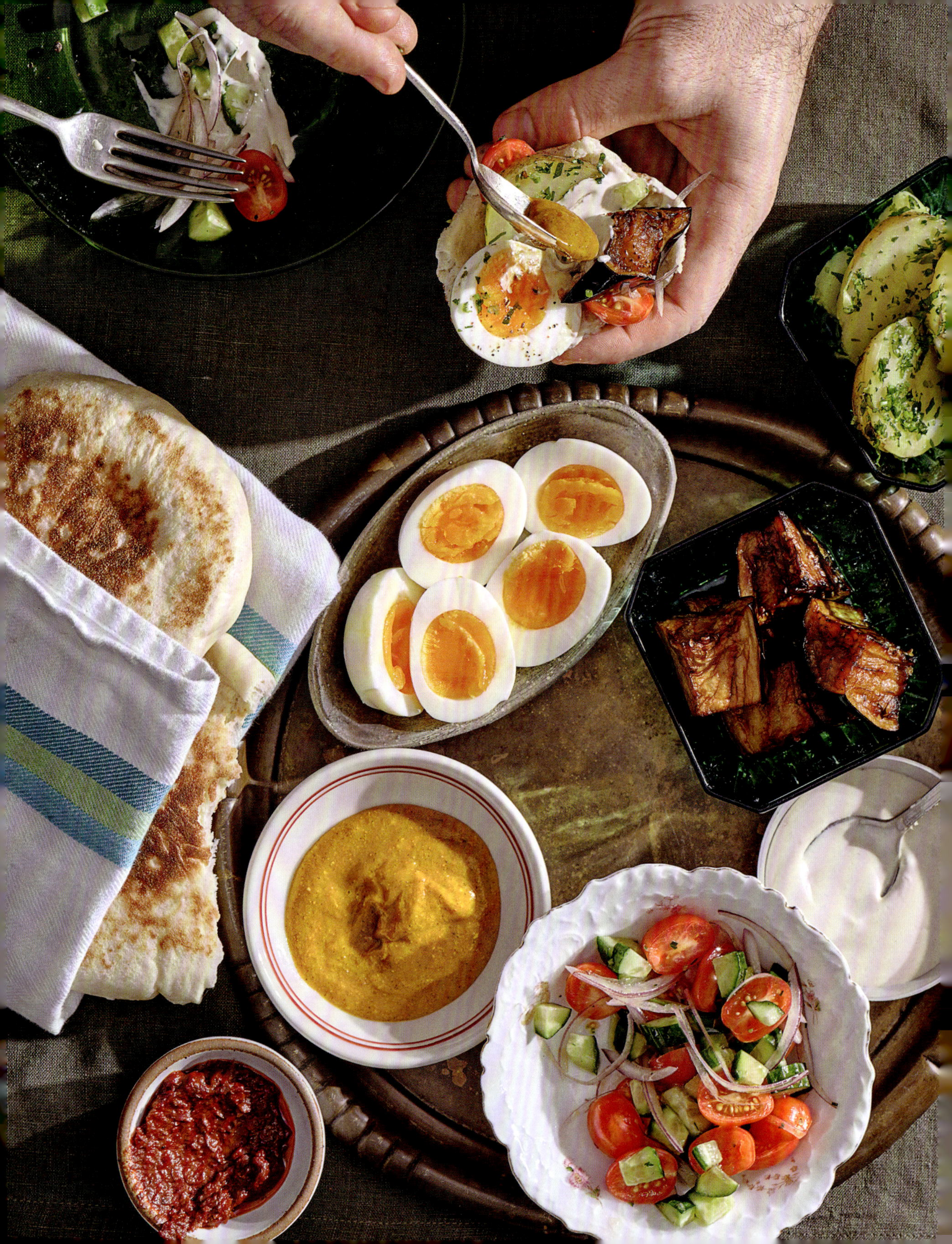

Juice of ½ lemon

2 tablespoons extra virgin olive oil, plus more for garnish

1 teaspoon gray salt

FOR THE POTATOES:

3 Dutch yellow potatoes, unpeeled and boiled in salty water until tender

¼ bunch of flat-leaf parsley, finely chopped

2 tablespoons extra virgin olive oil

1 teaspoon gray salt, for garnish

FOR SERVING:

4 large eggs, soft-boiled, peeled, and cut in half

1 small bowl Zikki's Quick Amba (page 60)

1 small bowl Harissa (page 50)

1 small bowl The Smoothest Tahini Dip (page 55)

4 Pitas (page 109)

4. Once you have achieved golden perfection, remove the eggplant from the frying oil using the slotted spoon and transfer to the prepared baking sheet to drain.

5. Repeat steps 3 and 4 until you have fried all the eggplant. Set aside.

6. Transfer the eggplant to two small plates. Plate the halved, soft-boiled eggs next to the eggplant. Drizzle with olive oil and finish with gray salt.

7. Assemble the salad: In a small bowl, combine the tomatoes, cucumbers, onion, lemon juice, olive oil, and gray salt. Serve piled high in a bowl with the eggplant and eggs.

8. Assemble the potatoes: Slice the boiled potatoes into ¼-inch rounds and add to a small bowl. Add the parsley, olive oil, and salt. Toss and transfer to a small plate.

9. Serve the deconstructed components alongside the amba, harissa, tahini, and some freshly baked pita!

ESSENTIAL TIP:

Frying the eggplant: Do not get discouraged if the first batch of eggplant isn't dark enough. It means that the oil isn't hot enough and that the eggplant is simply absorbing the oil instead of cooking in it. If this occurs, wait until the oil reaches the proper temperature before frying the next batch.

Marinated Peppers

semi-cooked

We can promise you one thing: this is not the first, nor is it the last time you will hear us rant about the superiority of charred vegetables. It is important to understand that charring vegetables is a way of life. Burning things on your gas range at home may seem insane, but it is without a doubt the BEST way to give your vegetables a totally invigorating transformation. In this instance, a regular crisp and crunchy bell pepper lets go of its form and becomes tender like a piece of meat. Once you fully char your peppers on a gas range (or over the flame on a grill), quickly transfer them into an airtight container and let them steam for at least 20 minutes. This allows the peppers to finish cooking, releasing their water weight and loosening the skin, while also cooling down enough for you to peel them and remove the seeds effortlessly. From there, you are 2 minutes away from an excellent Welcome Olives (page 39) dish. —ben & zikki

Serve it with: Tza-Zikki (page 87), Tel Avivian Focaccia (page 113)

Yield: Serves 4 to 6, makes 2 small plates

Total time: 30 minutes

Special tools: gas range or grill

---

3 red bell peppers

3 yellow bell peppers

1 garlic clove, thinly sliced

Juice of ½ lemon

1 teaspoon fine sea salt

¼ bunch of flat-leaf parsley, minced

¼ cup extra virgin olive oil, plus more for drizzling

1. Working one at a time, place a pepper on your gas range or grill on high heat and allow it to char. Using rubber tongs, turn the pepper every minute to expose a new side to the flame. Once the pepper is fully blackened, remove from the heat and place into an airtight container. Set aside for at least 20 minutes, or for up to 24 hours in the refrigerator. Repeat with the remaining peppers.

2. Once the peppers are cool enough to handle, peel off the burnt skin, seed them, and remove the stems. Slice the peppers lengthwise into quarters and add them to a medium bowl.

3. Add the sliced garlic to the pepper mixture. Combine and toss with the lemon juice, salt, parsley, and extra virgin olive oil. Allow the peppers to marinate for at least 10 minutes. Store the peppers in the refrigerator until you are ready to serve. When you are ready to serve, distribute the peppers evenly onto small plates and finish with a drizzle of olive oil.

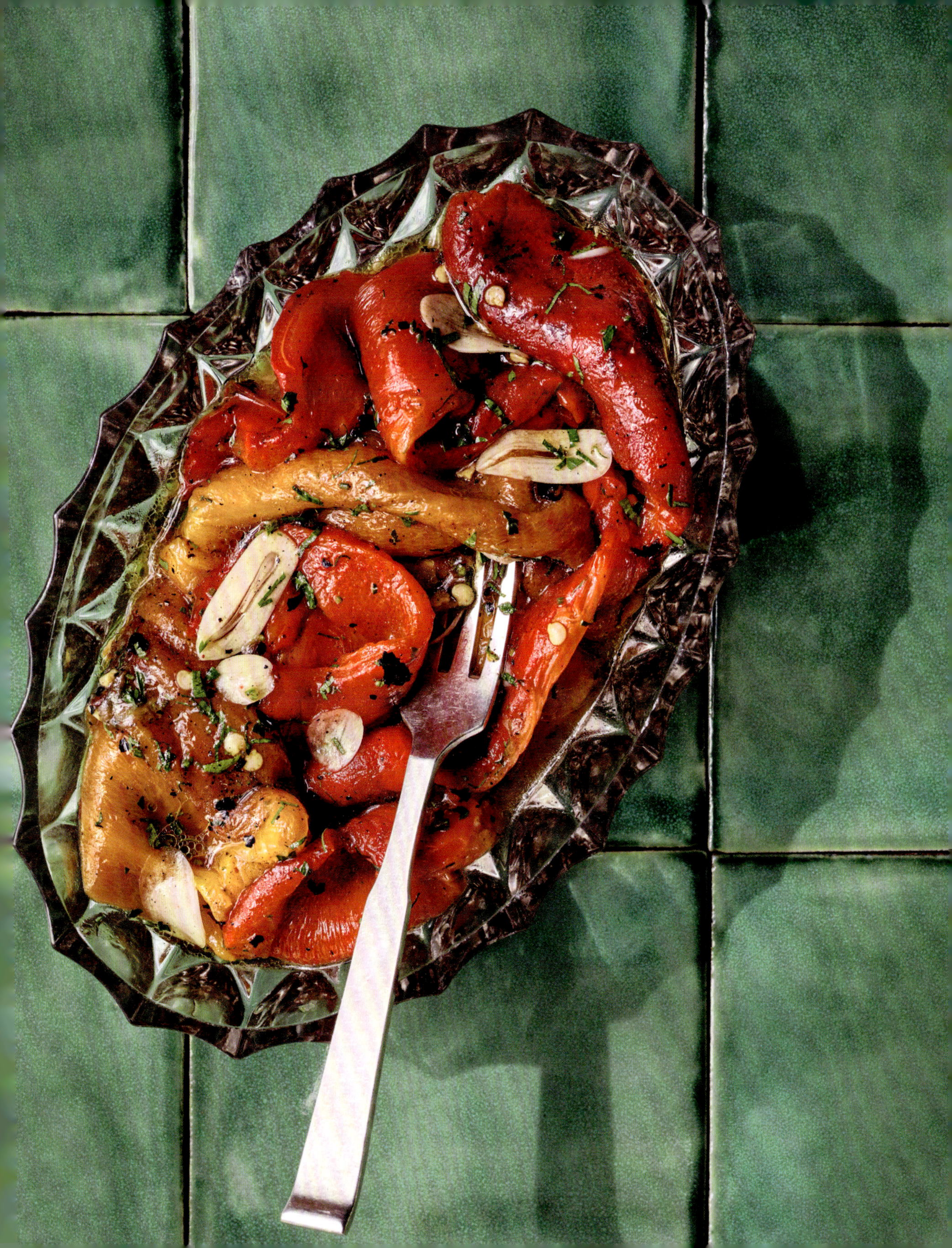

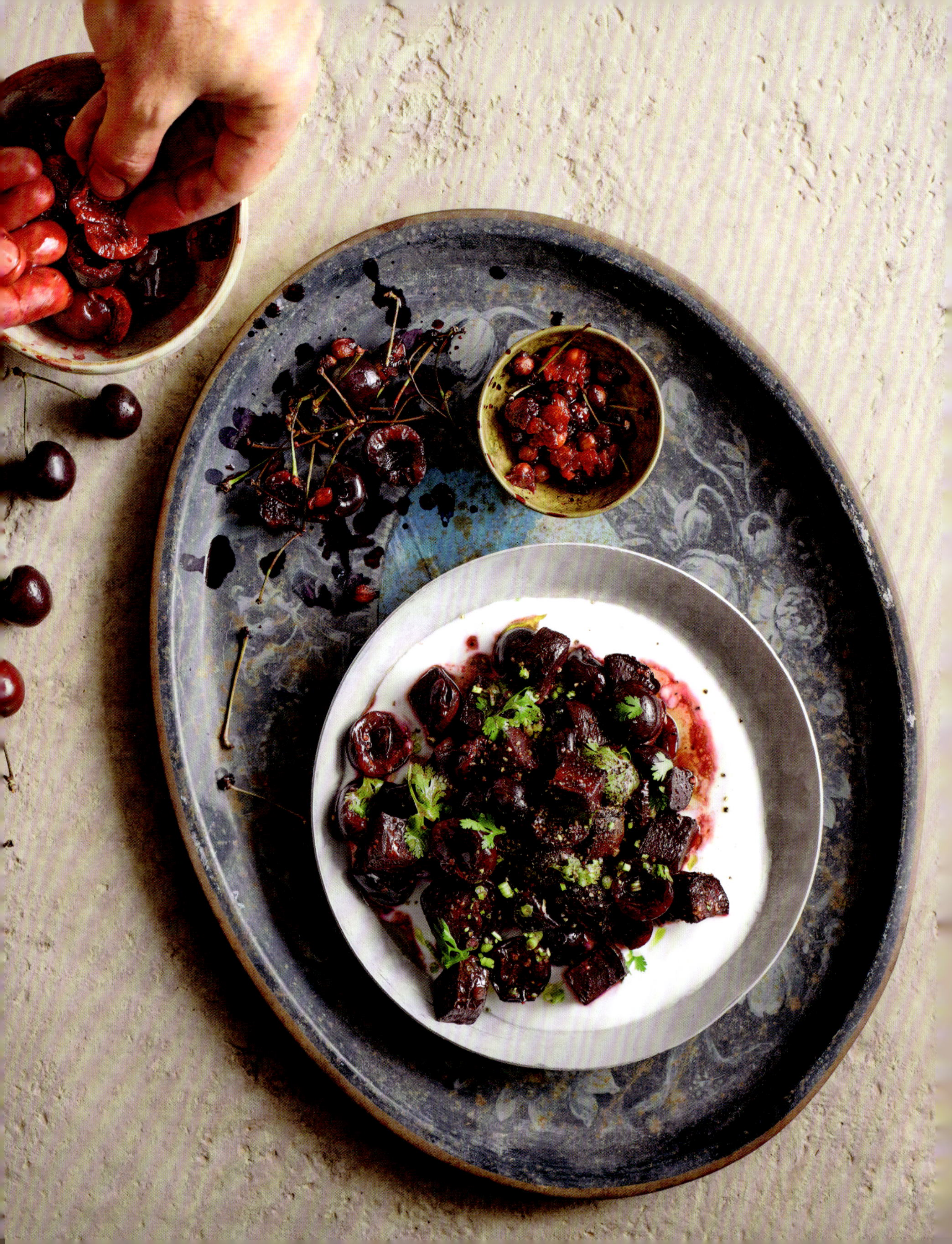

beet & cherry salad

semi-cooked

I am not a fruit guy, but this salad fully changed my mind about fruit in salads, especially cherries. When Zikki and I first met, she would make a cilantro and cherry salad every cherry season. I was always intrigued by the smell of the sweet cherries mixed with extra virgin olive oil and cilantro, but I felt that something else was missing—enter the beets! Who knew that beets and cherries were born to be a match?

The roasted beets in this salad not only elevate its flavor profile with their smoky, savory sweetness, but they add a textural element that has more bite and gives the salad more substance. Served over a bed of tangy and bright whole-fat yogurt, this hot-pink salad is a must at your next dinner party. —ben

Serve it with: Akko Crudo (page 247), Garlicky String Beans (page 203), Murtabak (page 127)

Yield: Serves 4 to 6, makes 3 small plates

Total time: 1 hour

For the Roasted Beets:

- 4 beets, cut into ¾-inch cubes
- 2 tablespoons extra virgin olive oil
- 1 teaspoon gray salt

For the Salad:

- 20 fresh, sweet cherries (such as Rainier), pitted
- Juice of ½ lemon
- 10 sprigs of cilantro, leaves and stems chopped
- ½ teaspoon gray salt
- Freshly cracked black pepper
- ¾ cup whole-fat yogurt, to serve

1. Roast the beets: Preheat the oven to 450°F (230°C). In a medium bowl, add the beets and toss with the extra virgin olive oil and salt. Spread the beets evenly on a baking sheet and roast for 35 minutes, or until crisp around the edges. Set aside to cool.

2. Assemble the salad: In a medium bowl, add the cherries, cooled beets, lemon juice, cilantro, salt, and pepper and toss to coat.

3. Spread the yogurt evenly onto three small plates using the rounded side of a wide spoon. Layer the salad on top of each and serve immediately.

Herby Marinated Eggplants

Back when we were living in a small Italian mountain town, Zikki and I often hosted friends in our tall-ceilinged, pink-kitchened home. They would come before school for a coffee, after school for a snack, and always on Friday evenings for Shabbat, or as we explained it to our non-Jewish friends, "Friday Family Dinner." One of our friends always came bearing this incredible eggplant dish, swimming in extra virgin olive oil, herbs, and garlic. Zikki was obsessed. She still claims that this was the day she fell in love with eggplant (though I would argue that it was on our first date). Anyway, from Italy to Israel to California and eventually to our home here in New York, this dish is a classic in our recipe book. It is amazing to make ahead of time—you can keep it in your refrigerator for up to a week! Frying the eggplant is not super fun and it's messy, BUT it is absolutely worth it. This is an excellent dish to make ahead of time!—BEN

Serve it with: Challah (page 117), Zikki's Peeled Tomato Salad (page 180), Jeweled Celery Salad (page 136)

Yield: Serves 4 to 6, makes 1 quart

Total time: 1 hour

Special tools: wire rack, digital kitchen thermometer

semi-cooked

For the Eggplant:

4 medium eggplants, sliced into ½-inch rounds

1 tablespoon kosher salt

Canola oil, for frying (about 1 quart)

For the Salad:

1 bunch of mint, roughly chopped

1 bunch of flat-leaf parsley, roughly chopped

½ bunch of dill, roughly chopped

1. Prep the eggplants: In a medium bowl, add the eggplant slices and toss with the kosher salt. Once coated, place them on a wire rack and allow them to sit for 15 minutes in order to release water. Then rinse the slices under cold water to wash off the excess salt. Place the rinsed eggplant rounds onto a dry kitchen towel and pat dry, pressing out all the moisture. Set aside until you are ready to fry.

2. Make the herb mixture: In a large bowl, combine the mint, parsley, dill, cilantro, garlic, and gray salt. Set aside.

3. In a medium skillet, heat 1 inch of canola oil over medium-high heat until it reaches 350° to 375°F (175° to 190°C) on a digital kitchen thermometer. Check the temperature periodically. This should take 5 to 7 minutes. Line a wire rack with an even layer of paper towels.

4. Once the oil is ready, add one layer of eggplant into the skillet without overlapping or layering. Fry for 5 minutes on each side, or until golden brown.

recipe and ingredients continue

EAT SMALL PLATES

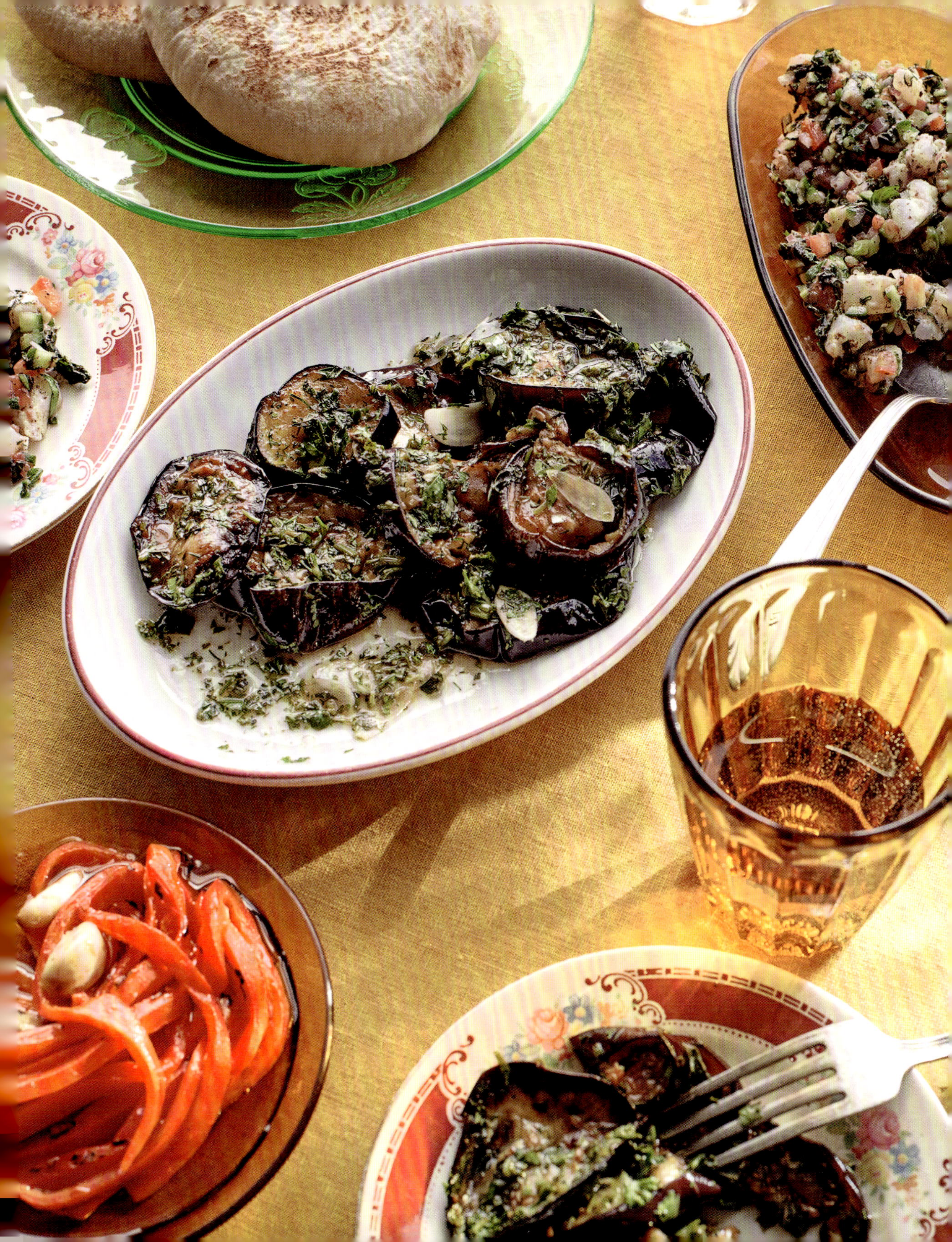

½ bunch of cilantro, roughly chopped

4 garlic cloves, thinly sliced

½ teaspoon gray salt

¼ cup red wine vinegar

½ cup extra virgin olive oil

5. Using a slotted spoon, transfer the eggplant to the prepared rack. Repeat steps 4 and 5 until all the eggplant slices have been fried.

6. Assemble the salad: While the eggplant slices are still hot but not burning, add the eggplant to the herb mixture and toss gently using your hands. Add the vinegar and olive oil, tossing gently again.

7. Serve immediately or store in an airtight container for a minimum of 2 hours (in order for the eggplants to marinate), or for up to 1 week in the refrigerator.

Chicken Shawarma Salad
Ben's "American Salad"

crispy, crunchy, or crushed

When Ben and I first met, I used to make salads from everything we had left over in the refrigerator, or so it seemed to him. Ben called these creations the "American Salad," and would poke fun at how many random things we could put in a bowl and combine to make a "salad." We've come a LONG way since those days. So much so that this here is Ben's very own "American Salad." Born from leftovers, this salad blew us away when Ben first made it one busy fall afternoon. It has since become a household staple we love to serve friends and family! It is colorful, crunchy, and fresh yet totally satisfying and comforting from the use of warm Middle Eastern spices. —*zikki*

Serve it with: Zikki's Quick Amba (page 60), Jerusalem Bagel (page 120)

Yield: Serves 4, makes 4 small plates

Total time: 30 minutes

For the Chicken Shawarma:

- 4 boneless, skinless chicken thighs
- 6 tablespoons olive oil
- ¼ cup shawarma spice mix (such as New York Shuk)
- 1 tablespoon gray salt

For the Dressing:

- 2 teaspoons balsamic vinegar
- 2 tablespoons sherry vinegar
- 1 teaspoon Dijon mustard

1. Prep the chicken: In a medium bowl, add the chicken thighs, 3 tablespoons of the olive oil, the shawarma spice mix, and salt. Toss to coat the chicken in the seasoning and then let it sit for at least 15 minutes or cover and refrigerate overnight.

2. When you are ready to cook the chicken, heat a medium skillet over medium heat and add the remaining 3 tablespoons olive oil. Once the oil is hot, add the chicken thighs to the skillet in a single layer. Let them sear undisturbed for 6 to 7 minutes on the first side, or until they develop a substantial golden-brown spice crust. Flip the chicken thighs and reduce the heat to medium. Continue cooking for an additional 6 minutes on the second side.

3. Once fully cooked, remove the chicken from the heat and allow it to cool completely. Using a sharp chef's knife, thinly slice the chicken thighs and set aside.

4. Make the dressing: In a small bowl, whisk together the balsamic vinegar, sherry vinegar, mustard, olive oil, and salt.

recipe and ingredients continue

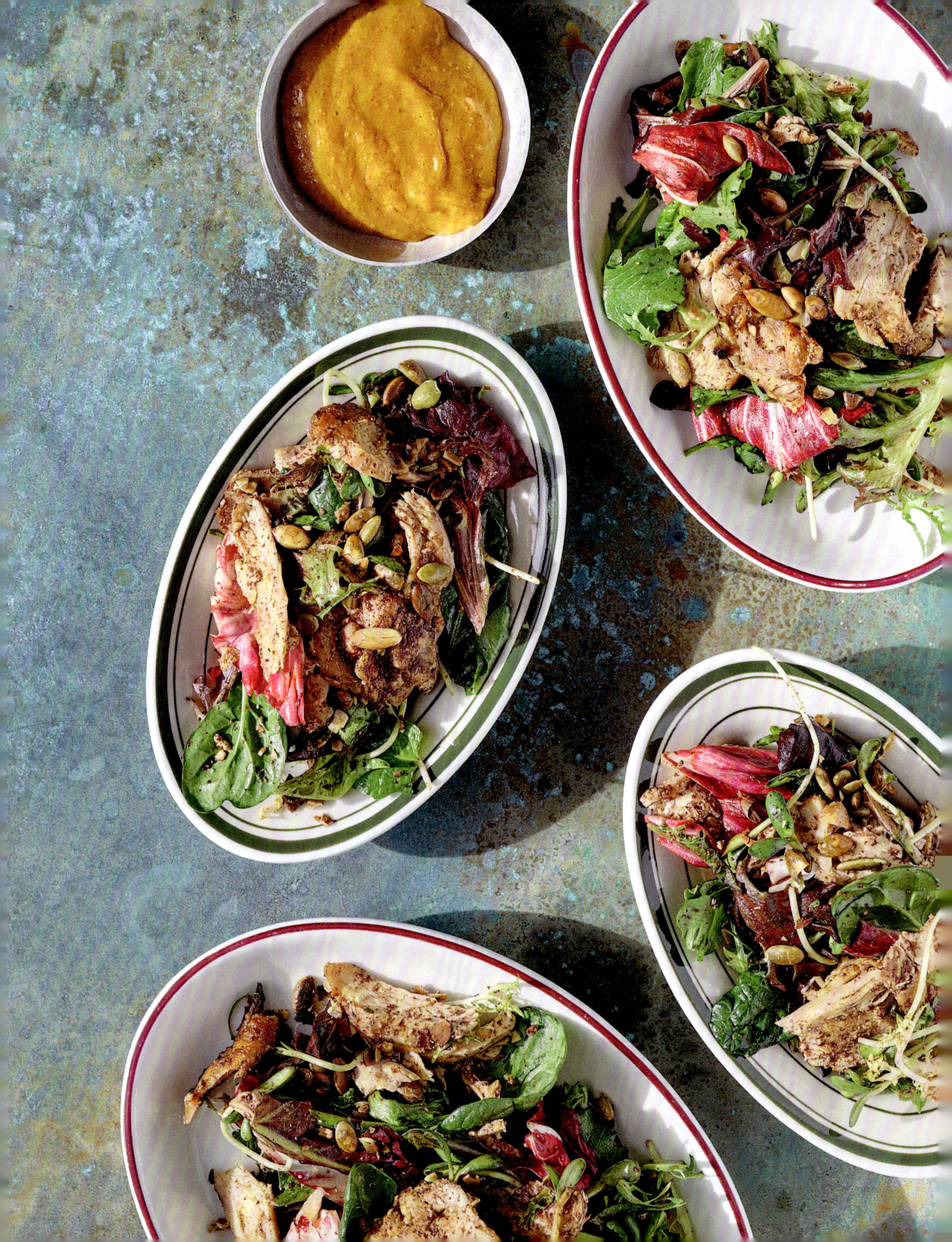

¼ cup extra virgin olive oil

½ teaspoon gray salt

For the Salad:

1 (10-ounce) bag mixed greens

½ small radicchio, thinly sliced

¼ cup raw pumpkin seeds

½ teaspoon sumac

Handful of sunflower sprouts

Zikki's Quick Amba (page 60), for serving

5. Assemble the salad: In a large bowl, add the mixed greens, radicchio, pumpkin seeds, sumac, sunflower sprouts, and the cooled chicken shawarma. Pour in the dressing and toss well using your hands.

6. Serve the salad immediately alongside a small bowl of amba.

breakfast salad

crispy, crunchy, or crushed

Let's get something straight. WE LOVE THIS SALAD! It is our go-to breakfast on any day, combining four of our all-time favorite ingredients: eggs, Persian cucumbers, Campari tomatoes, and extra virgin olive oil. There is a magic that happens when the yolk from the hard-boiled egg mixes with the tangy juices of the tomato, the coarse gray salt, and the aromatics of a really good extra virgin olive oil. Topped with freshly toasted homemade dukkah, this morning life-booster checks all our boxes: crunchy, fresh, tangy, salty, and absolutely delicious. Morning, noon, or night, it's always time for the Breakfast Salad. —BEN

Serve it with: Labneh Spread (page 84), Pita (page 109), small can of tinned fish (smoked trout or sardines)

Yield: Serves 2, makes 2 small plates

Total time: 20 minutes, plus 25 minutes for the dukkah (optional)

Special tools: food processor (for the dukkah)

---

3 large eggs, hard boiled, peeled, and roughly chopped

3 Persian cucumbers, cut into diamonds

6 Campari tomatoes, quartered

2 tablespoons extra virgin olive oil

½ teaspoon gray salt

Freshly cracked black pepper

Dukkah (recipe follows; optional)

---

1. In a medium bowl, add the eggs, cucumbers, and tomatoes. Then add the olive oil, salt, and pepper.

2. Using your hands, toss the salad. Be careful not to overtoss it as the eggs should maintain some structure and shouldn't be broken down completely.

3. Plate the salad and generously sprinkle it with dukkah, if using, for an extra crunch and spicy kick.

dukkah

½ cup raw shelled pistachios

1 cup sesame seeds

¼ cup cumin seeds

¼ cup coriander seeds

In a medium pan over medium heat, add the pistachios. Toast for 3 to 4 minutes, constantly moving the pan to toss the nuts and keep them from burning. Transfer the pistachios to a food processor.

recipe continues

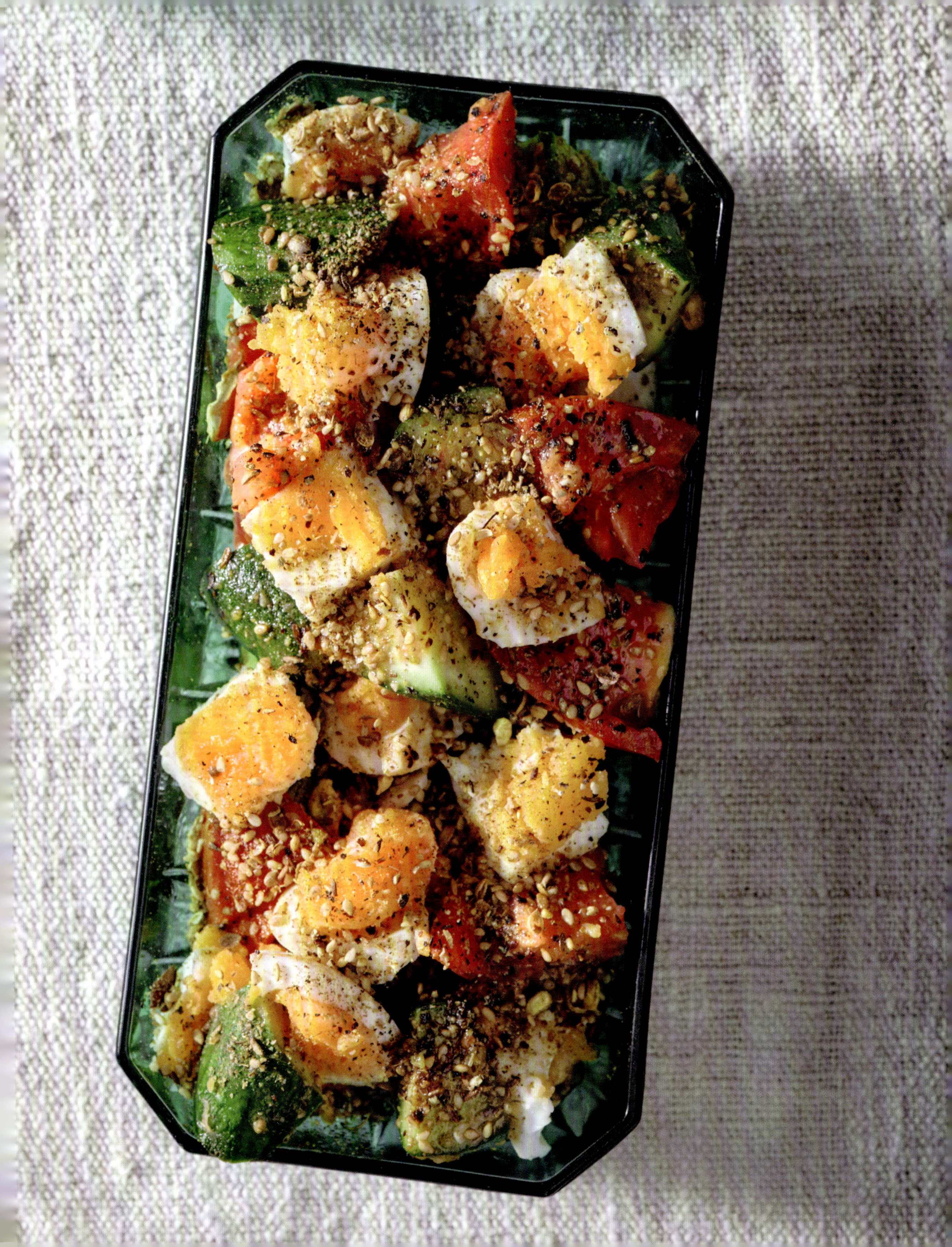

Using the same pan, toast the sesame seeds for 5 minutes, or until golden brown, again constantly moving the pan to toss. Remove the sesame seeds from the heat and add half to the food processor and the other half to a small bowl. Add the cumin and coriander seeds to the pan and toast for 2 minutes, or until fragrant. Transfer the spices to the food processor with the nuts. Pulse until a coarse, rough-textured powder is achieved, then transfer to the bowl of reserved whole sesame seeds. Toss and let cool. Use immediately on the breakfast salad or store in a tightly sealed jar for up to 2 months in a cool, dry place for use on any future salad.

Essential Tip:

Temperature of eggs: When making this recipe it is okay to use warm boiled eggs OR you can use precooked boiled eggs at fridge temp. Just make sure they are not super hot! A quick way to cool them down is to run them under cold water before peeling.

fennel, citrus & pistachio salad

crispy, crunchy, or crushed

It's funny, when you first lay eyes on this Sicilian-inspired salad, it looks like the most beautiful summer salad you've ever seen, given its bright coloring. But it is actually the best WINTER salad. When we were living in the little Italian mountain town of Bra, fennel was the most reliable winter vegetable we could get our hands on, and when paired with citrus, it tasted like a sunny day. The local co-op would receive bulk shipments of Sicilian citrus throughout the winter, so we'd often find ourselves in our quaint pink kitchen with loads of citrus and fennel. In addition to the killer orange upside-down cake that was born from this era in our life, this salad became a staple in our family, especially for the Shabbat dinners that we have hosted over the years. —BEN

Serve it with: NY Strip Steak (page 273), Zikki's Salty Baby Potatoes (page 204)

Yield: Serves 4 to 6, makes 6 small plates or 1 large plate

Total time: 20 minutes

Special tools: parchment paper

For the Dressing:

Juice of ½ lemon

½ teaspoon gray salt

1 teaspoon apricot jam or honey

2 tablespoons extra virgin olive oil

For the Salad:

¼ cup raw shelled pistachios, toasted (see page 22)

1 head of fennel, thinly sliced, fronds reserved (finely chopped)

1 navel orange, peeled (see note) and thinly sliced into rounds

1 blood orange, peeled (see note) and thinly sliced into rounds

1. **Make the dressing:** In a small bowl, whisk together the lemon juice, salt, apricot jam, and olive oil.

2. **Assemble the salad:** In a medium bowl, add the pistachios and fennel and pour in the dressing. Toss until the fennel is nicely coated in dressing and nuts.

recipe continues

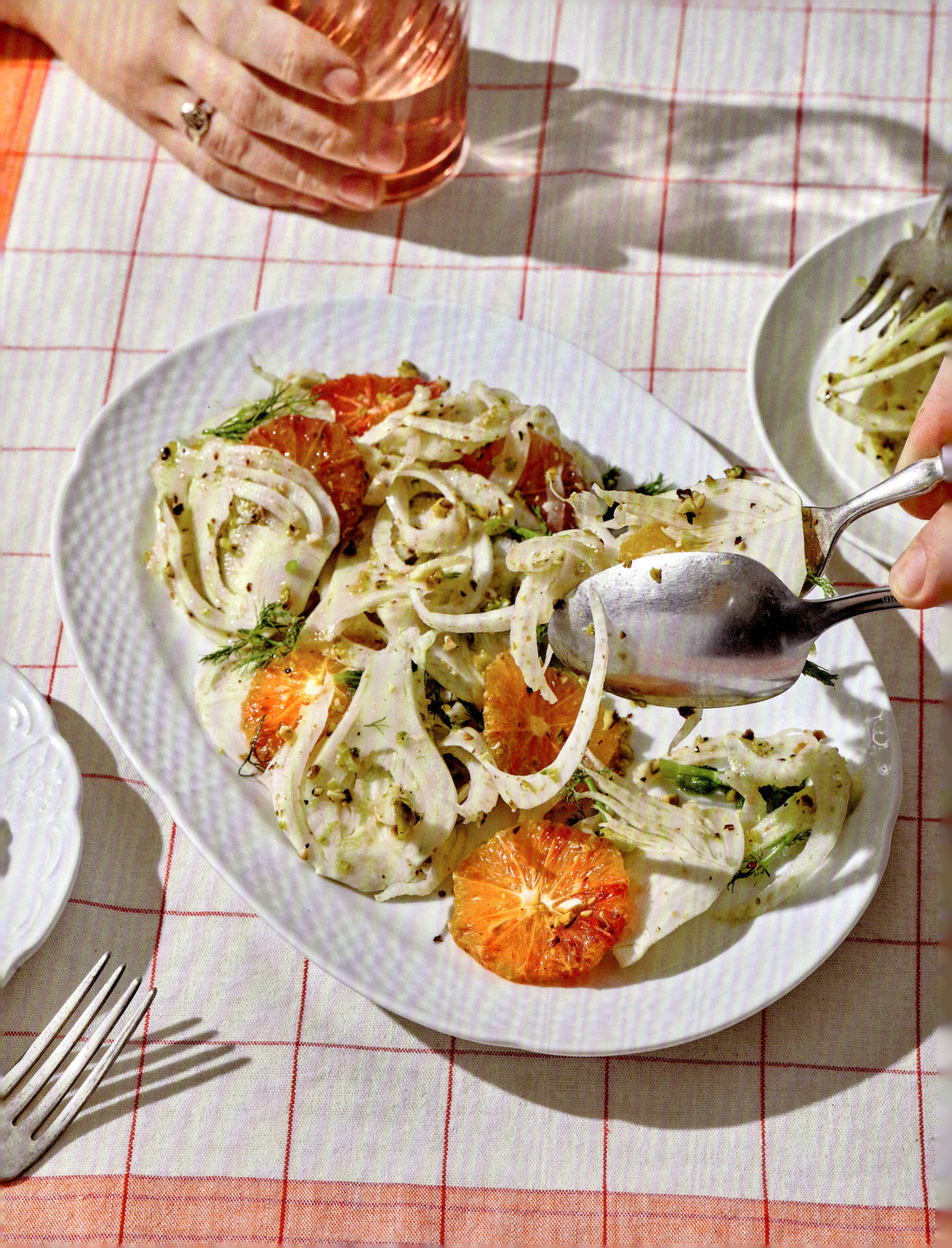

3. To the bowl of dressed fennel, add three-quarters of the citrus and fennel fronds. Lightly toss until combined and plate. Garnish with additional citrus and fronds and serve immediately.

ESSENTIAL TIP:

How to peel citrus: To neatly peel citrus for a salad like this, you need to separate both the peel and the pith from the citrus. Start by first slicing off the top and bottom of the fruit. Then, using your knife, slice the peel and pith from the citrus until all the segments are neatly exposed. From there you can either slice into rounds like seen in the salad image or carefully segment the citrus as you would for the Scallop Carpaccio (page 252).

NOT YOUR TYPICAL "CRISP VEG"

I would argue that everyone has had that dry and bland "crisp" veggie platter at one gathering or another. Am I wrong? I created this concept when a client requested a vegetable platter for an event because most of her guests didn't eat gluten. I wanted to make something a cut above the usual boring veggie plate.

For me, the perfect "crisp veggie" plate has beets, radishes, carrots, celery, and cucumbers. The key is to prepare each vegetable correctly so that it reaches its peak crunchiness. Root veggies require an ice bath before their grand performance. Then, you add the sliced cucumbers to the mix and toss everything in lemon juice and gray salt. We serve the vegetables together like a big salad, but you can also serve each one separately like a traditional veggie plate! That is totally up to you.—*zikki*

Serve it with: A Cashew Basil Dip Everyone Will Talk About (page 99), Beet & Goat Cheese Dip (page 88), Black Baba (page 94)

Yield: Serves 4 to 6, makes 3 small plates

Total time: 25 minutes

Special tools: mandoline

crispy, crunchy, or crushed

---

1 watermelon radish, thinly sliced with a mandoline

2 green radishes, thinly sliced with a mandoline or quartered

2 purple radishes, quartered lengthwise

1 candy cane beet, thinly sliced with a mandoline

1 yellow beet, thinly sliced with a mandoline

3 heirloom carrots, peeled and halved

2 celery ribs, sliced diagonally into ½-inch pieces (optional)

2 Persian cucumbers, sliced on a diagonal

Juice of 1 lemon

1 teaspoon gray salt

---

1. Prepare an ice bath in a large bowl that is one part water to three parts ice. Add all the radishes, the beets, carrots, and celery (if using) to the ice bath and let soak for at least 20 minutes.

2. When you are ready to serve, drain the vegetables and transfer to a medium bowl. Add the cucumbers.

3. Season the veggie mixture with the lemon juice and salt, toss, and serve immediately.

ESSENTIAL TIP:

What to look for when finding green radishes: Green radishes have a mild, crisp flavor, slightly less peppery than the more familiar red varieties. They're often available at farmers' markets or specialty grocery stores. When selecting green radishes, look for ones with smooth, firm skin and vibrant green tops, which indicate freshness. If you're unable to find green radishes, you can substitute them with daikon radishes for a similar mild taste and crunchy texture.

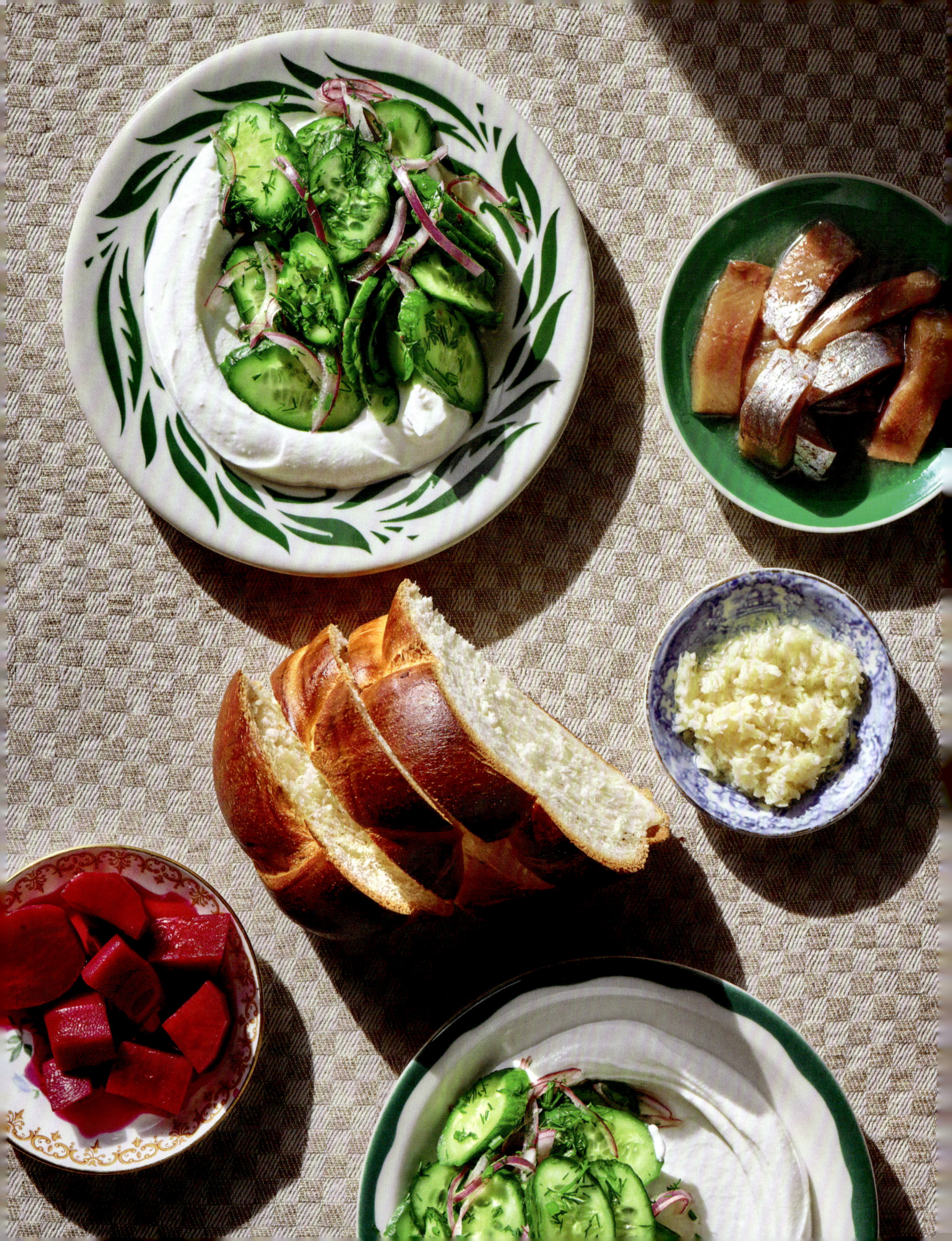

cucumber, dill, labneh & onion salad

crispy, crunchy, or crushed

Dill and cucumbers are staples in Ukrainian households. Now introduce a cute Israeli husband into the mix, and all of a sudden you have a gorgeous collision of culinary worlds. A cucumber, dill, and red onion salad tossed in sunflower seed oil, served over tangy, salty labneh is where the Middle East meets Eastern Europe. Pair it with pickled herring, fermented beets, and turnips and a few slices of fresh challah for a conversation-starting dish on food mobility. —*zikki*

Serve it with: Challah (page 117), Hot-Pink Turnips & Beets (page 238), grated horseradish, pickled herring

Yield: Serves 3 to 6, makes 3 small plates

Total time: 30 minutes

For the Quick-Pickled Cucumbers:

6 Persian cucumbers, thinly sliced on a diagonal

½ teaspoon kosher salt

For the Salad:

½ medium red onion, very thinly sliced

Juice of ½ lemon

2 tablespoons finely chopped dill

1½ tablespoons toasted sunflower oil, plus more for drizzling

Gray salt

For Serving:

¾ cup Labneh Spread (page 84)

1. Quick-pickle the cucumbers: In a medium bowl, toss the cucumbers with the kosher salt. Set aside for approximately 10 minutes, or until the cucumbers have released their water weight (you will know they are ready when they've lost their snap). Then rinse the slices under cold water to wash off the excess salt. Pat them dry with a paper towel and place them back into the bowl.

2. To the bowl with the cucumbers, add the onion, lemon juice, dill, and sunflower oil. Toss until combined.

3. Spread ¼ cup of labneh evenly onto each plate. Top each plate with the salad mixture and finish with gray salt and a drizzle of sunflower oil. Serve immediately.

PEAR, MUSTARD GREEN, MINT & CHALLAH CROUTON SALAD

crispy, crunchy, or crushed

This salad is what we refer to as a salad made of only the "good stuff." It includes ingredients that taste decadent: sweet, taffy-like Medjool dates; crisp, elegant pears; and buttery challah croutons, all tossed in a light sweet-and-sour dressing, and most importantly, it is served alongside a fat piece of blue cheese. The variety of flavors and textures of this dish are part of the magic, giving you the sense of eating a lavish charcuterie board but in salad form. —zikki

Serve it with: red wine, NY Strip Steak (page 273), The Best Green Salad of Your Life (page 184)

Yield: Serves 4, makes 2 small plates

Total time: 20 minutes

Special tools: parchment paper

FOR THE SALAD:

2 cups ½-inch cubes Challah (page 117)

2 Bosc pears, thinly sliced

8 Medjool dates, sliced into ¼-inch rounds

24 mint leaves

½ bunch of mustard greens

FOR THE DRESSING:

Juice of ½ lemon

2 tablespoons extra virgin olive oil

1 teaspoon apricot jam

½ teaspoon gray salt

FOR SERVING:

Blue cheese (Stilton)

1. Preheat the oven to 400°F (205°C). Line a baking sheet with parchment paper.

2. Add the challah cubes to the prepared baking sheet and bake for 10 minutes, or until golden brown. Remove from the oven and set aside.

3. Make the dressing: In a small bowl, whisk together the lemon juice, olive oil, apricot jam, and salt. Set aside.

4. In a medium bowl, add the challah croutons, pears, dates, mint leaves, and mustard greens.

5. Pour in the dressing and toss lightly until the salad is evenly coated. Divide immediately between two small plates and serve alongside a nice chunk of blue cheese.

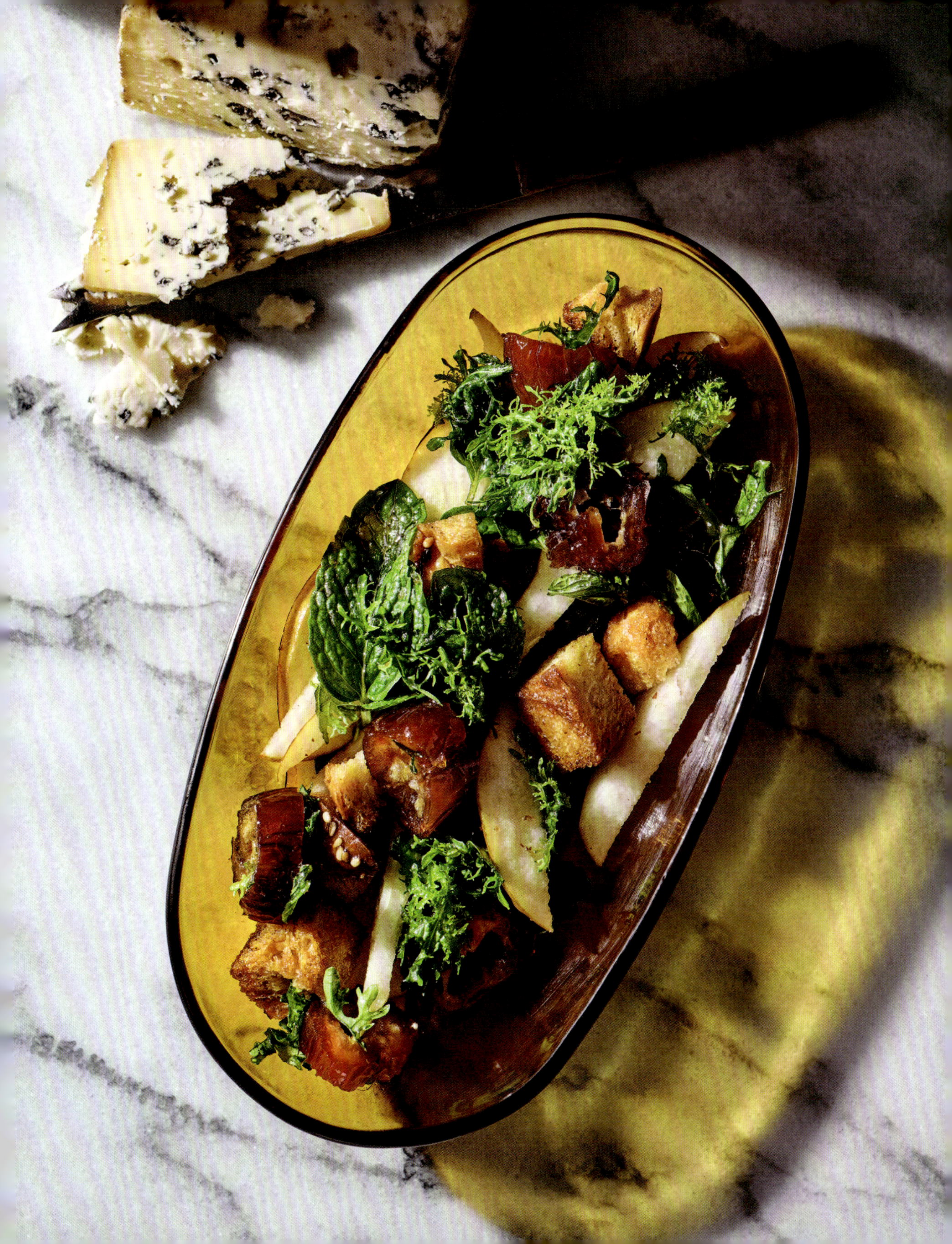

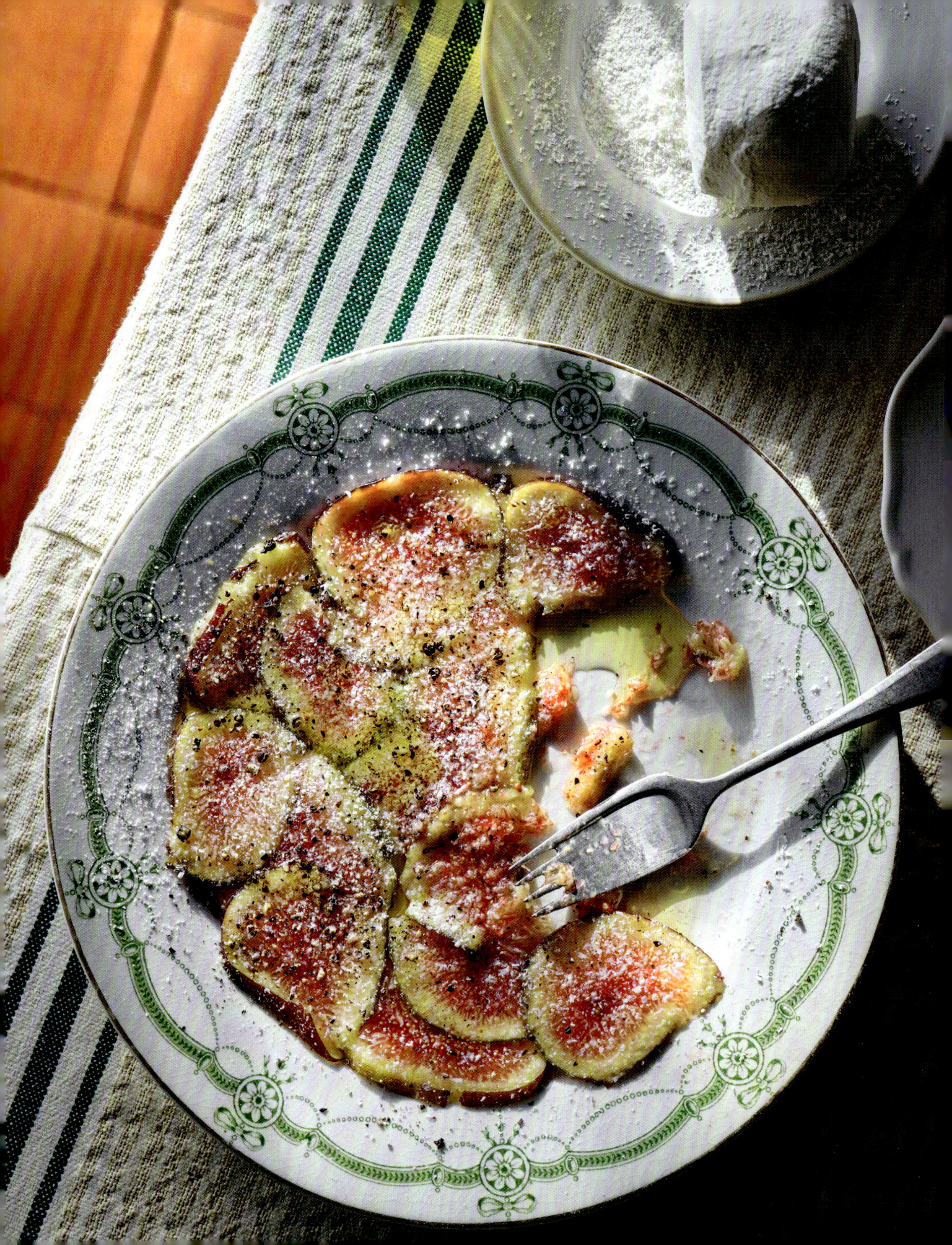

fig carpaccio

crispy, crunchy, or crushed

This is one of the dishes I made for Zikki when we first started dating. I still remember her initial reaction. She couldn't believe the crazy synergy between the delightful candy-like figs, bitter and aromatic extra virgin olive oil, and the tangy grated yogurt stone. It was salty and sweet, super light, and felt like the ultimate treat. Let's be honest. It is. It is unlikely that you will find twelve perfect figs for this recipe, but even if you find only five good ones, slice them up and make this carpaccio. Trust me, it's worth it. —BEN

Serve it with: Akko Crudo (page 247), Middle Eastern Caesar (page 187), Not Your Grandma's Fruit Salad (page 170)

Yield: Serves 2, makes 1 small plate

Total time: 20 minutes

Special tools: plastic wrap or parchment paper, Microplane

---

12 ripe figs, sliced into ¼-inch rounds

1 Yogurt Stone (page 85), for grating

½ teaspoon gray salt

Freshly ground black pepper

2 tablespoons extra virgin olive oil

---

1. Arrange the fig rounds evenly on the plate with about ¼ inch of space between each slice. Cover the plate with plastic wrap or parchment paper and gently press on the figs using your palm until they begin to bleed into one another, forming one cohesive base for your carpaccio. Remove the plastic wrap.

2. Using a Microplane, grate a generous amount of yogurt stone over the carpaccio so that all areas of the plate are covered. Season with the salt and pepper to taste and finish by drizzling the olive oil over the figs. Serve immediately and enjoy.

ESSENTIAL TIP:

Use the best-quality ingredients: This dish has very few ingredients, so it is imperative to the overall taste that you use the highest-quality produce. Make sure that the figs are tender and juicy when you cut them open. If they are instead dry and stiff, toss them aside. Unfortunately, they didn't ripen well and you shouldn't use them!

NOT YOUR GRANDMA'S fruit salad

crispy, crunchy, or crushed

This salad is all-caps SPECIAL. To me, this salad is Israel. To be clear, nothing specifically about it screams Israel, other than the fact that I made it many, many times at Ben's parents' house using the luscious fruit, herbs, and nuts available from the bountiful "shuk" or market. For our family, this salad is a staple, loaded with melons, stone fruit, herbs, and freshly toasted hazelnuts. When I think about the memories attached to this salad, they are encircled with pure love. I can almost taste the most abundant and juicy fruit of the season with a little lemon juice, extra virgin olive oil, apricot jam, and sea salt. I can see us all enjoying it together in the garden outside Ben's parents' house, chatting and simply relishing one another's company. —*zikki*

Serve it with: Tuna & Grapes (page 245), Fig & Young Cheese (page 303), Zikki's Eggplant (page 224), The Best Green Salad of Your Life (page 184)

Yield: Serves 6, makes 4 small plates

Total time: 20 minutes

Special tools: parchment paper

For the Dressing:

Juice of 1 lemon

1½ tablespoons apricot jam

3 tablespoons extra virgin olive oil

1 teaspoon gray salt

For the Salad:

¼ cantaloupe, sliced into ¼-inch pieces

¼ honeydew, sliced into ¼-inch pieces

1 nectarine, halved and thinly sliced

1 yellow plum, quartered and roughly chopped

Handful of flat-leaf parsley, stemmed

Handful of mint, stemmed

10 sprigs of cilantro, leaves finely chopped

½ cup raw hazelnuts, toasted and roughly chopped (see page 22)

Gray salt

1. Make the dressing: In a small bowl, whisk together the lemon juice, apricot jam, olive oil, and salt.

recipe continues

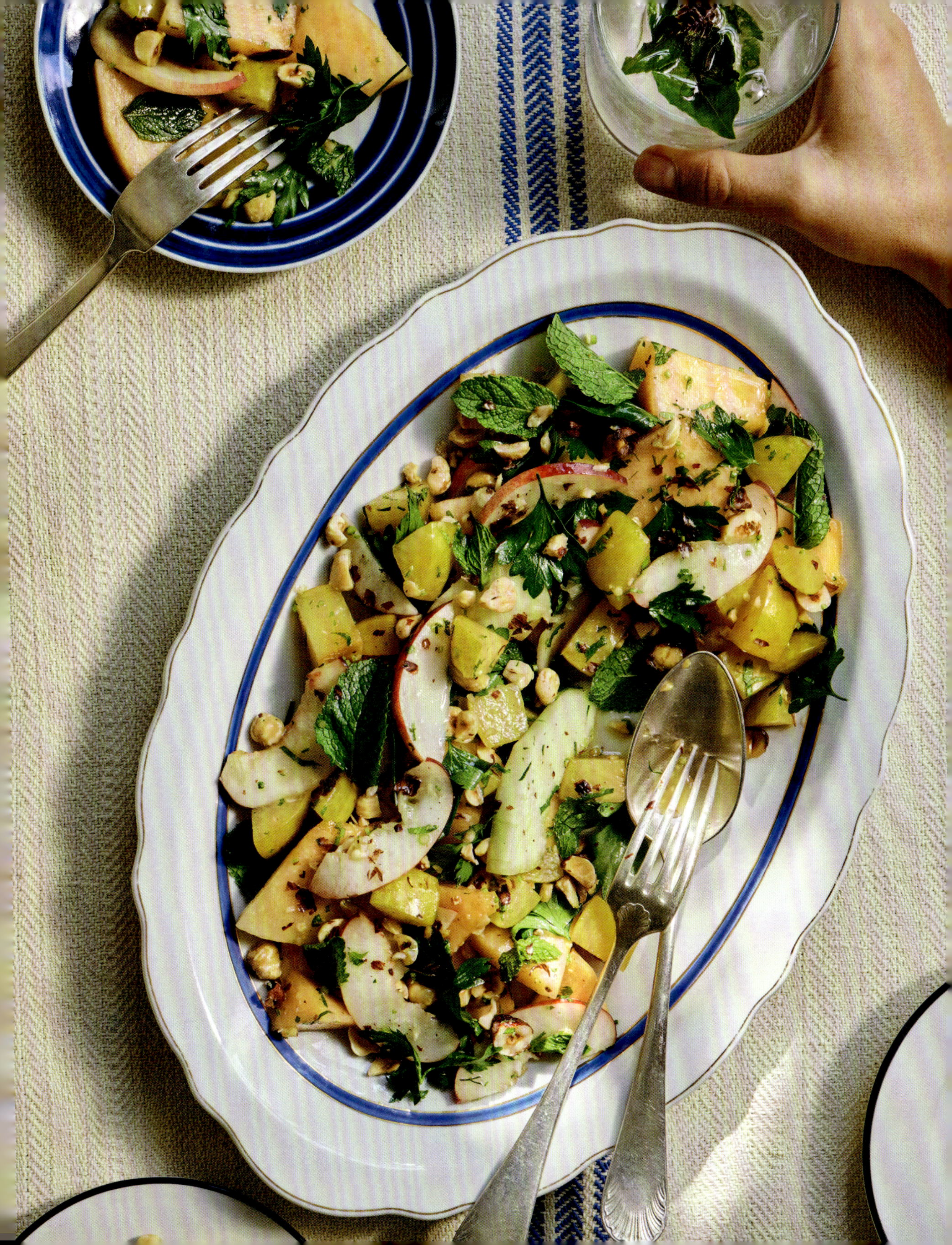

2. Assemble the salad: In a medium bowl, add the cantaloupe, honeydew, nectarine, plum, parsley, mint, and cilantro.

3. Set aside 2 tablespoons of the crushed hazelnuts and add the rest to the fruit mixture. Pour in the dressing and toss with your hands until combined. Adjust the salt to taste (it should be perfectly balanced between sweet and salty).

4. Plate the salad and garnish with the reserved hazelnuts. Serve immediately.

ESSENTIAL TIP:

Use seasonal fruit if you can: Keep in mind that this salad is meant to highlight the season's best fruit. So, if you find yourself with only honeydew or peaches, that is also OKAY. Feel free to riff on the base recipe using what you have available.

fattoush salad

tomato based

There are few things I love more in this life than the combination of ingredients in this salad. Not only are they always readily available in my refrigerator, but each ingredient is excellent on its own or exceptionally delicious combined all together. It's easy to forget how delicious this salad is as the ingredients seem almost TOO perfectly matched. The familiarity of the flavors might make the dish seem simple, but that simplicity is exactly what makes it so special. Plus, there's truly no better way to use leftover pita! —ben

Serve it with: Falafel (page 215), Vetrena Fries (page 227), Kubenia (page 261), My Uncle Tal's Lentil Masabacha (page 79)

Yield: Serves 4 to 6, makes 4 small bowls

Total time: 35 minutes

Special tools: parchment paper, basting or pastry brush

For the Za'atar Pita Chips:

2 leftover Pitas (page 109)

2 tablespoons olive oil

1 tablespoon za'atar

For the Salad:

1 large heirloom tomato, roughly chopped

6 cherry tomatoes, roughly chopped

2 cucumbers, roughly chopped

4 small radishes, quartered

½ small red onion, thinly sliced

2 scallions, thinly sliced

1 long green hot chili, thinly sliced

½ bunch of mint, stemmed

¼ cup flat-leaf parsley leaves

2 sprigs of oregano, stemmed

Juice of 1 lemon

1 teaspoon gray salt

Freshly cracked black pepper

2 tablespoons sumac

¼ cup extra virgin olive oil

For serving:

1 (7-ounce) piece feta, cut into ½-inch cubes or roughly crumbled

Extra virgin olive oil, for drizzling

Gray salt

1. Preheat the oven to 360°F (180°C). Line a baking sheet with parchment paper.

recipe continues

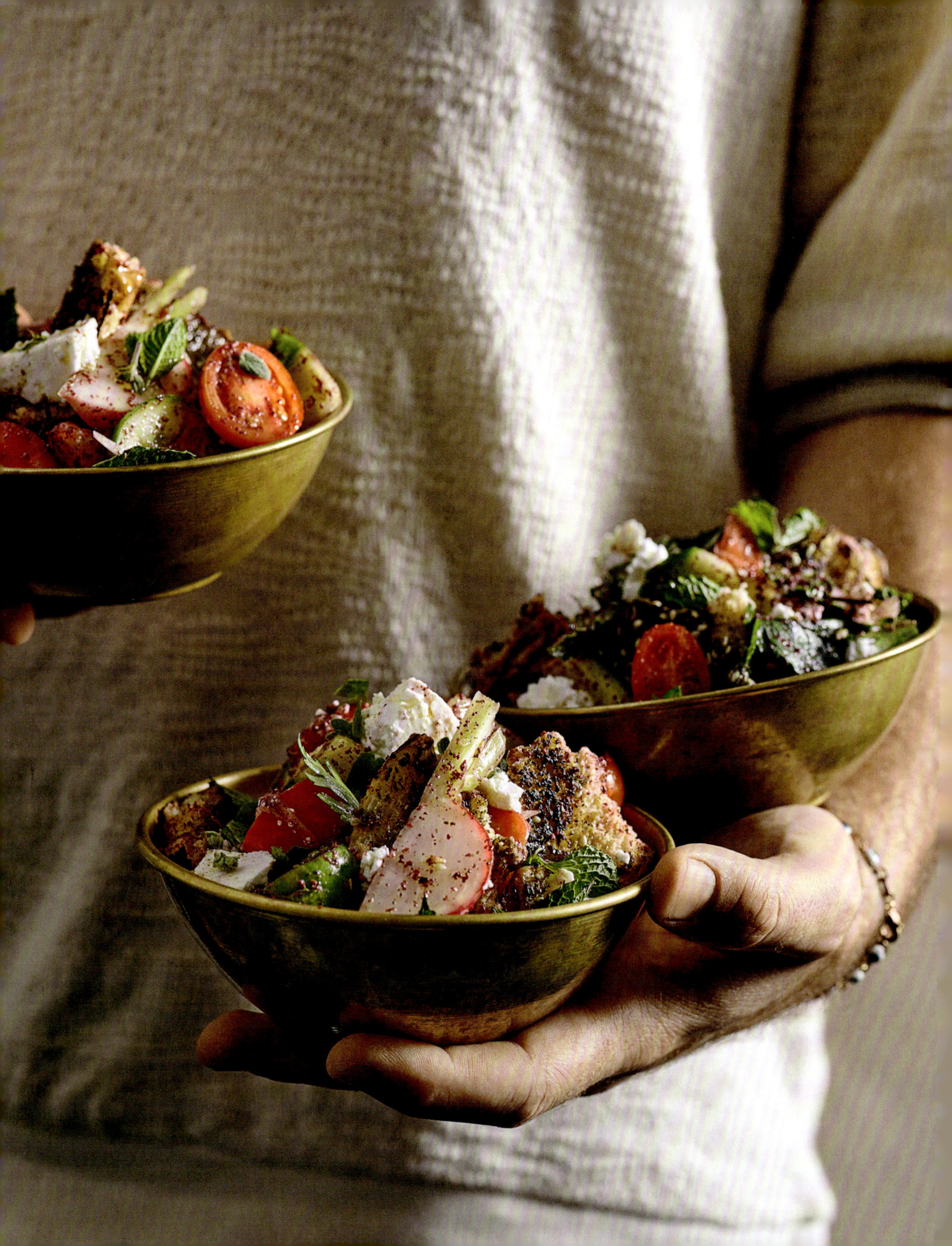

2. Make the pita chips: Split the pitas in half along the seam into two whole circles. Place the opened pitas on the prepared baking sheet and brush with the olive oil and sprinkle with the za'atar. Toast for about 8 minutes, or until golden brown. Remove from the oven and let cool. Once cooled, break them into bite-size pieces and set aside.

3. Assemble the salad: In a large bowl, add the tomatoes, cucumbers, radishes, onion, scallion, chili, mint, parsley, and oregano. Toss and season with the lemon juice, salt, pepper, sumac, and olive oil.

4. Before serving, add the pita chips and lightly toss to combine. Distribute the salad mixture evenly among small bowls. Top with the feta, a light drizzle of olive oil, and a sprinkle of salt. Serve immediately.

Peach & Tomato Salad with Mozzarella & Basil

tomato based

This gorgeous summer salad highlights the season's juicy vine-ripened tomatoes and succulent, tender peaches, but I would argue that the most important part of this salad is the copious amount of basil and freshly cracked black pepper. Here, basil is the main character, with its flowers adding an extra layer of herbaceous aroma. Quick to prepare for any party, it's a crowd-pleaser—especially the leftover juice. After the peaches, tomatoes, olive oil, salt, basil, and mozzarella meld together, they leave behind a pool of salty, sweet, tangy, and rich goodness, perfect for mopping up with fresh bread! —ben & zikki

Serve it with: Beef Tartare (page 259), Fried Barbouniot (page 269), Challah (page 117)

Yield: Serves 4 to 6, makes 1 large plate

Total time: 20 minutes

- 3 peaches, halved and sliced into thick half moons
- 1 large red or orange heirloom tomato, roughly chopped into ½-inch chunks
- 3 small yellow heirloom tomatoes, halved
- 10 cherry tomatoes, halved
- 1 bunch of basil (about 30 leaves), stemmed with flowers
- 2 tablespoons extra virgin olive oil
- 1 teaspoon gray salt, plus more for finishing
- 1 teaspoon freshly cracked black pepper, plus more for finishing
- 1 (8-ounce) ball of mozzarella, torn into bite-size pieces

1. In a medium bowl, add the peaches and tomatoes. Set a handful of the basil leaves and flowers aside for garnish and combine the rest of the basil leaves, including their flowers, with the tomato-peach mixture.

2. To the tomato-peach mixture, add the olive oil, salt, and pepper and toss until combined.

3. Plate the salad and garnish with the mozzarella, reserved basil leaves and flowers, and salt and pepper to taste. Serve immediately.

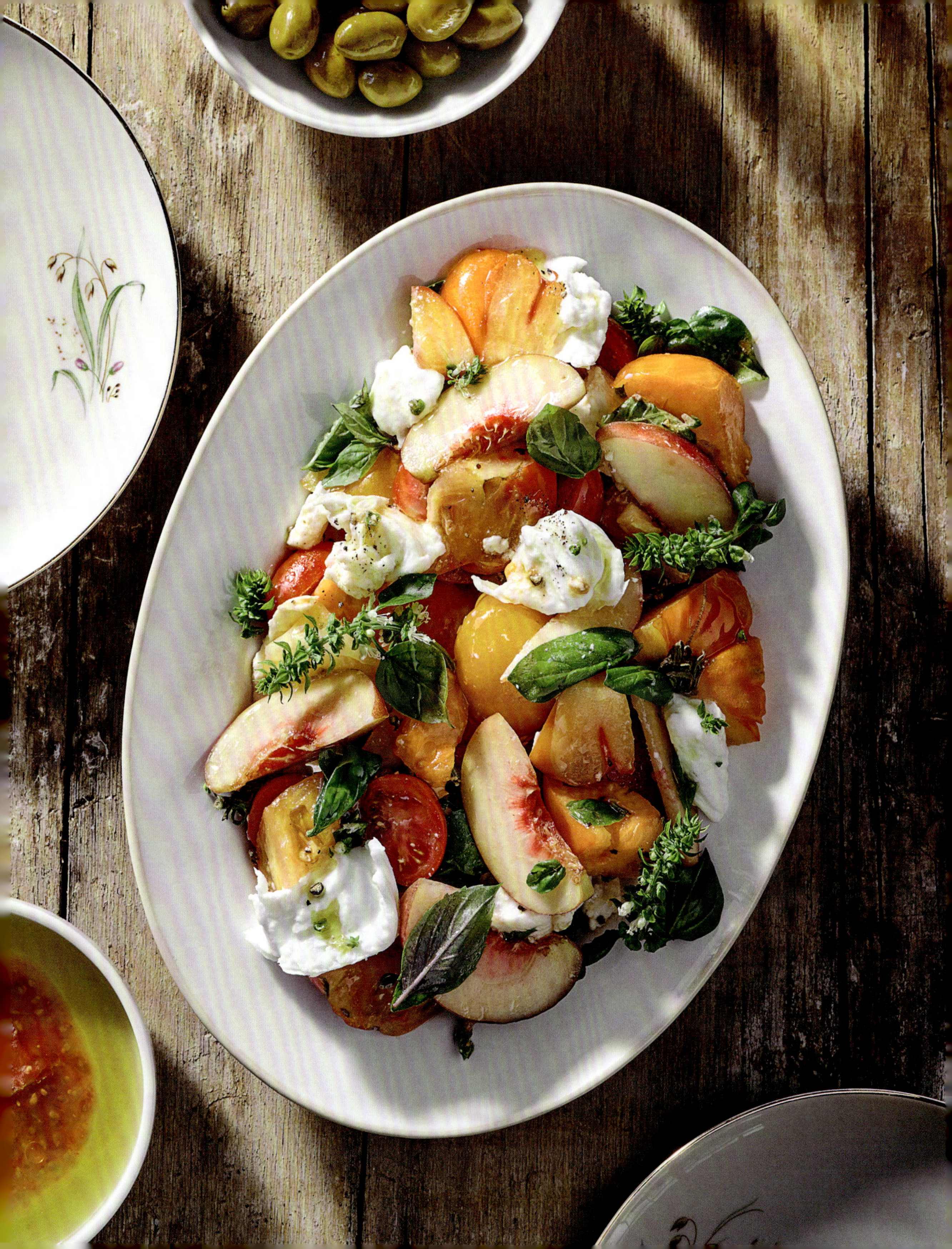

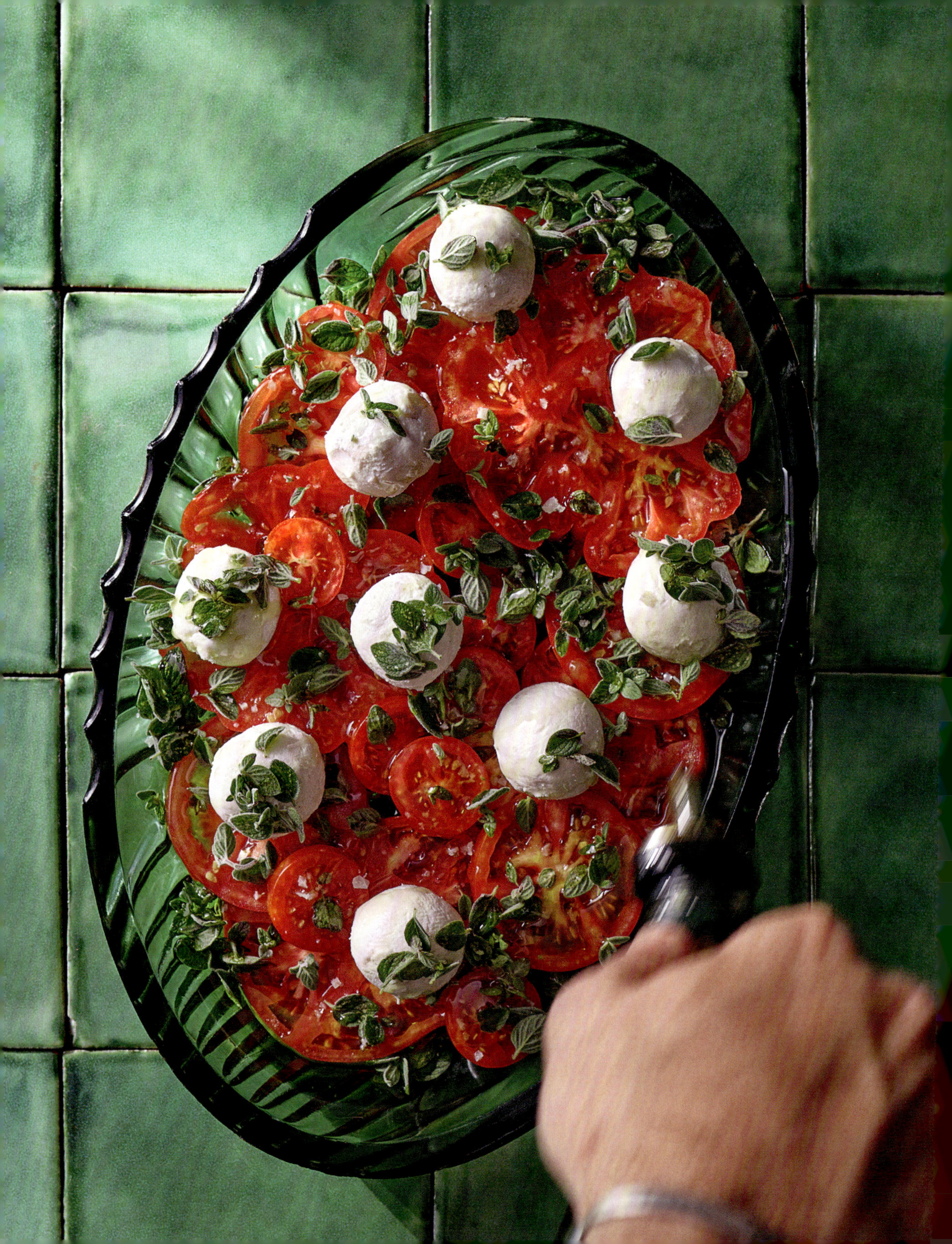

israeli caprese

tomato based

Tomatoes, herbs, and cheese. Voilà! A match made in heaven. Now, try this combination with homemade labneh balls, fresh oregano from the farmers' market, and the world's best extra virgin olive oil—you have yourself the ultimate Israeli caprese. This salad is super quick to whip up if you are in a bind and need to add a beautiful and simple dish to your menu. The labneh is tangy and salty, pairing perfectly with the earthy oregano we would usually use, which grows wild all over Israel. This dish is only as delicious as its ingredients and presentation, so please pay close attention to the details here! Choose a gorgeous oval plate and serve with a Jerusalem Bagel. —BEN

Serve it with: Zhug & Zucchini (page 211), Mackerel, Cucumber & Arugula Crudo (page 255), Jerusalem Bagel (page 120)

Yield: Serves 4 to 6, makes 1 large plate

Total time: 15 minutes

---

1 large red heirloom tomato, sliced crosswise into rounds

3 Campari tomatoes, sliced crosswise into rounds

8 Labneh Balls (page 85)

2 sprigs of oregano leaves, stemmed

½ teaspoon gray salt

3 tablespoons extra virgin olive oil

---

1. Presentation is everything in this salad. Start by arranging an even layer of overlapping heirloom tomato slices on an oval serving plate. Add the Campari tomatoes in a second layer. Then arrange the labneh balls on the plate, evenly spaced on top of the tomatoes.

2. Garnish the dish evenly with the oregano leaves, sprinkle with the salt, and drizzle with the olive oil. Serve immediately.

zikki's peeled tomato salad
when people say, "ukrainian food," i say . . .

tomato based

When I first traveled to Ukraine as an adult, it was for my master's thesis project, and I gathered data on something I called the New Wave Ukrainian Gastronomic Movement. As a child, I thought Ukrainian cuisine was heavy because my family usually only prepared traditional Ukrainian holiday food, which was richer than everyday meals. But when I visited Ukraine in 2019, all of a sudden I discovered a completely new, lighter side of the cuisine.

I made this salad for the first time at my apartment in Lviv, with homegrown tomatoes I bought from a little old lady on the street, freshly toasted sunflower seeds, and a drizzle of the local toasted sunflower oil. I topped it with Bryndza cheese (a young, tangy, crumbly, white sheep's milk cheese similar to feta). The dressing here is actually a magical moment shared between the juicy tomato seeds, sunflower oil, chopped dill, and salt. It's rich, decadent, and like nothing you've ever tasted before—I promise. —*zikki*

Serve it with: Cucumber, Dill, Labneh & Onion Salad (page 165), Hot-Pink Turnips & Beets (page 238), pickled herring

Yield: Serves 1 to 2, makes 1 medium plate

Total time: 15 minutes

---

8 Campari or Maggie tomatoes

1 tablespoon finely chopped dill

2 tablespoons toasted sunflower oil

½ teaspoon gray salt

2 tablespoons raw sunflower seeds

8 chunks Bryndza or feta

Freshly cracked black pepper

---

1. Using a very sharp knife, slowly and patiently peel the tomatoes (it is worth it, I promise!). Cut the tomatoes in half and add them to a medium bowl.

2. To the tomatoes, add the dill, sunflower oil, and salt. Toss lightly and set aside.

3. In a small pan over medium heat, toast the sunflower seeds for approximately 3 minutes, until golden brown and aromatic. Toss the seeds constantly so that they toast evenly and don't stick to the pan, then transfer them directly to the tomato mixture. Toss to combine.

4. Plate the tomato mixture and top with the Bryndza and pepper. Serve immediately.

ESSENTIAL TIP:

Don't skip peeling the tomatoes: This is a method we both learned as young cooks from the well-known Israeli chef Eyal Shani, and it absolutely transforms the tomato experience. Usually, only one or two surface areas of a tomato are exposed when you season a salad. But by peeling a tomato, you actually expose ALL of the fruit's juicy interior, and the tomato becomes truly seasoned.

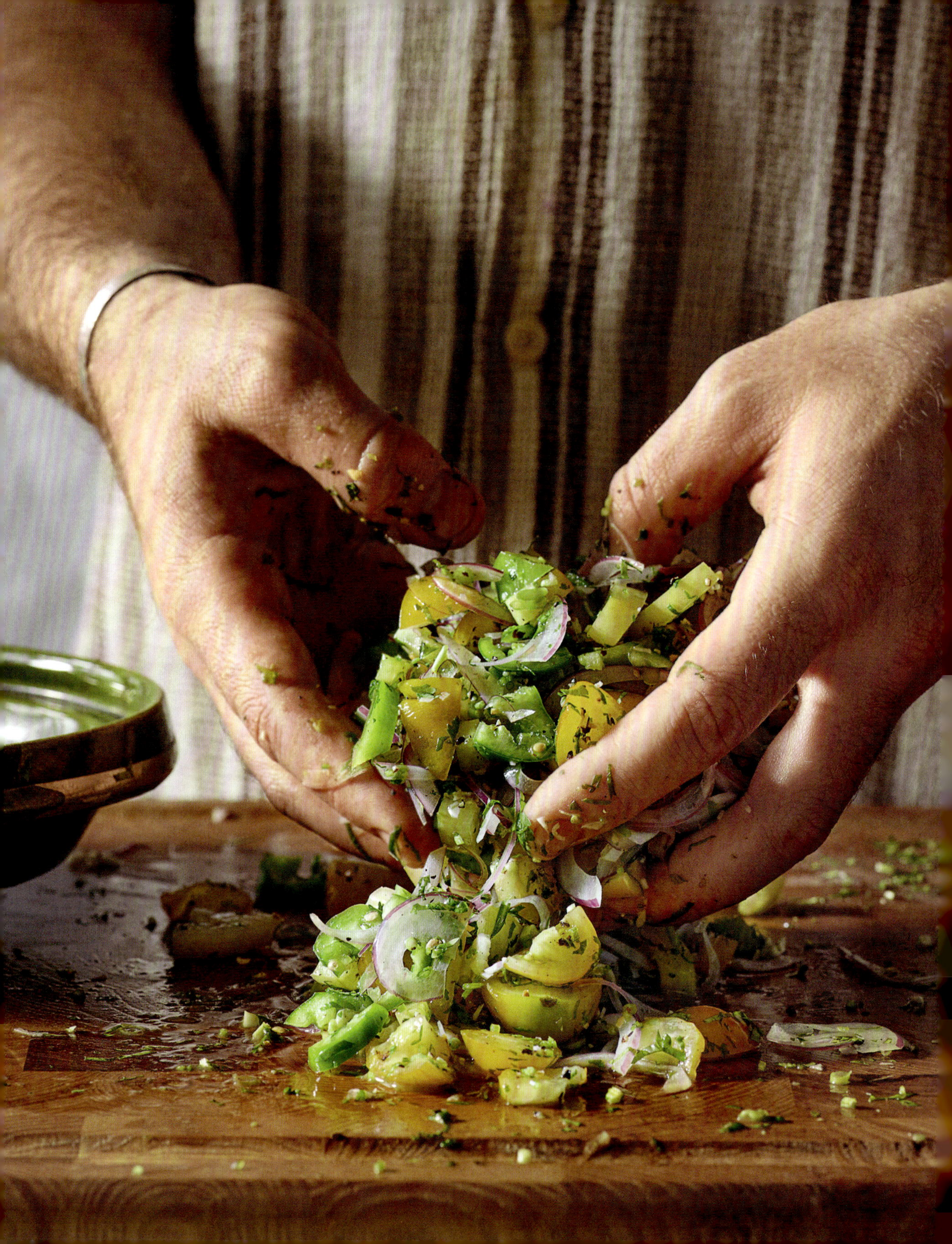

salat dudu

tomato based

The magic of this salad is the imperfectly cut tomatoes and chilies. Salat Dudu is the Israeli "pico de gallo" and pairs perfectly with any small plate, but especially with a pita with a meaty filling. In the summertime, when tomatoes are at their peak, you may get tired of eating only red tomatoes in your salads. Intentionally choosing yellow tomatoes for this dish provides a completely new experience and will transform your guests' previous opinions on tomato salads! —ben

Serve it with: Kebab (page 266), Zikki's Quick Amba (page 60), The Smoothest Tahini Dip (page 55), Pita (page 109)

Yield: Serves 2, makes 2 small bowls

Total time: 15 minutes

---

1 large yellow heirloom tomato, cut into ½-inch pieces

10 yellow cherry tomatoes, quartered

1 long green hot chili, halved lengthwise and thinly sliced

¼ medium red onion, thinly sliced

¼ bunch of flat-leaf parsley, finely chopped

Juice of ½ lemon

1 teaspoon gray salt

3 tablespoons extra virgin olive oil

In a medium bowl, add the tomatoes, chili, onion, parsley, lemon juice, salt, and olive oil. Toss and serve immediately.

ESSENTIAL TIP:

Enjoy the juices! You will inevitably end up with a lot of juices at the bottom of your salad bowl because raw tomatoes, especially when they are in season, release a lot of juice when they come in contact with salt. This is a GOOD problem and just means that you need lots of fresh bread to dip into the bottom of this fabulous salad. However, if you are serving this to a crowd and want the dish to look its best, feel free to drain off the juices and put them aside to make a fun salad dressing later on that same day!

The Best Green Salad of Your Life

leafy

Zikki and I love to eat. That is common knowledge. One of our favorite places to have a romantic date in New York City is Il Buco Alimentari on Great Jones Street in the Village. For a long time, this wasn't the case, as we had repeatedly misordered! But once we went with my uncle Tal and he ordered the whole menu—the food was unbelievable. But what specifically stood out to us? Their house salad. Holy smokes.

Zikki and I would go to Il Buco Alimentari simply to order two of these salads. After a few visits, she made it her mission to make her own version. The salad is crisp and crunchy. The kale leaves are perfectly massaged, the radishes have a solid bite, and the dressing is loaded with anchovies and tarragon. It is the perfect salad. Don't tell anyone, but I prefer Zikki's version to Il Buco Alimentari's—hers has more love. We like to serve this salad directly onto a guest's small plate from a giant bowl using tongs! It is grand and always leaves them craving more. —Ben

Serve it with: NY Strip Steak (page 273), Shrimp in Grated Tomato Butter (page 276), Garlicky String Beans (page 203)

Yield: Serves 4 (or 1 very eager eater), makes 1 large bowl

Total time: 30 minutes

Special tools: mandoline (optional), food processor or blender

For the Salad:

1 purple radish, thinly sliced (using a mandoline if available)

8 short, tender Tuscan kale leaves, bottom 1 inch trimmed

4 heads of Little Gem lettuce, or the hearts of 4 heads of butter lettuce with the outer leaves removed

1 bunch of mustard greens (optional)

1. **Prep the veggies:** In a medium bowl, prepare an ice bath that is one part water to three parts ice. Add the radish slices to the ice bath.

2. **Make the dressing:** Drain the anchovies, reserving the oil, and place them into a food processor or blender. Add the anchovy oil directly to a small skillet and set the pan aside.

3. To the food processor with the anchovies, add the tarragon, lemon juice, vinegar, mustard, honey, and salt. Blend until smooth. Slowly pour in the olive oil as the mixture continues to blend and thicken. Set the dressing aside.

4. **Make the breadcrumbs:** Heat the pan with the anchovy oil over medium heat for 10 seconds. Add the breadcrumbs, tossing

recipe and ingredients continue

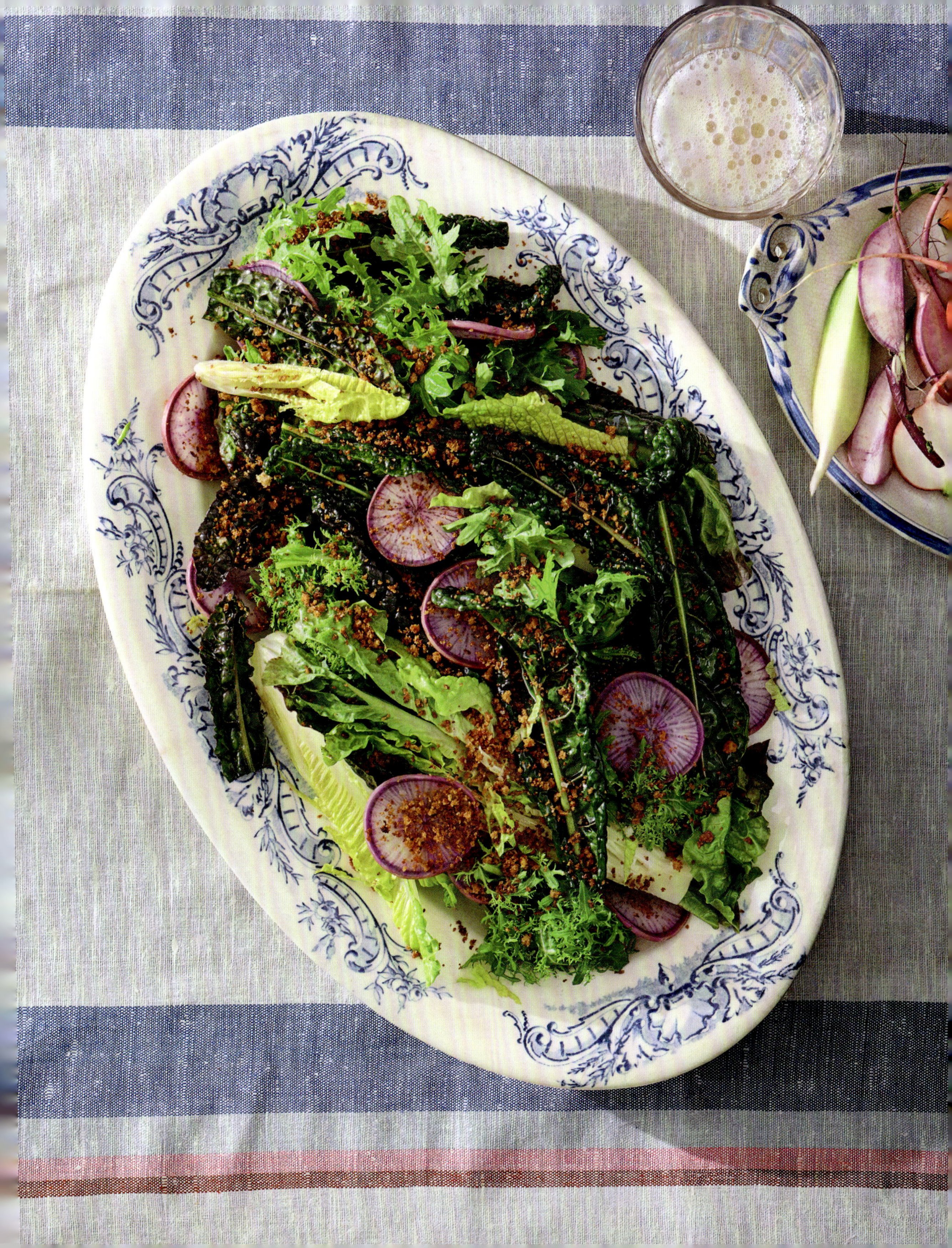

FOR THE TARRAGON DRESSING:

1 (2-ounce) can anchovies, oil reserved

½ cup tarragon, or 1 (0.75-ounce) container, stemmed

Juice of 1 lemon

2 tablespoons sherry vinegar

1 tablespoon Dijon mustard

1 teaspoon honey

1 teaspoon gray salt

½ cup extra virgin olive oil

FOR THE ANCHOVY BREADCRUMBS:

Oil from 1 (2-ounce) can anchovies

¾ cup panko breadcrumbs

½ teaspoon gray salt

---

continuously until they turn golden brown. Add the salt, mix, and remove from the heat. Set aside until ready to serve.

5. Assemble the salad: In a large bowl, add the kale and massage with a teaspoon of the dressing for at least 1 minute.

6. Drain the radishes, pat them dry with a towel, and add them to the bowl with the kale. Toss with an additional teaspoon of the dressing.

7. Add the lettuce and mustard greens (if using) to the bowl. Add the dressing 1 tablespoon at a time until the salad is dressed to your liking.

8. Plate your gorgeous salad and garnish with the toasted anchovy breadcrumbs. Serve immediately.

ESSENTIAL TIPS:

Use the best-quality ingredients: When shopping for the ingredients of this salad, prioritize freshness of ingredients over recipe precision. If you need to substitute a crisp romaine because the Little Gem lettuce is looking sad, absolutely do so. If purple radishes are nowhere to be found, use watermelon radishes.

Use kale with small leaves: When purchasing the Tuscan kale for this recipe, try to source the very smallest adult leaves, as they are far more tender than the stalky large leaves. They should be anywhere from 4 to 6 inches in length.

middle EASTERN CAESAR

leafy

I remember the first time Zikki and I made this salad for one of our events. We were going through a Caesar salad phase in life and wanted to find a way to include it in the menu we offered. The question was: How do we give this American classic a Middle Eastern twist? Enter pomegranate seeds, fresh za'atar-tossed challah breadcrumbs, and a zesty preserved lemon Caesar mash-up. To say it is a home run doesn't actually give this salad enough credit. The best part about this recipe? Everything can be made ahead of time, so when your guests come over, all you have to do is cut the lettuce in quarters, drizzle, garnish, and serve! —*ben*

Serve it with: NY Strip Steak (page 273), Zikki's Salty Baby Potatoes (page 204), Double-Dip Artichoke (page 198)

Yield: Serves 4 to 6, makes 1 large platter

Total time: 30 minutes

Special tools: food processor, Microplane, parchment paper

For the Preserved Lemon Caesar Dressing:

2 tablespoons Preserved Lemon (page 57), finely chopped

3 garlic cloves, peeled

¼ teaspoon gray salt

Juice of 1 lemon

1 (2-ounce) can anchovies

1 tablespoon Dijon mustard

½ cup extra virgin olive oil

1 pasteurized egg yolk

1. Make the dressing: In a food processor, add the preserved lemon, garlic, salt, lemon juice, anchovies and their oil, and mustard. Process until the mixture becomes homogeneous, then slowly drizzle in the olive oil as it continues to blend. Once the dressing is fully blended, add the egg yolk and blend for an additional 15 seconds. Transfer the dressing to a small bowl and set aside.

2. Prep the breadcrumbs: Preheat the oven to 425°F (220°C). Line a baking sheet with parchment paper.

3. In a medium bowl, toss the challah cubes in the olive oil and salt to combine. Evenly spread the challah cubes on the prepared baking sheet and bake for 10 minutes, or until golden brown. Remove the croutons from the oven and return them to the medium bowl. Add the za'atar and toss the croutons while still hot. Once the croutons have cooled, transfer them to the food processor and process until the breadcrumbs are just slightly bigger than panko (or coarse breadcrumbs). Set aside.

4. Assemble the salad: Remove any wilted leaves from the outside of the butter lettuce and slice ¼ inch off the bottom of the stem. Then, quarter each heart of lettuce.

recipe and ingredients continue

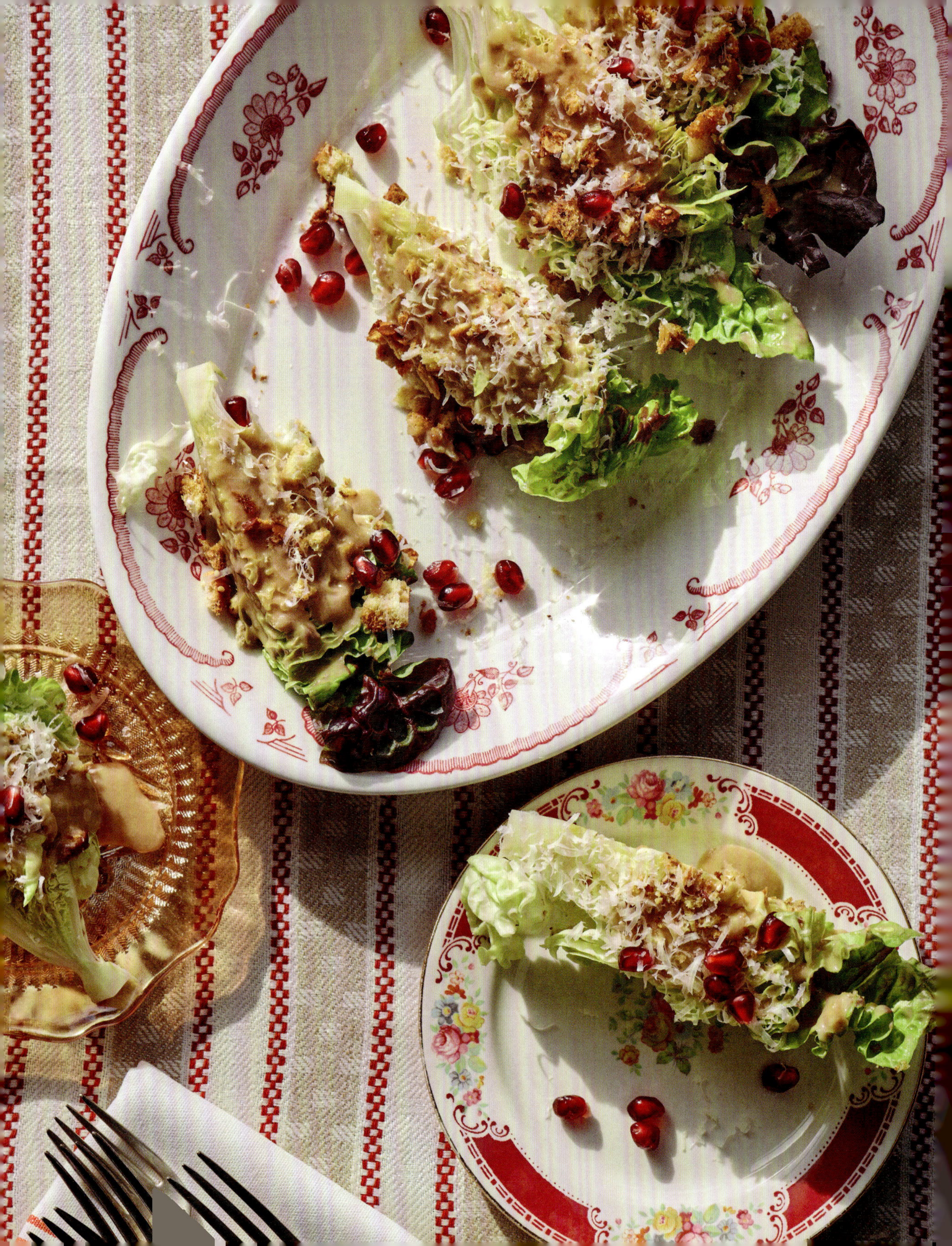

For the Za'atar Challah Breadcrumbs:

½ loaf Challah (page 117), cut into cubes

¼ cup olive oil

½ teaspoon gray salt

¼ cup za'atar

For the Salad:

4 hearts of butter lettuce

¼ cup grated Parmigiano Reggiano

¼ cup pomegranate seeds

5. When you are ready to serve, arrange the butter lettuce quarters on your serving plate. Using a spoon, spread ¼ cup of the dressing across the full surface area of the butter lettuce. Top with a handful of the breadcrumbs and finish with the Parmigiano Reggiano and pomegranate seeds. Serve immediately.

Essential Tips:

Don't skip the egg yolk in the dressing: The level of acidity from the preserved lemon and lemon juice requires a solid boost of fat at the end. The egg yolk will ensure your dressing goes from thin and tart to creamy and balanced.

Raw eggs can add that perfect creamy touch, but remember—there's a risk they could invite uninvited guests (like bacteria) to the party. Play it safe by using pasteurized eggs, which are treated to reduce bacteria.

Save any extra dressing: We love to serve the salad with a small bowl of leftover dressing on the side for dipping.

Breadcrumb yield: You will end up with about 1 cup of leftover breadcrumbs. Store in a tightly sealed container for up to 2 weeks in a cool, dry place.

Radicchio, Blue Cheese & Hazelnut Salad

leafy

On my thirtieth birthday, my parents took us out for lunch in Tel Aviv at Hotel Montefiore. The whole menu at this restaurant was reminiscent of times past. Decadent, detail oriented, and simply classic. We had a salad with just three ingredients: radicchio, blue cheese, and hazelnuts. It was divine. Zikki and I ran home that day to recreate it for ourselves, incorporating our own twists. Over time, the salad transformed into our own. We found that slicing the radicchio super thin gave the bitter green a completely new life. This salad is a delicate dance between three very powerful characters, and the goal is to find their perfect balance. —Ben

Serve it with: Shrimp in Grated Tomato Butter (page 276), Jerusalem Bagel (page 120), A Cashew Basil Dip Everyone Will Talk About (page 99)

Yield: Serves 4 to 6, makes 1 large plate

Total time: 20 minutes

For the Salad:

2 heads of radicchio

4 to 6 ounces blue cheese (the stinkier the better)

½ cup raw hazelnuts, toasted and crushed (see page 22)

Gray salt

For the Fig & Lemon Dressing:

Zest and juice of 2 lemons

½ cup extra virgin olive oil

3 tablespoons fig jam

1 teaspoon gray salt

1. Trim the stems and remove any wilting leaves from the radicchio. Then, cut the radicchio in half through the stem end. Cut each half into thin slices, like you are making a slaw. Add the radicchio to a medium bowl and set aside.

2. Make the dressing: In a small bowl, whisk together the lemon zest and juice, olive oil, fig jam, and salt.

3. Crumble a quarter of the blue cheese into the bowl of radicchio and add a quarter of the hazelnuts. Add half of the dressing and toss with your hands to fully incorporate. Adjust the dressing amount according to your preference. We recommend using only as much as you need; the salad should not be soaked.

4. Plate the salad and finish with the remaining blue cheese and crushed hazelnuts and a light drizzle of the remaining dressing. Serve immediately.

ESSENTIAL TIP:

Save the dressing: You may have leftover dressing—hold on to it! Transfer it to a glass jar or a tightly sealed container to preserve freshness. Store in the refrigerator for up to 1 week.

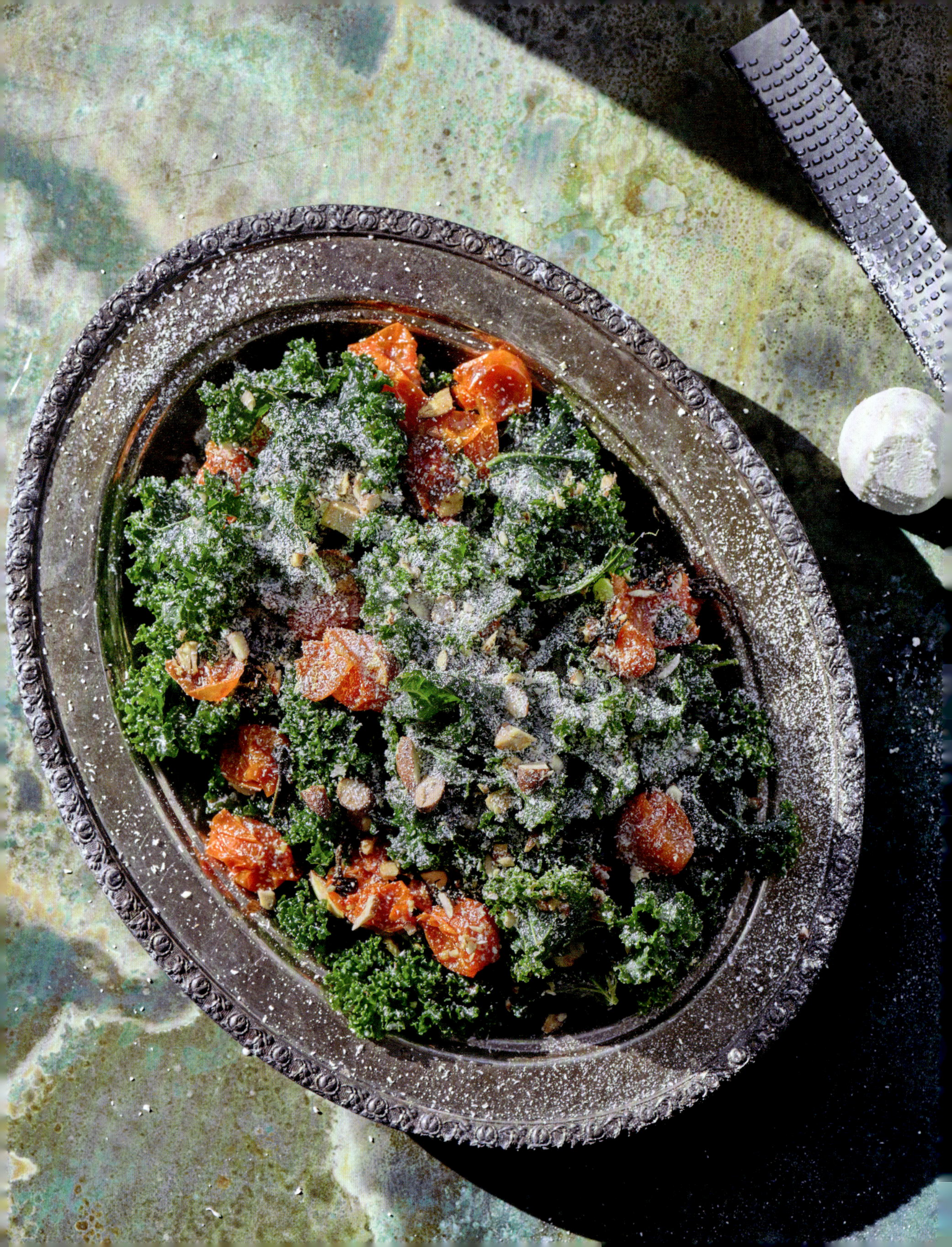

kale salad with roasted tomatoes & almonds

leafy

Kale. Either you absolutely LOVE it or you hate it. I truly believe that the only thing standing between most people and a delicious kale salad is the simple act of massaging the kale before serving. Massage your kale with your best extra virgin olive oil, lemon, and salt. Watch as it transforms from a stiff brassica to a luxurious and crazy-delicious tangy salad. It gets even better after a day or two in the refrigerator. It's excellent to make ahead and serve for a last-minute dinner party! —*zikki*

Serve it with: Garlicky String Beans (page 203), Shrimp in Grated Tomato Butter (page 276), Pear, Mustard Green, Mint & Challah Crouton Salad (page 166)

Yield: Serves 4 to 6, makes 3 small plates

Total time: 40 minutes

Special tools: parchment paper

For the Roasted Tomatoes:

2 (10-ounce) containers cherry tomatoes

¼ cup olive oil

1 teaspoon gray salt

For the Salad:

2 bunches of curly kale, torn into small pieces

Juice of 1 lemon

1 teaspoon gray salt

¼ cup extra virgin olive oil

½ cup raw almonds, toasted and crushed (page 22)

1 Yogurt Stone (page 85), grated, for garnish

1. Preheat the oven to 425°F (220°C). Line a baking sheet with parchment paper.

2. Add the cherry tomatoes to the prepared baking sheet. Drizzle with the olive oil and season with the salt. Holding the tray firmly on both sides, give it a light shake from side to side to make sure the tomatoes are evenly seasoned. Roast for 25 minutes, or until the tomatoes look as if they are about to burst. Remove from the oven and let cool to room temperature.

3. In a medium bowl, add the kale, lemon juice, salt, and olive oil and toss to combine. Using your hands, massage the kale for around 1 minute, or until it is evenly coated in the seasonings and softened.

4. Add the almonds, cooled tomatoes, and the juice from the pan to the kale mixture. Using your hands, toss and gently massage the tomatoes into the kale.

5. Plate the salad and finish with grated yogurt stone. Serve immediately.

VEGGIE bITES

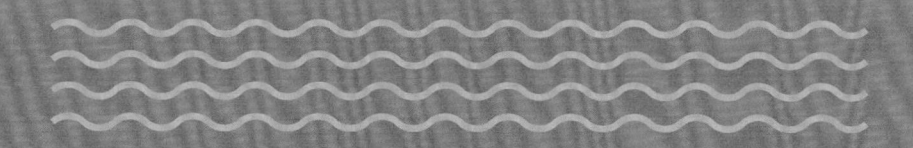

This chapter is very special for Ben and me. Since the beginning of our relationship, we have been cooking vegetables with the same respect that we give to meat. You know that moment when a steak has been cooked to perfection, allowed to rest, and then sliced on a particular angle? Well, vegetables deserve that same care and attention. They all have that peak point where they are cooked to the very best version of themselves. Our mission in this section is to teach you how to cook each vegetable beautifully and how to season it simply without overpowering it: because veggies are our friends.

The magic in this chapter isn't so much about the combination of flavors but rather about the cooking method we use to coax the best out of these beautiful earth-given vegetables.

Once you have that perfectly prepared vegetable, sometimes it is as simple as combining it with a dip you already have on hand in order to elevate it. Hence, the Zhug & Zucchini (page 211), the Sweet Potatoes on Labneh (page 214), and the Cauliflower & Tahini (page 212).—*zikki*

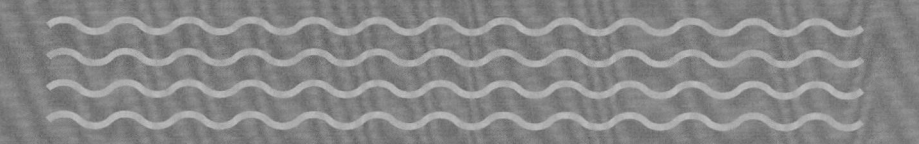

recipes

double-dip artichoke

moroccan carrots

garlicky string beans

zikki's salty baby potatoes

burnt beets & feta

corn off the cob

zhug & zucchini

cauliflower & tahini

sweet potatoes on labneh

falafel

let's talk eggplant: charred in three acts
charred eggplant 101 • charred eggplant with thick tahini • charred eggplant with chopped salad & hard-boiled egg • charred eggplant with labneh, zhug & dukkah

zikki's eggplant

vetrena fries

safta's skinny stuffed grape leaves

amit's fizzy veggie mix

my dad's fermented cucumbers

hot-pink turnips & beets

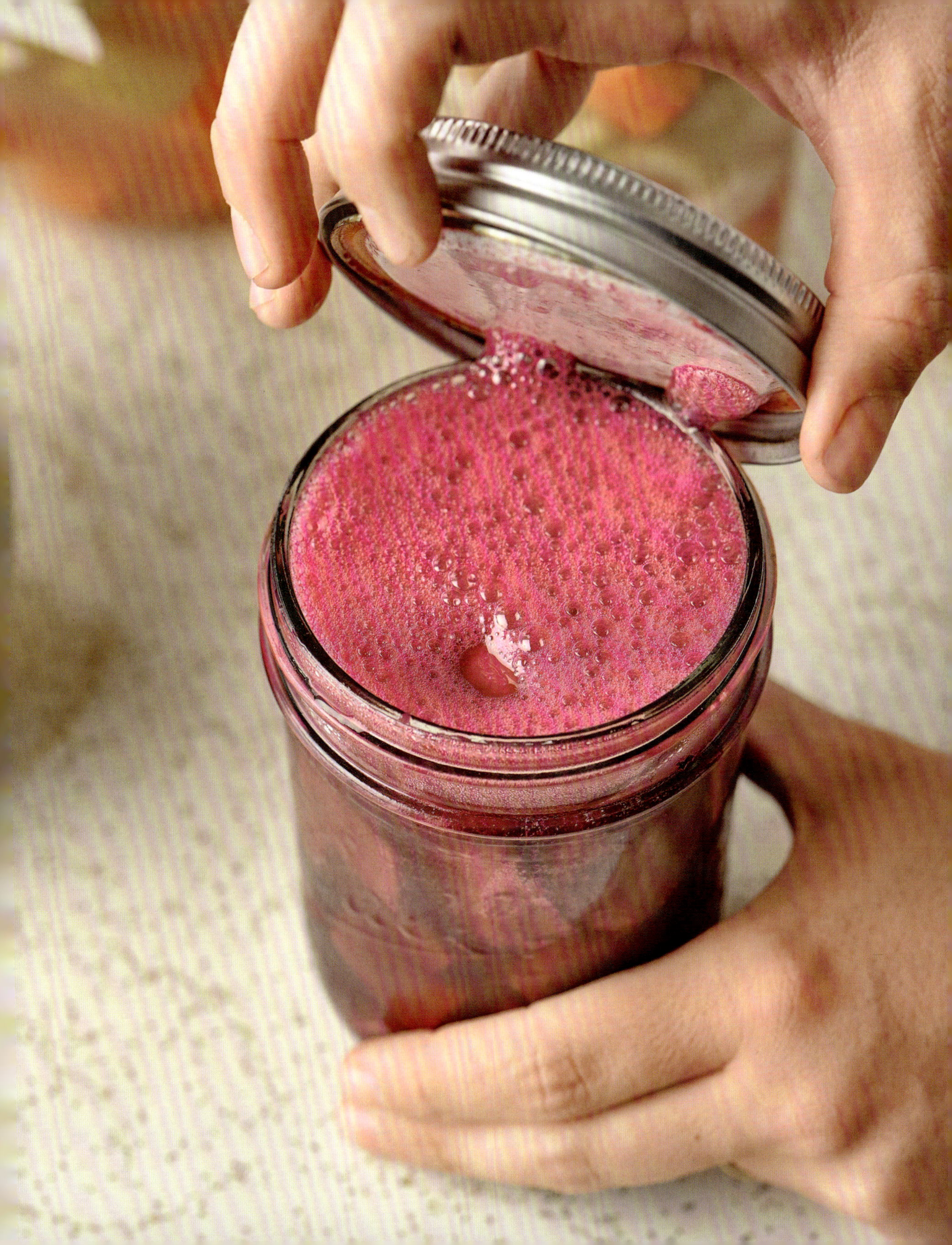

double-dip artichoke

The artichoke: A royal creature it is. One we treat with great respect in our home. To eat an artichoke is like going on a great culinary quest—starting first with the tender leaves and then continuing into the heart that first you must clear of "hairs" with a spoon!

In our opinion, this queen is best cooked in super-salty boiling water until she is tender and falling apart, then dipped in a crazy-delicious preserved lemon crema and double-dipped in anchovy breadcrumbs. Yo! Insane. Artichoke leaves, the original "dippers," may be the most fun food ever and are perfect for when you are hosting friends. It is the ultimate sharing food. —ben & zikki

Serve it with: Fig Carpaccio (page 169), Radicchio, Blue Cheese & Hazelnut Salad (page 190), NY Strip Steak (page 273)

Yield: Serves 3 to 6, makes 3 small plates

Total time: 1 hour 30 minutes

For the Artichokes:

3 artichokes

1½ tablespoons fine sea salt

½ lemon

For the Preserved Lemon Crema:

½ cup whole-fat Greek yogurt

1 tablespoon Preserved Lemon paste (page 57)

5 canned anchovy fillets, finely minced, oil reserved

For the Anchovy Breadcrumbs:

¼ cup panko breadcrumbs

1 teaspoon anchovy oil from a can of anchovy fillets (optional)

1 teaspoon extra virgin olive oil

½ teaspoon gray salt

1. Make the artichokes: Cut ½ inch off the stem of each artichoke. Place the whole artichokes in a large pot and fill it almost to the top with water. Add the fine sea salt and lemon half. Place a heavy plate over the artichokes so that they stay submerged and cover with a lid. Bring to a boil and cook over medium-high heat for 1 hour, or until the leaves are easily removed from the base.

recipe continues

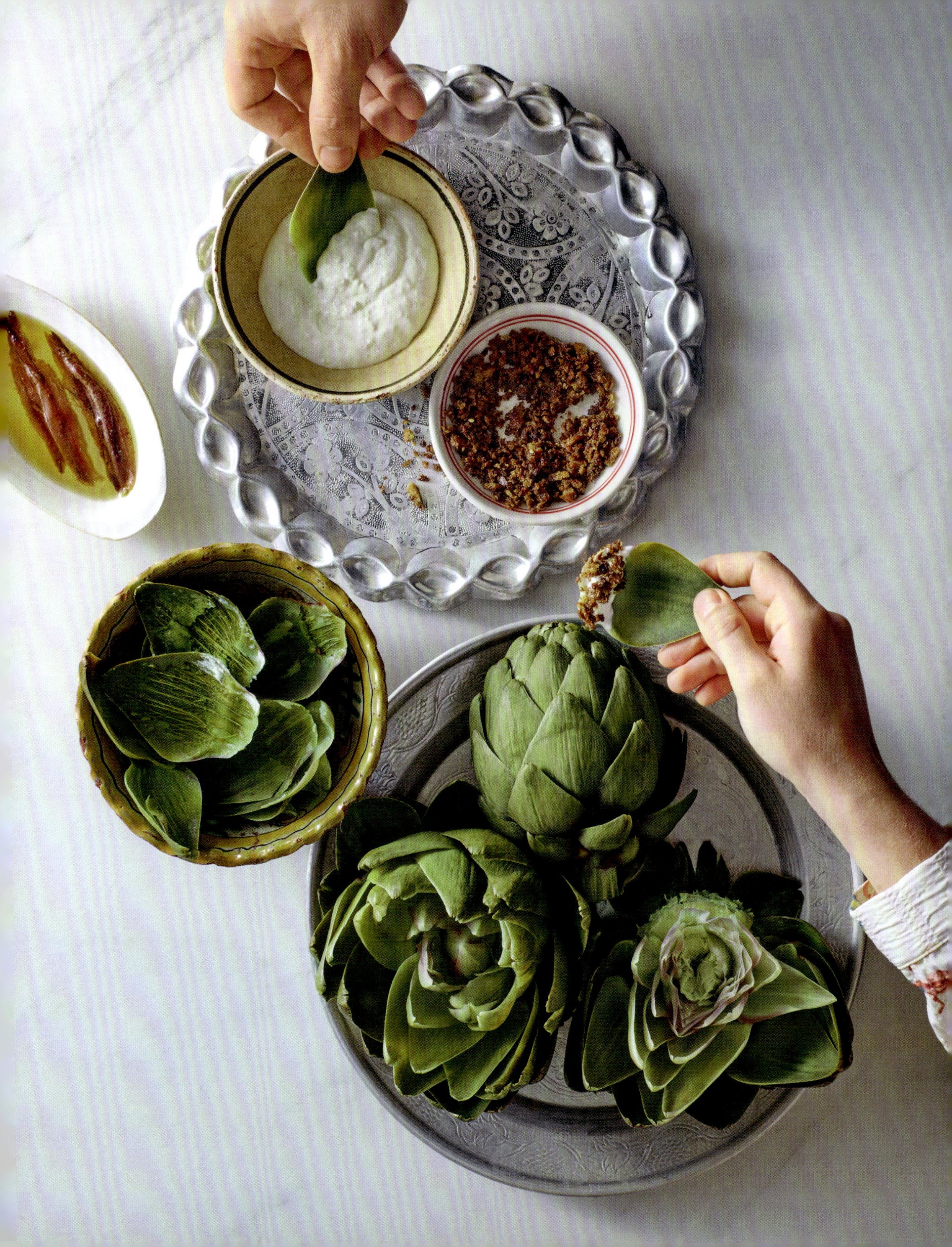

2. Make the crema: In a small bowl, add the yogurt, lemon paste, and anchovies. Stir to combine and set aside.

3. Make the breadcrumbs: In a small nonstick skillet over medium heat, toast the breadcrumbs, tossing them every few seconds, for 2 to 3 minutes, until they have browned. Add the anchovy oil (if using), the olive oil, and gray salt. Toss to coat the breadcrumbs evenly in oil. Once coated and golden brown, about 30 seconds, remove the pan from the heat.

4. Remove the artichokes from the boiling water and serve each one on a separate small plate by pressing the stem side of the artichoke into the plate and using your fingers to open up the flower. Serve alongside a bowl of preserved lemon crema and a bowl of the anchovy breadcrumbs.

ESSENTIAL TIPS:

Keep the artichokes underwater when they are boiling: Keeping the artichokes fully submerged during the whole cooking process is imperative to achieving a completely cooked vegetable.

Salt is nonnegotiable. This may be the biggest defining factor in someone fighting over the last leaf of the choke versus the whole head staying totally untouched. Salt the water like you mean it. The artichoke is a very fibrous thistle and requires a generous amount of salt to bring out its full flavor and salinity.

"Wait, how do I eat it?" If you have never eaten an artichoke before, you start with the leaves. Their meat is at the very bottom of each triangle and is best enjoyed dipped in the preserved lemon crema and then into the breadcrumbs. When you have finished the leaves, you will see the heart of the artichoke. It is covered in a ¼-inch layer of "hairs." When you get to the heart, using a spoon, remove the hairs. The remaining portion of the heart is not only edible but crazy delicious. Make sure to slather on more sauce and crumbs.

MOROCCAN CARROTS

Ben and I argue regularly about how to make Moroccan carrots (see photo, page 202). Ben prefers to keep things traditional by boiling the carrots and then adding ground cumin and chopped parsley. However, I think this salad could stand to be more interesting. This recipe is our combined version. We roast the carrots and incorporate freshly toasted and crushed cumin seeds with a scoop of our homemade harissa.

Keep in mind that this recipe calls for a large amount of carrots—as they roast in the oven, they will lose a lot of their volume. If you don't use enough, you will find yourself disappointed with the small amount of carrots that will be left after you are done secretly snacking on them. —*zikki*

Serve it with: Our Hassle-Free Matbucha (page 52), Classic Hummus (page 77), Labneh Spread (page 84), Tel Avivian Focaccia (page 113)

Yield: Serves 4, makes 3 small plates

Total time: 1 hour

Special tools: parchment paper, mortar and pestle

---

20 large carrots (2 pounds), peeled and cut diagonally into ½-inch pieces

½ cup extra virgin olive oil

1 tablespoon gray salt

1 tablespoon cumin seeds

1 tablespoon honey

2 tablespoons Harissa (page 50)

1. Preheat the oven to 425°F (220°C). Line a baking sheet with parchment paper.

2. In a medium bowl, toss the carrots with the olive oil and salt. Arrange the carrots on the prepared baking sheet and bake for 40 minutes, or until the carrots are tender and have begun to shrink. Remove them from the oven and place them in a large bowl.

3. While the carrots are roasting, place the cumin seeds in a small skillet and then turn the heat to medium. This allows the seeds and pan to rise in temperature together. Toss the seeds for 2 to 3 minutes, until they become fragrant.

4. Transfer the toasted cumin seeds to a mortar and crush with the pestle for about 2 minutes, or until they become a coarse powder.

5. To the bowl with the carrots, add the honey, cumin, and harissa. Toss to evenly coat, then serve.

garlicky string beans

moroccan carrots

tabbouleh

Garlicky String Beans

Garlic was ever-present in my childhood, with my mother using it raw, roasted, or cooked in extra virgin olive oil. She was absolutely obsessed and believed it could heal any ailment. While I don't use garlic in everything like she did, it is still nonnegotiable in certain dishes. Enter Garlicky String Beans.

This recipe combines two incredible vegetables cooked to their peak: blanched string beans and grated garlic lightly simmered in olive oil. The magic here? Timing. When you think that the string beans need another minute to cook, that is exactly the time to pull them off the heat. Don't wait until their bright color begins to turn darker or for the garlic to turn brown. Like meat, beans continue to cook even after you remove them from the heat. Simple to make, this dish will have your guests reaching for more. —*zikki*

Serve it with: NY Strip Steak (page 273), The Best Green Salad of Your Life (page 184), Fennel, Citrus & Pistachio Salad (page 159)

Yield: Serves 2 to 4, makes 4 small plates

Total time: 15 minutes

---

1 tablespoon fine sea salt

2 (12-ounce) bags string beans

½ cup extra virgin olive oil

4 large garlic cloves, grated

1 teaspoon gray salt

---

1. Bring a large pot of water to a boil and add the fine sea salt. Meanwhile, prepare an ice bath in a large bowl with one part water to three parts ice.

2. When the water reaches a boil, add the string beans and cook for 2 minutes, then immediately transfer them to the ice bath for 1 minute. Drain the cooled string beans and then transfer them to a large bowl. Set aside.

3. In a small saucepan, add the olive oil and garlic. Bring the oil to a light simmer over low heat and cook for about 1 minute, or until aromatic. Remove the pan from the heat and let the oil finish cooking the garlic for an additional 30 seconds.

4. Pour the hot oil over the string beans in the bowl. Add the gray salt and toss. Distribute the garlicky string beans evenly between four small plates and serve immediately.

zikki's salty baby potatoes

I really believe that sometimes the craziest mistakes can lead us to the wildest discoveries, especially in the kitchen. These Salty Baby Potatoes were born from exactly that. While cooking an extensive menu for our clients, I was boiling potatoes in salty water and forgot about them. I'd intended to smash them and then broil them (which honestly would have dried them out!). But before I knew it, the water in the pot had almost completely evaporated and there was a thin layer of salt on each potato. The texture on the inside was also shockingly tender and perfectly creamy. What might have seemed like a disaster was clearly a victory. The best part? The potatoes remained creamy, tender, and warm for a long time and were perfect for a large crowd. Being Ukrainian, I couldn't help but toss them in some butter and dill before serving them alongside sour cream and chrain, a pungent eastern European condiment made of grated horseradish and beets. The absolute best side dish, maybe ever. —*zikki*

Serve it with: NY Strip Steak (page 273), Zikki's Peeled Tomato Salad (page 180)

Yield: Serves 3 to 4, makes 2 to 4 small plates

Total time: 1 hour 20 minutes

Special tools: food processor

FOR THE CHRAIN (MAKES ONE 8-OUNCE JAR):

1 (6-ounce) horseradish root, 6 to 8 inches long

1 medium beet, cut into ¼-inch pieces

Juice of ½ lemon

1½ teaspoons honey

½ teaspoon gray salt

1. Make the chrain: Peel and chop the horseradish into ¼-inch pieces. In a food processor, add the horseradish, beets, lemon juice, honey, and gray salt and blend until the mixture is an even, hot pink color!

2. Prep the potatoes: In a large pot, add the potatoes and fine sea salt, adding enough water to cover the potatoes by about 2 inches. Place the pot over high heat and bring the water to a boil, then reduce to a low boil and cook for 45 minutes to 1 hour, until 90 percent of the water has evaporated, leaving about 1 inch of water in the bottom of the pot.

3. Turn up the heat to medium for about 2 minutes, keeping a very careful eye on the potatoes. As the remainder of the water boils off, a thin layer of salt will form on the potatoes and the bottom of the pot.

recipe and ingredients continue

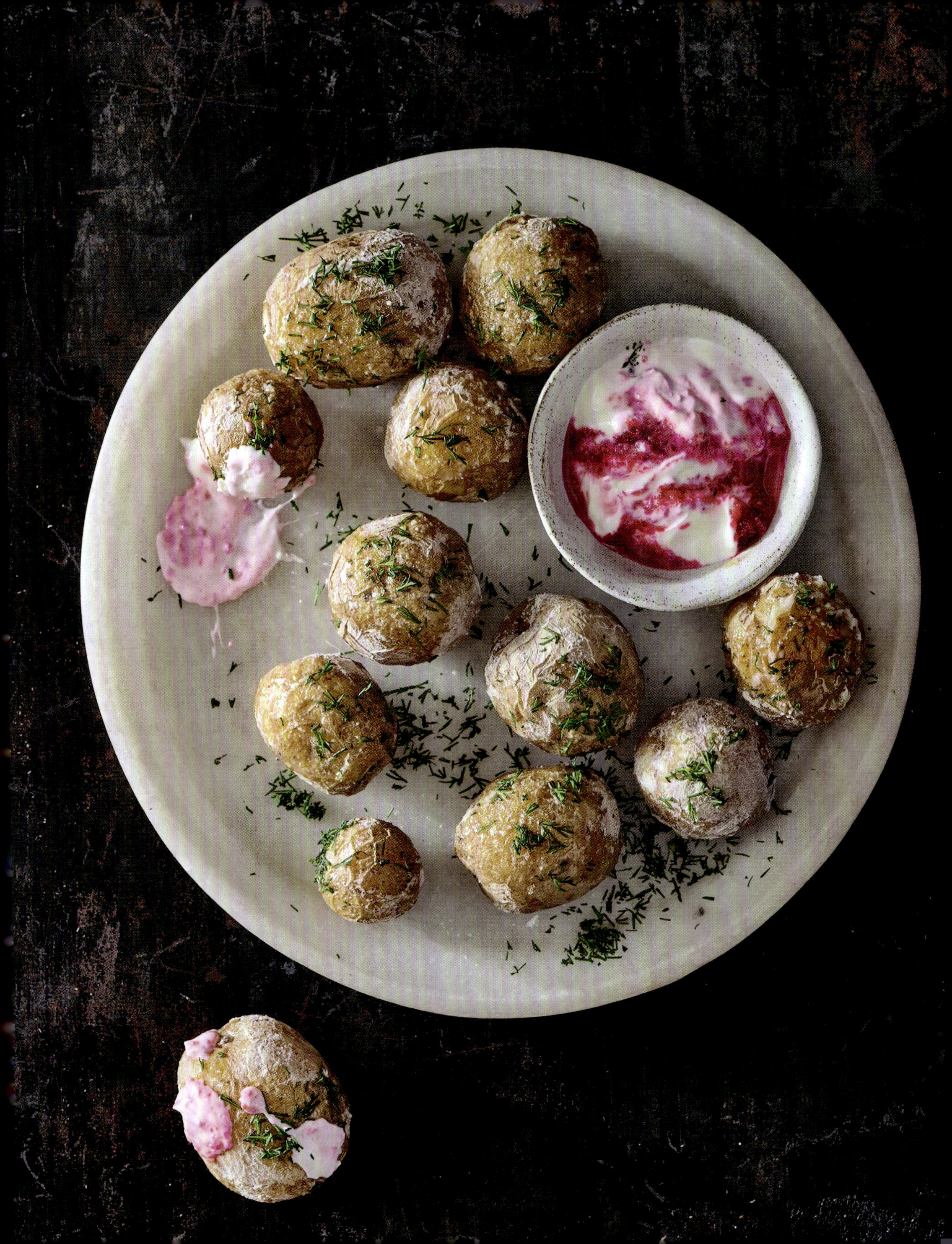

FOR THE POTATOES:

2 (1.5-pound) bags baby yellow potatoes

1 tablespoon fine sea salt

2 tablespoons salted Irish butter

2 tablespoons finely chopped dill

¼ cup sour cream, for serving

Turn off the heat the moment that all the water has evaporated.

4. Transfer the potatoes to a large bowl with the butter and dill. Gently toss immediately, being careful not to crack the skin of the potatoes.

5. Distribute the potatoes evenly onto small plates and serve immediately with a small side bowl of chrain topped with the sour cream.

ESSENTIAL TIP:

Long cook time but low effort: This recipe is awesome because it requires your full attention only for the last 5 minutes of the cook time.

burnt beets & feta

A beet is an overwhelmingly beautiful root vegetable that can be enjoyed in many forms: raw in a salad, grated with horseradish (my personal favorite), boiled in a soup, or roasted in salt and olive oil. Wherever she goes, she brings an incredible pop of color and an unparalleled sweet touch. Our favorite way to enjoy beets is by roasting them whole in their own skin (similarly to sweet potatoes) or sliced into chunky pieces, exposing their hot-pink flesh. The longer you roast them, the more tender and decadent they become. Now, tossed with tangy feta, crushed pistachios, and a kick of lemon? You've got an instant crowd-pleaser. Tangy, crunchy, and sweet (see page 208)!—ben

Serve it with: Zhug & Zucchini (page 211), Corn off the Cob (page 209)

Yield: Serves 4 to 6, makes 4 small plates

Total time: 1 hour

Special tools: parchment paper

---

2 large (or 5 small) beets, cut into eighths

1 teaspoon gray salt

¼ cup extra virgin olive oil, plus 1 to 2 tablespoons for garnish

¼ cup raw shelled pistachios, toasted and crushed (page 22)

Juice of ½ lemon

¼ cup roughly crumbled feta or goat cheese

20 mint leaves, thinly sliced

Hot honey, for garnish

Freshly cracked black pepper, for garnish

1. Preheat the oven to 425°F (220°C). Line a baking sheet with parchment paper.

2. In a medium bowl, add the beets, salt, and olive oil and toss to coat. Arrange the beets on the prepared baking sheet and roast for 35 minutes, or until the beets begin to shrivel and the edges become crisp. Remove the beets from the oven and allow them to cool to room temperature.

3. Set 1 tablespoon of the crushed pistachios aside for topping. In a small bowl, combine the cooled beets, lemon juice, and remaining pistachios. Toss and distribute evenly among four small plates.

4. Finish the plates with the feta, mint, the reserved pistachios, a drizzle of hot honey, extra virgin olive oil, and some freshly cracked black pepper.

essential tips:

Use a tangy feta: If high-quality, tangy feta isn't available, try goat cheese or crumbled Labneh Balls (page 85).

When to add the feta: Add the feta just before serving to prevent the beets from turning the cheese pink!

corn off
the cob

zhug &
zucchini

burnt beets
& feta

CORN OFF THE COB

Corn on the cob can be a little intimidating. Do you boil it? Do you grill it? How do you know when it is done? In theory it all seems obvious, but in application, corn is easily overcooked and does require a keen eye. We find that charring corn directly on a gas range is the absolute best way to cook it. A direct and quick fire on the surface area of the corn gives you the perfect cook. You may hear little pops, as the direct heat creates sugary pressure in the kernels, but fear not. You are only 2 minutes away from perfectly cooked corn. Once charred to perfection, you can gently cut the kernels off the cob and mix them into a quick and fresh side salad! —BEN

Serve it with: Burnt Beets & Feta (page 207), Zhug & Zucchini (page 211), Kebab (page 255)

Yield: Serves 2 to 4, makes 2 small bowls

Total time: 30 minutes

Special tools: gas range

FOR THE QUICK-PICKLED ONIONS:

1 medium red onion, thinly sliced

1½ teaspoons fine sea salt

1 tablespoon honey

½ cup red wine vinegar

½ cup boiling water

FOR THE CORN:

4 ears sweet corn, husks and silks removed

¼ cup Quick-Pickled Onions

¼ bunch of cilantro, chopped

1 teaspoon sumac

1. Quick-pickle the onions: In a heatproof pint container, add the onions, fine sea salt, and honey. Then pour in the vinegar and boiling water. Cover and set aside for at least 30 minutes, or until the onions begin to dye the water pink. You can set the onions aside to use for the corn or keep them in the refrigerator for up to 1 month.

2. Prep the corn: Working one at a time, arrange an ear of corn on a burner grate of your gas range and turn the heat to medium. Allow the corn to cook on each side for 15 to 20 seconds, until you hear small pops and the color of the kernels has turned from a pastel yellow to a bright yellow followed by a dark char. Rotate the corn until there are char marks on 60 percent of the cob, then turn off the gas and remove the corn from the heat. Repeat with the remaining corn. Set aside.

3. Place a small bowl upside down in a large bowl and stand the corn on the cob upright. Carefully cut the kernels off the cob from the top down using a sharp chef's knife. The kernels should fall into the large bowl. Once you have removed all the kernels from their cobs, remove the small upside-down bowl and set the large bowl of corn aside.

recipe and ingredients continue

1 teaspoon gray salt, plus more to taste

2 tablespoons extra virgin olive oil

Juice of 1 lime

4. In a separate bowl, combine ¼ cup of the pickled onions with the cilantro, sumac, gray salt, olive oil, and lime juice. Add the corn to the onion mixture and toss to coat.

5. Adjust the salt to taste and distribute the corn mixture evenly into two small bowls. Serve and enjoy!

ESSENTIAL TIP:

Cooking the corn: When cooking the corn on the gas, be very attentive. Once the heat is on, the entire cooking process is very fast. It will take only a matter of 15 to 20 seconds before you need to turn the corn. The goal when charring the corn is to get as much of the surface area of the corn exposed to the flame as possible.

ZHUG & ZUCCHINI

We genuinely feel that you can never have enough zucchini recipes, especially when it is zucchini season and the farmers' market is flooded with these tender summer squashes. Many times, this vegetable is overlooked because people overcook zucchini while simultaneously underseasoning it. Our method for cooking zucchini keeps the structural integrity of the vegetable intact and layers flavor using a two-part process of baking and then charring on a gas range. This dish is an instantly delicious, flavorful side, made even easier with last week's zhug from the fridge (see photo, page 208). —Ben

Serve it with: Burnt Beets & Feta (page 207), Arabic Ceviche (page 256), Jerusalem Bagel (page 120)

Yield: Serves 3 to 4, makes 3 small bowls

Total time: 30 minutes

Special tools: parchment paper, gas range

---

5 medium zucchinis

1 teaspoon gray salt, plus more to taste

Juice of ½ lemon

3 tablespoons My Grandfather's Zhug (page 49)

ESSENTIAL TIP:

Salting the zucchini: In step 5, coat the zucchini with salt and lemon juice first, then taste to ensure the salt is absorbed before adding the zhug. This step removes excess moisture, evenly seasons the zucchini, and balances the bold flavors of the zhug.

1. Preheat the oven to 500°F (260°C). Line a baking sheet with parchment paper.

2. Place the whole zucchinis on the prepared baking sheet and bake for 15 minutes, or until they begin to just darken in color.

3. Remove the zucchinis from the oven and place them, one at a time, directly on a burner grate of your gas range. Turn the heat to high and allow the flame to char the skin of the zucchini. Rotate every 20 seconds for 1 minute. Then remove it from the heat and set aside to cool for 5 minutes. Repeat with the remaining zucchinis.

4. Once cooled, slice the zucchinis down the middle lengthwise and then again into quarters. Cut the long quarters into 1-inch-thick pieces. Transfer to a medium bowl.

5. To the bowl with the zucchini, add the salt and lemon juice. Toss and adjust the salt to taste (see note). Add the zhug and toss again to coat. Serve immediately or store in the refrigerator to serve later that day.

CAULIFLOWER & TAHINI

Cauliflower and tahini is a staple dish in Israel. Zikki likes to drizzle the tahini over the cauliflower, but I grew up folding the tender cauliflower into the tahini and eating it in a pita—they work so well together that you can't differentiate between the creamy sesame sauce and the cauliflower. In this recipe, we meet somewhere in the middle. The real star here isn't the tahini but the cauliflower. What is the secret to the perfect cauliflower? Time, temperature, and oil. A cauliflower coated generously in extra virgin olive oil and given the proper amount of time to roast is destined for perfection. —BEN

Serve it with: Chicken Shawarma Salad (page 153), Sweet Potatoes on Labneh (page 214)

Yield: Serves 2 to 4, makes 2 to 4 small plates

Total time: 1 hour 20 minutes

Special tools: parchment paper

---

1 head of cauliflower

½ cup extra virgin olive oil

1 teaspoon gray salt

2 tablespoons za'atar

½ cup The Smoothest Tahini Dip (page 55)

---

1. Preheat the oven to 425°F (220°C). Line a baking sheet with parchment paper.

2. Using a sharp chef's knife, roughly cut the cauliflower into medium 2-inch pieces and place into a medium bowl. Toss with the olive oil and salt.

3. Arrange the cauliflower evenly on the prepared baking sheet and roast for at least 1 hour, until it has turned golden brown and crispy.

4. Remove the cauliflower from the oven and plate the large pieces on small plates, placing any small crispy pieces in a small bowl.

5. To the small bowl, add the za'atar and toss to combine with the small pieces.

6. Drizzle the tahini dip over the small plates of cauliflower and finish the dish with a generous sprinkle of crispy cauliflower za'atar crumbs. Serve immediately.

cauliflower & tahini

sweet potatoes on labneh

SWEET POTATOES ON LABNEH

There is a magic that happens when you cook a sweet potato in an extremely hot oven for a long period of time. The sugars condense, forming a sweet potato pillow as the flesh detaches from the skin. It is an incredible spectacle and requires little to no work. Simply bake, peel, and serve the sweet potatoes over any dip or spread you've got in your refrigerator. We love to serve these sexy sweet potatoes on a heaping bed of tangy and salty labneh, drizzled with extra virgin olive oil and sprinkled with gray salt (see photo, page 213). —BEN & ZIKKI

Serve it with: Cauliflower & Tahini (page 212)

Yield: Serves 4 to 6, makes 2 small plates

Total time: 2 hours 30 minutes

Special tools: parchment paper

---

4 medium sweet potatoes

½ cup labneh

Gray salt

Honey, for garnish

Extra virgin olive oil, for garnish

---

1. Preheat the oven to 500°F (260°C). Line a baking sheet with parchment paper.

2. Place the sweet potatoes whole on the prepared baking sheet and bake for 2 hours, or until the skin cracks to the touch and feels detached, airy, or hollow.

3. Remove the baking sheet from the oven and allow the sweet potatoes to cool for 10 minutes. Once cool enough to handle, peel the sweet potatoes with your hands, leaving the skin at one end for easy transfer to plates.

4. Spoon the labneh onto two small plates (¼ cup per plate) and, using the back of a spoon, spread the labneh evenly across the plates. Top the labneh with two peeled sweet potatoes per plate. Finish with salt to taste and a drizzle of honey and olive oil.

ESSENTIAL TIPS:

How to know the sweet potatoes are cooked: After 2 hours at 500°F (260°C), gently knock the skin. If it's still attached and dense, cook in 20-minute increments until it cracks and feels hollow.

Add a kick: Swap regular honey with hot honey for some heat.

falafel

As with hummus, everyone in Israel likes to claim that they know where the best falafel is made. Growing up in Rehovot, I was around falafel all the time. Falafel in my hometown is like pizza in New York City. Every other shop is a falafel shop. The special thing about falafel made in Israel is that it is bright green, which comes from copious amounts of fresh herbs. The falafel spot that I love the most is HaKosem, which happens to be the most successful falafel shop in Israel.

This recipe is inspired by HaKosem's, but I adjusted it by adding nigella seeds to the mixture. Nigella seeds are really special and date back to Egyptian times. They were found in Tutankhamen's tomb and are mentioned in the Old Testament. Using them is optional, but their incredible aroma will take your falafel game to the next level. Falafel can be eaten in a bowl alongside a couple of dips, or filled to the top of your pita sandwich. —ben

Serve it with: Pita (page 109), Classic Hummus with Tiny Tangy Chili Oil (page 77)

Yield: Serves 6 to 10, makes 30 medium falafel balls

Total time: 2 hours, plus at least 12 hours soaking

Special tools: meat grinder or food processor, mortar and pestle, digital kitchen thermometer, ice cream scoop or falafel press

FOR THE FALAFEL:

2½ cups (500 grams) dried chickpeas

2 medium yellow onions, diced

4 garlic cloves, minced

1 bunch of flat-leaf parsley, roughly chopped

1 bunch of cilantro, roughly chopped

1 teaspoon coriander seeds

1 teaspoon cumin seeds

1. In a large bowl, add the chickpeas and cover with cold water at least twice their volume. Let soak overnight, or at least 12 hours, then drain.

2. Using a food processor or meat grinder, blend or grind the chickpeas, onions, garlic, parsley, and cilantro until coarse but homogeneous. Transfer the mixture to a medium bowl and set aside.

3. In a small skillet, add the coriander seeds, cumin seeds, sesame seeds, and nigella seeds (if desired). Toast on medium-low heat for about 2 minutes, stirring frequently, until very fragrant. Remove from the heat.

4. Using a mortar and pestle, grind the coriander seeds, cumin seeds, sesame seeds, and nigella seeds and mix the spices into the chickpea mixture. Then add the salt, 1 teaspoon of water, and the baking soda to the chickpea mixture and mix until combined. Cover and chill in the refrigerator for 1 hour.

recipe and ingredients continue

pita

falafel

1 tablespoon sesame seeds

1 teaspoon nigella seeds (optional)

1 tablespoon gray salt

1 tablespoon baking soda

1 quart canola oil, for frying

For Serving:

The Smoothest Tahini Dip (page 55)

5. Once you are ready to start frying, in a deep, medium pot, heat the oil over medium heat until it reaches 350° to 375°F (175° to 190°C) on a digital kitchen thermometer. Check the temperature periodically. Line a baking sheet with paper towels.

6. Using a medium ice cream scoop or falafel press, form the falafel balls and fry them in the oil for 3 to 5 minutes, until dark brown in color. Do not crowd the falafel. We recommend making at most five falafel at one time. Once the falafel are ready, using a slotted spoon, transfer to the prepared baking sheet to drain. Repeat with the remaining falafel, allowing the oil to return to temperature between batches.

7. Serve immediately alongside a bowl of tahini dip.

Essential Tips:

Blending the chickpea mixture: When making the chickpea mixture for the falafel, especially if you are using a food processor, make sure not to overprocess it. It is best to blend it until it is a coarse texture, not a paste.

Chilling the falafel: It is important to chill the mixture for an hour so that it holds its shape better when you shape and fry the falafel.

Baking soda: Don't forget the baking soda! This is what gives falafel its fluffy texture.

Reheating instructions: If you want to serve falafel at your party but do not want to spend time frying, fry the falafel halfway to develop color and structure and then remove from the frying oil and bring to room temperature. Fifteen minutes before serving your falafel, place your half-cooked falafel balls on a parchment paper–lined baking sheet into a 425°F (220°C) oven for 10 minutes. Serve immediately.

let's talk eggplant: charred in 3 acts

charred eggplant 101

Yield: Serves 2, makes 1 small plate
Total time: 30 minutes
Special tools: gas range

I remember the first time I ever burned an eggplant for Zikki. It was our second official date. She came over to my apartment, which overlooked the mountains in the tiny town of Bra. We had bought a few ingredients at the farmers' market and decided to cook. I started by putting a whole eggplant directly on the fire of my gas range. She was in shock. She had literally never seen this cooking method before. Meanwhile, burning an eggplant is a normal Tuesday morning in Israel. Through Zikki's eyes, I really understood how truly magical a charred eggplant is. While it is best known for baba ganoush (page 92), it can be the base for any sauce, dip, spread, or meal (for any time of day). It has the power to absorb any flavor while adding an unparalleled smokiness. —ben

1 Italian eggplant, fat and round

1. Place the eggplant directly on the large burner grate of your gas range. Turn the heat to high. Char the eggplant for 10 to 12 minutes on the first side without flipping, until the skin is burnt and flaky and the flesh is soft. You can test this by turning off the heat, lifting the eggplant with your tongs, and tapping the charred side with your finger (being very careful not to burn yourself). The skin should cave in and crack when tapped.

2. With the opposite side down, place the eggplant back on the large burner grate. Turn the gas to high heat. Char the eggplant for 10 to

recipes continue

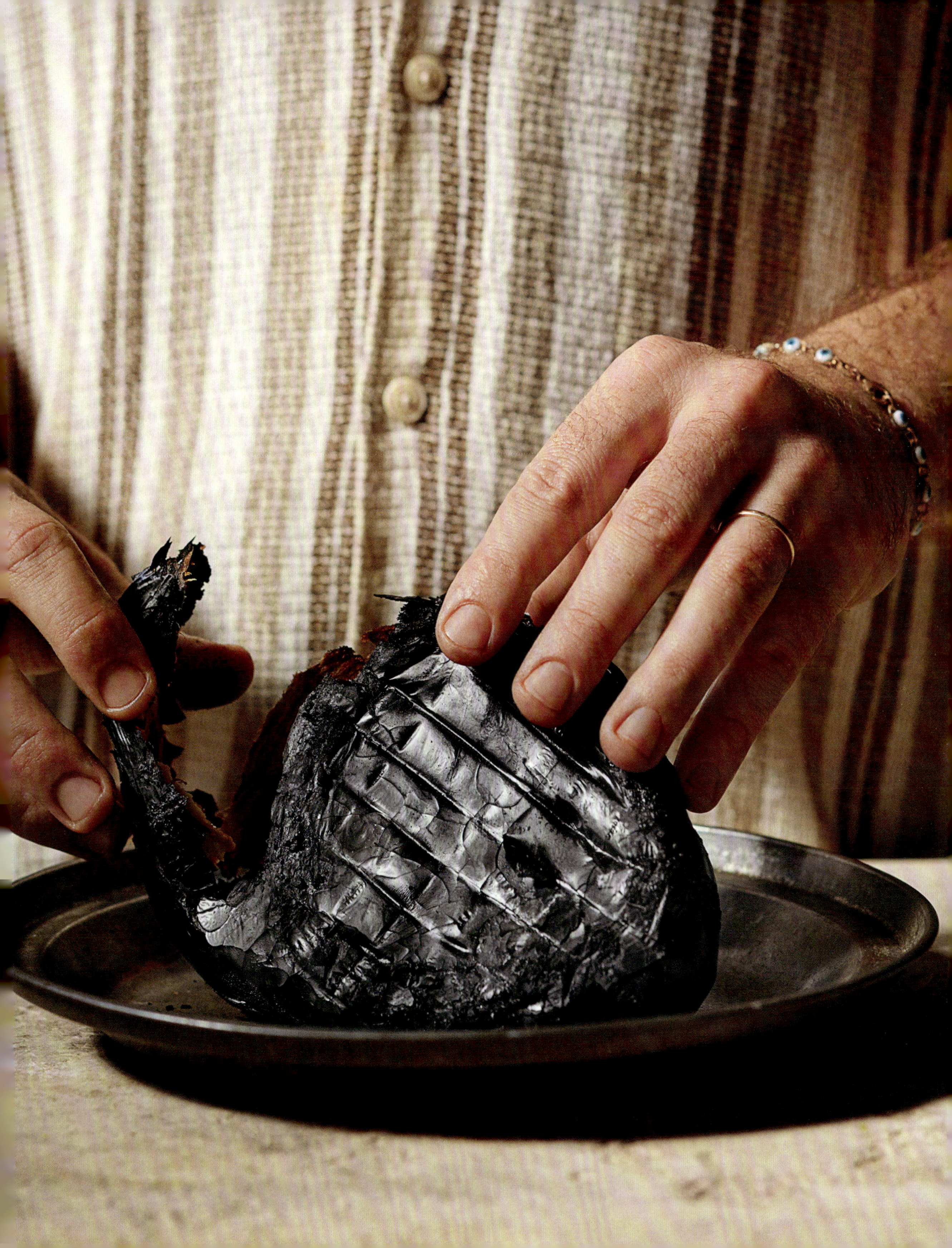

charred eggplant
with thick tahini

charred eggplant
with labneh,
zhug & dukkah

charred eggplant
with chopped salad
& hard-boiled egg

ESSENTIAL TIPS (FOR ALL CHARRED EGGPLANTS):

Why to keep the eggplant stem:
Leaving the stem attached not only keeps the eggplant looking whole and royal, but it also makes it easier to transfer to a plate.

12 minutes without flipping. When the skin of the second side is burnt and flaky and the flesh is soft, turn off the heat.

3. Place the charred eggplant into a colander in the sink standing stem up. Let the fluids of the eggplant drain as the it cools for around 15 minutes.

CHARRED EGGPLANT WITH THICK TAHINI

Yield: Serves 1 to 2, makes 1 small plate
Total time: 15 minutes

This is the original version of charred eggplant that I made for Zikki. Classic and absolutely delicious! —BEN

1 large eggplant
¼ cup The Smoothest Tahini Dip (page 55)
½ teaspoon sumac
½ teaspoon gray salt
1½ tablespoons extra virgin olive oil

1. Follow steps 1 through 3 from Charred Eggplant 101 (page 218).

2. Place the cooled, burnt eggplant flat on a cutting board. Hold the far-left side with your nondominant hand and, using a sharp chef's knife, gently remove the burnt skin from the top of the eggplant.

3. Using a spoon, gently scoop the eggplant flesh to detach it from the burnt skin on the bottom, leaving the rest of the skin intact to serve as a bowl for the flesh.

4. Spread the tahini dip evenly onto a plate. Leaving the stem of the eggplant attached, move the eggplant to the small serving plate on top of the tahini.

5. Finish by sprinkling the eggplant with the sumac and salt and drizzling with the olive oil.

recipes continue

veggie bites

Charred Eggplant with Chopped Salad & Hard-boiled Egg

Yield: Serves 1 to 2, makes 1 small plate
Total time: 25 minutes
Special tools: Microplane

This dish is the perfect breakfast salad. Quick, easy, satisfying, and a staple at our home! —BEN

1 large eggplant
1 hard-boiled egg
¼ cup When in Doubt Chopped Salad (page 139)
½ teaspoon gray salt
1½ tablespoons extra virgin olive oil
1 heaping tablespoon The Smoothest Tahini Dip (optional, page 55)

1. Follow steps 1 through 3 from Charred Eggplant 101 (page 218).

2. Place the cooled, burnt eggplant on a cutting board so that it is lying flat. Place your nondominant hand on one side of the eggplant and, using a sharp chef's knife with your dominant hand, gently run the knife directly under the skin from the opposite end to remove the burnt outer layer of skin from the cooked eggplant flesh.

3. Using a spoon, gently scoop the eggplant flesh to detach it from the burnt skin on the bottom, but leave the remaining skin of the eggplant intact as a sort of bowl to contain the flesh.

4. Leaving the stem of the eggplant attached, move the eggplant to the small serving plate.

5. Using a Microplane, grate the hard-boiled egg onto the side of the eggplant. Plate the chopped salad next to the charred eggplant and hard-boiled egg.

6. Finish the eggplant by sprinkling it with the salt, drizzling with the olive oil, and dolloping with the tahini dip (if desired).

CHARRED EGGPLANT WITH LABNEH, ZHUG & DUKKAH

Yield: Serves 1 to 2, makes 1 small plate
Total time: 25 minutes

This eggplant is a little fancier but all the more fun. —BEN

1 large eggplant
¼ cup Labneh Spread (page 84)
1 tablespoon My Grandfather's Zhug (page 49)
1 tablespoon Dukkah (page 156)
1½ tablespoons extra virgin olive oil
¼ teaspoon gray salt

1. Follow steps 1 through 3 from Charred Eggplant 101 (page 218).

2. Place the cooled, burnt eggplant on a cutting board so that it is lying flat. Place your nondominant hand on one side of the eggplant and, using a sharp chef's knife with your dominant hand, gently run the knife directly under the skin from the opposite end to remove the burnt outer layer of skin from the cooked eggplant flesh.

3. Using a spoon, gently scoop the eggplant flesh to detach it from the burnt skin on the bottom, but leave the remaining skin of the eggplant intact as a sort of bowl to contain the flesh.

4. Using a large, wide spoon, evenly spread the labneh onto a small plate. Leaving the stem of the eggplant attached, place the eggplant on top of the labneh.

5. Dollop the zhug on the side and evenly sprinkle the dukkah on top of the eggplant. Finish with the olive oil and salt. Serve and enjoy!

veggie bites

zikki's eggplant

This is my favorite way to eat eggplant, ever. Charred to perfection, this beast is then loaded with tangy tomato seeds, quick-pickled chilies, and extra virgin olive oil. Make sure that you have some pita or other bread to mop up all the juices or you'll be licking the plate clean. I promise. —*zikki*

Serve it with: Pita (page 109)
Yield: Serves 1 to 2, makes 1 small plate
Total time: 25 minutes

For the Charred Eggplant:

1 large eggplant

3 Campari tomatoes

1½ tablespoons extra virgin olive oil

½ teaspoon gray salt

For the Quick-Pickled Chili:

1 long green hot chili, sliced into really thin rounds

Juice of 1 lemon

½ teaspoon gray salt

1. Follow steps 1 through 3 from Charred Eggplant 101 (page 218). Place the eggplant on a small plate and set aside.

2. Quick-pickle the chili: In a small bowl (or jar), add the chili, lemon juice, and salt. Toss and set aside.

3. Place the cooled, burnt eggplant on a cutting board so that it is lying flat. Place your nondominant hand on the far side and, using a sharp chef's knife with your dominant hand, gently run the knife directly under the skin on the opposite end to remove the burnt outer layer of skin from the cooked eggplant flesh.

4. Using a spoon, gently scoop the eggplant flesh to detach it from the burnt skin on the bottom, but leave the remaining skin of the eggplant intact as a sort of bowl to contain the flesh.

5. Leaving the stem of the eggplant attached, place the peeled, charred eggplant on a small plate.

6. Cut the bases off the tomatoes, squeeze their seeds onto the eggplant, and discard the remaining tomato shell (or use it for something else). Place the quick-pickled chili pieces on top of the eggplant and add a few spoonfuls of the spicy chili and lemon juice mixture.

7. Finish the eggplant by drizzling it with the olive oil and sprinkling with the salt.

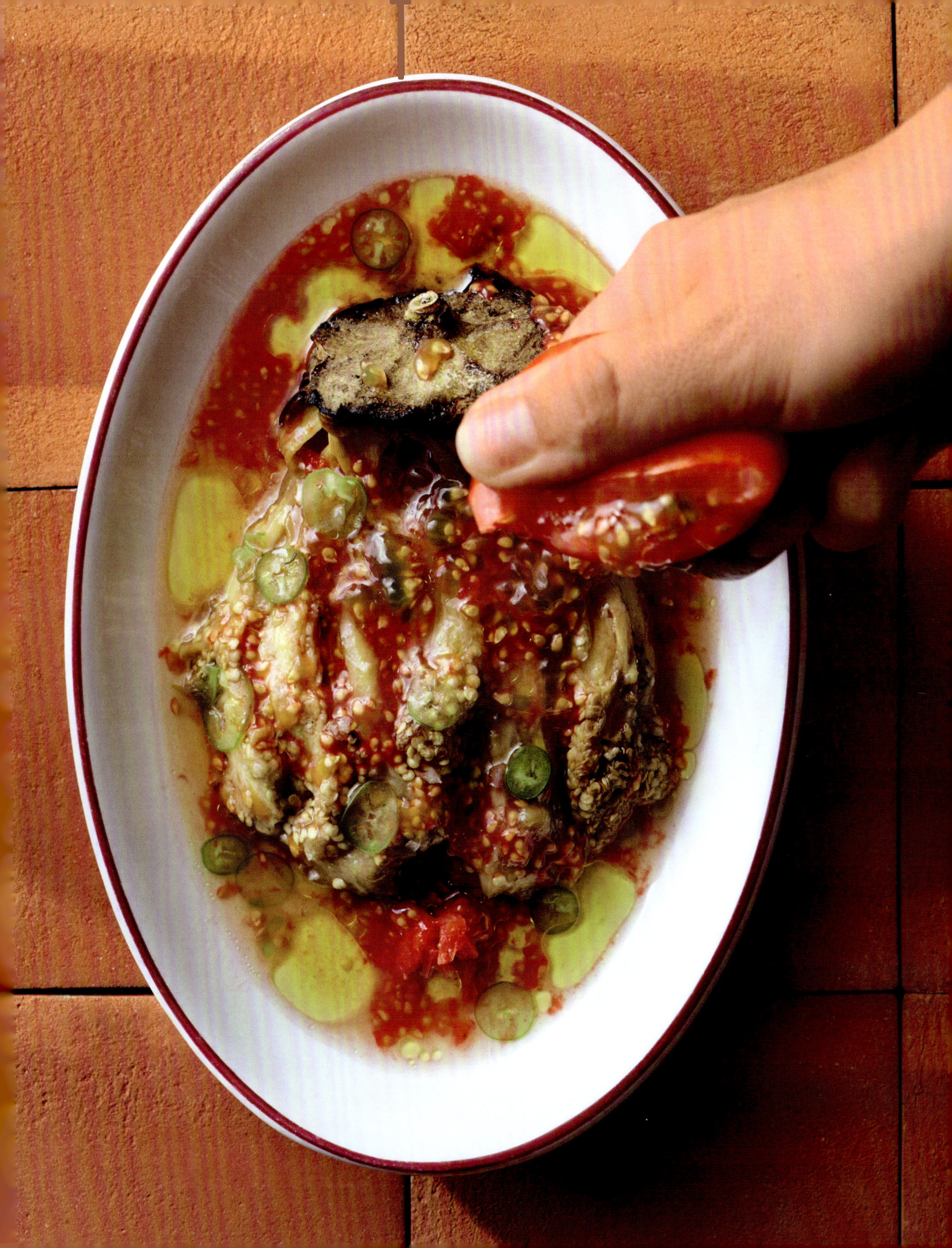

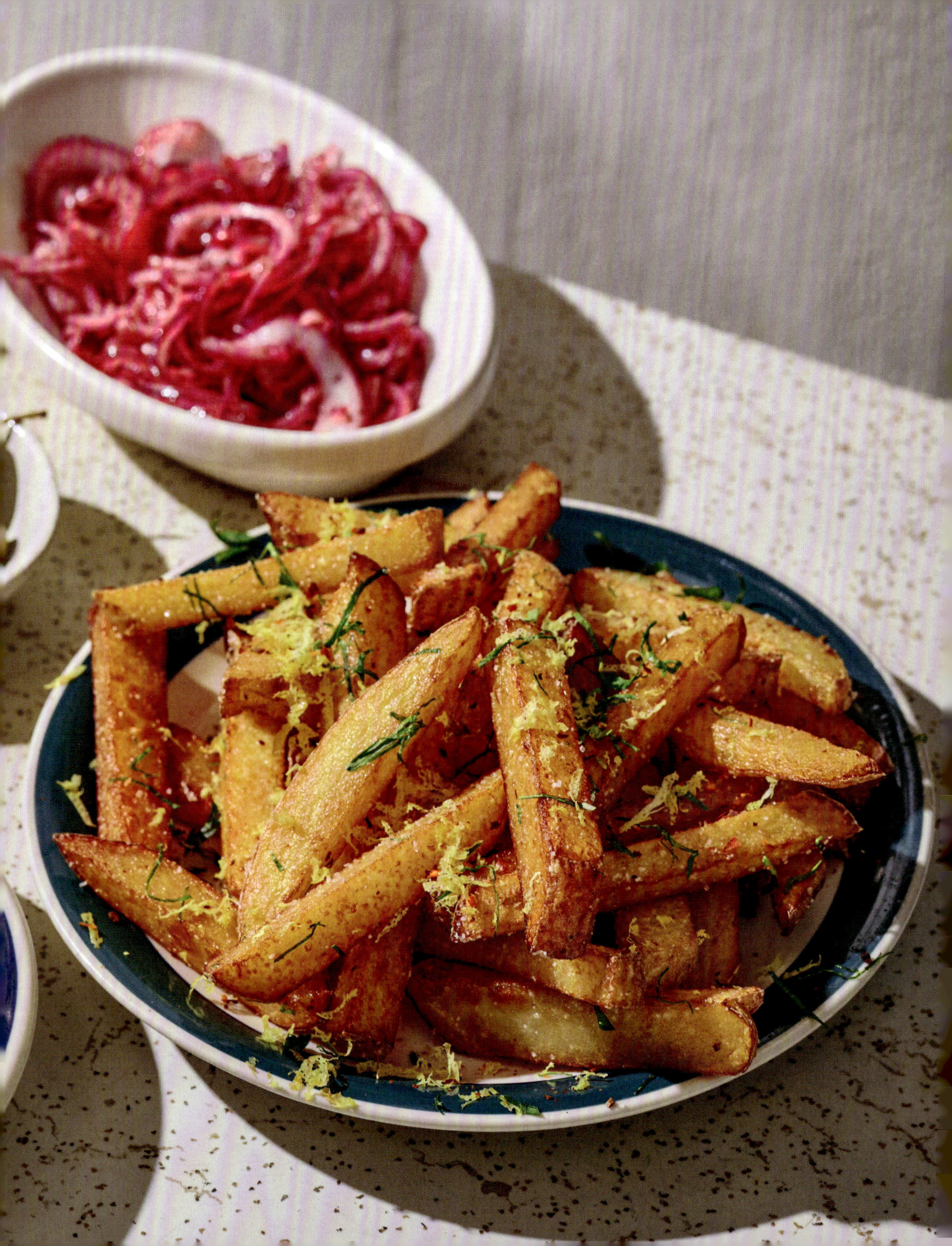

VETRENA fries

When I worked for Eyal Shani's restaurant in Tel Aviv, there was a place next door called Vetrena. It was a high-end burger and hot dog spot that was known for its zesty french fries. To this day, I still dream about those fries, which were tossed in copious amounts of herbs, garlic, and lemon zest. They had a beautiful tang and an excellent kick. I've recreated them in this recipe—I often make french fries at home when I'm done frying schnitzel and have leftover oil. My girls absolutely love them. —BEN

Serve it with: Falafel (page 215), Uncle Tal's Lentil Masabacha (page 79), red onions tossed with a pinch of sumac and gray salt

Yield: Serves 4, makes 2 small plates

Total time: 50 minutes

Special tools: Dutch oven, digital kitchen thermometer

---

4 large Idaho potatoes, peeled

1 quart canola oil, for frying

½ teaspoon fine sea salt

Zest of 2 lemons

1 garlic clove, grated

¼ bunch of cilantro, finely chopped

½ teaspoon gray salt

Freshly cracked black pepper, for garnish

---

1. Using a sharp chef's knife, cut the potatoes into ½-inch-thick uniform sticks.

2. Place the potatoes into a large bowl and cover them with cold water. Allow the potatoes to soak for at least 30 minutes to remove the excess starch.

3. Drain and thoroughly dry the potatoes. The drier the potatoes, the crispier the fries!

4. In a Dutch oven, heat the oil over medium heat until it reaches 330°F (165°C) on a digital kitchen thermometer. Line a baking sheet with paper towels.

5. Fry the potatoes in small batches for 3 to 4 minutes until partially cooked. Transfer with a slotted spoon to the baking sheet to drain. Repeat for all potatoes, allowing the oil to return to temperature between batches.

6. Turn up the heat to increase the oil temperature to 375°F (190°C). Fry the potatoes in small batches for 2 to 3 minutes, or until golden. Remove with a slotted spoon, place on the baking sheet, and season with fine sea salt. Repeat until all potatoes are fried.

7. Toss fries evenly with lemon zest, garlic, cilantro, gray salt, and pepper. Serve immediately.

Safta's Skinny Stuffed Grape Leaves

I've never met anyone who doesn't like stuffed grape leaves. They are incredibly delicious and come in such a variety of flavors. They are also a substantial snack due to the rice. Here in the US, you will find them mostly in the deli section at the supermarket or in cans, and most of them are pretty thick. On one of our trips to the north of Israel we met Jalila, who taught my family and me how to make stuffed grape leaves as they should be. The rule of thumb is to roll them thinner in width than your pinky. The secret? Always use LESS filling than you think. —ben

Serve it with: The Smoothest Tahini Dip (page 55), Labneh (page 82), Fattoush Salad (page 173)

Yield: Serves 7 to 10, makes 60 grape leaves

Total time: 2 hours 30 minutes

For the Filling:

- 1 cup rice
- 2 tablespoons finely chopped flat-leaf parsley
- 2 tablespoons finely chopped cilantro
- 2 tablespoons finely chopped mint
- 2 Campari tomatoes, finely chopped
- ¼ celery rib
- ¼ onion, finely chopped
- 1½ teaspoons baharat
- 1½ teaspoons gray salt

1. Make the filling: Soak the rice in hot water in a medium heatproof bowl for 20 minutes. Drain and transfer the rice to a small bowl.

2. In a medium bowl, combine the parsley, cilantro, mint, tomatoes, celery, onion, and rice. Add the baharat and salt and toss the ingredients together.

3. Assemble the stuffed grape leaves: Submerge the grape leaves in water and soak for 15 minutes so that they are easier to separate. Drain and separate the leaves. Organize your grape leaf filling station, with the rice mixture ready to go in a bowl and the grape leaves neatly stacked on the side!

4. Working on one leaf at a time, lay the leaf flat on a cutting board with the textured side facing up and the stem side closest to you. Place a thin layer of the rice filling (a little more than a teaspoon) along the stem-side edge of the grape leaf. Fold the left and right sides of the leaf over the filling and roll the grape leaf away from you, continuing to tuck the left and right sides as you roll it into a cigar shape. It should be tight but not too tight so that the rice has room to expand as it cooks. Set the filled grape leaf aside and repeat filling and folding until all the filling is used.

For the Grape Leaves:

60 grape leaves, washed and stemless

3 to 5 lemons, thinly sliced (to line the bottom of the pan)

For the Pomegranate-Molasses Mixture:

1 teaspoon gray salt

1 tablespoon pomegranate molasses

5. Make the pomegranate-molasses mixture: In a small bowl, combine 1 cup of water, the salt, and the pomegranate molasses. Set aside.

6. In a large, wide, and shallow pan, neatly arrange the lemon slices in one layer across the bottom. Neatly arrange the grape leaves in rows, seam side down and on top of the lemons, covering the full surface area of the pot.

7. Pour the pomegranate-molasses mixture over the arranged grape leaves in the pot until it covers them by ½ inch. Bring the water to a boil, then turn the heat down so that it remains at a low simmer. Cover and cook for 1 hour, or until all the liquid has evaporated.

8. After 1 hour, remove the pot from the heat and let rest with the lid closed for an additional 30 minutes. Serve.

Essential Tips:

Serving tips: This is a great dish to make in the morning as it can be ready for lunch and then served again as a small-plate appetizer for dinner. Traditionally, you can keep the grape leaves in the pot you cooked them in out of the refrigerator for an entire day due to the presence of the acidity in the dish. It will only get more delicious as the day goes on and the flavors marry.

Pomegranate-molasses mixture: If you do not have pomegranate molasses, use pomegranate juice.

Amit's Fizzy Veggie Mix

The students Zikki and I went to school with in Bra were extraordinarily talented, creative, and gastronomically inquisitive. One Saturday morning, we joined our friends Amit and Daphna for breakfast with their little baby girl, Lily. Within the first five minutes, Amit brought out several jars from his fermented vegetable collection. Zikki and I were in a BIG fermentation phase and had just hosted our first fermentation workshop, so we were eager to taste his treats. There was one mix that Amit made that sent Zikki over the moon—it was a jar of fizzy and crunchy carrots, celery, and turnips. To this day, whenever we travel to Israel, we always stop to visit Amit. And every time, Zikki peeks into his refrigerator to see what he's got fizzing away.

If you've never had fermented celery or turnip, we recommend that you make this recipe immediately. We serve this mix as a snack at all of our events and to accompany martinis.

Before you start on this glorious bacterial adventure, read our notes on fermentation (see page 236). It will help. We promise.

—Ben & Zikki

Serve it with: Welcome Olives (page 39), Chopped Liver, Better Than Your Grandma's (page 73), Falafel (page 215)

Yield: Four 32-ounce jars

Total time: 40 minutes (active time), plus 11 days for fermentation

Special tools: 4 fermentation weights, four 32-ounce sterilized wide-mouth mason jars (see page 72)

For the Brine:

10 teaspoons (60 grams) fine sea salt

For the Mixture:

8 small carrots, peeled and cut into ½-inch rounds

8 celery ribs, sliced into ½-inch pieces

5 small purple-and-white turnips, peeled and cut into ½-inch cubes

1. Make the brine: In a medium pot, bring 1 quart of water to a boil. Add the salt and stir to dissolve. Then add an additional 1 quart of cold water and stir again to combine. Set aside. You can make the brine ahead of time or even the day before you start your ferment!

2. In a large bowl, add the carrots, celery, and turnips and toss to combine.

3. Assemble the jars: To the bottom of each of four mason jars, add 1 garlic clove, half of a jalapeño, 1 bay leaf, and 1 teaspoon whey (if using). Divide the vegetable mixture evenly among the jars, tightly packing the vegetables and leaving about 1 inch of headspace at the top of each jar. Place a fermentation weight into each jar to hold your veggies down.

recipe and ingredients continue

amit's fizzy
veggie mix

hot-pink turnips & beets

my dad's fermented cucumbers

4 garlic cloves, crushed

2 jalapeños, halved lengthwise

4 bay leaves

4 teaspoons whey (optional, see page 237)

4. Pour the brine into each jar, fully submerging the vegetables and covering the top of the weight with an additional ¼ inch of brine. It is important that the vegetables remain submerged in the brine so that there is a protective layer from outside bacteria.

5. Seal your jars and place them in a dark place to rest, such as a pantry cabinet. After 24 hours, "burp" the jars by slightly opening the lid then closing it. Place the jars back into the dark resting place and repeat the "burping" process for 3 consecutive days.

6. On day 4, after burping the jar, taste the brine. If it has soured to your liking, place the jars into the refrigerator for at least 1 week to finish the fermentation.

7. After 1 week in the refrigerator, the ferment is ready to be eaten and served.

fermentation schedule

Day 1	Day 2	Day 3	Day 4
• Make the brine	• "Burp" the jar	• "Burp" the jar	• "Burp" the jar
• Load the jars with vegetables and brine	• Put the jar back into the dark place for 24 hours	• Put the jar back into the dark place for 24 hours	• Taste the liquid. If soured to your liking, move to the refrigerator.
• Seal the jars and put into a dark place for 24 hours			

my dad's fermented cucumbers

One of the greatest pleasures in coming home to visit my parents in Israel has to be their kitchen. It is not grand or outrageous, but simply perfect—always loaded with a vast array of vegetables fresh from the market, a cheese drawer filled with local goat cheeses, and a never-ending row of freshly toasted nuts hanging out in quart containers ready to be snacked on. At any point, you can stand over the sink looking out into the garden at a cactus that has been in my family for over a decade, with my dad's fermented pickles on the windowsill, bubbling away and souring into the following week's treat!

Typically when Zikki and I ferment things at home, we add a bay leaf or grape leaf to the mixture. The tannin in the leaves keeps the vegetables crisp as they transform. But my dad taught us that we can also use dried chickpeas to serve the same purpose! They're his secret for extra-crisp pickles. —ben

Serve it with: Chopped Liver, Better Than Your Grandma's (page 73), Chicken Shawarma Salad (page 153)

Yield: Three or four 32-ounce jars

Total time: 30 minutes (active time), plus 11 days for fermentation

Special tools: 3 or 4 fermentation weights, three or four 32-ounce sterilized wide-mouth mason jars (see page 72)

For the Brine:

5 teaspoons (30 grams) fine sea salt

For the Cucumbers:

9 garlic cloves, smashed

9 dried chickpeas

1 bunch of dill

2 pounds kirby or Persian cucumbers, sliced into ½-inch rounds or kept whole

1. **Make the brine:** In a medium pot, bring 1 quart of water to a boil. Add the salt and stir to dissolve. Then add an additional 1 quart of cold water and stir again to combine. Set aside. You can make the brine ahead of time or even the day before you start your ferment!

2. **Assemble the jars:** Add 3 garlic cloves, 3 chickpeas, and one-third of the dill to the bottom of each of the three mason jars (depending on the size of your cucumbers and whether you decide to keep them whole, you may need an extra jar). Divide the cucumbers (whole or sliced) evenly among the jars, tightly packing them in and leaving about 1 inch of headspace at the top of each jar. Place a fermentation weight into each jar to hold your cucumbers down.

3. Pour the brine into each jar, fully submerging the cucumbers and covering the top of the weight with an additional ¼ inch of brine. It is important that the cucumbers remain submerged in the brine so that there is a protective layer from outside bacteria.

recipe continues

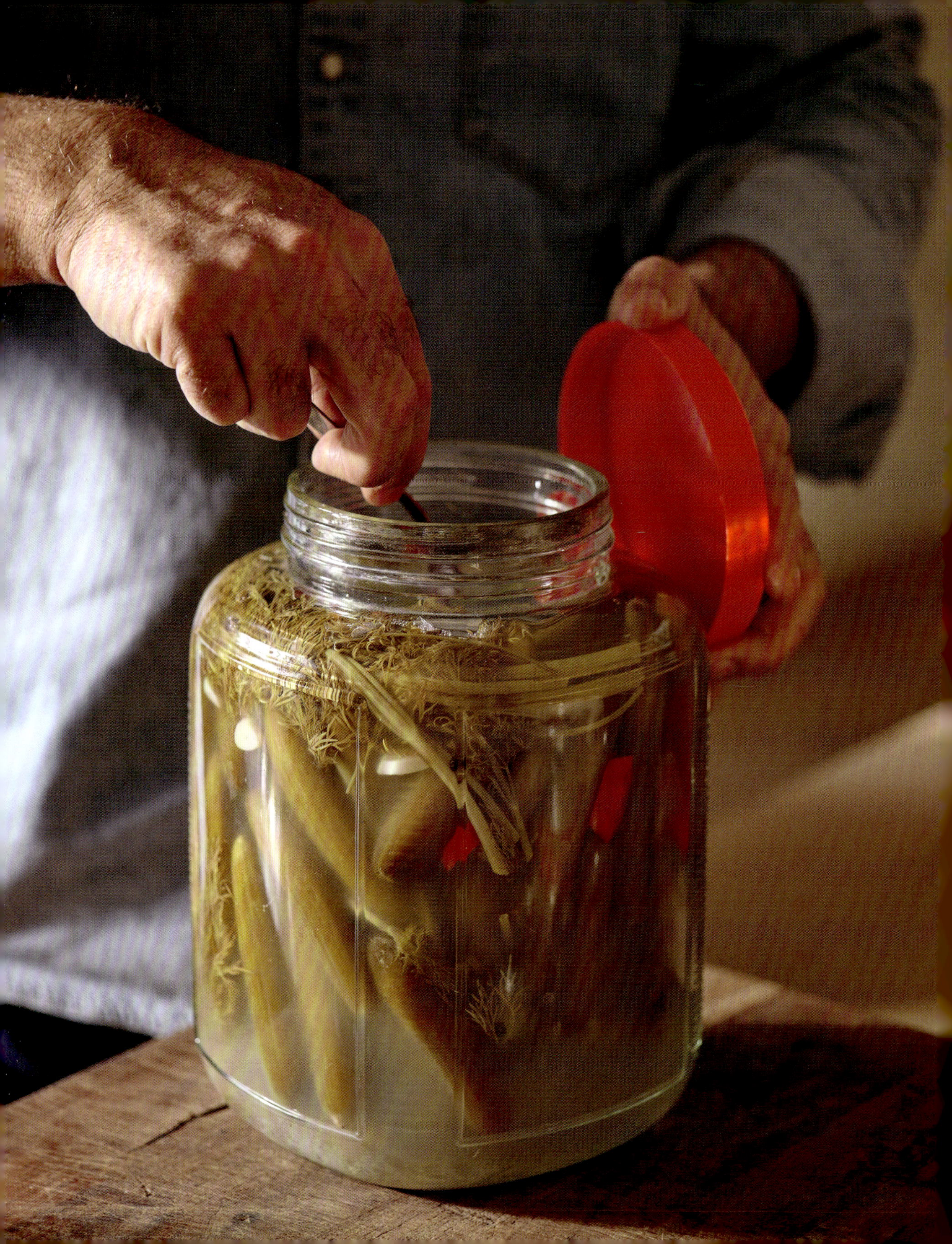

4. Seal your jars and place them in a dark place to rest, such as a pantry cabinet. After 24 hours, "burp" the jars by slightly opening the lid then closing it. Place the jars back into the dark resting place and repeat the "burping" process for 3 consecutive days.

5. On day 4, after burping the jar, taste the brine. If it has soured to your liking, place the jars into the refrigerator for at least 1 week to finish the fermentation.

6. After 1 week in the refrigerator, the pickles are ready to be eaten and served.

Essential Tip:

Keep the leftover brine! You may have some leftover brine depending on the type of jar you use for the pickles. Feel free to use it to pickle other things, such as Amit's Fizzy Veggie Mix (page 230)!

fear not—go forth & ferment

fermentation rules to live by

As I scoop a big bite of homemade sauerkraut into my mouth, my hope is that this list of rules to live by will inspire you to make fermentation part of your day-to-day life! Fermentation, which gives us all kinds of fizzy treats, is meant to be done casually when you have an abundance of fresh and seasonal vegetables! Not only is fermentation a great solution for preventing spoilage, fermented foods are an incredibly healthy thing to add to your diet! #probioticsbaby —*zikki*

1. **Go organic:** We recommend using exclusively organic vegetables. This allows your fermentation project to run smoothly with no start-up setbacks.

2. **Keep veggies crisp:** We use bay leaves and dried chickpeas in our ferments, but other people use grape leaves or cherry leaves. These leaves and legumes release tannins (a compound found in wine that gives it a natural dry tartness) into the mixture and preserve the crisp crunch of the vegetables. If you *don't* use one of these tannin(ators), you will be dealing with mushy, soggy, weird, and icky old vegetables in salt water.

3. **Use a kitchen scale:** It is really important to use a scale when making your brine in order to measure out exactly how much salt you will need. Having too much or not enough salt will affect the way the lactic bacteria develop in the fermentation!

4. **Pack the vegetables:** It is important that the vegetables remain submerged in the brine as that is their protective layer from outside bacteria. In the brine, the sugars from the vegetables combine with the salt to create lactic acid, which in turn preserves the vegetables, changing their flavor profile and texture forever.

5. **Leave room at the top of the jars:** This space is for your fermentation weight, which will keep your vegetables submerged in the brine (and away from icky bacteria) as they begin to ferment. The term *fermentation weight* quite literally refers to a heavy piece of glass

(you can order this online) specifically shaped to hold down vegetables in a jar during the process of fermentation. But a fancy weight isn't necessary—I sometimes use a piece of celery, which I break in half and create an X at the top of the jar to keep the vegetables submerged.

6. Ensure a successful start: To make sure you have a successful growth of bacteria, or "activation," we recommend adding a tablespoon of homemade whey to your raw vegetable and brine mixture. A great time to ferment is after you make homemade Labneh (page 82). Whey is the white-looking liquid released when the yogurt is combined with salt and left to hang. You can leave out the whey if you are confident about the quality and freshness of your veggies.

7. Don't refrigerate right away: We recommend fermenting your mixture for 3 days before putting your jars in the refrigerator. Refrigerating does not stop the fermentation, but it drastically slows it down. After 3 days of major transformation, a week in the refrigerator allows the fermenting process to finish slowly and tenderly. Ferments can last in your refrigerator for up to 6 months.

HOT-PINK TURNIPS & BEETS

Our love affair with this incredible pink goody started with its mesmerizing hue. Tell me you wouldn't be interested in tasting something that is naturally hot pink? No? We used to buy fermented turnips for all our events. They were tangy, salty, and gorgeous, and flew off the table like hotcakes. So, we started making them ourselves—and the result? To die for. Root vegetables were born to be combined with salt in water and left to do their thing.

Try this . . . At the beginning of your meal, serve a small plate of these hot-pink turnips, a few sliced homemade pickles (page 233), and a small bowl of Amit's Fizzy Veggie Mix (page 230) and watch people snack away. There is nothing more satisfying than something crunchy, juicy, light, and salty to start a meal. —BEN & ZIKKI

Serve it with: Welcome Olives (page 39), Cucumber, Dill, Labneh & Onion Salad (page 165)

Yield: Two 32-ounce jars

Total time: 30 minutes (active time), plus 11 days for fermentation

Special tools: 2 fermentation weights, two 32-ounce sterilized wide-mouth mason jars (page 72)

FOR THE BRINE:

5 teaspoons (30 grams) fine sea salt

FOR THE TURNIPS AND BEETS:

2 medium beets, peeled and cut into ½-inch cubes

4 purple-and-white turnips, peeled and cut into ½-inch cubes

2 garlic cloves, peeled

1 jalapeño, halved lengthwise

2 bay leaves

2 teaspoons whey (optional, see page 237)

1. Make the brine: In a large pot, bring 1 quart of water to a boil. Add the salt and stir to dissolve. Then add an additional 1 quart of cold water and stir again to combine. Set aside.

2. In a large bowl, add the beets and turnips and toss to combine.

3. Add 1 garlic clove, half of the jalapeño, 1 bay leaf, and 1 teaspoon of the whey (if using) to each mason jar. Divide and pack the beet and turnip mixture evenly among the jars, leaving about 1 inch of headspace. Place a fermentation weight in each jar to keep the vegetables submerged.

4. Pour brine into each jar to submerge vegetables, covering the weight with ¼ inch of brine to protect against bacteria.

5. Seal the jars and place them in a dark place, such as a pantry cabinet. After 24 hours, "burp" the jars by slightly opening the lid then closing it. Place the jars back into the dark resting place and repeat the "burping" process for 3 consecutive days.

6. On day 4, after burping the jar, taste the brine. If it is sufficiently sour, refrigerate jars for at least 1 week to finish the fermentation.

7. After 1 week in the refrigerator, the turnips and beets are ready to be eaten and served.

ANIMAL BITES

Proteins are a funny thing in our house. We serve them sparingly, and always family-style, so that you can share, enjoy, and relish with your lovers. This chapter is broken into two sections: raw and cooked. The raw treats are delicate yet exhilarating, while the cooked classics are absolute comfort staples.

We prioritize quality over quantity—hence the wild number of raw dishes swimming through this section. Because we purchase the best protein possible, we feel comfortable eating it in its raw form. In Israel, eating raw meat and fish is very common and highly celebrated. Whether it is a crudo at a restaurant in Tel Aviv or a gorgeous kubenia from a Druze community in a small village in northern Israel, we just love it raw.

Each dish in this chapter deserves the spotlight. If you happen to be hosting a little soiree, we recommend choosing three dips, two salads, and one animal bite for the evening ahead!

—ben & zikki

recipes

RAW
tuna & grapes
akko crudo
tuna nectarine tartare
scallop carpaccio
mackerel, cucumber & arugula crudo
arabic ceviche
beef tartare
kubenia

cooked
ben's schnitzel fingers
kebab
fried barbouniot
ny strip steak
stuffed onions
shrimp in grated tomato butter

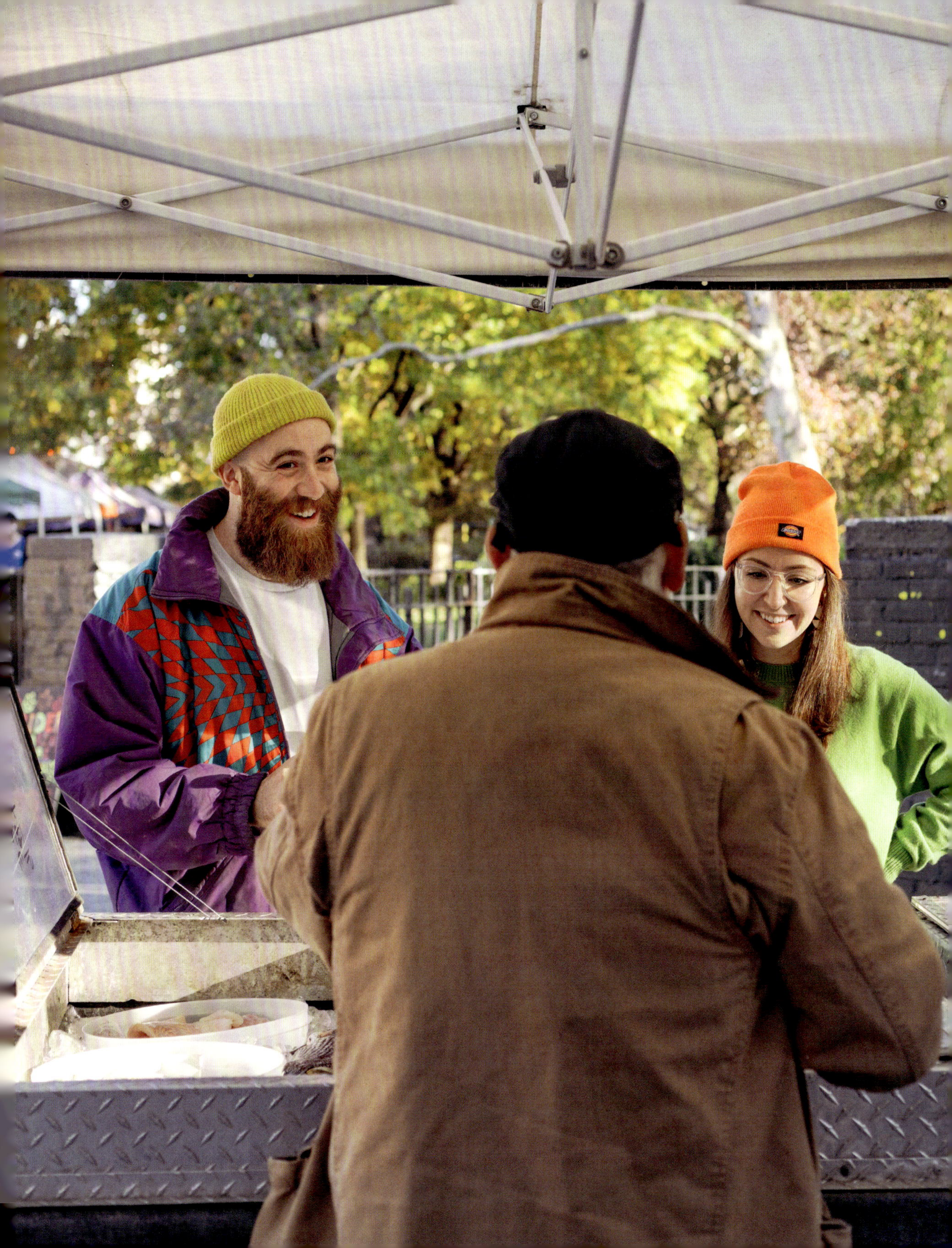

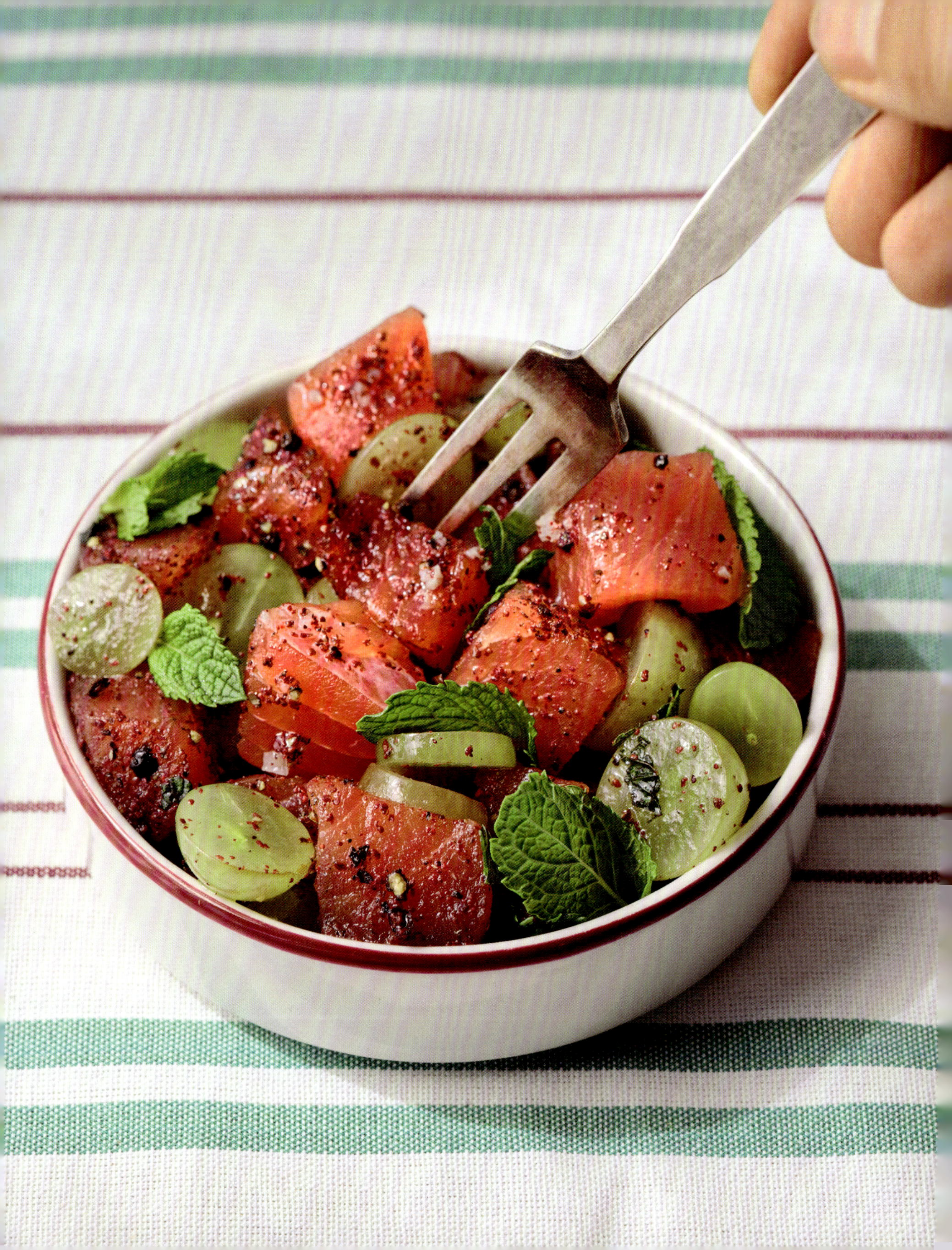

TUNA & GRAPES

raw

Last summer, when Zikki and I were in Israel, my baby brother asked me for a unique birthday present. He wanted us to prepare a bountiful brunch for him and his friends, so we did exactly that. Zikki and I gathered the most outrageous and fresh ingredients from all our favorite producers in Israel. At the time, the grapes in the market were explosively sweet and just calling to be used. When I originally thought about this dish, I was imagining a watermelon and grape summer salad. However, I then thought it would be much more fun to swap the watermelon for tuna, keeping the chunks of the tuna small and bite-size like the grapes. In Israel, especially, we love the combination of raw fish and fruit, as they complement each other so well. Paired with fragrant fresh mint, citrus, sumac, and a gorgeous flaky gray salt—I promise this will be a fan favorite. Plus, it is always fun to see people's reaction when they discover this is a savory dish made with tuna and not watermelon. —ben

Serve it with: Not Your Grandma's Fruit Salad (page 170), Zikki's Eggplant (page 224), Pita (page 109)

Yield: Serves 2 to 4, makes 2 small plates

Total time: 15 minutes, plus 30 minutes for curing

Special tools: wire rack

½ teaspoon fine sea salt

10 ounces tuna steak (¾ inch thick; see page 246)

16 green grapes

20 mint leaves, roughly torn into small pieces

1 teaspoon sumac

¼ teaspoon freshly cracked black pepper

½ teaspoon gray salt

1½ tablespoons extra virgin olive oil

Juice of ½ lemon (optional, see note)

1. Place a wire rack on top of a baking sheet. Sprinkle the fine sea salt over the full surface area of the tuna to begin the curing process. Place the tuna on the prepared baking sheet and put the rack in the refrigerator for 30 minutes.

2. Remove the tuna from the refrigerator and pat dry using a paper towel. Using a sharp chef's knife, cut the tuna into ½-inch cubes. The cubes should not be much bigger than the halved grapes.

3. Using a sharp chef's knife, halve 12 of the green grapes. Slice the remaining 4 grapes into ⅛-inch medallions.

4. In a medium bowl, add the grapes, tuna, mint, sumac, pepper, gray salt, olive oil, and lemon juice (if using). Toss and serve immediately.

recipe continues

ESSENTIAL TIPS:

Prep ahead of time: You can prepare the tuna ahead of time—just cut it and store it in the refrigerator until you are ready to combine it with the rest of the ingredients. But the finished dish cannot sit and wait; it must be eaten immediately for the best result!

Doubling the recipe: This recipe is meant to be an appetizer that serves 2 to 4 people. If you'd like it to be more of a substantial main dish, double the recipe so that each person is served 5 ounces of tuna. The ratio of tuna cubes to grapes should be equal, so it is best to make individual small bowls of tuna rather than combining all the ingredients to make it in one big batch. Serve with miniature forks.

Adding lemon: If you choose to use lemon in the dish, you will need to serve the dish very quickly after it is added, as it will begin to cook the tuna. To preserve the shiny, bright-pink color of the tuna, omit the lemon and simply add more sumac for additional tang.

sashimi-grade fish

In America, it is rare to find sashimi-grade fish that isn't tuna or salmon. So, if you want to eat other types of fish raw, we suggest that you find a very reliable fish market that will sell you the freshest fish. Also, if you do not want to fillet your own fish, kindly ask your butcher to fillet and remove the skin from your fish.

quick-curing the fish

When we buy fish, Ben fillets, then salts the loins before putting them into the refrigerator for 30 minutes to 1 hour for a quick cure. "Salting" the fish in this chapter means generously sprinkling fine sea salt over the entire surface area of the raw fish. Quick-curing uses salt to draw out moisture through the process of osmosis. It helps firm up and remove water from the fish, resulting in a better texture and enhanced flavor.

akko crudo

raw

When we travel to Israel, Ben goes out of his way to make sure I always feel at home. He plans incredible trips and outings to the very best restaurants, where we always end up chatting with the staff for hours over a good bottle of wine. One such experience took us to a seaside restaurant in Akko, where our friend Habibi owns an Arabic seafood restaurant. During our first meal there, he served us a crudo dish that blew my mind. He used crushed pistachios and olive oil to "marinate" the fish and layered it with regional flavors like fresh mint leaves, sliced chili, harissa, preserved lemon paste, feta, and an incredible local olive oil. The use of the crushed pistachios to coat the fish is the heartbeat of this dish. Combining the pistachio crust with the olive oil transforms the fish and nuts into one—something unexpectedly necessary and absolutely unforgettable. —zikki

Serve it with: The Best Green Salad of Your Life (page 184), Mackerel, Cucumber & Arugula Crudo (page 255), Tel Avivian Focaccia (page 113)

Yield: Serves 2 to 4, makes 2 small plates

Total time: 45 minutes

Special tools: wire rack

FOR THE RED SNAPPER:

½ teaspoon fine sea salt, for curing

1 red snapper fillet (6 to 8 ounces)

2 tablespoons raw shelled pistachios, toasted and crushed (see page 22)

1 teaspoon gray salt

2 tablespoons extra virgin olive oil

20 mint leaves

2 ounces feta, crumbled coarsely

1. Cure the snapper: Place a wire rack on top of a baking sheet. Sprinkle the fine sea salt on the full surface area of the snapper to begin the curing process. Place the snapper on the prepared rack and refrigerate for 30 minutes.

2. Remove the snapper from the refrigerator and pat dry using a paper towel. Using a sharp chef's knife, cut the snapper into ¼-inch cubes. These pieces should be slightly larger than those for a tartare.

3. In a small bowl, combine the cubed snapper, pistachios, gray salt, and olive oil. Set aside until ready to serve.

4. Quick-pickle the chili: In a separate small bowl, add the chili, gray salt, and lemon juice. Mix until the salt is dissolved. Set aside until ready to serve.

5. Prep the harissa sauce: In a separate small bowl, add the yogurt, preserved lemon paste, and harissa. Mix until fully homogeneous. Set aside until ready to serve.

recipe and ingredients continue

ANIMAL BITES

For the Quick-Pickled Chilies:

½ long green hot chili, sliced into very thin rounds

¼ teaspoon gray salt

Juice of ¼ lemon

For the Sauce:

¼ cup yogurt

1 tablespoon Preserved Lemon paste (page 57)

1½ teaspoons Harissa (page 50)

6. Add the mint leaves and quick-pickled chilies to the snapper mixture and toss.

7. Assemble the crudo: Add 1 tablespoon of the harissa sauce to each of two plates and, using a spoon, spread it evenly across the plate by pushing the round edge of the spoon against the sauce while moving the plate clockwise. Spoon the Akko crudo onto the plate and finish with some crumbled feta. Serve and enjoy immediately!

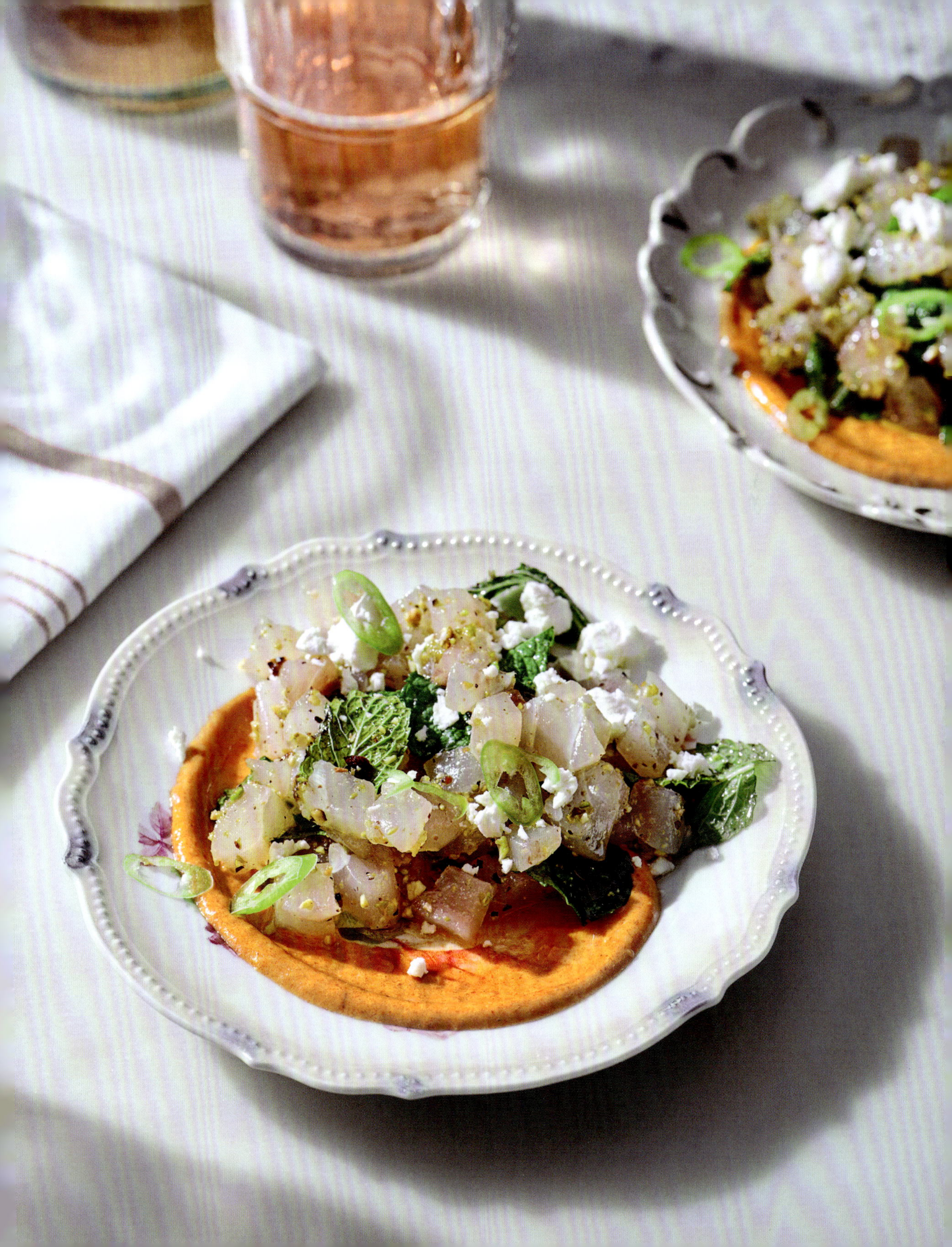

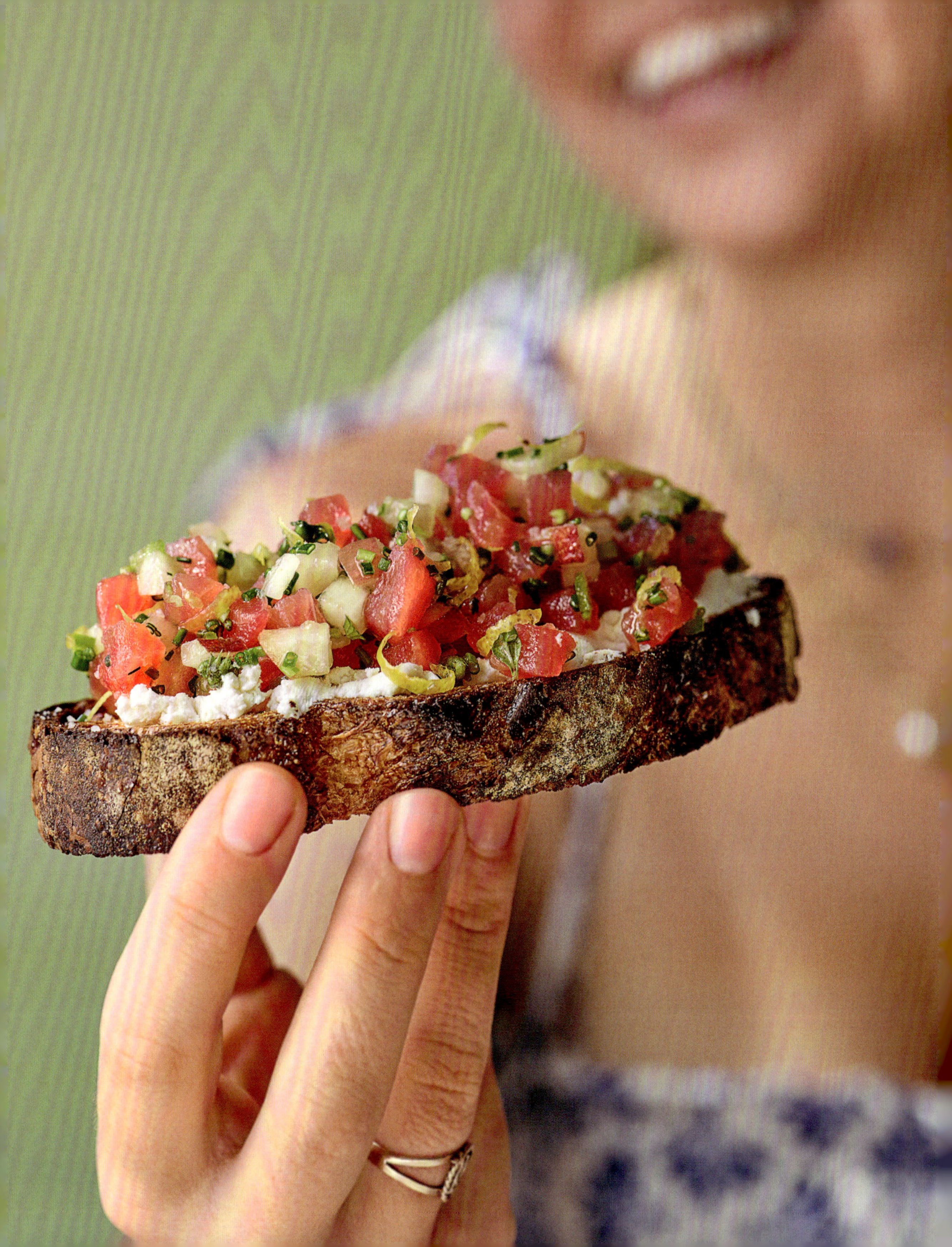

TUNA NECTARINE TARTARE

raw

Have you ever had tuna tartare served on a piece of toasted sourdough lathered in homemade labneh? Probably not unless you've spent some time in Tel Aviv. This is a very common combination of flavors and textures in that city and one we are always missing in New York. This dish makes eating raw fish casual, and I just love that because it should be. No fuss, crazy delicious, and totally out of the box. —*zikki*

Serve it with: Tuna & Grapes (page 245), Peach & Tomato Salad with Mozzarella & Basil (page 176)

Yield: Serves 2 to 4, makes 2 toasts

Total time: 15 minutes

4 ounces tuna, cut into ½-inch cubes

1 nectarine, finely diced

8 cilantro stems, finely chopped

10 chives, finely chopped

1 teaspoon finely diced long green hot chili

1 tablespoon extra virgin olive oil

Zest of 2 lemons

½ teaspoon gray salt, plus more to taste

2 slices of sourdough bread, 1-inch-thick slices

¼ cup Labneh Spread (page 84)

1. In a small bowl, combine the tuna, nectarine, cilantro stems, chives, chili, olive oil, lemon zest, and salt. Toss and adjust the salt to taste.

2. Toast the sourdough slices. Lather each slice generously with the labneh.

3. Top each slice of toast with a heaping amount of the tuna nectarine tartare and serve immediately.

scallop carpaccio

raw

When Ben and I moved back to the Lower East Side of New York City, we were obsessed with the restaurant Thai Diner. We ate there at least once a week. If you don't know this about us, we are obsessed with Thai food. A favorite dish of ours at Thai Diner is their sliced scallops, which are served as part of their raw bar menu. The first time we had it was the first time we'd tasted scallops raw, as well as the first time we had raw scallops with passion fruit. It was life-changing. I'm not sure we've ever been the same. This scallop carpaccio is our take on that dish and that especially joyous time in our life—a symbol of a new era for me personally, rediscovering the ever-evolving city I was born in and the endless (food) adventure that lies within. —*zikki*

Serve it with: Not Your Grandma's Fruit Salad (page 170), Tuna & Grapes (page 245)

Yield: Serves 2 to 4, makes 2 small plates

Total time: 15 minutes

---

4 scallops, sliced horizontally into ¼-inch medallions

2 tangerines, sectioned

Juice of 1 tangerine

1 tablespoon finely diced long green hot chili

½ teaspoon gray salt

2 passion fruits, halved

1 tablespoon extra virgin olive oil

---

1. Arrange the sliced scallops in an even layer on two small plates. Set aside.

2. In a small bowl, add the sectioned tangerines and tangerine juice, chili, and salt. Squeeze the passion fruit into the tangerine mixture and toss everything together.

3. Layer the tangerines on top of the scallops, then spoon the remaining tangerine mixture over them, distributing the chili, passion fruit pulp, and juices evenly. Drizzle each plate with ½ tablespoon of the olive oil.

ESSENTIAL TIPS:

How much sushi per scallop: Each average-sized scallop should yield about four ¼-inch pieces of sashimi.

Slicing the scallop: Place the scallop upright on a cutting board. Hold it steady with your nondominant hand and slice ¼-inch medallions in slow, assertive motions.

Sectioning the tangerine: Section the tangerine over a bowl to catch the juice for the sauce.

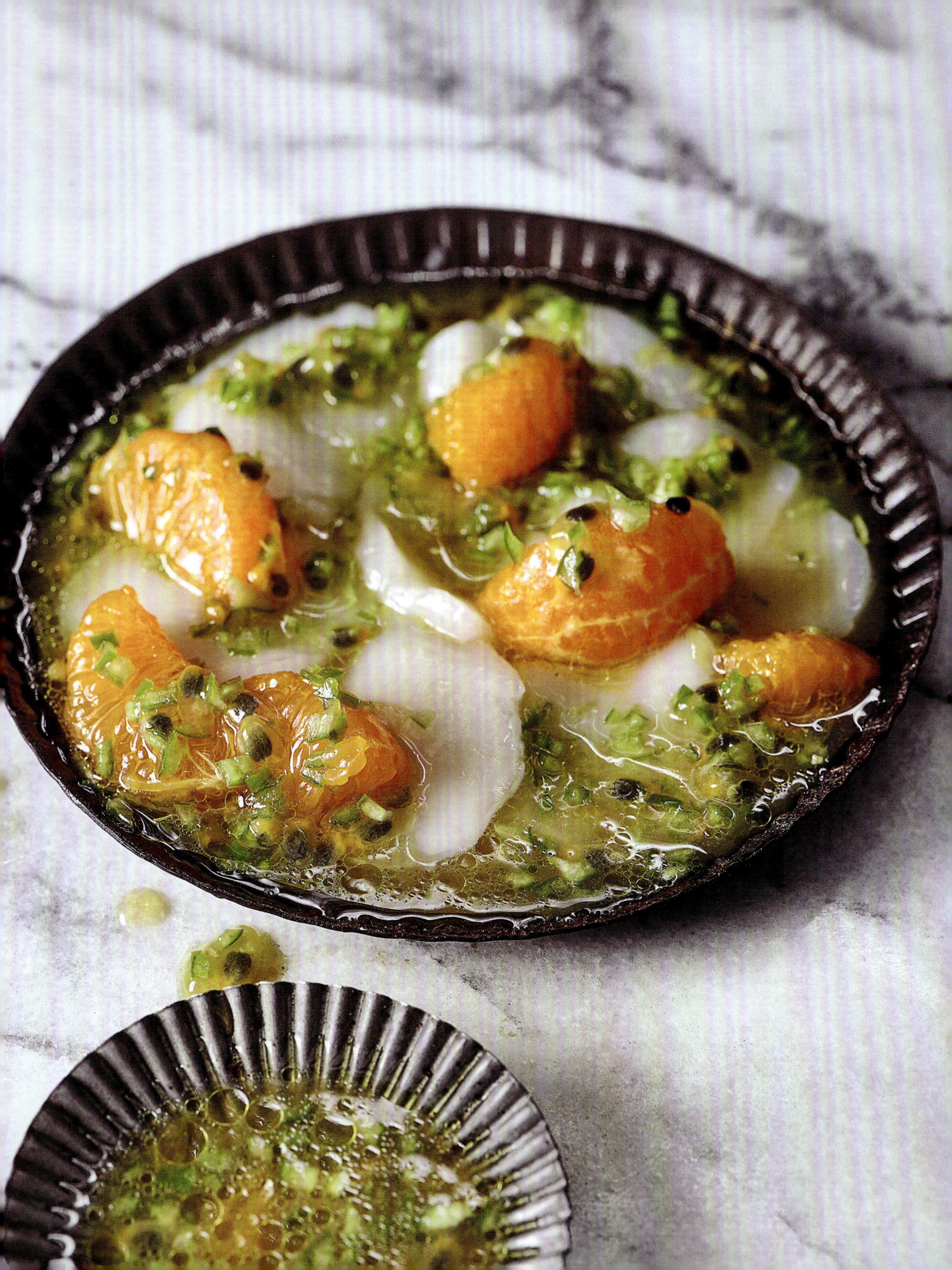

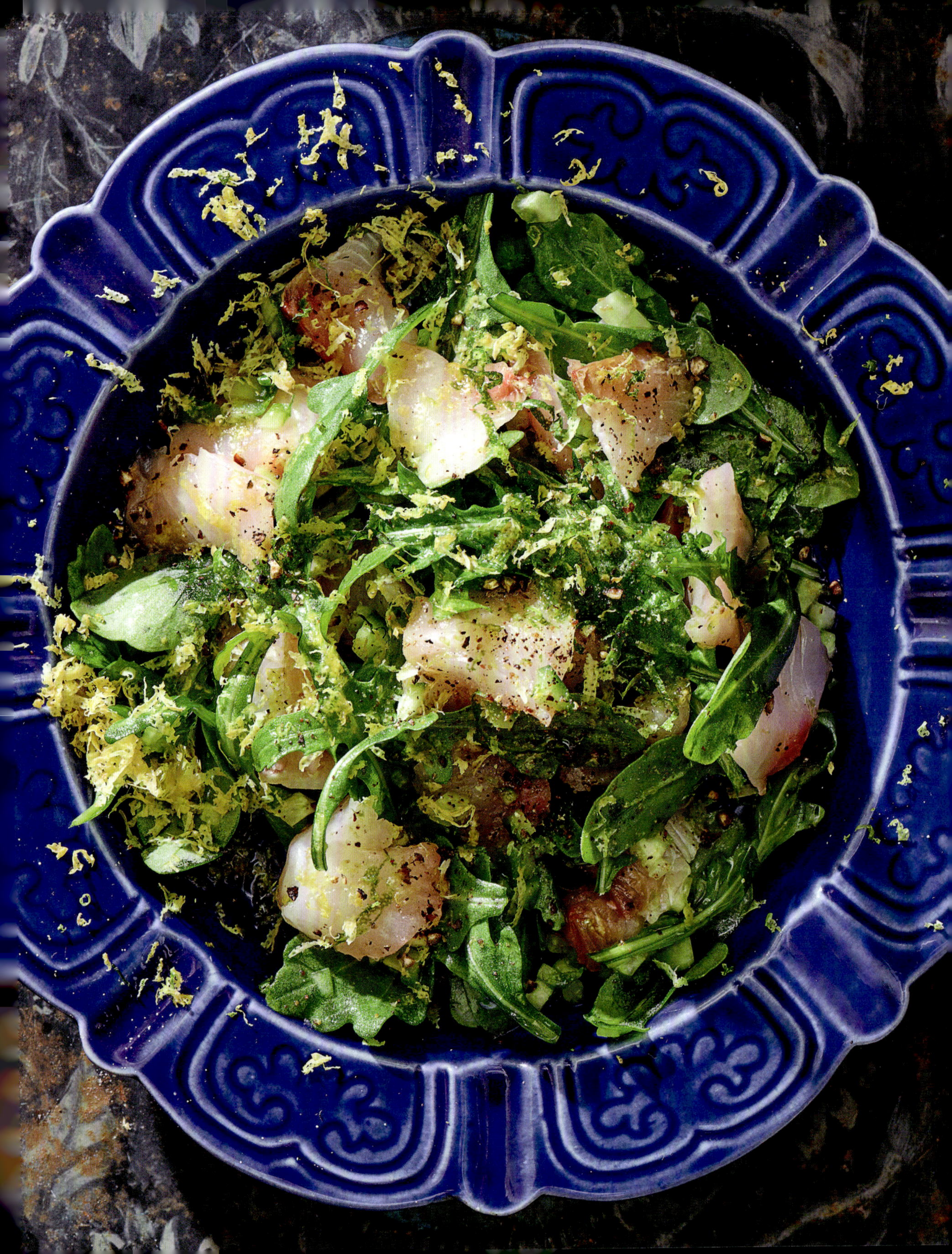

Mackerel, Cucumber & Arugula Crudo

raw

Every time Ben and I eat raw fish, we find ourselves daydreaming and thinking about opening a small place called White & Raw that serves the best white wine and raw fish dishes.

Plating and serving raw fish is truly an art form, and raw fish can be paired with absolutely anything. We created this gorgeous Mackerel, Cucumber & Arugula Crudo after taking an early-fall Sunday walk on the streets of NYC, and stopping in Aqua Best in Chinatown to pick up mackerel for a light sashimi dinner. It is simple, delicate, and a perfect addition to any menu! —*zikki*

Serve it with: A Cashew Basil Dip Everyone Will Talk About (page 99), Tel Avivian Focaccia (page 113), Charred Eggplant with Thick Tahini (page 221)

Yield: Serves 2, makes 1 to 2 small plates

Total time: 30 minutes

Special tools: wire rack

½ mackerel fillet (4 to 6 ounces)

½ teaspoon fine sea salt

1 Persian cucumber, finely diced

Zest of 1 lemon

Juice of ½ lemon

1 tablespoon extra virgin olive oil

Gray salt

Freshly cracked black pepper

2 cups baby arugula

---

1. Place a wire rack on top of a baking sheet. Sprinkle the fine sea salt on the full surface area of the mackerel to begin the curing process. Place the mackerel on the prepared baking sheet and place the rack in the refrigerator for 30 minutes.

2. Remove the mackerel from the refrigerator and pat dry using a paper towel. Using a sharp chef's knife, make thin, even slices by cutting through the loin on a slight angle and against the grain for a smoother cut. It is best to slice the fish in smooth, long strokes rather than straight down.

3. In a small bowl, add the mackerel and cucumber. Season with lemon zest and juice, olive oil, and gray salt and pepper to taste.

4. When you are ready to serve, add the baby arugula to the cucumber mixture. Toss and serve immediately.

animal bites

ARABIC CEVICHE

raw

Does anyone else get the urge to add raw fish to everything? I first felt this way during an event Zikki and I were hosting. I had made the most legendary chopped salad of all time. It was bursting with herbs, lemon, sumac, glorious summer tomatoes, and cucumbers. But I couldn't help feeling that the salad was missing raw fish, which would perfectly soak up the "juice" of the veggies.

This dish plays on a traditional citrus and herb ceviche base but comes to life with the use of my hometown favorites like mint, lemon, and sumac. This dish is a staple on our hosting menu, and we highly recommend it if you are just getting started with preparing raw fish dishes at home! —BEN

Serve it with: Labneh Spread (page 84), Fried Barbouniot (page 269), Jerusalem Bagel (page 120), Tza-Zikki (page 87)

Yield: Serves 3 to 6, makes 2 to 3 small bowls

Total time: 20 minutes

½ bunch of cilantro

½ bunch of flat-leaf parsley

½ bunch of mint

1 fluke fillet (4 to 6 ounces), cut into ¼-inch cubes

3 Persian cucumbers, finely diced

1 medium heirloom tomato, finely diced and excess juices drained

½ medium red onion, finely diced

½ teaspoon sumac

1 teaspoon gray salt

Juice of 1 lemon

2 tablespoons extra virgin olive oil

1. For each bunch of herbs, stem and stack the leaves on top of one another. Roll the leaves up like a cigar and hold the rolled leaves in one hand with your fingers tucked under. Using a sharp chef's knife, thinly slice the rolled-up leaves, working perpendicularly to the cigar shape and moving your fingers back as you cut.

2. In a medium bowl, add the chopped herbs, fluke, cucumbers, tomato, onion, sumac, salt, lemon juice, and olive oil. When you're ready to serve, toss and plate immediately in bowls, piled high.

ESSENTIAL TIP:

Timing for tossing: It is important to toss all the ingredients together just before you are ready to serve this dish. If not, you will have a pool of liquid at the bottom of each bowl, as the tomatoes and cucumbers release a lot of juice when they come into contact with salt.

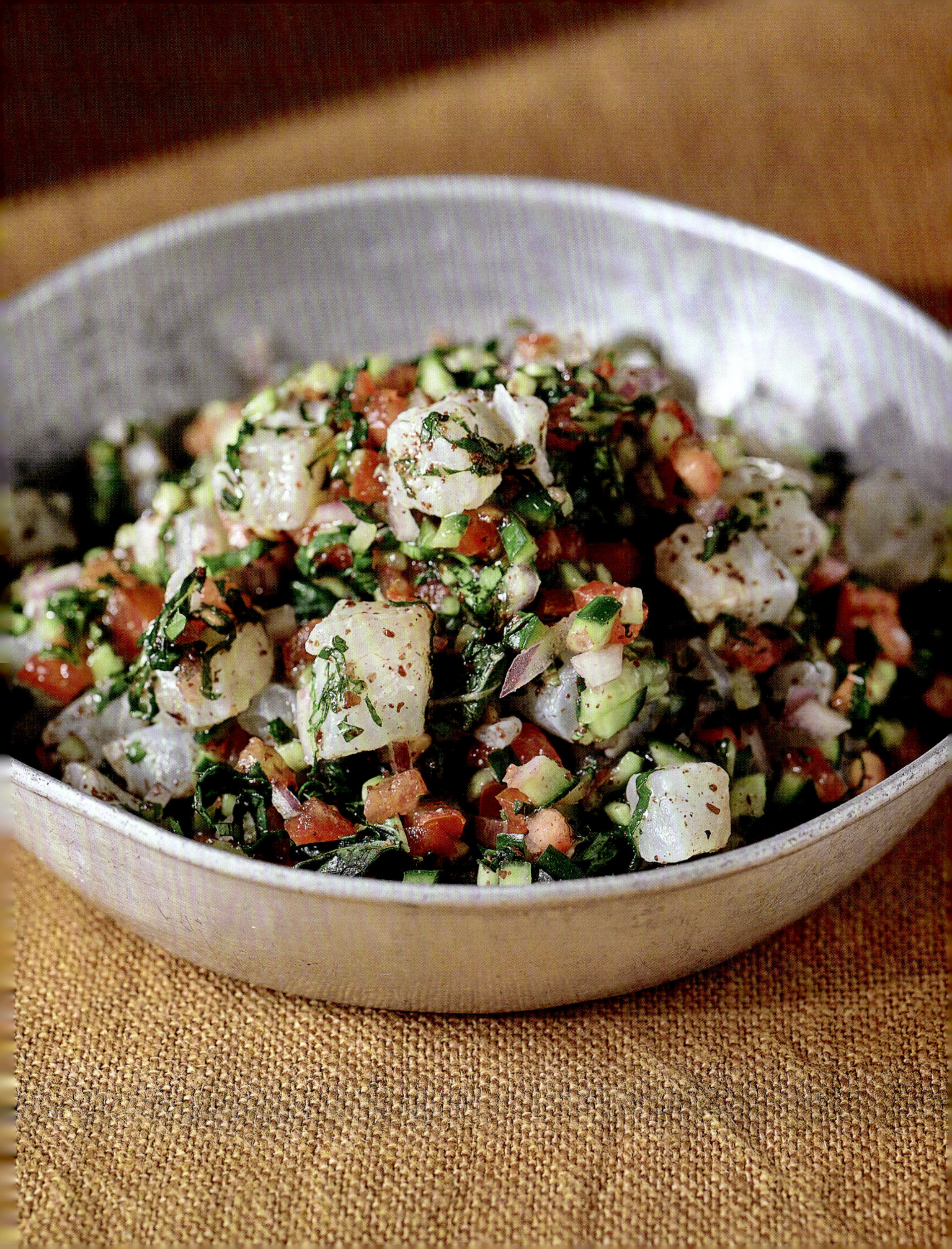

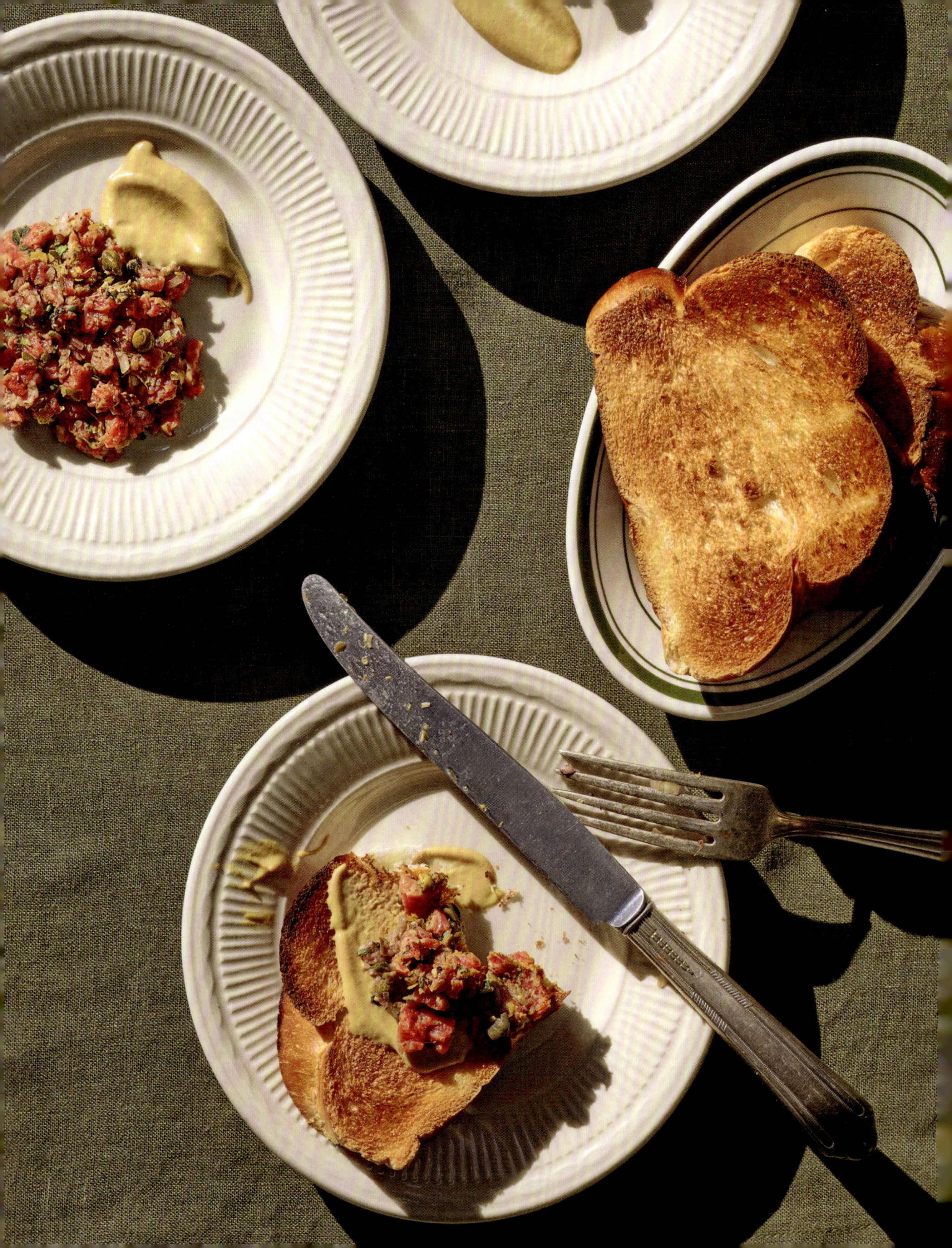

beef TARTARE

raw

I know we've covered only raw fish up to now, but the moment has arrived for raw beef. Beef tartare is typically made with egg yolk to bind the ingredients, but I find that it detracts from the pure flavor of the meat and the rest of the fixings. This beef tartare is the opposite of the classic dish. It is briny, salty, tangy, and absolutely irresistible. It features our pantry favorites, including capers, Dijon mustard, and Preserved Lemon paste.

For beef tartare, you should use a tender, lean cut of the highest quality, as it will be served raw. The best cuts for beef tartare are beef tenderloin or top sirloin. Just keep in mind when buying meat for your beef tartare, make sure you are buying the highest-quality protein. Go to a trusted butcher and ask them for a recommendation for what can be eaten raw. We always recommend grass-fed organic beef from a local spot. —ben

Serve it with: Challah (page 117), Breadsticks (page 123), Middle Eastern Caesar (page 187), Amit's Fizzy Veggie Mix (page 230)

Yield: Serves 2 to 4, makes 2 to 3 small plates

Total time: 15 minutes

FOR THE BEEF TARTARE:

8 ounces beef chuck tender

½ shallot, minced

7 anchovies, finely chopped

7 sprigs of fresh oregano, stemmed and leaves finely chopped

¼ red hot chili, thinly sliced

2 tablespoons capers, finely chopped

Zest of 1 lemon

1 teaspoon Preserved Lemon paste (page 57)

1 tablespoon Dijon mustard

1 tablespoon extra virgin olive oil

1 tablespoon sumac

½ teaspoon freshly cracked black pepper

Gray salt

FOR SERVING:

4 teaspoons salted Irish butter

4 slices Challah (page 117), toasted

4 teaspoons Dijon mustard

recipe continues

ANIMAL BITES

1. Using a sharp chef's knife, slice the beef very thin, about ⅛ inch thick. Then, stack a few slices at a time and cut the beef crosswise, again forming ⅛-inch-thick strips. Finally, gather a few strips together and dice crosswise, cutting the beef into ⅛-inch cubes. Repeat with the remaining slices.

2. In a small bowl, add the cubed beef, shallot, anchovies, oregano, chili, capers, lemon zest, preserved lemon paste, mustard, extra virgin olive oil, sumac, pepper, and salt to taste. Toss and adjust the seasoning to taste.

3. Spread the butter on the challah toasts and serve two toasts per plate. Plate the beef tartare on the side of the toast or right on top, along with a teaspoon of mustard on the side of each toast. Serve and enjoy!

kubenia

raw

The Druze, who live mainly in the north, are one of the many distinct communities in Israel. They have a unique cuisine, and one of the most famous dishes they serve is kube, a meat-stuffed, deep-fried bulgur dumpling. *Nia* means "raw" in Arabic and *kubenia* refers to raw kube. I learned to make this dish during one of our visits to the Druze communities and I've been obsessed since then. Traditionally served in the center of the table, kubenia can be presented either as a thin, pressed layer on a plate or as individual bites featuring the knuckle imprint of the person who made it—adding a very personal touch. —BEN

Serve it with: Fattoush Salad (page 173), Our Hassle-Free Matbucha (page 52), White Baba (page 92)

Yield: Serves 6 to 8, makes 25 to 30 kubeniot

Total time: 60 minutes

For the Beef:

1 pound beef sirloin

2 tablespoons extra virgin olive oil

1 white onion, chopped

¾ cup bulgur, cooked according to package instructions

Zest of 2 lemons

1 heaping teaspoon baharat

1 tablespoon Harissa (page 50)

1 tablespoon champagne vinegar

1 tablespoon gray salt

1 teaspoon freshly cracked black pepper

For Serving:

1 head of butter lettuce

½ cup Labneh Spread (page 84)

Extra virgin olive oil, for drizzling

Gray salt, for seasoning

1. Trim the fat from the beef. Place the fat cuts into a small saucepan with the extra virgin olive oil and onion. Slowly cook (confit) the fat on low heat for 45 minutes, or until it completely melts in your mouth upon tasting. Remove the pan from the heat and strain the oil through a colander. Set the oil aside and, if desired, use the remaining fat and onions as a topping in another recipe. If you do not plan to use, you can discard.

recipe continues

2. Using a sharp knife, mince the remaining sirloin and add to a medium bowl along with the confit oil, cooked bulgur, lemon zest, baharat, harissa, vinegar, salt, and pepper. Mix until evenly combined.

3. Scoop out a portion of the mixture and place it into the ridge between your fingers and your palm. Press until you create a knuckle imprint in the raw beef like the shape seen in the photo on the preceding page. Repeat this process until you have 25 to 30 kubeniot.

4. Separate the leaves from the head of the butter lettuce, being careful to maintain the cup shape for serving. Add ½ teaspoon of labneh at the base of each leaf. Then place each kubeniot into a leaf.

5. Plate the leaves and finish them with a drizzle of olive oil and a sprinkle of salt.

Essential Tip:

Alternative use for the beef and onion mixture: Don't throw away the leftover beef and onion mixture! After the oil is drained from the confit, use it as a topping for white rice and enjoy.

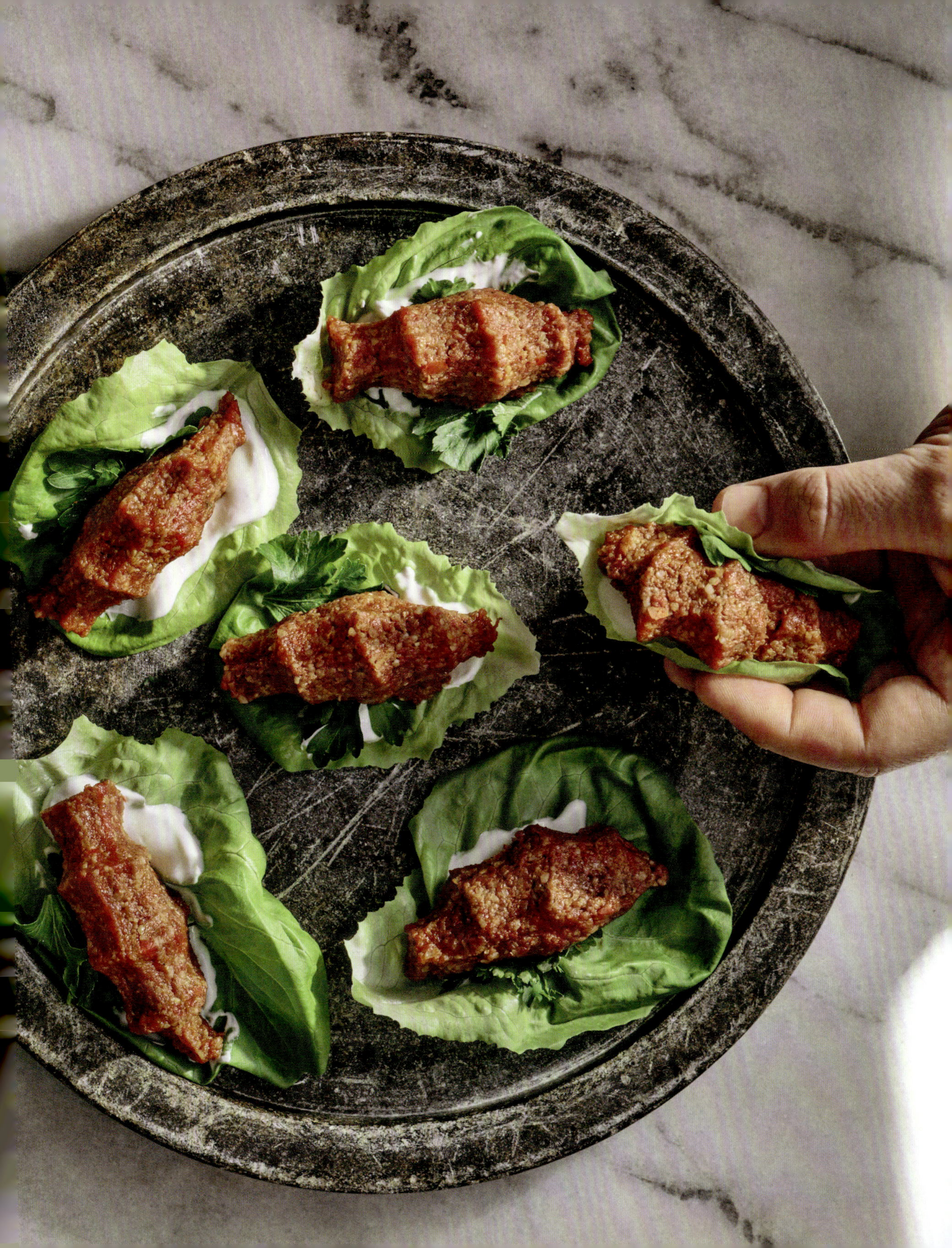

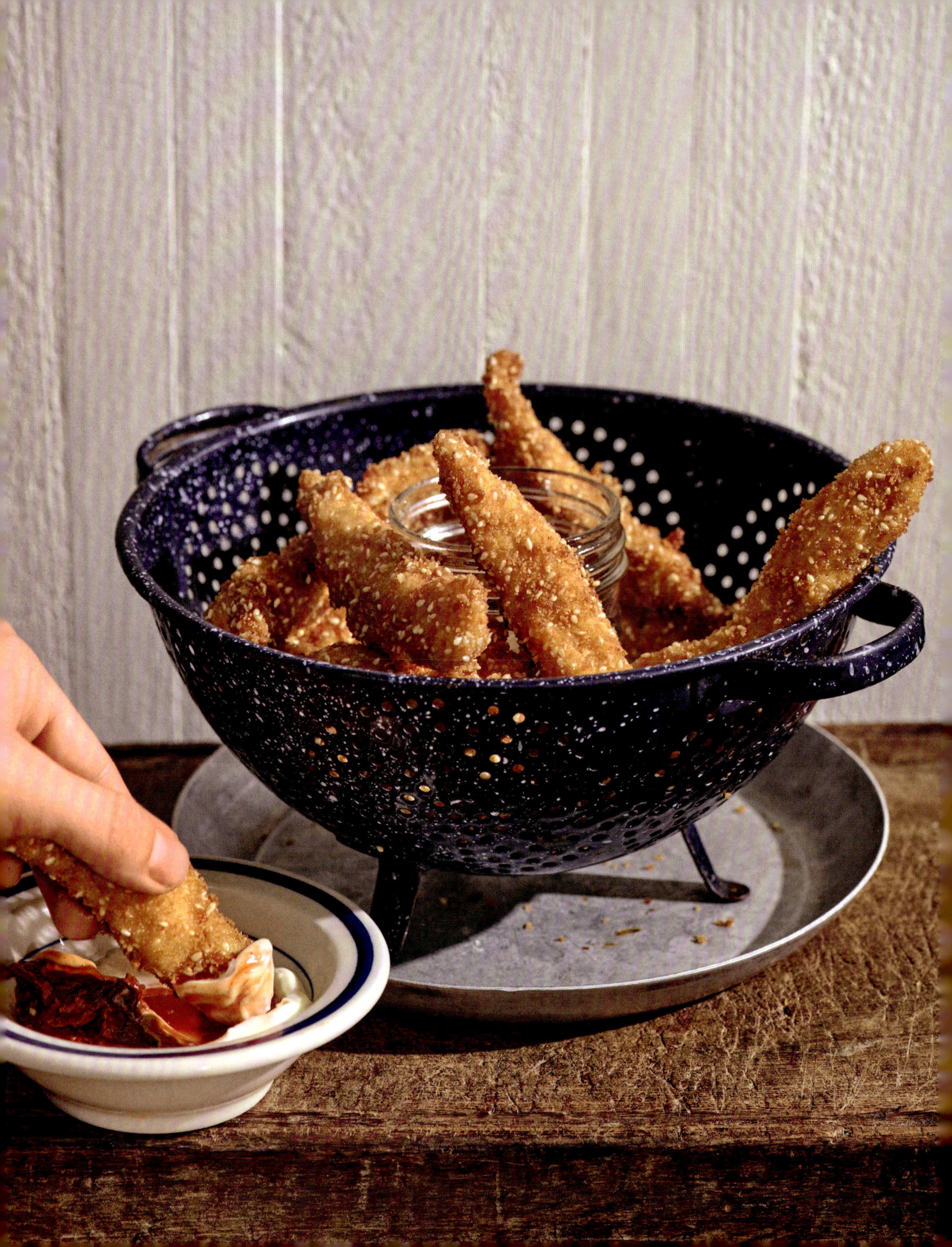

ben's schnitzel fingers

cooked

Is there anything that reminds you more of your childhood than deep-fried chicken cutlets? I mean, really. The most common schnitzel in Israel is made from chicken and coated with golden breadcrumbs and spices. As a child, I loved incorporating sesame seeds for an extra crunch and aroma. As an adult, I upgraded the mix with hawaij, a Yemeni spice blend of cumin, black pepper, turmeric, and cardamom. Hawaij gives the dish a little kick, and I've never been able to go back. You'll see; it changes the schnitzel fingers game. —ben

Serve it with: Vetrena Fries (page 227), When in Doubt Chopped Salad (page 139), Chrain (page 204)

Yield: Serves 2 to 4, makes 10 to 15 schnitzelonim

Total time: 35 minutes

For Ben's Schnitzel Fingers:

- 1 pound organic chicken tenders
- 2 large eggs
- 1 tablespoon Dijon mustard
- 1½ cups panko breadcrumbs
- 1 teaspoon hawaij
- 1 teaspoon sesame seeds
- 1 teaspoon fine sea salt
- 1 quart canola oil, for frying
- Gray salt, for seasoning

For Serving:

- ¼ cup ketchup
- 1 tablespoon Harissa
- ¼ cup mayo

1. Pat the chicken tenders dry with a paper towel. Using a sharp chef's knife, slice them into long finger-size strips.

2. In a small bowl, whisk together the eggs and mustard, then pour the mixture into a wide shallow bowl or deep plate. In a medium bowl, combine the panko, hawaij, sesame seeds, and fine sea salt.

3. Working one at a time, dip the chicken tenders into the egg mixture, coating both sides and all edges, and set aside on a baking sheet. Once they've all been coated with egg, dip them into the breadcrumb mixture, ensuring again that both sides and all edges are fully coated. Repeat until you cover all the chicken tenders with the panko mixture. Set aside.

4. In a wide, deep medium skillet, heat the oil over medium heat until it reaches 350°F (175°C) on a digital kitchen thermometer. Check the temperature periodically. Line a baking sheet with paper towels.

5. Once the oil is ready, add the chicken in small batches and fry for 3 to 4 minutes on each side, until golden brown. Using a slotted spoon, transfer the chicken to the prepared baking sheet to drain. Immediately sprinkle with gray salt. Repeat until all the chicken is fried, allowing the oil to return to temperature between batches.

6. Serve the schnitzel fingers immediately as they are best right after they are fried. Serve with a small plate of ketchup, harissa, and mayo.

kebab

cooked

Kebab is one of the most popular barbecued dishes around the world. Traditionally, it's a spiced minced meat attached to a skewer and grilled to perfection over an open flame. In our version, we skip the skewers and cook the kebab on the stovetop. Everyone has their own spice mix and ingredients for the kebab. What makes ours special is the generous use of fresh herbs and raw onion. These two ingredients give the kebab a light and fresh texture, balancing the overwhelming amount of fat in the meat. We love to serve tahini, amba, and garlic toum alongside our kebab. Drop-dead delish. —ben

Serve it with: The Smoothest Tahini Dip (page 55), Zikki's Quick Amba (page 60), Garlic Lovers ONLY Toum (page 61), Jeweled Celery Salad (page 136)

Yield: Serves 8 to 10, makes 30 to 40 kebabs

Total time: 1 hr 30 minutes to 13 hours 30 minutes (optional)

---

2 pounds ground lamb

1 bunch of mint, finely chopped

1 bunch of cilantro, finely chopped

1 white onion, grated

3 garlic cloves, grated

1 tablespoon gray salt

1 teaspoon freshly cracked black pepper

1 heaping teaspoon sumac

2 heaping teaspoons baharat

3 tablespoons olive oil

1. In a large bowl, add the lamb, mint, cilantro, onion, garlic, salt, pepper, sumac, and baharat. Mix until all the ingredients are evenly distributed.

2. Cover with a kitchen towel and let the mixture sit at room temperature for at least 1 hour. For best results, let it sit overnight in the refrigerator with plastic wrap. The longer it sits, the deeper the flavor will be.

3. When you're ready to cook the kebabs, remove the mixture from the refrigerator. Using your hands, shape the mixture into cigars and set aside. They should be slightly thicker than a man's finger.

4. Preheat a large skillet over medium heat for 1 minute, then add the olive oil. Immediately add the kebabs (spaced at least 1 inch apart) to the pan and fry for 1 minute on each of the four sides. Once the kebabs have turned dark brown in color, remove from the pan and set aside. Repeat until all the kebabs are pan-fried. Serve immediately and enjoy.

the smoothest
tahini dip

garlic lovers
ONLY toum

zikki's quick amba

tza-zikki

fried barbouniot

cooked

As a child, I remember going to an Arabic restaurant at the Jaffa Port with my parents and being surrounded by what seemed like millions of colorful small plates on the table. The only thing we needed to decide on was the main dish—the rest of the small plates were chosen for us. Barbouniot, a deep-fried mini fish, was always the dish that we ordered as a family to share. While red mullet is typically used in fried barbouniot, we recommend using smelt, anchovies, or sardines as great alternatives. Golden and crispy with a fresh squeeze of lime, it is one of my favorite snacks to enjoy by the sea. —ben

Serve it with: Tza-Zikki (page 87)

Yield: Serves 4 to 5, makes 20 fried barbouniot

Total time: 30 minutes

Special tools: digital kitchen thermometer, wire rack

¾ cup semolina flour

2 tablespoons cornstarch

½ teaspoon fine sea salt

20 small fish (smelt, anchovies, or sardines), gutted and cleaned

2 quarts canola oil, for frying

Gray salt, for seasoning

1 lime, cut into quarters

1. In a large bowl, combine the semolina flour, cornstarch, and fine sea salt.

2. Add the fish to the flour mixture and toss, making sure that the full surface area of each fish is covered.

3. In a deep medium skillet or Dutch oven, heat the oil over medium heat until it reaches 350°F (175°C) on a digital kitchen thermometer. Check the temperature periodically. Line a wire rack with paper towels.

4. Once the oil is ready, add the fish in small batches (3 to 4 at a time) and fry for 4 minutes to achieve the ideal crispiness. Using a slotted spoon, transfer the fish to the prepared wire rack. Repeat with the remaining fish, allowing the oil to return to temperature between batches.

5. Season with a generous pinch of gray salt and serve immediately with lime wedges on the side.

stuffed onions

cooked

The first time Ben told me he was craving a stuffed onion, I thought he was absolutely out of his mind. I'm very open to new flavors and textures, but for some reason this felt like a crazy idea. Though like most everything new we taste together, I easily and blindly fell in love. Stuffed onions are an unexpected magic. First boiled whole, the little spheres are perfect for stuffing. We load ours with rice, herbs, meat, and spices, then line them up perfectly in a pan and generously drizzle with a tangy pomegranate sauce. This all happens before they melt into one another in the oven for over an hour. You will be eager to eat them immediately, but traditionally and in our house I let them sit overnight on the stove at room temperature to really develop flavor, and then I heat them up again for lunch the next day! Served with a big dollop of tahini, there is nothing better. —*zikki*

Serve it with: The Smoothest Tahini Dip (page 55), Fattoush Salad (page 173)

Yield: Serves 8 to 10, makes 1 pan of stuffed onions or approximately 28 pieces

Total time: 4 hours

Special tools: parchment paper

For the Stuffed Onions:

9 medium yellow onions, 8 for stuffing and 1 for grating

½ cup basmati rice

8 ounces ground beef, 15% fat

½ bunch of flat-leaf parsley, finely chopped

½ bunch of cilantro, finely chopped

2 teaspoons gray salt

1 teaspoon freshly cracked black pepper

2 teaspoons sumac

1. Prep the onions: Grate 1 onion using a box grater and set aside. Using a sharp chef's knife, remove the top and the bottom stems from the remaining 8 onions for stuffing. Peel each onion and then stand it upright. Place the tip of the knife on the core of one of the onions and slice all the way to the bottom, making an incision from the core to the outermost part of the onion. The goal is for the onion to open up and have room to expand as it boils. Repeat this cut in each of the onions and then place them in a large pot. Fully submerge the onions in water (covered by at least 2 inches of water) and boil for 30 minutes. Then remove them from the water and allow them to cool completely.

2. Prep the rice: Place the rice in a fine-mesh strainer and rinse under cold water. In a small pot, add the rice and ¾ cup of water. Bring the water to a boil, cover, and cook for 7 minutes, or until the rice is 80 percent cooked. Remove from the heat and let cool to room temperature.

recipe and ingredients continue

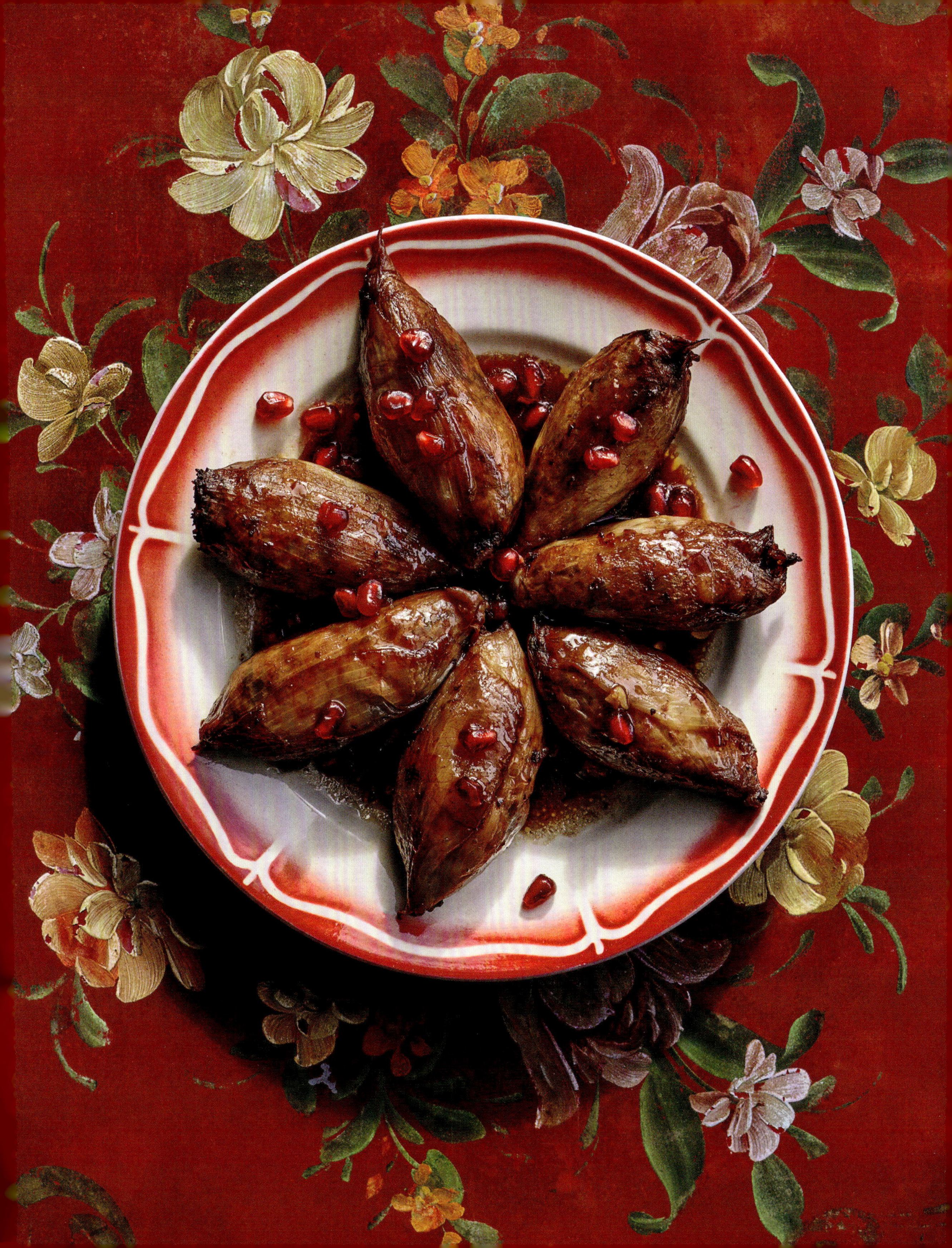

1 teaspoon baharat

Olive oil, for coating the pan

½ cup The Smoothest Tahini Dip (page 55), for serving

For the Pomegranate Sauce:

3 tablespoons pomegranate molasses

2 tablespoons silan (date honey)

1 teaspoon gray salt

1 teaspoon freshly cracked black pepper

1 teaspoon ground cinnamon

¼ cup extra virgin olive oil

1 tablespoon honey

3. Prep the filling: In a medium bowl, combine the cooled rice, ground beef, parsley, cilantro, grated onion, salt, pepper, sumac, and baharat. Mix until all the ingredients are evenly distributed.

4. Make the pomegranate sauce: In a medium bowl, whisk together the pomegranate molasses, silan, salt, pepper, cinnamon, olive oil, and honey. Set aside.

5. When the onions are cool enough to handle, carefully remove the outer layers of each onion (about 5 to 6 layers per onion) and set aside.

6. Arrange the onions for baking: Evenly coat an ovenproof deep, wide pot or Dutch oven with olive oil. Then take one onion layer and hold it open in the base of your palm. Add 1 tablespoon of the filling into the base of the layer and then roll the onion skin into itself to seal the stuffed onion. Place the onion into your pan seam side down. Repeat until all the onion skins are stuffed and packed into the pan. Make sure that they are tightly packed so that the filling doesn't come out. Once all the onions are packed, preheat the oven to 350°F (180°C).

7. In the meantime, pour the pomegranate sauce evenly over the onions to submerge them. You should be able to see the top of the onions popping out, but they should still be surrounded by sauce.

8. Cover the pan with a layer of parchment paper and then a layer of aluminum foil. Place the lid of the pot on top of the aluminum foil and then place into the oven. Bake for 3 hours, or until all the liquid has been absorbed and the rice is fully cooked.

9. Remove the pan from the oven and serve alongside a big bowl of the tahini dip.

Essential Tip:

Rest time: Traditionally, this dish sits overnight to develop deeper flavors. However, if you have concerns about food safety, you can let it rest at room temperature for 2 hours before placing it in the refrigerator. It will be just as delicious.

NY Strip Steak

cooked

Ben and I rarely eat steak at home, but it is a crowd favorite among our clients, so I have learned a great deal about cooking and serving it to perfection. If we do eat it at home, we don't have it as a main course. Never. Instead, we serve it on a small plate to share, so that everyone gets a taste or two to simply satisfy the craving. You don't need more of such a grand treat, and this way you can buy the best cut available.

My secret? I always buy the steak the same day I will be cooking it, and I do not put it in the refrigerator. Instead, I let it come to room temperature and do a quick cure by salting the surface area, which allows it to release any remaining moisture. Once patted dry, I season it with freshly cracked coarse black pepper and let it rest until I'm ready to sear. For the best results, be sure to cook only one steak at a time in the cast-iron skillet. —*zikki*

Serve it with: Middle Eastern Caesar (page 187), Shrimp in Grated Tomato Butter (page 276)

Yield: Serves 2 to 4, makes 2 small plates

Total time: 30 minutes, plus 1 hour of curing

Special tools: gas range, cast-iron skillet

FOR THE STEAK:

2 tablespoons gray salt

2 (10- to 14-ounce) NY strip steaks, room temperature

1 tablespoon freshly cracked black pepper

FOR THE BURNT SCALLION CHIMMI:

1 bunch of scallions

1 long green hot chili, finely chopped

Juice of 1 lemon

1. Quick-cure the steaks: Sprinkle the salt on the full surface area of the steaks to begin the curing process. Cover the steaks loosely with the same paper they came in or parchment paper, giving them room to breathe. Let rest for at least 1 hour.

2. Make the burnt scallion chimmi: Turn a gas burner to high heat. Using tongs, place the entire bunch of scallions directly on the burner, moving it every couple of seconds until it begins to char. Continue cooking until the entire bunch is bright green and charred on 60 percent of its surface area. Remove from the heat.

3. Using a chef's knife, thinly slice through the entire charred bunch of scallions and add to a small bowl. Add the chili, lemon juice, salt, and olive oil. Toss to combine and set aside until ready to serve.

4. After the steaks are done resting, using a paper towel, pat the steaks on both sides to remove any excess moisture. Season the steaks on both sides with the pepper.

recipe and ingredients continue

Animal bites

ny strip steak

shrimp in grated tomato butter

¼ teaspoon gray salt

1 tablespoon extra virgin olive oil

5. Heat a cast-iron pan over medium heat for 1 minute. To know when your cast-iron pan is hot enough, you can use the water droplet test: Flick a few drops of water into the pan after it's heated for a minute. If the droplets sizzle and evaporate almost immediately, the pan is ready. Once the pan is hot enough, place one steak into the pan fat side down. Sear for 2 minutes. Then, lay the steak onto one side and cook for 3 minutes. Flip the steak and cook on the other side for an additional 3 minutes. Remove the steak from the pan and set aside to rest for at least 10 minutes before slicing. Repeat with the second steak.

6. Arrange the plates: After the steaks have rested, use a sharp chef's knife to cut them into slices. Serve each steak on its own plate alongside the burnt scallion chimmi.

Essential Tips:

Cook the steak at room temperature: Remove the steak from the refrigerator 45 to 60 minutes before cooking to allow it to fully reach room temperature.

Run your stove vents: If you are making the steak indoors, make sure that the vent above your stove and any air purifiers are on since it will get smoky in your kitchen.

Let the steak rest: Do not skip the mandatory 10-minute rest period before slicing the steaks. Resting allows it to finish cooking and fully tenderize.

SHRIMP IN GRATED TOMATO BUTTER

When Ben and I first moved to New York City, we were living on the Upper West Side in a tiny studio apartment. Ben was filming baking videos from home, and I took a job at Eyal Shani's restaurant North Miznon. I remember my first night in the kitchen. It was Saturday night and we had 220 tables. I had never worked in a professional kitchen before, and the adrenaline rush was the most intense of my life. I was on fire. I was HOME. Chef Nadav Greenberg's food and the energy during service were just dynamite, and I knew I had found my people and the next chapter.

That night, I tasted one of the dishes, and it completely changed my understanding of sauce: shrimp in tomato seed butter. It is made with Madagascar shrimp with the head and shell on, quickly seared in a superhot pan and finished with tomato seeds, long green hot chilies, and butter. Nothing more, nothing less. Pure perfection. Our version is made with grated tomato. There's no waste and way more sauce to soak up with a thick slice of challah (page 117). —*zikki*

Serve it with: NY Strip Steak (page 273), Middle Eastern Caesar (page 187)

Yield: Serves 2 to 4, makes 3 small plates

Total time: 30 minutes

Special tools: kitchen scissors or paring knife

cooked

---

10 jumbo Madagascar shrimp, head and shell on

4 tablespoons extra virgin olive oil

1 teaspoon gray salt

4 tablespoons salted Irish butter

½ long green hot chili, super thinly sliced

6 Campari tomatoes, grated

---

1. If your shrimp are not already deveined, using scissors, start by making a shallow cut in the spine of each shrimp from head to tail to ensure even cooking and easy peeling. Then, using a colander, rinse the shrimp under cold water to ensure that there is no sediment left along the spine. Pat the shrimp dry using a paper towel and place into a medium bowl. Toss with 2 tablespoons of the extra virgin olive oil and the salt.

2. Before you begin cooking, have your butter, chilies, and grated tomatoes ready to go as the cooking process will move quickly.

3. Heat a large nonstick skillet over high heat for 1 minute. Add the remaining 2 tablespoons extra virgin olive oil. Once the pan is hot, add the shrimp and sear for 30 to 45 seconds, until they turn pink with a salt crust. (You want a good crust.) Flip the shrimp and sear for an additional 20 to 30 seconds. Then quickly add the butter and chilies to the pan. Once the butter is about 90 percent melted and the chilies have begun to change color (about 10 seconds), add the grated tomatoes.

5. Holding the handle of the pan, move the shrimp around in the sauce to coat by swirling the pan for about 30 seconds, or until the sauce is fully homogeneous. Using tongs, quickly remove the shrimp from the pan and divide them among three small plates. Then continue cooking the sauce for 10 more seconds, or until it becomes slightly thicker. Look for a rapid simmer in the sauce, as it reduces quickly. Immediately remove the pan from the heat and evenly divide the sauce among the plates of shrimp.

6. Serve the shrimp with plenty of napkins and explain to your guests that you must peel the shrimp before you eat them. Trust me, it is worth the fuss.

Essential tips:

Subbing the shrimp: You can substitute 8 ounces of shell-on, headless large shrimp for the Madagascar shrimp.

Make sure your pan is hot: If your pan is not hot enough, your shrimp will get rubbery and take longer to cook. Searing both sides of the shrimp in a superhot pan will create a crust.

If the sauce breaks: If the sauce separates, add 1 teaspoon of water and mix until homogeneous again. Remove the pan from the heat.

Cook in small batches: This recipe is meant to serve 2 to 4 people. You may be tempted to double it, but it is best to make the shrimp in small batches of 10 (max) because this will ensure that the sauce comes together and that the shrimp are perfectly cooked. There is nothing worse than gummy, overcooked shrimp!

SOME-THING SWEET

This chapter is an ode to my all-time favorite desserts. Some have deep-rooted familial legacies taking me back to my childhood, when my friends and I would sneak my mom's Chocolate Balls (page 291) out of the freezer on hot summer afternoons. And others are recipes and memories I've collected over the years as an adult with a far less picky palate. We made sure that this chapter has something for every level of dessert mastery! If you want to make something grand, lean into the daylong process of making Rogalach (page 283). If you prefer something quick but equally satisfying, jump into the Jaffa Sundae (page 299). If you want to make something far in advance that can be served anytime—we've got that too! Mix and match these gorgeous treats for the perfect way to close a meal.—BEN

recipes

rogalach

knafeh

malabi

chocolate balls

tahini truffles

ma'amoul

jaffa sundae

citrus basbousa

fig & young cheese

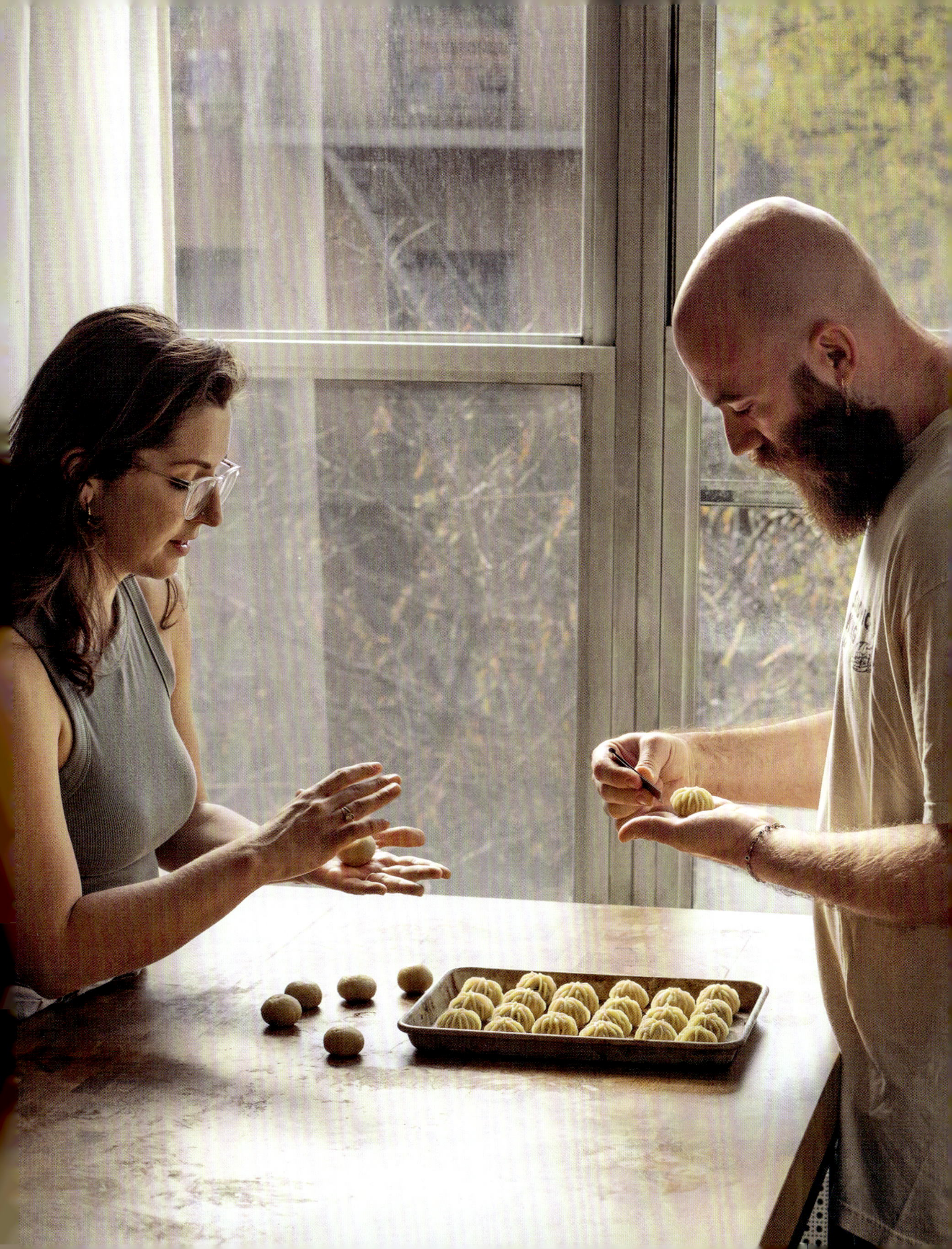

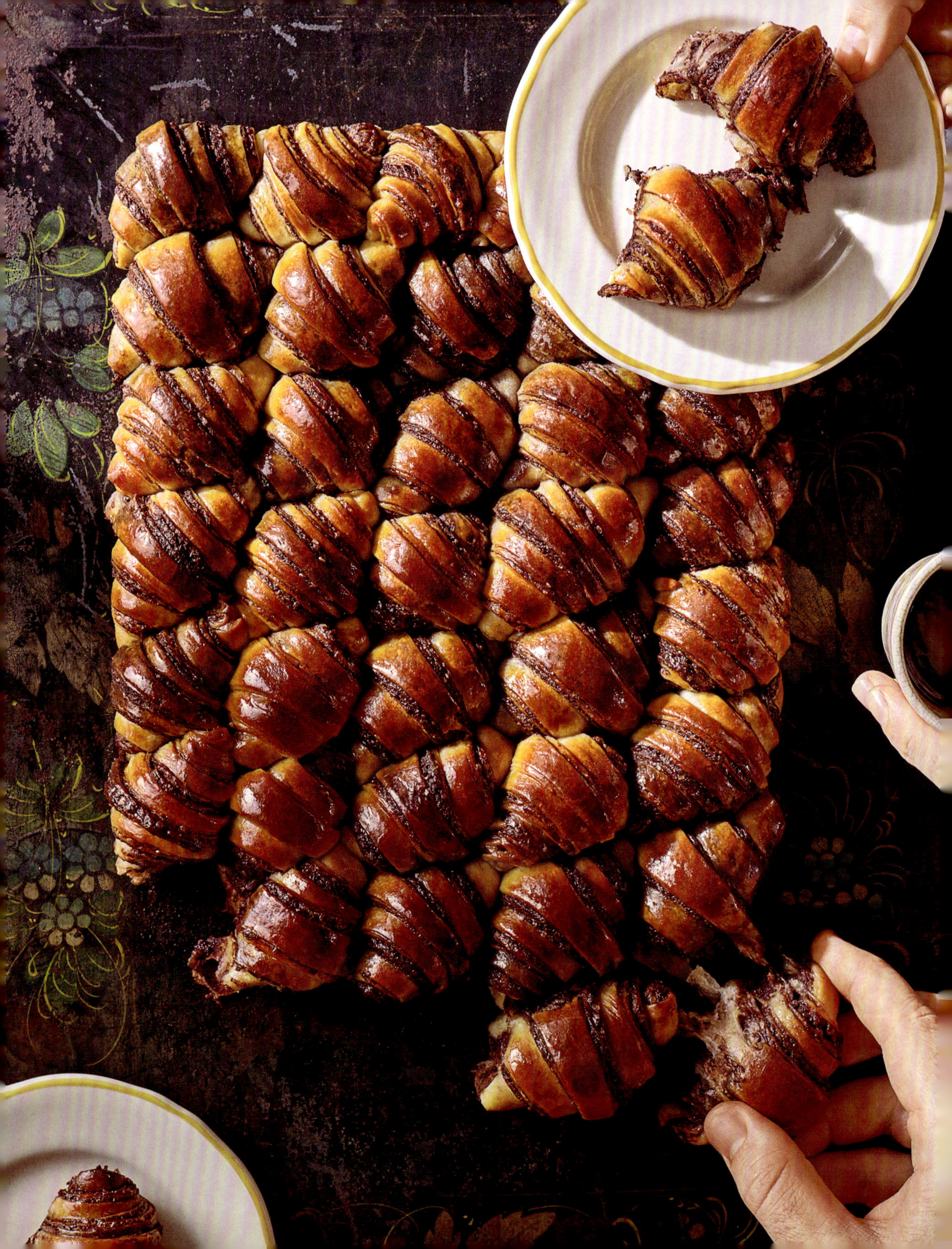

ROGALACH

I'm confident enough to tell you that I prefer rogalach over croissants. There, I said it. Rogalach always reminds me of my childhood. Every Friday, my parents would wake up early to go shopping for Shabbat dinner, and the first stop was always the bakery. They would return from the bakery before heading to the market and leave a box of mini rogalach for me and my siblings to snack on. I've seen some people try to elevate rogalach by adding a Nutella filling, but I have to say, nothing beats the classic taste of the brown sugar, cocoa, and butter mixture. We love it this way!

I always place the rogalach close together in the pan so that they are touching as they bake. This way, you can enjoy this sweet treat as a pull-apart rogalach cake. This is such a wonderful dessert to offer your loved ones! —ben

Yield: Makes 35 to 40 mini rogalach

Total time: 5 hours

Special tools: stand mixer, rolling pin, parchment paper, pastry brush

For the Dough:

500 grams all-purpose flour, plus more for dusting

10 grams active dry yeast

90 grams sugar

150 grams milk

2 large eggs

100 grams unsalted butter, softened to room temperature

10 grams fine sea salt

1. Make the dough: In the bowl of a stand mixer fitted with the dough hook, add the flour, yeast, and sugar. Mix on the lowest speed until combined. Add the milk and eggs and continue mixing on the lowest speed until almost no flour remains in the bowl. Add the softened butter and continue mixing. Once the butter has been fully incorporated, add the salt. Continue to mix on the lowest speed for 5 minutes, or until the dough is smooth and elastic.

2. Round the dough and place into a large bowl. Cover with plastic wrap and let the dough rest for 1 hour to 1 hour 30 minutes, or until it has almost doubled in size.

3. While the dough is proofing, make the syrup: Preheat the oven to 365°F (180°C). In the meantime, in a small saucepan over medium-low heat, combine the water and sugar. Once the sugar has completely dissolved, remove the syrup from the heat and let cool. Transfer to the refrigerator.

recipe and ingredients continue

For the Syrup:

100 grams water

100 grams sugar

For the Filling:

200 grams brown sugar

150 grams unsalted butter, melted

50 grams extra virgin olive oil

100 grams unsweetened cocoa powder

For Brushing:

2 large eggs

Essential Tip:

Prepping ahead of time: You can prepare the syrup in advance and in bigger quantities to keep in the refrigerator. I always have a cold syrup ready to be poured over my baked goods the moment they come out of the oven.

4. After proofing, transfer the dough to a lightly floured work surface to prevent sticking. Gently press the dough with your hands to flatten it slightly before rolling it. Using a rolling pin, roll out the dough into a ¼-inch-thick rectangle, approximately 12 × 24 inches. Make sure to roll from the center outward, rotating the dough as needed to maintain an even thickness. If the dough starts to stick, sprinkle a little more flour on the surface and rolling pin.

5. Make the filling: In a medium bowl, add the brown sugar, melted butter, olive oil, and cocoa powder. Mix until fully combined.

6. Evenly spread half of the filling onto the rolled-out dough. Fold the dough in half and roll into a ¼-inch-thick rectangle again. Evenly spread the remaining filling onto the rolled-out dough. Fold the dough in half and roll out the dough again into a ¼-inch-thick rectangle, approximately 12 × 24 inches.

7. Line a baking sheet with parchment paper. Using a sharp chef's knife or a pizza wheel, cut the dough into long, narrow rectangles, about 2 × 6 inches each. Cut each rectangle from opposite corners to create two triangles. Then, taking one triangle, create a crescent shape by rolling the triangle down, starting from the wide side, to the tip. Repeat until all the crescents are formed. Arrange each one closely on the prepared baking sheet so that they form into one unit when baked.

8. In a small bowl, whisk the eggs. Using a pastry brush, brush the rogalach with the egg wash. Bake for 15 to 20 minutes, or until golden brown.

9. Remove the rogalach from the oven and, using a pastry brush, immediately brush with the cooled syrup. Brush the syrup on very slowly, allowing the Rogalach to absorb it before applying more. It is very important that the syrup is cold and the rogalach is hot! Serve immediately or wrap tightly with plastic and store at room temperature for 3 days.

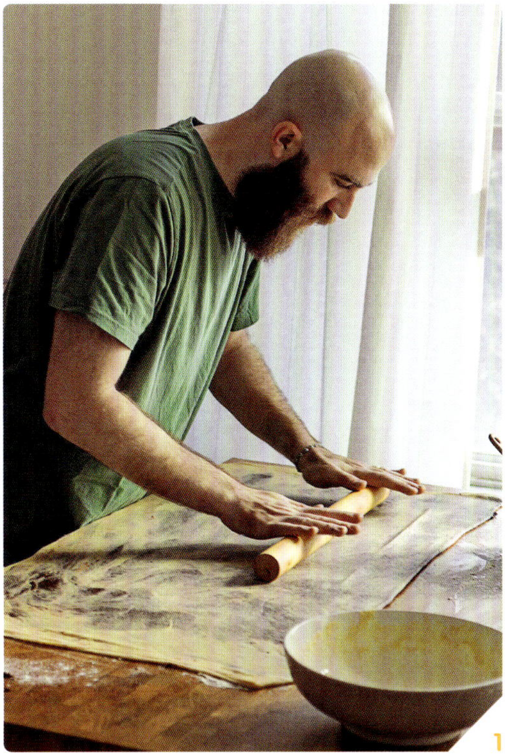
1

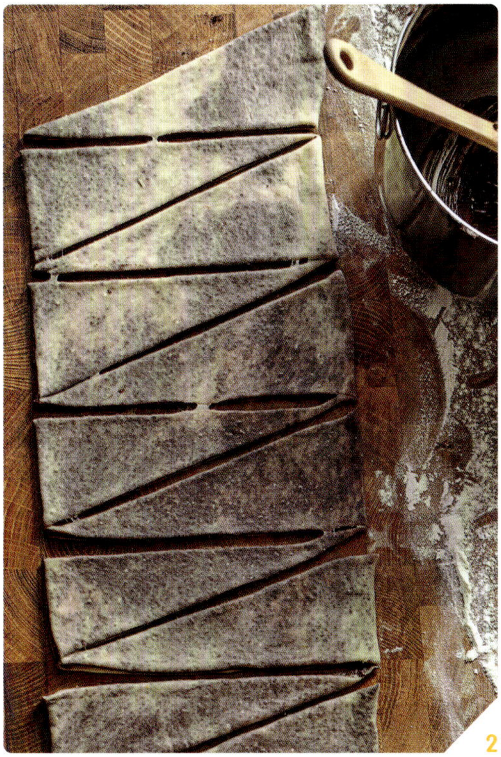
2

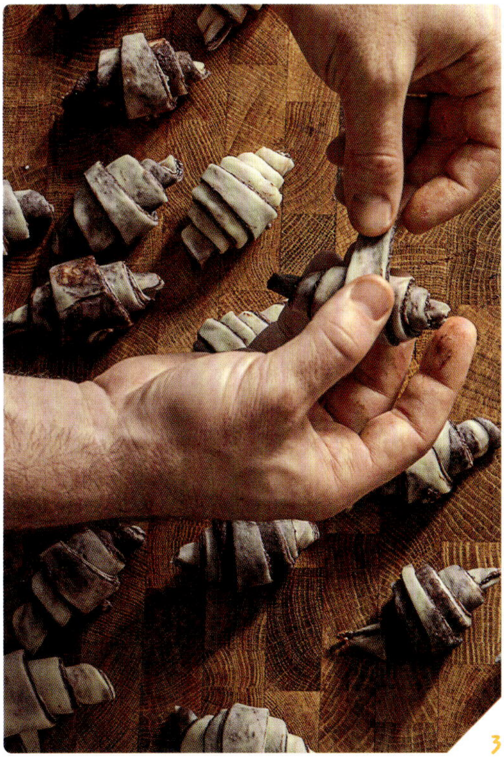
3

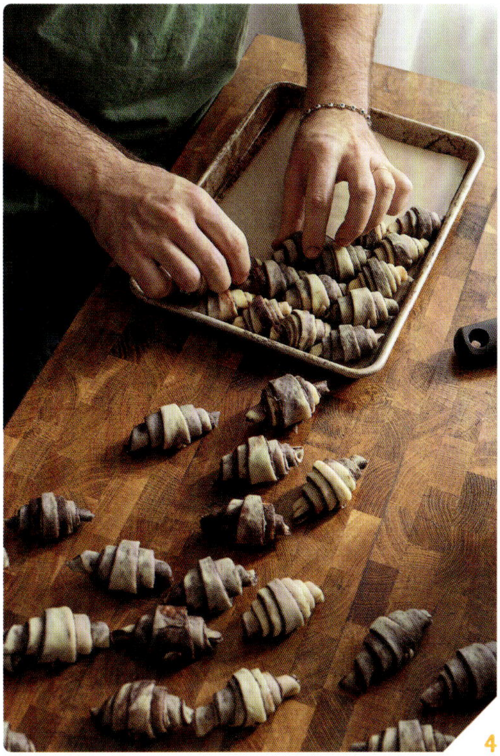
4

ESSENTIAL TIP:

Prepping ahead of time: You can complete steps 1 through 3 ahead of time and store the uncooked, layered knafeh in the refrigerator for up to 2 days. Remove it from the refrigerator an hour before cooking and then continue with steps 4 through 6.

knafeh

Knafeh is not just delicious but also a really good way to impress your guests with minimal effort. It is a traditional Middle Eastern dessert of shredded phyllo dough (kataifi) layered with cheese, soaked in syrup, and decorated with green pistachios. What I love about this dessert is that you can make it as sweet as you like, depending on how much syrup you add. It's a perfect way to please all your guests, from those concerned about sugar levels to those with a strong sweet tooth.

I know you may ask yourself, "Where do I find this shredded phyllo dough?" and the answer is either in your local Middle Eastern grocery shop or online. You can keep the dough in your freezer for a few months, so it is no problem if you don't use it right away. —ben

Yield: Makes 4 small knafeh
Total time: 30 minutes
Special tools: kitchen scissors

For the Syrup:

- 200 grams water
- 200 grams sugar
- Zest of 1 lemon

For the Knafeh:

- 227 grams kataifi (shredded phyllo dough)
- 227 grams unsalted butter, melted
- 454 grams mozzarella, hand shredded

For Serving:

- ¼ cup raw shelled pistachios, toasted and crushed (see page 22)

1. Make the syrup: In a small saucepan over medium-low heat, combine the water, sugar, and lemon zest. Once the sugar has completely dissolved, remove the syrup from the heat and let cool.

2. Prep the kataifi. Using kitchen scissors, cut the kataifi into 1-inch pieces. In a large bowl, combine the kataifi with the melted butter.

3. Using a small 6- to 8-inch skillet, arrange a ⅓-inch-thick layer of the kataifi. Then, sprinkle a ⅓-inch-thick layer of the shredded mozzarella on top, followed by another ⅓-inch-thick layer of the kataifi. After combining these three equally thick layers (two of the kataifi and one of the mozzarella), the knafeh should be 1 inch thick.

4. Cook over medium-low heat for about 5 minutes, or until the knafeh's bottom is golden and crispy. Use a spatula to check the color, then remove from heat when ready.

5. Place a small plate upside down on the knafeh and, using oven mitts, flip the skillet so the crispy golden layer is on top. Carefully slide the knafeh back into the skillet and cook for 3 minutes, or until the bottom matches the top. Transfer to a serving plate.

6. Pour the syrup over the knafeh and top with the pistachios. Serve immediately or store in the refrigerator for up to 3 days.

MA'AMOUL

Since I was a child, I've always had a sweet tooth. I think I got it from my mama as she is the biggest fan of sweets I have ever known. She loves ice cream, cookies, and chocolate, to be more specific. And dates. My mom LOVES dates. So much so that she always has them on hand in her freezer (yes, it's a great place to keep your dates). As a family of date lovers, our favorite type of cookies are ma'amoul.

Ma'amoul are butter semolina cookies filled with spiced dates, then topped with powdered sugar. They are so mesmerizing due to their unique decoration and the fact that they always have a special personality, shaped by the person who makes them. When developing this recipe, our food stylist, Amit, brought ma'amoul cookies that he made for us to taste. They were so good that they became our official recipe. Thank you, Amit! —BEN

Yield: Makes 35 to 40 cookies
Total time: 2 hours
Special tools: ma'amoul tongs

For the Dough:

250 grams all-purpose flour

125 grams semolina flour

30 grams sugar

2.5 grams baking powder

100 grams unsalted butter, softened to room temperature

50 grams olive oil

90 grams water

2.5 grams rose water

Powdered sugar, for sprinkling

1. Make the dough: In a large bowl, add the all-purpose flour, semolina flour, sugar, and baking powder. Mix until combined, then add the butter, olive oil, water, and rose water, mixing until a cohesive dough is formed. Be careful to mix and not knead, as it will develop the gluten structure of the dough, which will result in hard cookies.

2. Make the filling: In a separate medium bowl, add the date paste, cinnamon, and nutmeg. Mix with your hands until combined.

3. Divide the dough into 1-inch balls. Set aside. Then divide the date filling, forming it into balls a bit smaller than the dough balls. Line a large baking sheet or two medium-sized baking sheets with parchment paper.

4. Place one dough ball in your hand and, using your thumb, press into the center of the dough ball, creating a small well. Insert the date ball into this well with your other hand and wrap the outside dough layer around the date filling to cover it entirely. Roll the dough with your hands to seal the filling, then place it on the baking sheet. Repeat until all cookies are formed.

recipe and ingredients continue

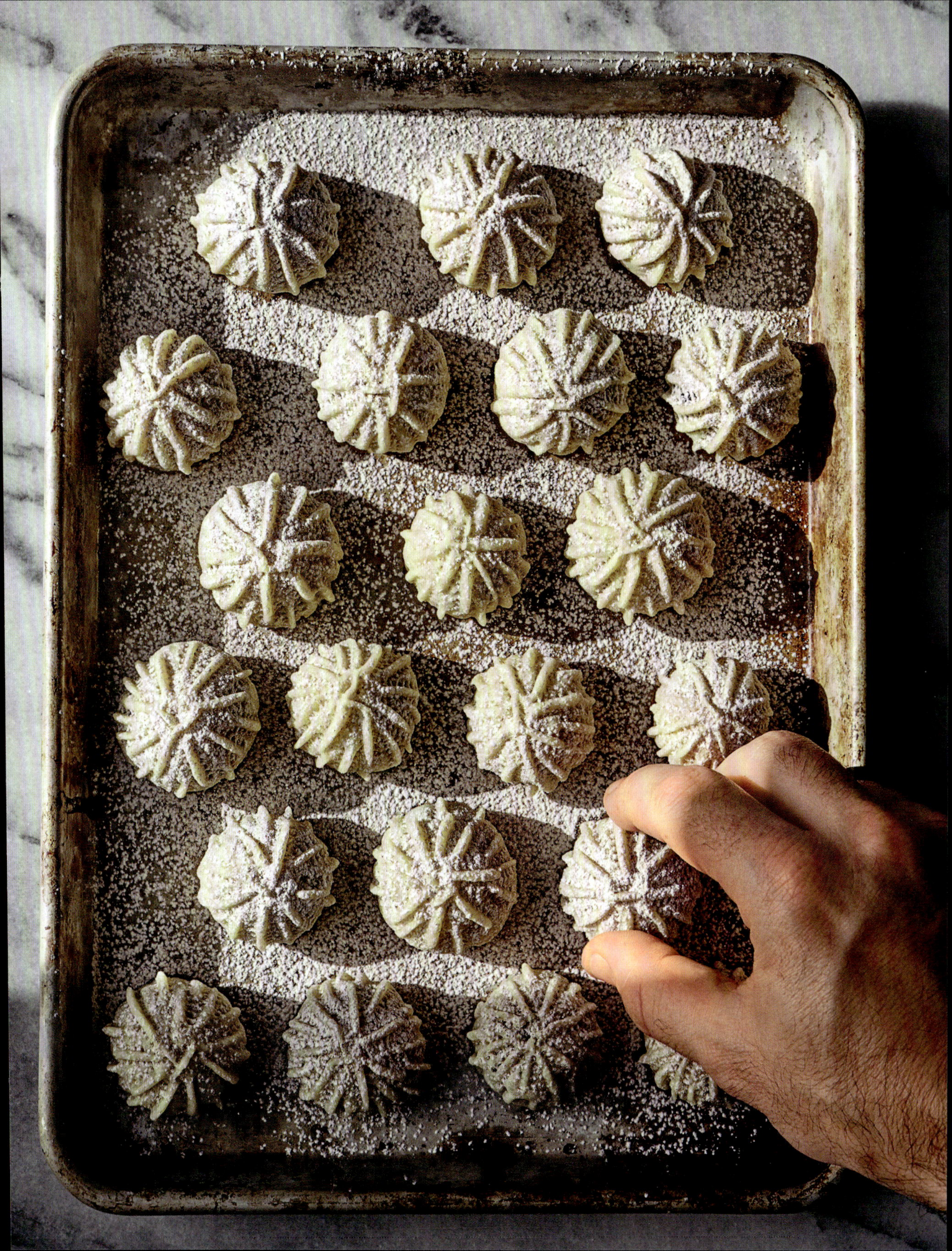

For the Filling:

14 ounces date paste

1 teaspoon ground cinnamon

¼ teaspoon grated nutmeg

5. Preheat the oven to 340°F (170°C).

6. Using ma'amoul tongs (see note), squeeze 8 to 10 ridges into the top of the cookies, working clockwise and pressing well to ensure that the pattern will remain visible after baking.

7. Bake for 12 to 14 minutes, or until the cookies are lightly browned on the bottom.

8. Let the cookies cool to room temperature before sifting a light layer of powdered sugar on top. Serve or store in an airtight container at room temperature for 1 to 2 weeks.

Essential Tip:

Using ma'amoul tongs: The beauty of these cookies lies in their decoration, and ma'amoul tongs, small tweezers specifically designed to pinch and press intricate patterns into the dough, are perfect for this.

chocolate balls

Every Friday, kindergarten children across Israel bring home a challah and chocolate balls to share with their family. While the quality of the challah is debatable, you can't go wrong with the chocolate balls. Chocolate balls were and still are a staple sweet in my house. During my childhood, my father crafted this super-easy recipe, and ever since, my mom has overseen the operation, making sure the freezer is always stocked with them! Whenever we are back in Israel visiting my parents, my friends come over and always take a peek in the freezer to sneak a ball.

This recipe offers many variations, but the basics include buttery cookies (specifically Petit Beurre), chocolate, and a coating of shredded coconut or sprinkles. My father's recipe guarantees success each time. —ben

Yield: Makes 40 chocolate balls
Total time: 2 hours
Special tools: rolling pin

For the Dough:

1 pound simple butter cookies (we recommend Petit Beurre)

8 ounces heavy cream

12 ounces chocolate hazelnut spread

1 ounce rum or whiskey (optional)

For the Topping:

¾ cup raw shelled pistachios, toasted (see page 22)

1 cup shredded unsweetened coconut

1. Place the butter cookies in a tightly sealed plastic bag and crush using a rolling pin on a hard surface. Some prefer the cookies to be a finer powder, and others prefer to have more chunks for the crunch—it is up to you! Set aside.

2. Place the pistachios in a tightly sealed bag and use the rolling pin to apply even pressure, rolling back and forth over the pistachios until they are crushed to your desired size. Set aside.

3. In a microwave-safe bowl, combine the cream and chocolate hazelnut spread. Heat in 30-second intervals, stirring in between each interval, until homogenous and smooth.

4. Add the crushed cookies to the heavy cream–hazelnut mixture and add the rum, if desired. Mix until combined.

5. Cover the bowl tightly with plastic wrap and place in the freezer for at least 1 hour, or until firm.

recipe continues

6. Once the mixture is firm, remove it from the freezer. Using a teaspoon, scoop the mixture into your hands and roll to form a ball about 1 inch in diameter. Repeat this process until you have about 40 balls. If the mixture is too hard at first, let it warm up for a couple of minutes at room temperature so it is easier to work with.

7. Fill two seperate medium bowls with the toppings: shredded coconut and crushed pistachios. Drop the balls in the coating of your choice and lightly shake the bowl until the balls are fully covered with an even layer. This is the best method to achieve a light, even coating without leaving finger marks.

8. Arrange the balls in a tightly sealed container and store in the freezer until you are ready to serve, up to 3 months.

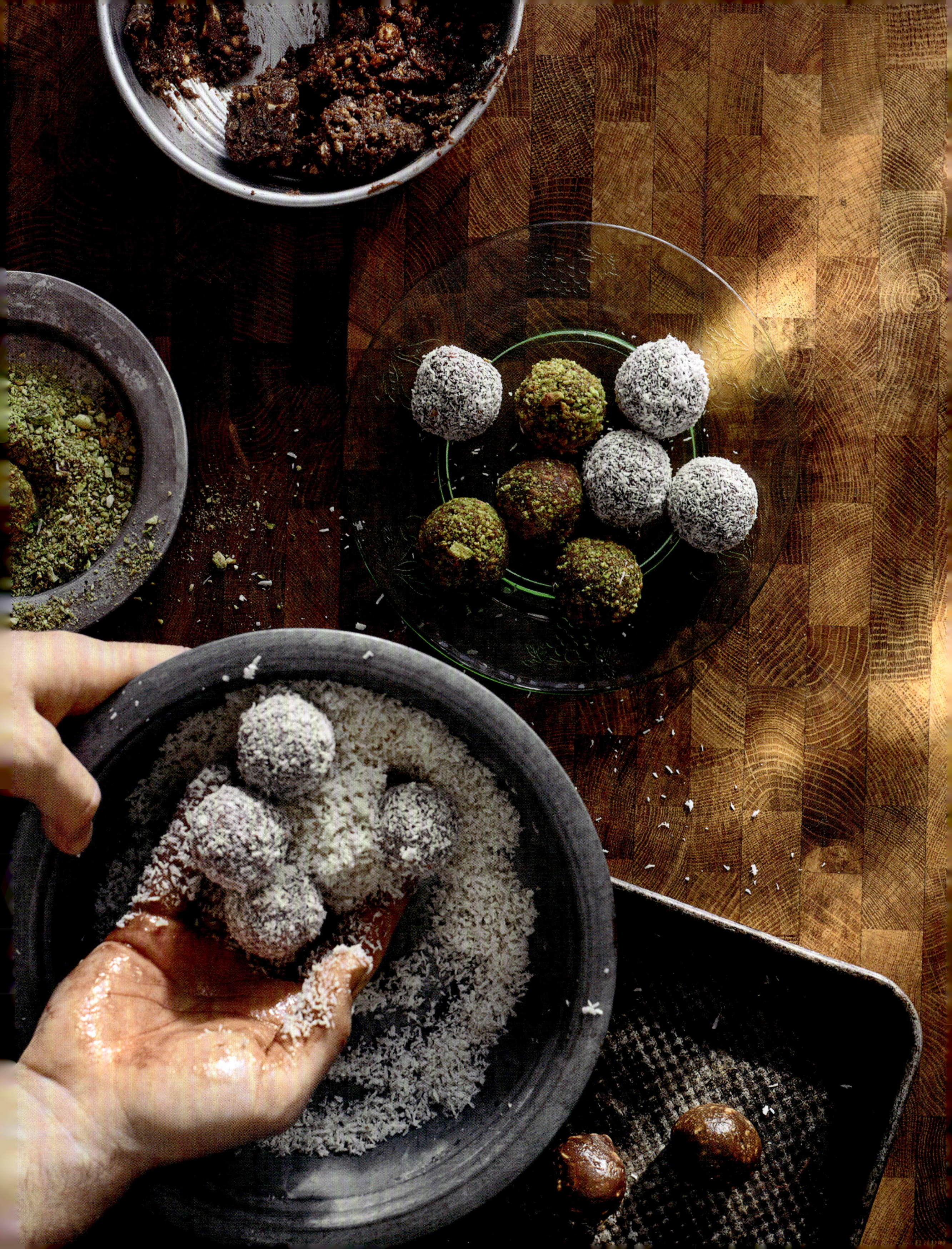

ESSENTIAL TIP:

Serving options: Some people enjoy the truffles directly from the refrigerator, while others prefer to let them sit at room temperature for a couple of minutes, which makes the texture more fudgy. They are amazing both ways!

Make it vegan: Use very dark vegan chocolate.

TAHINI TRUFFLES

These fudgy tahini truffles were my childhood addiction when visiting my grandmother Aviva. They are balanced with the perfect amount of sweetness from the chocolate and a delightful nutty flavor from the raw tahini. There is also an added kick from the cinnamon and a pinch of salt, so we are set from all angles. Serve these cuties alongside Turkish coffee. —BEN

Yield: Makes 20 to 30 small tahini truffles

Total time: 4 hours

Special tools: parchment paper

1 pound dark chocolate chips

1 cup raw tahini

½ teaspoon ground cinnamon

Pinch of gray salt

½ cup unsweetened cocoa powder, for coating

ESSENTIAL TIP:

Melting the chocolate: If you do not have a heatproof bowl, you can place the chocolate chips in a microwave-safe bowl and melt them in 30-second intervals, stirring between intervals until completely smooth.

1. Bring a medium pot of water to a simmer. Place a heatproof bowl on top, ensuring that the bottom of the bowl does not come into contact with the water, and add the chocolate chips. Allow the chocolate to start melting in the bowl, stirring occasionally to prevent burning, until the chocolate is completely smooth.

2. Transfer the melted chocolate to a medium bowl and add the raw tahini, cinnamon, and salt. Stir to combine. Line a flat, shallow 9 × 9-inch baking pan (so the mixture sets evenly and quickly) with parchment paper and pour the mixture into the dish. Transfer to the refrigerator to chill for at least 2 hours.

3. Once the truffle mixture has set, scoop it into small mounds, about 2 teaspoons per truffle. For larger truffles, scoop into 1-tablespoon mounds. Roll the mounds in between your fingers to form individual balls and place on a plate. This will get a bit messy and that's okay. Return the truffles to the refrigerator to chill for 20 to 30 minutes.

4. In a medium bowl, add the cocoa powder. After chilling, reroll the truffles with your hands. Add all the truffles into the bowl with the cocoa powder and shake the bowl until the truffles are fully coated.

5. Transfer the truffles back to the refrigerator and store there until ready to serve, or up to 1 week.

Malabi

Better known as the Middle Eastern panna cotta, malabi is a popular summer dessert in Israel, often enjoyed after a day at the beach. Topped with strawberry syrup, toasted coconut, and pistachios, it's a light, refreshing treat. Instead of cooking jam, we let sugar naturally break down strawberries into syrup, preserving their raw flavor. A sprinkle of freshly toasted coconut elevates the malabi to a whole new level. —ben

Yield: Six 4-ounce dessert bowls
Total time: 4 hours

For the Malabi:

500 grams whole milk

250 grams heavy cream

80 grams sugar

35 grams cornstarch

10 grams rose water

For the Strawberry Syrup:

10 strawberries, diced

100 grams sugar

10 grams sumac

For Topping:

¼ cup shredded unsweetened coconut

¼ cup raw shelled pistachios, toasted and crushed (see page 22)

1. Make the malabi: In a medium saucepan, add the milk, cream, sugar, cornstarch, and rose water. Whisk until there are no lumps of cornstarch visible.

2. Place the saucepan over medium heat and cook, stirring constantly, just until the mixture starts to thicken. Quickly remove it from the heat and pour into a heatproof measuring cup. Immediately begin dividing the mixture evenly among six 4-ounce bowls, leaving about ½ inch on top for the toppings.

3. Tightly cover the bowls with plastic wrap and place in the refrigerator to chill for at least 3 hours, or up to 3 days.

4. Make the syrup: In a medium bowl, mix the strawberries with the sugar and sumac. The sugar will break down the strawberries into a thick, rough syrup after 15 to 20 minutes. Set aside until you are ready to serve.

5. Prepare the topping: In a small skillet over medium-low heat, add the coconut in an even layer. Toast, stirring frequently, for 3 to 5 minutes, or until it is lightly browned and fragrant. Remove from the heat and set aside to cool.

6. Assemble the malabi: When ready to serve, top each bowl with 2 tablespoons of the strawberry syrup and a sprinkle of the toasted coconut and pistachios. Serve immediately.

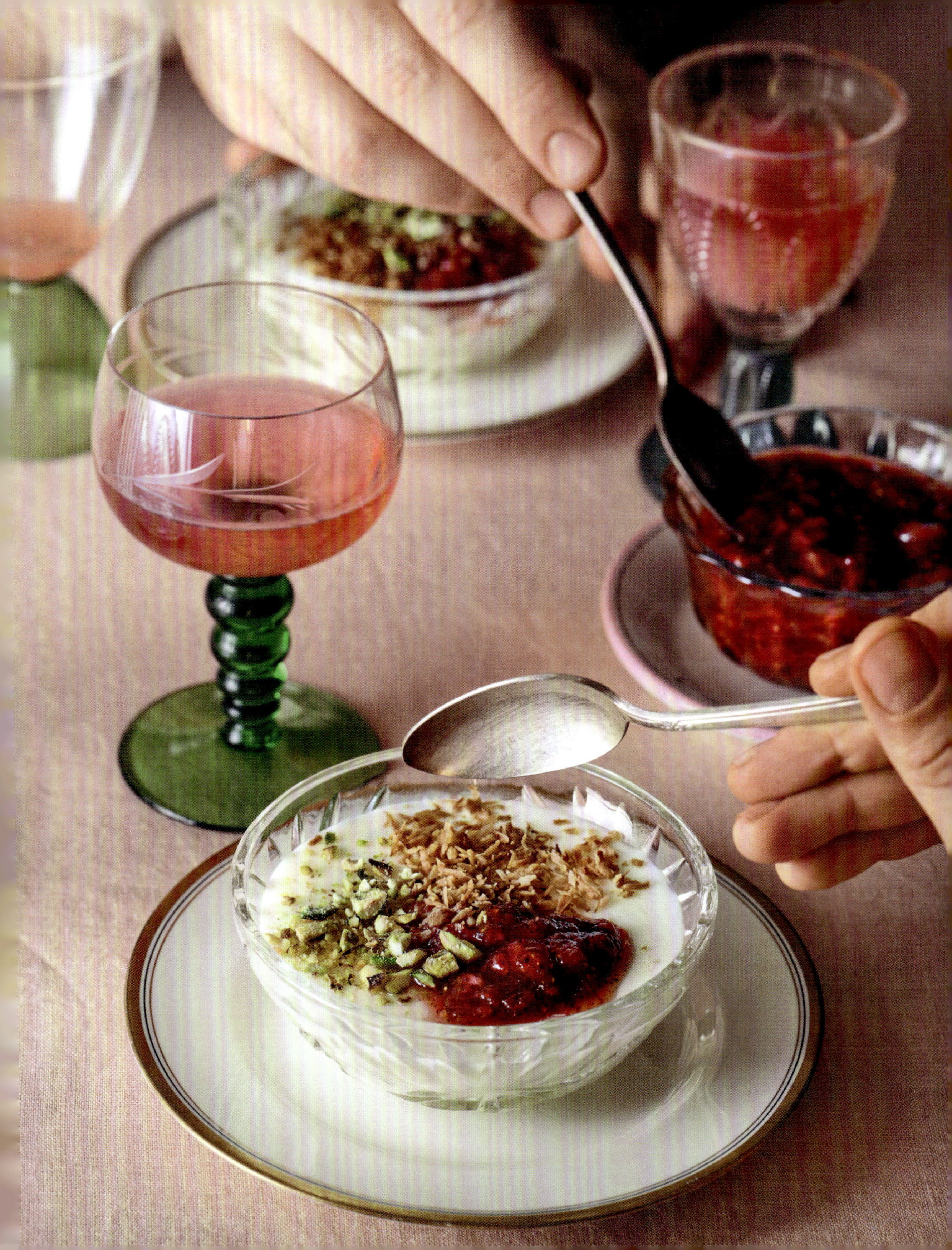

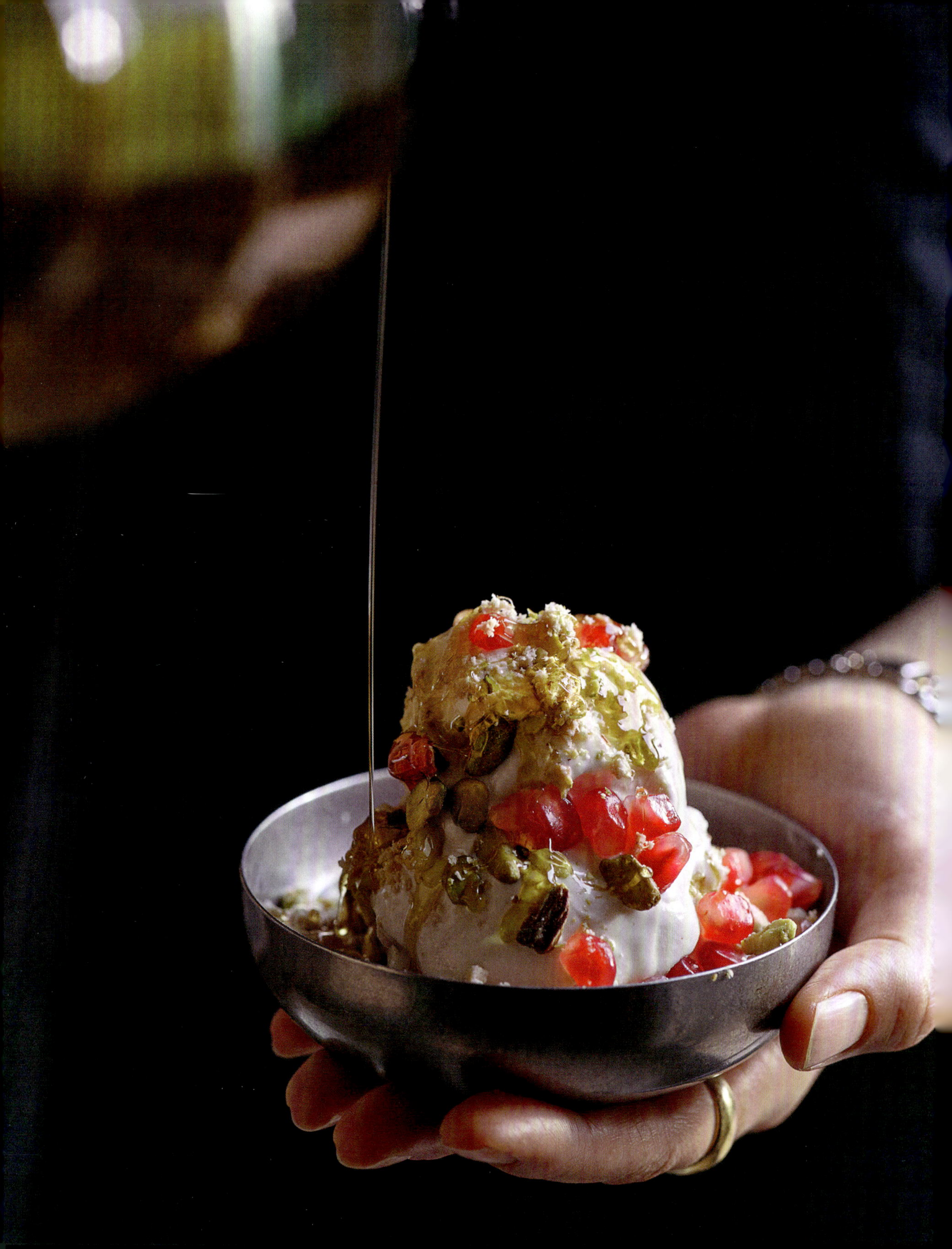

Jaffa Sundae

This dessert is really special and quick to make. Excellent for the everyday! Zikki used to make it on a base of Greek yogurt (which you can totally do!), but recently we began making it with a creamy, decadent, and classic American vanilla ice cream. This sundae comes together in exactly 10 minutes and highlights all the gorgeous products found in a Middle Eastern pantry and refrigerator. Topped with tangy, juicy pomegranate seeds, crunchy and aromatic toasted pistachios, decadent halva, raw honey, extra virgin olive oil, and gray salt, the Jaffa Sundae has us nostalgic for long summer days on the beach in Tel Aviv. —BEN

Yield: Makes 4 sundaes
Total time: 10 minutes
Special tools: ice cream scoop

Ingredients

- 8 scoops vanilla ice cream
- ¼ cup raw shelled pistachios, toasted and crushed (see page 22)
- ¼ cup crumbled halva
- ½ cup pomegranate seeds
- Extra virgin olive oil, for drizzling
- Raw honey, for drizzling
- Gray salt, for seasoning

Instructions

1. Remove the ice cream from the freezer 30 minutes before you plan to make the sundaes. (The worst thing on earth is a hard ice cream when you are building a sundae.)

2. In a small bowl, combine the pistachios and halva.

3. In each of four small serving bowls, add 2 scoops of the softened vanilla ice cream. Top each bowl with 2 tablespoons of the pistachio-halva mixture, 2 tablespoons of the pomegranate seeds, a drizzle of olive oil, a drizzle of honey, and a pinch of salt. Feel free to adjust the toppings to your liking and serve immediately.

Citrus Basbousa

Basbousa, a beloved semolina-based cake from the Middle East, means "sweet" in Arabic and is often used as a term of endearment. My Citrus Basbousa adds a zesty twist to the classic with freshly squeezed orange juice. It's the perfect cake to enjoy with morning tea or as a subtly sweet after-dinner treat—so light you'll definitely be reaching for a second slice. Best of all, it's incredibly easy to make: one bowl, a quick mix, and straight into the oven.—Ben

Yield: Makes one 9-inch square cake or about 16 pieces

Total time: 1 hour 30 minutes

Special tools: parchment paper

For the Cake:

4 large eggs

220 grams sugar

240 grams extra virgin olive oil

240 grams freshly squeezed orange juice

120 grams all-purpose flour

130 grams semolina flour

75 grams shredded unsweetened coconut, plus 40 grams for topping

10 grams baking powder

For the Syrup:

150 grams freshly squeezed orange juice

100 grams sugar

1. Preheat the oven to 340°F (170°C). Line a 9-inch square cake pan with parchment paper.

2. Make the batter: In a large bowl, whisk the eggs and sugar for 5 minutes, or until the mixture becomes airy and pale yellow. Whisk in the olive oil and the orange juice until combined.

3. Add the all-purpose flour, semolina flour, 75 grams of the shredded coconut, and the baking powder into the wet ingredients and fold until combined, ensuring that no flour lumps remain. If you are having trouble breaking up the flour lumps, you can briefly switch to a whisk, but be careful not to overwhisk the batter as it can result in a dense cake.

4. Pour the batter into the prepared pan and bake for 45 to 50 minutes, or until a toothpick inserted into the center comes out clean. This will indicate that the crumb is fully set and no excess moisture remains.

5. Make the syrup: While the cake bakes, in a small saucepan, bring the orange juice and sugar to a boil. Once boiling, reduce the heat to a simmer and cook for 5 minutes, or until the mixture becomes glossy and homogenous. Remove from the heat.

6. Remove the cake from the oven and immediately pour the syrup on top in an even layer. Sprinkle the remaining 40 grams shredded coconut on top. Let cool to room temperature and serve. Store at room temperature, covered tightly with plastic wrap, for up to 2 days.

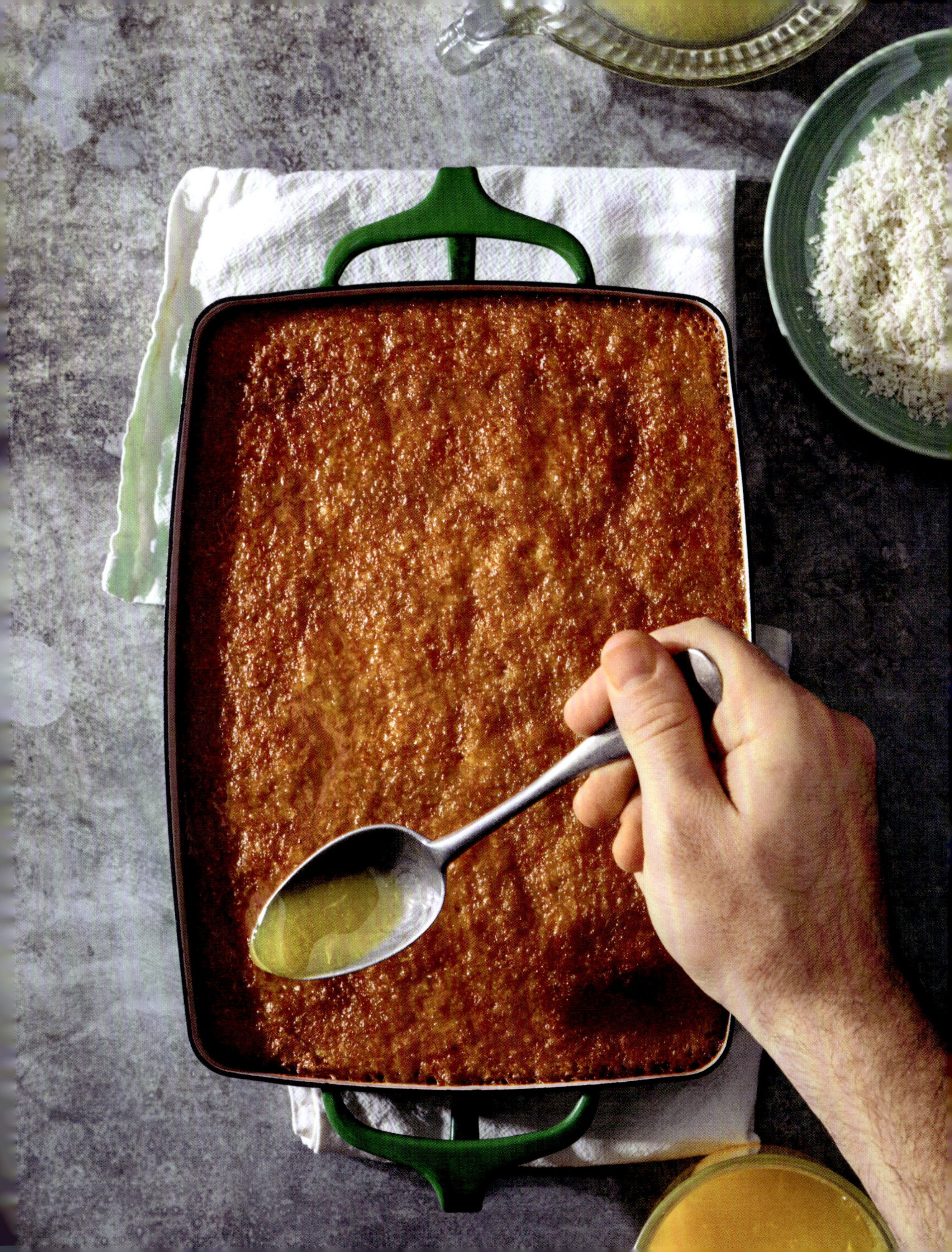

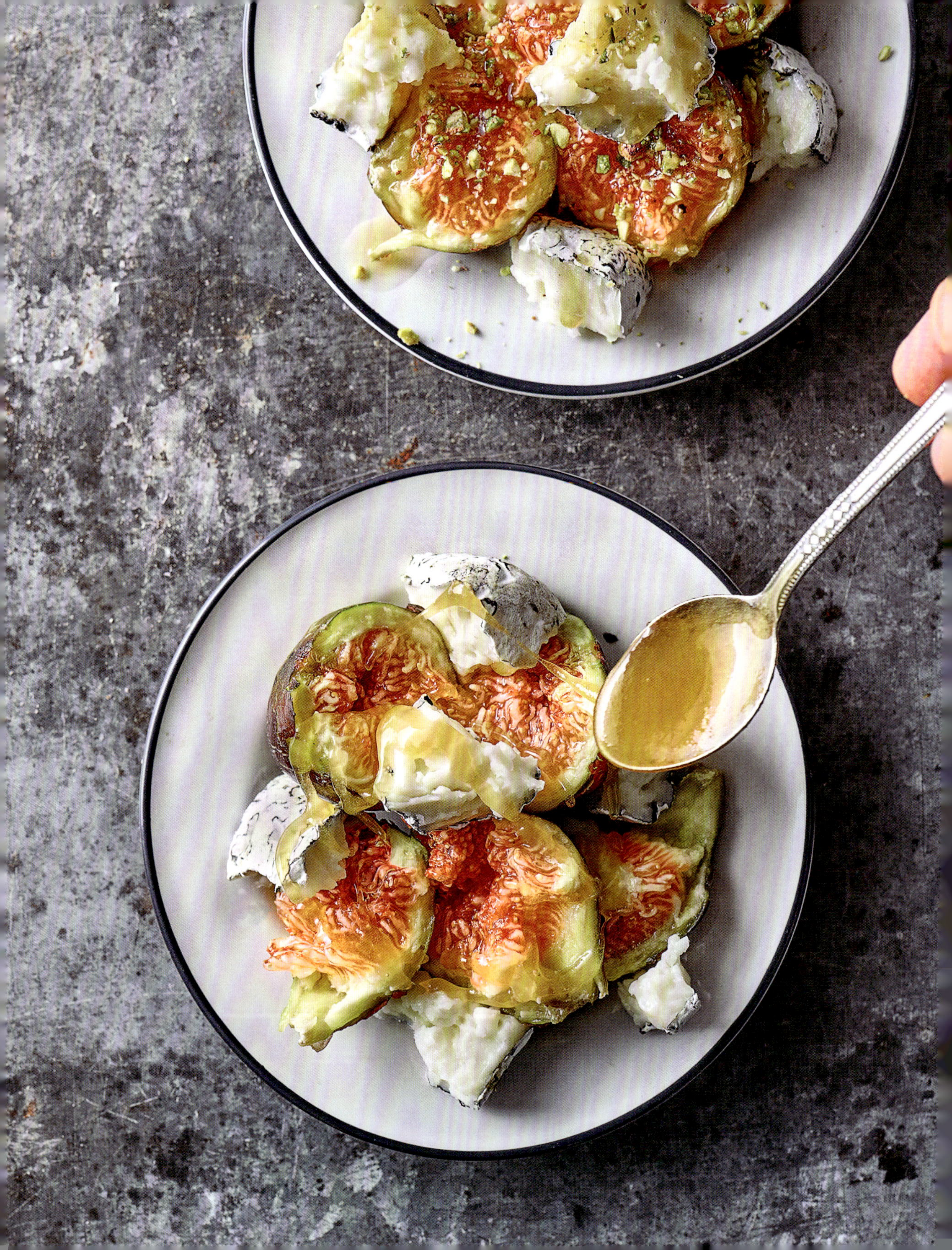

fig & young cheese

Not every dessert requires pastry chef skills. Sometimes less is more, like this dish: a seasonal ripe fruit opened wildly with your hands, paired with a blue goat cheese and topped with pistachios and honey. Any fruit can work here, but keep in mind it must be fully ripe and in peak season. And for us, when fig season arrives, it's time to party! —*zikki & ben*

Yield: Makes 4 small plates

Total time: 5 minutes

6 to 8 ripe figs

8 ounces mold-ripened goat cheese (such as Humboldt Fog)

¼ cup raw shelled pistachios, toasted and crushed (see page 22)

Gray salt, for seasoning

2 tablespoons raw honey

1. Using your hands, open the figs in half and break the cheese into rough, uneven pieces.

2. Arrange the cheese and figs on four small plates. Evenly sprinkle the pistachios and salt on top with a drizzle of raw honey before serving.

tips, tricks & sample menus

We designed this book to be your ultimate hosting cheat sheet.
   The magic of this book is that you can choose a recipe from every single chapter and combine those six dishes together into one hell of a dinner party. Each dish is strong enough to stand alone but also fits perfectly into a menu alongside any of our other dishes. They all speak the same language. Now, if you feel like going above and beyond, you can even choose a dish from every subchapter of a chapter. For example, the salad chapter has five subchapters: chopped; semicooked; crispy, crunchy, or crushed; tomato based; and leafy. Even if you were to throw a party for just salads (check out Let's Make It Light, Casual & Salad-Heavy, Babe), you would have a fabulous array of diverse textures and flavors.
   Now, if you don't feel like building your own menus—don't worry. We've got you covered.

absolutely love a breakfast spread

dips & spreads
labneh spread (page 84)
my grandfather's zhug (page 49)
preserved lemon butter (page 69)
silan & onion jam (page 71)

breads
pita (page 109)
jerusalem bagel (page 120)

salads
breakfast salad (page 156)
fig carpaccio (page 169)
not your grandma's fruit salad (page 170)

veggie bites
charred eggplant with thick tahini (page 221)

something sweet
ma'amoul (page 288)

i'm feeling euro nostalgic, but make it hip

dips & spreads
chopped liver, better than your grandma's (page 73)

breads
challah (page 117)

salads
zikki's peeled tomato salad (page 180)

cucumber, dill, labneh & onion salad (page 165)

veggie bites
zikki's salty baby potatoes (page 204)

burnt beets & feta (page 207)

my dad's fermented cucumbers (page 233)

animal bites
ben's schnitzel fingers (page 265)

pickled herring (jarred store-bought)

something sweet
rogalach (page 283)

craving sushi, but make it middle eastern

dips & spreads
black baba (page 94)

beet & goat cheese dip (page 88)

breads
breadsticks (page 123)

salads
middle eastern caesar (page 187)

veggie bites
safta's skinny stuffed grape leaves (page 228)

animal bites
scallop carpaccio (page 252)

tuna nectarine tartare (page 251)

mackerel, cucumber & arugula crudo (page 255)

tuna & grapes (page 245)

something sweet
malabi (page 296)

let's make it light, casual & salad-heavy, babe

dips & spreads
garlic confit (page 63)

a cashew basil dip everyone will talk about (page 99)

breads
tel avivian focaccia (page 113)

salads
the best green salad of your life (page 184)

jeweled celery salad (page 136)

radicchio, blue cheese & hazelnut salad (page 190)

veggie bites
garlicky string beans (page 203)

animal bites
beef tartare (page 259)

something sweet
jaffa sundae (page 299)

omg! i forgot we are hosting shabbat!

dips & spreads
- tza-zikki (page 87)

breads
- challah (page 117)

salads
- the best green salad of your life (page 184)
- pear, mustard green, mint & challah crouton salad (page 166)

veggie bites
- garlicky string beans (page 203)
- double-dip artichoke (page 198)
- sweet potatoes on labneh (page 214)

animal bites
- ny strip steak (page 273)
- shrimp in grated tomato butter (page 276)

dessert
- jaffa sundae (page 299)

this is awkward . . . i'm actually vegan

dips & spreads
- a cashew basil dip everyone will talk about (page 99)
- my uncle tal's lentil masabacha (page 79)
- the smoothest tahini dip (page 55)

breads
- tel avivian focaccia (page 113)

salads
- when in doubt chopped salad (page 139)
- herby marinated eggplants (page 150)

veggie bites
- moroccan carrots (page 201)
- vetrena fries (page 227)
- falafel (page 215)

something sweet
- tahini truffles (page 295)

i'm hosting a grand feast—the welcome olives

not a recipe
- sumac cucumber spears (page 43)
- 5-minute goat cheese stuffed dates (page 43)

dips & spreads
- labneh spread (page 84)
- mashwiya (page 98)
- beet & goat cheese dip (page 88)
- white baba (page 92)
- our hassle-free matbucha (page 52)

breads
- jerusalem bagel (page 120)
- pita (page 109)

salads
- not your typical "crisp veg" (page 162)
- jeweled celery salad (page 136)

veggie bites
- zhug & zucchini (page 211)
- safta's skinny stuffed grape leaves (page 228)

- garlicky string beans (page 203)
- zikki's eggplant (page 224)

animal bites
- arabic ceviche (page 256)
- kebab (page 266)

something sweet
- citrus basbousa (page 300)
- ma'amoul (page 288)

307

TIPS, TRICKS & SAMPLE MENUS

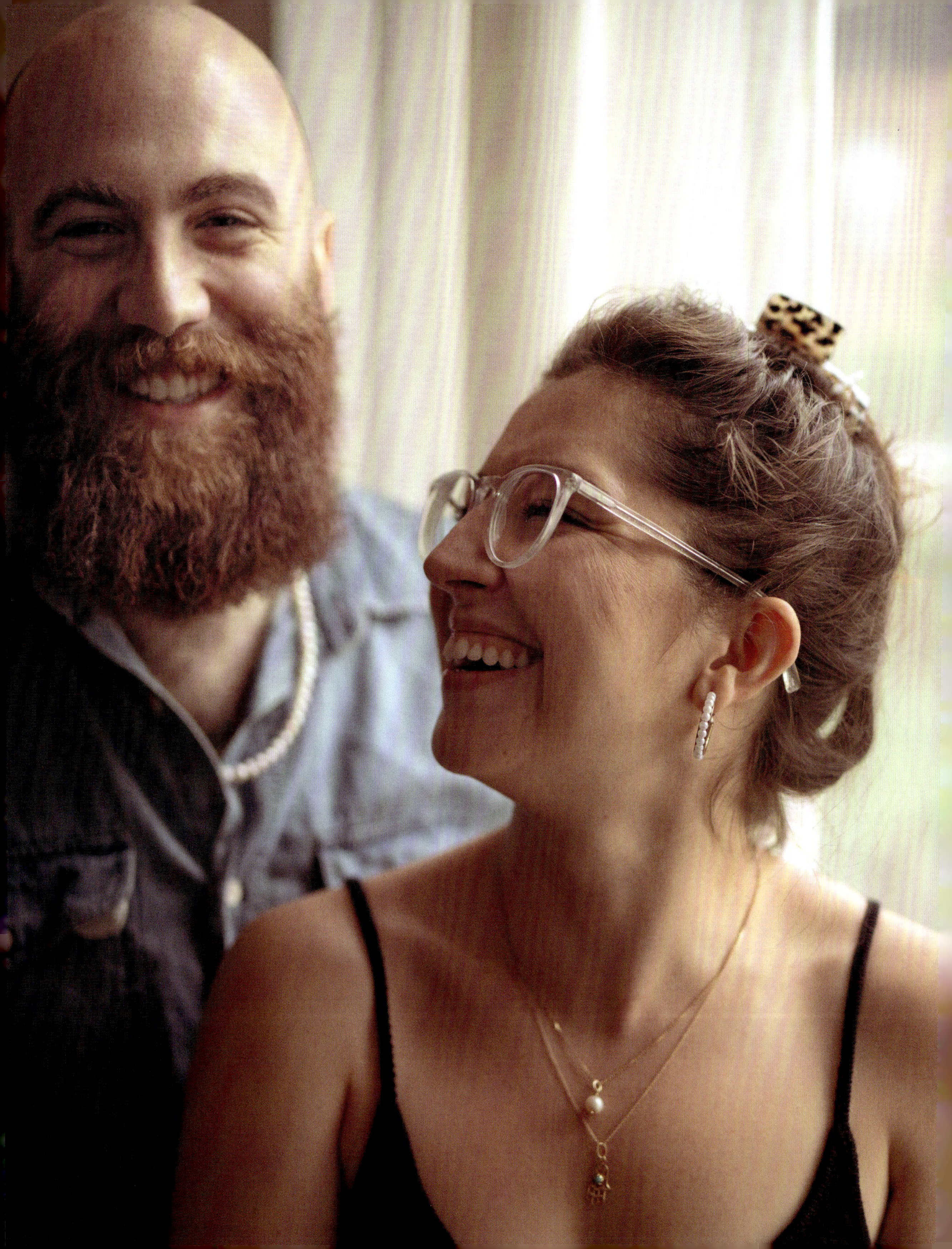

acknowledgments

First and foremost, I want to express my endless gratitude to my wife, Zikki. Without her, this project would never have been created. From conceptualizing the vision for this book and recipe testing to spending endless months writing the copy, editing, and handling me through the entire process. Zikki, you are not only my partner in all our culinary adventures but truly the best partner in this wild and unpredictable life.

Before we jump in to thank all of the beautiful people who helped us make this book come to life, we want to share with you that we take a great pride in calling all the people who are involved in this book our friends. All of them are very close to us, and we love spending time together. Thanks to these unique and genuine relationships, this book is a true reflection of our life—real and raw. It fully captures this current wave of our life and all the joy and adventure woven throughout. They know us, and we know them. And together we worked as a strong, united team.

To photographer Dan Perez, thank you for your ability to understand our vision and bring it to fruition. We are amazed by your talent of controlling natural light and making our food shine in every part of the day. Natural light is the medium we use to talk about our food. Real. Untouched. Organic. As it should be.

To stylist Amit Farber, first I want to thank you for your ma'amoul recipe. It's the best one I've ever had. Thank you for dedicating so much time to selecting the unique props and dishware for the shoot. I'm so happy I was able to find someone who shares the same love and passion for this type of food and knows how to make it look its best. Every set you designed was exactly as we imagined it in our mind.

To our beloved literary agent Sarah Passick, who emotionally and professionally supported us throughout the process of writing this book. Sarah is our cookbook mama, and she accompanied us through this invigorating project with so much patience. Sarah, you are such a good friend, and I'm so grateful for the time our kids are spending together. It's so freaking cute.

To Omer Kaplan, our lifestyle photographer. Thank you for capturing us in our urban playfulness in apartment 4A, amongst the chaos, in the raw, and doing what we love most. Cooking and hosting.

To Itamar Levy, our production assistant, for always being there for us, in developing recipes, providing unfiltered feedback (always keeping it real), and helping us make the photoshoot marathon happen seamlessly. We will never forget the twelve-hour days on set. Thank you for every single time you moved the small plate collection back to its original spot.

To Carli Gordon, our "Girl Friday." Thank you for willingly and joyfully stepping in to help with every bit and piece of the editing process. It was extremely reassuring and directional to have you on our editorial team. You went above and beyond to help Zikki and me review every inch of the manuscript before our submission, every single time. Thank you for reading the book so many times (haha!) and for your keen eye and fabulous taste on set! You da best!

To Brandon Tacconelli and Dana Kurylyk, for recipe testing our book. Your dedication and feedback on every single recipe made this book bulletproof and accurate for any cooking level. We so deeply appreciate your attention to detail and your excitement when it comes to the food we cook!

To Jake Cohen, for not just being a wonderful friend but also for introducing us to Sarah and guiding us through the process from your experience. Your help was so unbelievably valuable.

To my uncle Tal Siman Tov. First for instilling in me the love and passion for food, but more importantly for life. You always pushed me to go after my dreams, and I could never imagine all of this happening without you and your support. Second, I want to thank you for helping us conceptualize the book. Our time together in your kitchen always inspires us to be creative. You are the best uncle.

To Ali Teniuch, Kira Yearwood, and Ryan Zawojski, thank you for joining us for the "Feast Table 101" photoshoot and eating our food oh so beautifully.

To Lucia Watson, Isabel McCarthy, Ashley Tucker, and the whole Avery team—thank you for your endless patience, support, willingness, and excitement that surrounded our debut book.

To our dear family in Israel and here in the United States. You are our everything. We love you deeply. You've made us the people that we are today. Your patience, love, and support have given us the ability to take on the world. We are better parents, people, and friends because of your guidance.

...all have loved... Love u, miss u, think about u everyday! Yuvi ♥

2+B Thanks for having me in your lovely place! Can't wait to meet baby Simon-Tov <3 The Fylish family

Thank you so much man I said whenever I come to N.Y I have to meet you. I really enjoy every single minute with you. Good luck with your baby B+Z, hope we can bake together next year. Love, Beshan

B+Z, Thank you for being kind & authentic people. Can't wait to become ♥ good friends :) Love, [signature]

That our... in life. What ... as a business relationship evolved into a friendship unlike I could've ever imagined. Cheers to many more years growing something special together. Love Jo...

...yeast! ...reddsters

...thing ...thony ...to be reminded of family but I am west coast but I am

B+Z, From the back of a Prius, to approaching parenthood— Love you two always! More life, more bread. ♥ Charlie

Proud to be 1st, love you 4ever Pita;

Thank you for trusting me w/ beautiful Olivia! Can't wait to meet the new babe. ♥ Chelsea

Proud to be pita's love, and to get to meet you, till next time. ♥ Shahar 20.6.21

Zikki and Ben I just love you guys so much. Thank you for bringing Olivia to our life. Mor

Bitch don't kale my vibe 🌿 Love you to BRA and back Achi. ♥

B+Z ♥ You are the heartbeat of it all! It's impossible not to be infected by your stylization, impenetrable kindness & LOVE. Love always, Larissa ♥

벤 & 지키! 초대해주셔서 너무 감사합니다. 이렇게 예쁜 커플을 만나게되어 영광입니다. 다음에 또 주방을 어지럽힐 생각을하니, 벌써 두근두근 하네요! :) 알렉스 :-)

...you both for having ...your apt + lives all the ...u guys always brighten m... ...ss time we hang. Can't ...e all you have achieved ...oth. Can't wait to meet ...her T.

hello sir (Ben) and queen of the universe (Zikki), ∞ to be blessed with a friendship as one that you have given, is one of the coolest gifts ♥ may your home always be blessed with an abundance of love, may you all be protected and experience some of the most iconic chapters of your life in this home. You guys are the most visionary trailblazers that deserve every inch of ♥ and blessings coming your way.

בן וזיקי! ... ...מצוין... Ben & Zikki, Love you so much!! — Zekey

Mr. Be... Thank... the los... hugs. ... I will OLIVI...

You invited me into your home. Fed me, wined & dined me. Chatted w/ me. You two always will have a pla...

index

Note: *Italicized* page numbers indicate material in tables or illustrations.

A

acacia raw honey, 25
acid, 21
Akko Crudo, 247–49
alcohol, 30
almonds
   Jeweled Celery Salad, 136–37
   Kale Salad with Roasted Tomatoes & Almonds, 193–94
   as Welcome Olives, 40*t*
amba: Zikki's Quick Amba, 60, *267*
Amit's Fizzy Veggie Mix, 230–32
Anaheim chiles, 25
anchovies
   Anchovy Breadcrumbs, 184–86, 198–200
   Beef Tartare, 258–60
   Fried Barbouniot, 268–69
   as pantry essential, 25
   Tarragon Dressing, 186
   as Welcome Olives, 40*t*
Animal Bites, 240–77
   Akko Crudo, 247–49
   Arabic Ceviche, 256–57
   Beef Tartare, 258–60
   Ben's Schnitzel Fingers, 264–65
   on the feast table, *36*
   Fried Barbouniot, 268–69
   Kebab, 266–67
   Kubenia, 261–63
   Mackerel, Cucumber & Arugula Crudo, 254–55
   NY Strip Steak, 273–75
   sample menus, 305–6
   Scallop Carpaccio, 252–53
   Shrimp in Grated Tomato Butter, 276–77
   Stuffed Onions, 270–72
   Tuna & Grapes, 244–46
   Tuna Nectarine Tartare, 250–51
apple cider vinegar, 21
apricot jam, 25, 40
Arabic Ceviche, 256–57
artichokes
   Cilantro Pistachio Artichoke Dip, 102–3
   Double-Dip Artichoke, 198–200
   as pantry essential, 25
   as Welcome Olives, 40*t*
arugula: Mackerel, Cucumber & Arugula Crudo, 254–55

b

bagels: Jerusalem Bagel, 120–22
baharat, 24
baking commandments, 106–7
Basbousa, Citrus, 300–301
basil
   A Cashew Basil Dip Everyone Will Talk About, 99–101
   Peach & Tomato Salad with Mozzarella & Basil, 176–77
beef
   Beef Tartare, 258–60
   Kubenia, 261–63
   NY Strip Steak, 273–75
   Stuffed Onions, 270–72
beets
   Beet & Cherry Salad, 148–49
   Beet & Goat Cheese Dip, 88–89
   Burnt Beets & Feta, 207
   Hot-Pink Turnips & Beets, *231*, 238–39

Zikki's Salty Baby Potatoes, 204–6
Ben's Schnitzel Fingers, 264–65
Best Green Salad of Your Life, 184–86
Black Baba, 94
black pepper, 21
blue cheese: Radicchio, Blue Cheese & Hazelnut Salad, 190–91
breadcrumbs
　Anchovy Breadcrumbs, 184–86, 198–200
　Za'atar Challah Breadcrumbs, 187–89
Breads, 104–31
　baking commandments for, 106–7
　bread, butter, and jam boards, 66–67
　Breadsticks, 123–25
　Challah, 116–19
　for feast tables, 33*t*
　Jerusalem Bagel, 120–22
　Lahuh, 129–31
　Murtabak, 126–28
　Pita, 108–12, *216*
　sample menus, 304–6
　Tel Avivian Focaccia, 113–15
　as Welcome Olives, 40*t*
breakfast
　Breakfast Salad, 156–58
　sample menu for, 304
bulgur: Tabbouleh, 140
Burnt Beets & Feta, 207, *208*
Burnt Scallion Chimmi, 273–75
burrata, 39, 40*t*
butter lettuce: Middle Eastern Caesar, 187–89
butters
　bread, butter, and jam boards, 66–69
　Compound Butters, 68–69
　Preserved Lemon Butter, 69

Sage & Leek Butter, 69
Shrimp in Grated Tomato Butter, 276–77
storing, 69

C

Caesar salad, 187–89
cakes: Citrus Basbousa, 300–301
canned pantry items, 25
canola oil, 20
cantaloupe: Not Your Grandma's Fruit Salad, 170–72
carrots
　Amit's Fizzy Veggie Mix, 230–32
　Moroccan Carrots, 201
A Cashew Basil Dip Everyone Will Talk About, 99–101
cauliflower
　Cauliflower & Tahini, 212–13
　Tabbouleh, 142
celery
　Amit's Fizzy Veggie Mix, 230–32
　Jeweled Celery Salad, 136–37
ceviche: Arabic Ceviche, 256–57
Challah
　recipe for, 116–17
　Za'atar Challah Breadcrumbs, 189
champagne vinegar, 21
charcuterie, 39, 40*t*
Charred Eggplant 101, 218–21
Charred Eggplant with Chopped Salad & Hard-Boiled Egg, *220*, 222
Charred Eggplant with Labneh, Zhug & Dukkah, *220*, 223
Charred Eggplant with Thick Tahini, *220*, 221
cheeses
　Beet & Goat Cheese Dip, 88–89

Burnt Beets & Feta, 207
Fattoush Salad, 173–75
Fig & Young Cheese, 302–3
5-Minute Goat Cheese Stuffed Dates, *42*, 43
Peach & Tomato Salad with Mozzarella & Basil, 176–77
Radicchio, Blue Cheese & Hazelnut Salad, 190–91
tips on feta, 207
as Welcome Olives, 39, 40*t*
cherries: Beet & Cherry Salad, 148–49
chicken
　Ben's Schnitzel Fingers, 264–65
　Chicken Shawarma Salad, 153–55
chickpeas
　Classic Hummus, 76–78
　cooking, 78
　Falafel, 215–17
chilies
　Burnt Scallion Chimmi, 273–75
　Harissa, 50–51
　Mashwiya, 98
　My Grandfather's Zhug, 48–49
　Our Hassle-Free Matbucha, *51*, 52–53
　Quick Pickled Chile, 247–49
　Salat Dudu, 182–83
　Tiny Tangy Chili Oil, 78
　Zikki's Eggplant, 224–25
chocolate
　Chocolate Balls, 291–93
　Tahini Truffles, 294–95
　tips for melting, 295
Chopped Liver, Better Than Your Grandma's, 73–75
Chrain, 204–6
chutney: My Grandfather's Zhug, 48–49, *131*
cilantro
　Arabic Ceviche, 256–57

cilantro *(continued)*
   Cilantro Pistachio Artichoke Dip, 102–3
   Falafel, 215–17
   Jeweled Celery Salad, 136–37
   Kebab, 266–67
   My Grandfather's Zhug, 48–49, *131*
   Stuffed Onions, 270–72
   Tabbouleh, 140–42
citrus
   Citrus Basbousa, 300–301
   Fennel, Citrus & Pistachio Salad, 159–61
   Not Your Grandma's Fruit Salad, 170–72
   peeling, 161
   Scallop Carpaccio, 252–53
   Tuna Nectarine Tartare, 250–51
   See also lemon
Classic Hummus, 76–78
coconut, shredded
   Chocolate Balls, 291–93
   Malabi, 296–97
colors of the food, 35
Compound Butters, 68–69
confits, 62–65
cookies
   Chocolate Balls, 291–93
   Ma'amoul, 288–90
Corn off the Cob, 208–10
crackers, 40, 40*t*
cranberries
   Cranberry & Sumac Jam, *66*, 70
   Jeweled Celery Salad, 136–37
crunchy foods as Welcome Olives, 40*t*
cucumbers
   Arabic Ceviche, 256–57
   Breakfast Salad, 156–58
   Cucumber, Dill, Labneh & Onion Salad, 164–65
   Deconstructed Sabich, 143–45
   Fattoush Salad, 173–75

   Mackerel, Cucumber & Arugula Crudo, 254–55
   My Dad's Fermented Cucumbers, *231*, 233–35
   Sumac Cucumber Spears, 43
   Tabbouleh, 140, 142
   Tza-Zikki, 86–87, *268*
   When in Doubt Chopped Salad, 138–39
cumin, 24
cutlery, 33

d

date honey (silan)
   buying, 71
   as pantry essential, 25
   Silan & Onion Jam, *66*, 71
dates
   5-Minute Goat Cheese Stuffed Dates, *42*, 43
   Ma'amoul, 288–90
   Pear, Mustard Green, Mint & Challah Crouton Salad, 166–67
   as Welcome Olives, 40*t*
Deconstructed Sabich, 143–45
desserts, 278–303
   avoiding omission of, 28, 30–31
   Chocolate Balls, 291–93
   Citrus Basbousa, 300–301
   Fig & Young Cheese, 302–3
   Jaffa Sundae, 298–99
   Knafeh, 286–87
   Ma'amoul, 288–90
   Malabi, 296–97
   Rogalach, 282–85
   sample menus, 304
   Tahini Truffles, 294–95
dill: Cucumber, Dill, Labneh & Onion Salad, 164–65
Dips & Spreads, 43–105
   Beet & Goat Cheese Dip, 88–89

   Black Baba, *93*, 94
   A Cashew Basil Dip Everyone Will Talk About, 99–101
   Chopped Liver, Better Than Your Grandma's, 73–75
   Cilantro Pistachio Artichoke Dip, 102–3
   Classic Hummus, 76–78
   Cranberry & Sumac Jam, *66*, 70
   on the feast table, *36*
   Garlic Lovers ONLY Toum, 61
   Harissa, 50–51, *54*
   Labneh 3 Ways, 82–85
   Let's Burn a Veggie and Make a Spread, 90–91
   Mashwiya, 98
   My Grandfather's Zhug, 48–49, *54*, 56, *131*
   My Uncle Tal's Lentil Masabacha, 79–81
   Our Hassle-Free Matbucha, *51*, 52–53
   Persimmon & Thyme Jam, *66*, 71
   Preserved Lemon, 57–59
   Preserved Lemon Butter, *67*, 69
   Sage & Leek Butter, *66*, 69
   sample menus, 304–7
   Silan & Onion Jam, *66–67*, 71
   The Smoothest Tahini Dip, 54–55, 56
   Sumac, Lemon & Oregano Butter, *65–66*, 68
   Three Confits, 62–65
   Tza-Zikki, 86–87, *268*
   White Baba, 92–93
   Zaalouk, 95–97
   Zikki's Quick Amba, 60, *267*
Double-Dip Artichoke, 198–200
dressings
   for The Best Green Salad of Your Life, 184–86

for Chicken Shawarma Salad, 153
for Fennel, Citrus & Pistachio Salad, 159
Fig & Lemon Dressing, 190–91
for Not Your Grandma's Fruit Salad, 170
for Pear, Mustard Green, Mint & Challah Crouton Salad, 166
Preserved Lemon Caesar Dressing, 187–89
Tarragon Dressing, 186
Dukkah
  Charred Eggplant with Labneh, Zhug & Dukkah, *220*, 223
  as pantry essential, 24
  recipe for, 156–58

E

eggplants
  Black Baba, *93*, 94
  Charred Eggplant 101, 218–21
  Charred Eggplant with Chopped Salad & Hard-Boiled Egg, *220*, 222
  Charred Eggplant with Labneh, Zhug & Dukkah, *220*, 223
  Charred Eggplant with Thick Tahini, *220*, 221
  Deconstructed Sabich, 143–45
  frying, 145
  Herby Marinated Eggplants, 150–52
  White Baba, 92–93
  Zaalouk, 95–97
  Zikki's Eggplant, 224–25
eggs
  Breakfast Salad, 156–58
  Charred Eggplant with Chopped Salad & Hard-Boiled Egg, *220*, 222
  Deconstructed Sabich, 143–45
  Spiced Jammy Eggs, 43
extra virgin olive oil (EVOO)
  on the feast table, *36–37*
  as pantry essential, 19, 20
  and Welcome Olives, 40*t*

f

Falafel, 215–17
fast meals, 43
Fattoush Salad, 173–75
feast tables, 32–35, *36–37*, 307
Fennel, Citrus & Pistachio Salad, 159–61
fermented foods
  Amit's Fizzy Veggie Mix, 230–32
  basic rules of, 236–37
  fermentation schedule, 232*t*
  Hot-Pink Turnips & Beets, *231*, 238–39
  My Dad's Fermented Cucumbers, *231*, 233–35
  as Welcome Olives, 40*t*
feta
  Burnt Beets & Feta, 207
  essential tips on, 207
  Fattoush Salad, 173–75
figs
  Fig & Lemon Dressing, 190–91
  Fig & Young Cheese, 302–3
  Fig Carpaccio, 168–69
  fig jam, 25, 40
fish
  Akko Crudo, 247–49
  Anchovy Breadcrumbs, 184–86, 198–200
  Arabic Ceviche, 256–57
  Beef Tartare, 258–60
  Fried Barbouniot, 268–69
  Mackerel, Cucumber & Arugula Crudo, 254–55
  as pantry essential, 25
  pantry essentials, 25
  quick-curing, 246
  salmon, smoked, 40*t*
  sashimi-grade, 246
  Tarragon Dressing, 186
  Tuna & Grapes, 244–46
  Tuna Nectarine Tartare, 250–51
  as Welcome Olives, 39, 40*t*
5-Minute Goat Cheese Stuffed Dates, *42*, 43
flowers, 33
fluke: Arabic Ceviche, 256–57
focaccia: Tel Avivian Focaccia, 113–15
food processors, 100
Fried Barbouniot, 268–69
fries: Vetrena Fries, 226–27
fruits
  Beet & Cherry Salad, 148–49
  Citrus Basbousa, 300–301
  Cranberry & Sumac Jam, *66*, 70
  Fennel, Citrus & Pistachio Salad, 159–61
  Fig & Lemon Dressing, 190–91
  Fig & Young Cheese, 302–3
  Fig Carpaccio, 168–69
  fig jam, 25, 40
  5-Minute Goat Cheese Stuffed Dates, *42*, 43
  Jeweled Celery Salad, 136–37
  Ma'amoul, 288–90
  Not Your Grandma's Fruit Salad, 170–72
  Peach & Tomato Salad with Mozzarella & Basil, 176–77
  Pear, Mustard Green, Mint & Challah Crouton Salad, 166–67
  peeling, 161
  Persimmon & Thyme Jam, *66*
  Safta's Skinny Stuffed Grape Leaves, 228–29
  Scallop Carpaccio, 252–53

fruits *(continued)*
    selecting seasonal, 172
    Tuna & Grapes, 244–46
    Tuna Nectarine Tartare, 250–51
    as Welcome Olives, 40*t*
    Zikki's Quick Amba, 60
    See also lemon; pomegranates/pomegranate seeds; *specific fruits*

g

garlic
    Amit's Fizzy Veggie Mix, 230–32
    Garlic Confit, 63
    Garlicky String Beans, 202–3
    Garlic Lovers ONLY Toum, 61, *267*
    Middle Eastern Caesar, 187–89
glassware, 28
goat cheese
    Beet & Goat Cheese Dip, 88–89
    Fig & Young Cheese, 302–3
    5-Minute Goat Cheese Stuffed Dates, *42*, 43
grapes
    Safta's Skinny Stuffed Grape Leaves, 228–29
    Tuna & Grapes, 244–46
    as Welcome Olives, 40*t*
grape syrup, 182–73
gray Atlantic sea salt, 20, 40*t*
greens
    The Best Green Salad of Your Life, 186
    Chicken Shawarma Salad, 153–55
    Kale Salad with Roasted Tomatoes & Almonds, 193–94
    Middle Eastern Caesar, 187–89
    Pear, Mustard Green, Mint & Challah Crouton Salad, 166–67
    Radicchio, Blue Cheese & Hazelnut Salad, 190–91
grissini (breadsticks), 123–25

h

halva, 25
harissa
    Deconstructed Sabich, 143–45
    as pantry essential, 25
    recipe for, 50–51, *54*
    tahini combined with, 56
hawaij, 24
hazelnuts
    Radicchio, Blue Cheese & Hazelnut Salad, 190–91
    as Welcome Olives, 40*t*
hazelnut spread: Chocolate Balls, 291–93
Herby Marinated Eggplants, 150–52
honeydews: Not Your Grandma's Fruit Salad, 170–72
hosting, 26–43
    burnout with, 31
    cleaning up after, 31
    feast tables, 32–35, *36–37*, 307
    fundamentals of, 28
    guests, 31–32
    joy of, 27–28
    plating food, 39
    preparing for, 28–31
    sample menus, 304, 306
    Welcome Olives, 38–43
hot (spicy) ingredients, 24–25
Hot-Pink Turnips & Beets, *231*, 238–39
humboldt fog, 40*t*
Hummus, 76–78

i

ice, 28
ice cream: Jaffa Sundae, 298–99
immersion blenders, 100
Irish butter, 21
Israeli Caprese, 178–79

j

Jaffa Sundae, 298–99
jalapeños: Amit's Fizzy Veggie Mix, 230–32
jams
    bread, butter, and jam boards, 66–67, 70–72
    Cranberry & Sumac Jam, 70
    as pantry essential, 25
    Persimmon & Thyme Jam, 71
    Silan & Onion Jam, 71
    storing, 72
    as Welcome Olives, 40, 40*t*
Jerusalem Bagel, 120–22
Jeweled Celery Salad, 136–37

k

kale
    The Best Green Salad of Your Life, 186
    Kale Salad with Roasted Tomatoes & Almonds, 193–94
Kebab, 266–67
kitchen scales, 107
Knafeh, 286–87
kraft paper, 33
Kubenia, 261–63

l

labneh, 82–85
    Charred Eggplant with Labneh, Zhug & Dukkah, *220*, 223

Cucumber, Dill, Labneh & Onion Salad, 164–65
Labneh Balls, 85, 178–79
Labneh Spread, 84, 87, 250–51
   salt content in, 83
   Sweet Potatoes on Labneh, *213*, 214
   as Welcome Olives, 40*t*
   Yogurt Stone, 85
Lahuh, 129–31
lamb: Kebab, 266–67
leeks
   Chopped Liver, Better Than Your Grandma's, 73–75
   Leek & Sage Confit, 64–65
   Sage & Leek Butter, *66*, 69
lemon
   Garlic Lovers ONLY Toum, 61
   Not Your Grandma's Fruit Salad, 170–72
   as pantry essential, 19, 21
   Preserved Lemon, 57–59
   Preserved Lemon Butter, *67*, 69
   Preserved Lemon Caesar Dressing, 187–89
   Preserved Lemon Paste, 58–59
   Radicchio, Blue Cheese & Hazelnut Salad, 190–91
   Safta's Skinny Stuffed Grape Leaves, 228–29
   The Smoothest Tahini Dip, 54–55
   Sumac, Lemon & Oregano Butter, 68
   Tarragon Dressing, 186
   zesting, 87
lentils: My Uncle Tal's Lentil Masabacha, 79–81
Let's Burn a Veggie and Make a Spread, 90–91
liver: Chopped Liver, Better Than Your Grandma's, 73–75

M

Ma'amoul, 288–90
Mackerel, Cucumber & Arugula Crudo, 254–55
Malabi, 296–97
mangos: Zikki's Quick Amba, 60
Marinated Peppers, 146–47
masabacha: My Uncle Tal's Lentil Masabacha, 79–81
Mashwiya, *96*
matbucha, *51*, 52–53
meat. *See* Animal Bites
Middle Eastern Caesar, 187–89
mint
   Akko Crudo, 247–49
   Arabic Ceviche, 256–57
   Herby Marinated Eggplants, 150–52
   Jeweled Celery Salad, 136–37
   Kebab, 266–67
   Pear, Mustard Green, Mint & Challah Crouton Salad, 166–67
   Tabbouleh, 140–42
   Tuna & Grapes, 244–46
Moroccan Carrots, 201
mozzarella: Peach & Tomato Salad with Mozzarella & Basil, 176–77
Murtabak, 126–28
mustard greens: Pear, Mustard Green, Mint & Challah Crouton Salad, 166–67
My Dad's Fermented Cucumbers, *231*, 233–35
My Grandfather's Zhug, 48–49, *51*, *54*, 56
My Uncle Tal's Lentil Masabacha, 79–81

N

nectarines
   Not Your Grandma's Fruit Salad, 170–72
   Tuna Nectarine Tartare, 250–51
Not Your Grandma's Fruit Salad, 170–72
nuts
   Akko Crudo, 247–49
   Chocolate Balls, 291–93
   Cilantro Pistachio Artichoke Dip, 102–3
   Dukkah, 156–58
   Fennel, Citrus & Pistachio Salad, 159–61
   Fig & Young Cheese, 302–3
   Jaffa Sundae, 298–99
   Jeweled Celery Salad, 136–37
   Kale Salad with Roasted Tomatoes & Almonds, 193–94
   Malabi, 296–97
   as pantry essential, 21–23
   Radicchio, Blue Cheese & Hazelnut Salad, 190–91
   toasting, 22–23
   as Welcome Olives, 39, 40*t*
NY Strip Steak, 273–75

O

oils for cooking, 20
olive oil
   on the feast table, *36–37*
   as pantry essential, 19, 20
   and Welcome Olives, 40*t*
olives, 40, 40*t*
onions
   Cucumber, Dill, Labneh & Onion Salad, 164–65
   Kebab, 266–67
   Quick Pickled Onions, 208–10
   Silan & Onion Jam, *66*, 71
   Stuffed Onions, 270–72
orange blossom water, 25
oranges: Fennel, Citrus & Pistachio Salad, 159–61
oregano: Sumac, Lemon & Oregano Butter, 68

Our Hassle-Free Matbucha, *51*, 52–53
ovens, variability in, 107

P

pantry essentials, 18–25
parsley
   Arabic Ceviche, 256–57
   Falafel, 215–17
   Herby Marinated Eggplants, 150–52
   Jeweled Celery Salad, 136–37
   Stuffed Onions, 270–72
   Tabbouleh, 140–42
passion fruits: Scallop Carpaccio, 252–53
Peach & Tomato Salad with Mozzarella & Basil, 176–77
Pear, Mustard Green, Mint & Challah Crouton Salad, 166–67
pepper, black, 21
peppers
   charring, 146
   Harissa, 50–51
   Marinated Peppers, 146–47
   Mashwiya, 98
Persimmon & Thyme Jam, *66*, 71
phyllo dough, 286–87
pickled goodies, 40, 40t.
   See also fermented foods
pistachios
   Akko Crudo, 247–49
   Chocolate Balls, 291–93
   Cilantro Pistachio Artichoke Dip, 102–3
   Dukkah, 156–58
   Fennel, Citrus & Pistachio Salad, 159–61
   Fig & Young Cheese, 302–3
   Jaffa Sundae, 298–99
   Malabi, 296–97
Pita, 108–12, *216*
plates, 28, 33

plating food, 39
plums: Not Your Grandma's Fruit Salad, 170–72
pomegranates/pomegranate seeds
   Jaffa Sundae, 298–99
   Jeweled Celery Salad, 136–37
   Middle Eastern Caesar, 187–89
   Pomegranate Sauce, 261–63
   pomegranate syrup, 25
   Tabbouleh, 142
potatoes
   Deconstructed Sabich, 143–45
   Vetrena Fries, 226–27
   Zikki's Salty Baby Potatoes, 204–6
Preserved Lemon
   preparing, 57–59
   Preserved Lemon Butter, *67*, 69
   Preserved Lemon Crema, 198–200
   Preserved Lemon Paste, 58–59
proofing dough, 107
prosciutto, 39, 40t
proteins. *See* Animal Bites

Q

Quick Pickled Chile, 247–49
Quick Pickled Onions, 224–25

R

Radicchio, Blue Cheese & Hazelnut Salad, 190–91
radishes, green, 163
red peppers: Harissa, 50–51
rice
   Safta's Skinny Stuffed Grape Leaves, 228–29
   Stuffed Onions, 270–72
Rogalach, 282–85
rose water, 25

S

Safta's Skinny Stuffed Grape Leaves, 228–29
sage
   Leek & Sage Confit, 64–65
   Sage & Leek Butter, *66*, 69
Salads, 132–93
   acids that enhance, 21
   Beet & Cherry Salad, 148–49
   The Best Green Salad of Your Life, 184–86
   Breakfast Salad, 156–58
   Chicken Shawarma Salad, 153–55
   Cucumber, Dill, Labneh & Onion Salad, 164–65
   Deconstructed Sabich, 143–45
   Fattoush Salad, 173–75
   on the feast table, *36*
   Fennel, Citrus & Pistachio Salad, 159–61
   Fig Carpaccio, 168–69
   Herby Marinated Eggplants, 150–52
   Israeli Caprese, 178–79
   Jeweled Celery Salad, 136–37
   Marinated Peppers, 146–47
   Middle Eastern Caesar, 187–89
   Not Your Grandma's Fruit Salad, 170–72
   Not Your Typical "Crisp Veg," 162–63
   Peach & Tomato Salad with Mozzarella & Basil, 176–77
   Pear, Mustard Green, Mint & Challah Crouton Salad, 166–67
   Radicchio, Blue Cheese & Hazelnut Salad, 190–91
   Salat Dudu, 182–83
   sample menus, 304–6
   Tabbouleh, 140–42
   When in Doubt Chopped Salad, 138–39, 222

Zikki's Peeled Tomato Salad, 180–81
salami, 40*t*
Salat Dudu, 182–83
salmon, smoked, 40*t*
salt
 on the feast table, *36–37*
 as pantry essential, 19, 20
 Preserved Lemon, 57–59
 and Welcome Olives board, 40*t*
 Zikki's Salty Baby Potatoes, 204–6
salumi, 39
sample menus, 304–7
sardines
 Fried Barbouniot, 268–69
 as pantry essential, 25
 as Welcome Olives, 40*t*
scales, 107
scallions: Burnt Scallion Chimmi, 273–75
Scallop Carpaccio, 252–53
Schnitzel Fingers, Ben's, 264–65
sealing and storing foods, 72
sea salt, 20
serving dishes, 28, 33
sesame seeds: Dukkah, 156–58
shabbat, sample menu for, 306
sherry vinegar, 21
Shrimp in Grated Tomato Butter, 276–77
silan (date honey)
 buying, 71
 as pantry essential, 25
 Silan & Onion Jam, *66*, 71
smelt, fried, 268–69
The Smoothest Tahini Dip
 with Charred Eggplant with Labneh, Zhug & Dukkah, 222
 combining zhug or harissa with, 56
 Deconstructed Sabich, 143–45
 recipe for, 54–55, *267*

snapper: Akko Crudo, 247–49
sparkling water, 28
Spiced Jammy Eggs, 43
spices (pantry essentials), 23–24
spicy (hot) ingredients
 in Harissa, 50
 as pantry essential, 24–25
 "spicy plate" with meals, 51
steak, 273–75
sterilizing foods, 72
storing foods, guidelines for, 72
Strawberry Syrup, 296–97
String Beans, Garlicky, 202–3
Strip Steak, NY, 273–75
Stuffed Onions, 270–72
sumac
 Cranberry & Sumac Jam, *66*, 70
 as pantry essential, 23
 Sumac, Lemon & Oregano Butter, *65–66*, *67*, 68
 Sumac Cucumber Spears, 43, *96*
sunflower oil, toasted, 20
Sweet Potatoes on Labneh, *213*, 214
sweets/sweet ingredients
 as pantry essential, 25
 as Welcome Olives, 40, 40*t*
 See also desserts

T

Tabbouleh, 140–42
tahini
 Cauliflower & Tahini, 212–13
 Charred Eggplant with Labneh, Zhug & Dukkah, 222
 Charred Eggplant with Thick Tahini, *220*, 221
 Deconstructed Sabich, 143–45
 harissa combined with, 56
 as pantry essential, 21

The Smoothest Tahini Dip, 54–55, *267*
Tahini Truffles, 294–95
zhug combined with, 56
tangerines: Scallop Carpaccio, 252–53
tangy foods as Welcome Olives, 40*t*
Tarragon Dressing, 184–86
Tel Avivian Focaccia, 113–15
Three Confits, 62–65
thyme: Persimmon & Thyme Jam, *66*, 71
Tiny Tangy Chili Oil, 78, 88, *89*
tomatoes
 Arabic Ceviche, 256–57
 Breakfast Salad, 156–58
 Deconstructed Sabich, 143–45
 draining, 139
 Fattoush Salad, 173–75
 Israeli Caprese, 178–79
 Kale Salad with Roasted Tomatoes & Almonds, 193–94
 Our Hassle-Free Matbucha, 52–53
 Peach & Tomato Salad with Mozzarella & Basil, 176–77
 peeling, 181
 Safta's Skinny Stuffed Grape Leaves, 228–29
 Salat Dudu, 182–83
 Shrimp in Grated Tomato Butter, 276–77
 Tabbouleh, 140–42
 Tomato Confit, 64
 as Welcome Olives, 39
 When in Doubt Chopped Salad, 138–39
 Zaalouk, 95–97
 Zikki's Eggplant, 224–25
 Zikki's Peeled Tomato Salad, 180–81
tomato sauce, 43
tomato vinegar, 21

toum: Garlic Lovers ONLY Toum, 61
trout, smoked, 25, 40*t*
truffles, 294–95
tuna
  as pantry essential, 25
  Tuna & Grapes, 244–46
  Tuna Nectarine Tartare, 250–51
turnips
  Amit's Fizzy Veggie Mix, 230–32
  Hot-Pink Turnips & Beets, *231*, 238–39
Tza-Zikki, 86–87, *268*

V

vegan options, 306
vegetables
  charring, 91
  Let's Burn a Veggie and Make a Spread, 90–91
  See also specific vegetables
Veggie Bites, 194–239
  Amit's Fizzy Veggie Mix, 230–32
  Burnt Beets & Feta, 207
  Cauliflower & Tahini, 212–13
  Charred Eggplant 101, 218–21
  Charred Eggplant with Chopped Salad & Hard-Boiled Egg, *220*, 222
  Charred Eggplant with Labneh, Zhug & Dukkah, *220*, 223
  Charred Eggplant with Thick Tahini, *220*, 221
  Corn off the Cob, 208–10
  Double-Dip Artichoke, 198–200
  Falafel, 215–17
  on the feast table, *36*
  fermentation guide, 236–37
  Garlicky String Beans, 202–3
  Hot-Pink Turnips & Beets, *231*, 238–39
  Moroccan Carrots, 201
  My Dad's Fermented Cucumbers, *231*, 233–35
  Safta's Skinny Stuffed Grape Leaves, 228–29
  sample menus, 304–6
  Sweet Potatoes on Labneh, *213*, 214
  Vetrena Fries, 226–27
  Zhug & Zucchini, *208*, 211
  Zikki's Eggplant, 224–25
  Zikki's Salty Baby Potatoes, 204–6
Vetrena Fries, 226–27
vinegars, 21

W

Welcome Olives
  about, 38–43
  avoiding omission of, 28
  function of, 30
  sample menus, 306
When in Doubt Chopped Salad, 138–39, 222
White Baba, 92–93
whole-fat yogurt, 83
wine, 28

Y

yogurt
  Labneh 3 Ways, 82–85
  from whole-fat, 83
  Yogurt Stone, 168–69

Z

Zaalouk, 95–97
za'tar
  as pantry essential, 24
  Za'atar Challah Breadcrumbs, 187–89
  za'atar olive oil, 43
zhug
  Charred Eggplant with Labneh, Zhug & Dukkah, *220*, 223
  My Grandfather's Zhug, 48–49, *131*
  as pantry essential, 25
  tahini combined with, 56
  Zhug & Zucchini, *208*, 211
Zikki's Eggplant, 224–25
Zikki's Peeled Tomato Salad, 180–81
Zikki's Quick Amba
  Chicken Shawarma Salad, 153–55
  Deconstructed Sabich, 143–45
  recipe for, 60, *267*
Zikki's Salty Baby Potatoes, 204–6
Zucchini
  salting, 211
  Zhug & Zucchini, *208*, 211